INSPECTION THREATENS THE VICTORIAN PUBLIC SCHOOL

PRACTICE, PERSONALITY AND SCANDAL

© Michael Cullen 2024

First independently published in 2024 by Amazon KDP

All rights reserved. No part of this publication may be reproduced, stored on a retrieval system, or transmitted in any form or by any means without the prior permission of the copyright owner. Michael Cullen is hereby identified as author of this work in accordance with Section 77 of the Copyright, Designs and Patents Act 1988.

ISBN 979-83456082-9-6

Set in 11/14 Melior
Design by www.simprimstudio.com

INSPECTION THREATENS THE VICTORIAN PUBLIC SCHOOL

PRACTICE, PERSONALITY AND SCANDAL

Michael Cullen

The Lower School, Eton College

CONTENTS

	Introduction	i
	Preface	1

Part One — Background

Chapters	1	Eton's Long Chamber	6
	2	Keate	19
	3	Rough and Tumble	35
	4	Voices of Protest	44
	5	Diverse Schoolings	48
	6	Eton and King's	55
	7	Agents of Change	60
	8	Mid-Century Eton	81

Part Two — The Clarendon Report

Chapters	9	Trouble Ahead	111
	10	Setting up The Commission	121
	11	Eton Investigated	127
	12	The Other Clarendon Eight	146
	13	Just What Got Learnt?	163
	14	Debate Resumed	171
	15	The Public School Act of 1868	176

Part Three — Sequels

Chapters	16	Departures	180
	17	Later Lives	200
	18	Gladstone's Table Talk	264
	19	A.C.Benson's assessment	268
	20	Afterword	272

	Notes	275
	Bibliography	291
	Index	293

Cover quote from *Fraser's Magazine*, June 1864

ILLUSTRATIONS

The Lower School, Eton College	Front cover
Image of Keate from paper-cut silhouette	34
William (Johnson) Cory	59
Edward Craven Hawtrey: Headmaster	80
View of Eton College Chapel	95
Rev. C.Wolley	96
Rev. R.Day	96
Rev. S.Hawtrey	96
Rev. E.Hale	96
Rev. F.E.Durnford	97
Rev. J.E.Yonge	97
W.Johnson	97
Rev. J.L.Joynes	97
The Eton Eleven of 1858	98
Charles Old Goodford: Eton Headmaster and Provost	110
Provost Hawtrey	126
Edmond Warre. Circa 1858	179
James John Hornby: Eton Headmaster and Provost	198
William Cory with Rosa and Andrew in Madeira	199
Warre as Headmaster in 1905	220

Note on currency : Estimates of how much an 1864 pound would be worth today vary widely, depending on the assumed rate of interest. Two answers are £122 and £189.

INTRODUCTION

Required at Durham in 1964 to write a thesis on a historical aspect of education, the Clarendon Report of 1864 seemed a promising subject to research : the reason being that as it only considered nine schools there ought to be an interesting amount of detail about each. So it proved, and a residual interest in the controversy surrounding the report has remained.

One didn't though need to read too much contemporary source material before realising that concerns about one school, aired largely in the periodical Press, had brought it about.

That school was Eton. That being the case, there seemed good reason to delve a little further back into its history and practices as well as the issues aired in the debate of the 1860's. The richness of its historical archive provides another reason to do so.

This makes no claim to be comprehensive and approaches the report circuitously, perhaps lingering longer over interesting source material than a more rigorous academic study could do. Attempt is made to give a sense of the essence of Victorian schoolboys' life as well as the preoccupations, habits, and quirks of their masters, three of whom along with a pupil are followed into later life. The report itself though is the central topic.

Berwick-upon-Tweed
2020

PREFACE

In 1888 the Rev. Charles Wilkinson recorded his reminiscences of Eton where he'd been a boy during the latter part of Keate's regime (1809-1834). He began with an affectionate nod towards *'the dear old place'* then promptly launched into a scathing critique of the education offered in his time.

'I think it was simply disgraceful that, in return for all that was paid for us, and often many years of the curriculum at that time, we should – or might as some did, come away without writing a respectable hand; without any knowledge of the etymology of our language, or, in simple terms, without being able to spell; without knowing how to do a rule-of-three sum; without any acquaintance with common geography not only of the world, but not even of Great Britain, scarcely perhaps of England; without knowing whether the sun went round the earth, or the earth went round the sun, or whether the moon was, or was not 'made of green cheeese';without any knowledge of history except the stories they learnt at home in the nursery of Alfred and the cakes, of Canute and his courtiers on the sea-shore who would perhaps astonish many by rattling off verses in Latin and Greek, and by saying hundreds of lines every week for the poets of the Classical languages, and yet had no idea of English grammar, and could not write an essay or even a letter in their own language; who, upon the introduction of competition for the professions, had need to go to crammers.' [1]

Captain F.M. Norman, R.N., from the vantage point of 1899, looking back on his days at Harrow in the 1840's, recalled an education that was *'exclusively classical throughout'*.[2] It involved a good deal of repetition with such tasks as a hundred lines of Virgil being set for the 'Trials'. Little beyond the Classics was studied, or of anything actually taught. Despite that some 'swots' managed to win awards, their labours appreciated as they usually brought about a half-holiday. The prevailing notion was that all necessary other subject knowledge was *'picked up by gentleman's sons at home or under tuition'*.³ This he was sure was an illusion, that many boys left with very partial and limited knowledge. *'Now, in this connection, I have often heard people remark that "Public School education is a fraud"'*.⁴ Indeed, it made English education something of a laughing stock for *'the foreigner regards our system with amusement and wonder, declaring that the bulk of our boys are ignoramuses'*.⁵ He appreciated that what was taught was not the sole reason for going to a Public School, that it provided a *'sphere for the formation and development of the habits, character, and physique of the English gentleman'* but there was *'no disguising the fact that the almost universal necessity for a coach is a standing reproach to our Public Schools'*.⁶

It was a similar picture at Westminster where Captain F. Markham (1849-1855), looking back from 1903, recalled a Classically dominated curriculum with other subjects, Arithmetic, Maths, and French being *'at a discount'* and taught only in the afternoon of half-school days.⁷

* * * * *

Classics had the advantage of a historic prevalence in the curriculum. It was noted that of Eton in the Nineteenth Century had altered little from its Eighteenth-Century version.

Parallels could be found stretching much further back. Pochin, an Etonian of the 1860's, to whom the writing of Latin verse was a constant bugbear, was heard vexedly trying to fit 'Samvel' into a properly scanning line.⁸ Paston, writing home in 1468, had lamented the same trouble.⁹ Nor had the Latin grammar in use altered much from Malim's Tudor version.

The effect of this heavy emphasis on the Classics was often to effectively stream boys into two groups. There were those who enjoyed a measure of success with their school work and who from time to time would be *'sent up for good'* to feel the warm glow of Headmasterly approbation, win awards in school and for university, see their name set in gold on a schoolroom panel, or gain a more specific prize such as unmilled Maundy coins at Westminster.¹⁰ Yet those who either couldn't, or wouldn't, get to grips with it and who relied on cribs or conspiratorial help from more proficient friends to see them through lessons gained little. For should a boy failing at the Classics enjoy more success at Maths or French that never compensated and boys making inadequate progress found their form promotions tardy.

Something of this divide persisted in adult life. Cognoscenti enjoyed swapping quotes and embellishing their writings and speeches with Latin quotations and tags, drawing strength from this shared culture which also had an excluding effect, and which was *'the test of a gentleman'*.[11] To many, such as Gladstone, the Classics were a lifelong interest. Some retained an active involvement. The Fourteenth Earl of Derby, a Prime Minister, in old age applied himself to a translation of Homer.[12] On the other hand Thackeray observed that *'stout men in the bow-windows of clubs (for such young Etonians by time become) are not generally remarkable for a taste of Aeschylus'*.[13]

By the mid-Nineteenth Century Science could not be entirely ignored though the Public Schools; with the partial exception of Rugby, tried their best to do so. As Colin Shrosbree remarked, Shrewsbury School and Ironbridge were not far apart but they might just as well have been on different planets.[14] The Industrial Revolution, the chemistry craze, the great Exhibition – none of the knowledge generated by these and other developments was thought fit for more than the occasional lecture. For all it was said to offer was sterile fact in contrast to the vibrant humanity of the Classics. Some voices, the Edinburgh Review being particularly strident, pointed out that this was a damagingly anachronistic attitude and that such influential schools could not afford to ignore Science, *'on which the wealth of the nation depends'*.[15]

This Classical focus had hampering consequences. Charles Darwin had not learnt sufficient Maths to be able to take up a place studying Natural Philosophy at Cambridge.[16] Looking back on his years at Shrewsbury he considered that *'the school as a means of education to me was simply a blank'*.[17] He did though allow that it had given him a lifelong love of Horace's odes.[18] To some the experience of Public School could even be regressive. The Rev. W. Tuckwell recalled being quite good at quadratic equations at the age of twelve but far less so after his time at Winchester.[19]

It was not though academic limitations that led to calls for a Royal Commission but an altogether murkier business.

* * * * *

'There was, without gainsaying, a great deal of the rod in those years', recalled W.H.Tucker (Eton, 1811-1822) and like Wilkinson looking back much later (1891) involving *'a lively crop of convicts assembled in the library to be made better boys'*.[20] It was something of an event. *'Execution hour was an amusement. Many gathered to see their friends*

under the amelioration system.' At Westminster by contrast the regular punishment by the Headmaster was a caning on the back of the hand. Birching was rare and conducted in private. More regular and heavier thrashings were left to the boys.

Few thought a Public School could be run without some degree of corporal punishment. Endorsement came even from Royalty. Dr. Markham, Bishop of Chester, a former Headmaster of Westminster, future Archbishop of Canterbury, and an ancestor of the Markham already met – another was a general – was made Governor to the Princes George and Frederick. He asked George III in what manner he wished them educated. *'Like the son of any private English gentleman; if they deserve it let them be flogged. Do as you used to do at Westminster.'* [21] The formality of the process was marked by the ceremonial presentation of the birch to a new Eton Headmaster. Westminster had a rod-room full of rods *'most artistically made by College John'.*[22]

Images remained lodged in the mind. At Harrow there was 'Billy' who taught the third and fourth forms, holding a candle in one hand while performing with the other,[23] and an occasion when Dr. Wordsworth, Headmaster, *'a high-minded and kind-hearted gentleman'* but *'not a successful schoolmaster'* made a rare appearance in his D.D. gown, *'walked up to the form on which the pose had been effected, inflicted six rapid, slashing cuts, and then tossing the rod back into its receptacle, suddenly retired with a demeanour that showed how disgusted he was with the whole business'.*[24] Charles Vaughan, Wordsworth's sucessor, used the rod a good deal to secure better order, dealing in 6, 8, or 10 cuts. Chastisement finished he was wont to remark, *'Thankyou, my dear boy, I won't trouble you further'.*[25] Legends grew up around the birch, that at Harrow being that if the Head raised his hand above his shoulder he had to give the beaten boy five shillings and a bottle of wine.[26] Bent double though, the boy was hardly best placed to judge that, even had he had the temerity to do so. At Eton the first boy flogged by a new Headmaster was said to be presented with the birch and a dozen bottles of champagne though by 1850 that had become myth.[27] Other ways were found of painfully making a point. *'Bring your ears here,'* an Eton tutor would command.[28]

Roger Ascham, Queen Elizabeth's tutor suggested that if a boy failed to make adequate progress it might be more appropriate to beat the master than the boy, but somehow that never caught on.[29]

An imposition was though a commoner punishment.

" Judson! 600 lines!" was the exasperated response of a Harrow master

to further misbehaviour, on that occasion for pouring liquid down the back of a boy's collar.[30] Other diversions included chalking ASS on a boy's back, fastening a paper tail under the jacket collar so as to make him look ridiculous if called out, or putting cobbler's wax on a seat so as to glue a boy fast.

Living near Harrow before Norman's time was a professional line writer to whom the tiresome business of writing lines could be outsourced.[31] Then boys sometimes invested in their disciplinary future by writing out a heap of lines in the holidays then freewheeling in class until the stock began to run low. That though was ended when boys were made to go to their form master for special line-writing paper. Things could be speeded up by binding pens together – called 'coaches' at Westminster – and writing two or even three lines at once. In some quarters though there was recognition that regular line-writing had a deleterious effect on handwriting and an increased tendency to ask for learning by heart, the disadvantage of that being that time had to be found to hear the set task.

Masters could be instructive, ineffectual, kind, strict, humorous, grim, demanding, or lax, but they were generally rather distant figures. The tenor of a boy's life was far more affected by his contemporaries in what were, especially for boarders, largely communities presided over by older boys who made heavy demands on younger boys who, in turn, later found themselves in positions of some potency.

Whether or not boys learnt much was not though, to many, the real issue. The right spirit mattered more.

CHAPTER I: ETON'S LONG CHAMBER

IN 1832, THE NINE-YEAR-OLD WILLIAM JOHNSON, ALONG WITH HIS ELDER BROTHER Wellington, took his outside seat on the Barnstaple Stagecoach ready for the lengthy journey to Eton where he would be a new boy. On a later occasion, sat under an umbrella on the outside in pouring rain, he fell asleep, lost the umbrella, and reached Eton drenched.

He would have got only a blurred view of the surrounding countryside, being chronically short-sighted since birth. A sharper view of things only came about when he acquired a telescope at the age of twenty-three.[1]

He was leaving behind a comfortable home at Torrington in North Devon, an area with which the family had had connections since the time of the Domesday Book. His father, Charles, had made his fortune in India and was then busying himself with such local matters as buying and adapting houses and the control of roads – he was an early enthusiast for Macadam.[2]

Nine might seem a tender age at which to be thrust into the hurly-burly of Eton but it was not uncommon at the time. It wasn't until the later Victorian period, with the huge expansion of independent education when Preparatory Schools came to be numerous, that entry at twelve or thirteen became the norm. Arriving at such a tender age could result in a lengthy spell at Eton. Frank Tarver arrived in 1834 and was to be there for the next fourteen years, later becoming the French master.[3] In William Johnson's case it was to be nine years.

Doubtless William had already heard bits of comment about Eton from his elder brother. Wellington though would have had no experience of life in College which was where William, who'd won a scholarship, was heading and to face the daunting challenge of life in Long Chamber.

* * * * *

William Tucker did not face any particularly stiff challenge in order to enter Eton as a Colleger.[4] He was asked merely to give a Latin response to this question : 'Qua de villa vel urbe?' (Which town do you come from ?). This was simple enough if it was London, harder if Huddersfield. Yet it was known well in advance that that was to be the sole question, giving even the least promising Classicist time to get the response right. The system was then rather lax, he later reflected. He was eight and a half on admission and was to spend the next eleven years at Eton.

There was no time for niceties on arrival, dressed in shorts, trousers having been banned but allowed again after 1814. Boys were not though allowed to wear white dabs, nankeen, or jean. He was at once *made to have a fighting round or two with a boy about my size, but older, to see which was the better man'*,[5] an initiation from which he seemingly emerged with some credit. College gave him a serge gown, about all it would give him, which he was required to wear at all times, even to games, and he was introduced to Long Chamber where he was to spend countless hours.

This was *'no joke in my time, if taken in the light of dust, smoke, and peculiar atmosphere'*. It was *'lofty, airy, full of draughts and windows, many broken; and when lighted up from top to bottom with fifty dips and two roaring fires, it would have presented to the casual visitor a somewhat pleasing and suggestive sight'.*[6] To a new boy though the reality could be uncomfortable and alarming once the doors were locked at eight o'clock and he found himself part of a community of fifty Collegers while twenty more were housed in Carter's Chambers below. Keate, Headmaster, appeared in the evening to call Absence but for the rest of the time boy rule prevailed.

There was a practical difficulty. While there were enough beds there were too few bedsteads with the result that some boys had their bedding on the floor between beds. Tucker recalled how his bedding got trodden on and besmirched during the making of the beds on either side. This consisted of *'a thin flock mattress which lasted through my ensuing eleven years; three blankets, thin also; sheets, bolster, no pillow and a woollen horse-rug'.*[7] Sometimes beds were shared and nothing was thought odd about that. Until the end of the Eighteenth Century more had to be paid for a single bed. Tucker did though add that *'repeated and strong home complaints'* [8] secured additional bedsteads.

Each boy had a 'Universal Desk' beside his bed. This contrivance, about four foot square, contained a shelf, pigeon holes, side cupboard, and served as a stand-up desk.[9] It contained all his belongings – books, football trousers, clothes from which to find the 'long costume' necessary for a night in Long Chamber. On top might, if he'd been prudent, be the remains of a candle, usually held in a stick made from text book pages, which he could light to see to dress by when he heard Cartland, Keate's servant, going round with the bell in the morning.[10]

The winter cold seeped through cracks in the walls and the broken windows. The only chairs were those which some senior boys had procured for themselves. It had been entirely unheated until 1784 when two fireplaces had been put in. There was nowhere to wash – Tucker recalled a passing wash at a tap in his Dame's yard when returning muddied from football – save a sixth form shelf. The whole chamber stank of decaying rats' corpses, ordure and urine. In 1858 the floorboards were taken up and two cartloads of rats' corpses taken away. [11]

The saving grace was that Collegers had other resources. Each was allocated a Dame's house where he could take his clothes to be washed and laundered and go if unwell. Also, the habit was to take a usually shared room in Windsor at the standard charge of half a crown. One such Tucker secured with two other boys. This was *'an enormous convenience'*.[12] Windsor was quite out of bounds *'and yet, there are sixty Collegers, if not more, with authorised rooms high and low all over the town. Surely we are a strange people'*. [13]

* * * * *

The day started with meagre rations, Collegers being given a half-pint of milk and a penny roll and butter. With nowhere to consume it Tucker would do so outside if fine, or on his Dame's dresser if wet. For the rest of the day one sheep was the allotted College allowance meaning that the one hot meal of the day provided an unrelieved diet of mutton served without vegetables. Fags had first to cater for their seniors and that wasn't easy. *'Now, some of us were very small, and the carrying of a great, heavy, round pewter dish with a heavy joint upon it full of gravy, up some twenty steps from the kitchen to the Hall, and then down the tables... was a trial; and no wonder that the cooling gravy and grease invaded our waistcoats.'*[14] Often all that was left of this animal for them was scrag so that they scavaged leftovers for remains, or went hungry. The inadequacy of this diet did not escape notice. Parental complaint resulted in some increased provision with, for example, a quantity of loin previously shared by six then given for four.[15] Later on a Summer's day was 'Bever', when bread and beer were put out in Hall. Supper was at 6 o'clock in which the remainder of the mutton reappeared. It was voluntary and few turned up. Small wonder that the nine or ten year old Tucker *'slept and dreamed of feasts and banquets'*. The College cook, Worthy, always had some tempting delicacies if boys had the money to buy them. There was a question as to whether this slim fare didn't stunt later growth. [17]

Oppidans called the Collegers 'tugs' in view of their relentless consumption of tug mutton and made fun of their monotonous diet.

> 'Brown bread all the week,
> Pudding on a Sunday:
> And 'cause it is allowance day,
> Some porter on a Monday.' [18]

The porter was perhaps an improvement on the daily beer which came along in gallon tins and was in Tucker's opinion *'vile, villainous and detestable – a disgrace to the College'*,[19] undrinkable save to an unquenchable thirst. Boys though found that by putting it in stone bottles of the kind used for ginger beer, adding three or four raisins and molasses of sugar they would after four or five days have rather a good beer which they called 'Bumble'. That they were able to do this suggests that what they were given was not properly fermented. According to Tucker, College beer was still *'abortive'* decades later.

There were though brighter occasions. On Founder's Day Collegers were given half a roast chicken and on Election Saturday, at the end of the summer half, raspberry and currant tart.[20] Then it was possible to supplement the College's dire beer with better brews. Gowns and hollowed out folios that Keate viewed with justified suspicion could be employed to hide drinks hastily bought at the Christopher. Pride of place though was given to Bulstrode, a *'strong heady porter from the Duke of Portland's estate'*.[21] It cost a shilling a quart but its kudos was such that all had to have it. 'Drinking-in' was a communal event financed by surplus money from the games subscription. This followed a feast at the Christopher Inn and saw the downing of *'a succession of fiery twelve shilling bowls of Bishop, a highly spiced black strap port. ...... The whole thing was coarse – a very orgie'.* (sic) These nights ended in confusion. *'The Lower Boy servitors, half tipsy themselves, had difficulty and trouble enough to get their thoroughly tipsy masters to bed.'* [22]

* * * * *

A newcomer to the Chamber had then to rapidly accustom himself to his position as a fag. The Sixth Form Collegers could ask any of the thirty or so lower boys to do as they asked. Much of it was mundane with boys being asked to run errands, fetch provisions, or to go and saw logs – the last particularly unpopular. At the same time there was an attachment to a specific master. As far as the young Colleger was concerned, a good deal depended on the character of the master. Tucker was unlucky, being set to work for *'a hard and dreaded master'*.[23] Later in life they met socially and became good friends.

After a day of performing various tasks a fag might have been hoping for a quiet night. That though didn't always happen. Failings were given short shrift. Not making his master's bed in the approved manner could see him roughly pulled out of bed and kicked howling round the chamber. That might happen too if he was heard snoring. Or he might have his face slapped until it was 'red hot'. Other testing episodes were tossing in a blanket, *'pricking for sheriff'* [24] in which the victim was rolled up in a cloth and then pricked through it with needles and *'taking the omens'* in which the requirement was to dance on a heap of lighted paper. (With the number of open fires, guttering candles, and other pursuits such as this it seems providential that there seems not to have been any serious fire, at any rate within the time scale of this work, at any of the three Collegiate main dormitories at Eton, Westminster or Winchester).

Other demands on a lower boy must have been tedious in the extreme, such as 'mowing nights' when a senior's hair and whiskers had to be attended to while he lounged back in his chair, perhaps reading the latest raciest novel. This lengthy procedure meant a very late night. One master noticed that some lower boys could hardly keep awake in his class, asked questions, but no-one was saying much.

The Captain of College was the presiding supremo and he usually doubled as Captain of the Fireplace, in which role he would keep a close watch on the two fags set to prepare the fire, making sure that the three huge coals were correctly placed and using a rug string to check.[25]

If two boys fell out it was to him that they had to go to get permission to fight. If granted, a ring was formed and a few rounds contested. They usually ended amicably.

A welcome stage in a boy's career was reached when he progressed to 'liberty', at which point he could neither be fagged nor fag others. Once in the Fifth he had joined the aristocracy and could start to throw his weight around.

Drinking apart, there were other rousing events in Long Chamber. One was the rat hunt. Rats were such frequent visitors that some came to be individually recognised such as a large one with a pronounced limp. By way of preparation all known rat holes were stopped up, baited stockings left out then, when the rustling presence of enough was heard, the hunt began. Caught, their skins were *'carefully stretched and dried, and then nailed in rows over the broad fireplace from the ceiling downwards'*.[26] About forty were thus displayed with another two or three rows of them in Carter's Chamber. Wilkinson too remembered these hunts. *'It really was glorious fun – try it, some of you young fellows.'* [27]

Drama had an enduring popularity. Props of all kinds were made, some readily convertible to various objects, and kept none too well hidden in the dormitory, Keate rather turning a blind eye to them. The presence of Charles Kean's son was something of a stimulant. It reached the point at which boys were hiring out rooms in Windsor and giving regular performances until Keate, thinking it was getting rather out of hand, stopped it.

Collegers had two playing fields of their own. They excelled at cricket, that most cerebral of team sports, and always expected to beat the Oppidans. Keate, who took a keen interest in all College matters, was vexed if they lost. When on one occasion they did, the defeat was so taken to heart that their bats were covered in black crepe and stood along the wall. Bowling was under arm, eight balls to an over, and played without pads or guards. The stumps were raised in height to make it easier to dislodge such *'blockers and stickers'* as Sir Christopher Willoughby who carried his bat through an innings for seven and was not known ever to score a two.[28] That cricket matches were only patchily recognised as significant social events was shown by the 1818 Eton v Harrow Lords match when only three Etonian players turned up and the remainder had to be recruited from the crowd. Unsurprisingly, Harrow won.[29]

Football was voluntary and involved *'smart and prolonged rouges'* (scrimmages).[30] Wilkinson recounted how boys would take to the field wearing improvised pads consisting of old book covers inserted in stockings so that *'we took to the field, looking like half-swathed mummies, or gouty old codgers'*.[31] If they were school books that was risky as appearing in school with a coverless text book was a beatable offence. That though changed in 1825 when a boy called Barker turned out in knee breeches and silk stockings after which pads were discarded.[32] Neither Tucker nor Wilkinson gives much sense of the flow of the game though the latter wrote of the bully, presumably the same as a rouge, free kicks, and catching a ball in order to have a shy at the goals as aspects of it. Tucker denied that the Wall Game, of which it was later said that its rules *'have always been unintelligible except to a limited number of its professors'* [33] was *'rough, rude, and brutal'* [34] though he did allow that College v Oppidan games could be fierce.

Bathing had incurred the ominous prophecy that a boy would drown every three years. No-one taught swimming apart from a chap on the bank waving his arms about and *'telling us to strike our arms and legs together'*.[35] A handsome, vigorous young fellow named Hayes was one fatality. It was feared that a boy called Moore was another after he'd sunk and been submerged for five or ten minutes. He was though pulled out and resuscitated. Another boy, Collins, was remembered as being able to dive but not swim. G.A.Selwyn, or Selwyn Major in school terms, *'a grand athlete'* and future Metropolitan of New Zealand, took the danger of drowning seriously enough to demonstrate how to undress in the water, and even under water, in the event of falling in.[35] That didn't though meet the case of a boy deliberately entering the water naked, as was the custom, and then getting into difficulties.

There were other impromptu or occasional diversions. Boys might come chasing out of class at 12.00 or 4.00 p.m. with a game of 'Egg in the Hat' in mind.[36] This began with top hats being placed in a line crown down. From a distance boys then began to aim balls at them. If a ball lodged inside a hat all but the owner of the hat ran away while he ran for the ball and shied it at them. It involved various forfeits. Top hats also did as wickets for cloister cricket played with a fives ball so got rather battered. Fives itself could be played between the chapel buttresses. Hoops were in vogue during the hoops half by the end of which most were no longer usable as such but transformed into weapons of war for a grand Colleger/Oppidan battle.[37] In the half hour of freedom given after 8 o'clock Fifth and Sixth Formers occasionally took to 'Royal Mail' which involved hurtling round the College an armchair fitted with wheels, making regular stops at the same spots, and trying to get back on the dot of 8.30 p.m. One ingenious youth invented a 'rolling skate' without being able to make the wheels sufficiently frictionless to be of practical use.[38]

There was too some coarser sport. There was widespread betting on contests between bull and dog, after which the bull was killed and roasted. Recalled, Tucker saw this as an occasion of *'sottish, coarse, and drunken revelry'*. [39] There was too an occasion when two swans were shot *'for coarse food'*. That though *'was a vile act'*.[40] Wilkinson could add cock-fighting and badger-baiting, including an episode when a boy was flogged for badger-baiting and keeping a badger in his room.[41]

* * * * *

Tucker records rather ambivalent emotions of his early years in College. Time he had to himself was hard to fill either enjoyably or profitably with little being offered for junior recreation so that *'listless and motiveless was the whole of leisure '*.[42] There were a large number of whole or half-day holidays occurring on a regular basis with Saints' days and, in Tucker's time, holidays to celebrate Peninsular War victories. These occasions were though often *'rather desolate'*.[43] Go up to Long Chamber while the pupil room was shut up and he risked getting fagged. Altogether the Windsor room was a great relief.

As a result, perhaps, significant events were savoured. One was the visit of the Duke of Wellington who avoided formal encounters with gowned personages. *'When I first saw him, he had jumped upon, and was running along the Long Walk wall, followed by his two young sons, and a bevy of young noblemen's and gentlemen's sons whose fathers he knew ... and went on and stood laughing, chattering to the boys, and the boys laughing and chattering back until he jumped down in the middle of them – the veriest boy of all'*.[44] He went back to his old house and found his initials still visibly inscribed on the kitchen door alongside which was the maids' room, optimistically styled the Virgins' Bower. A very different affair was the funeral of George III which the top hundred boys in the school attended by royal command and every Eton boy wore black.[45]

As the prospect of the end of his lengthy spell at Eton came nearer his thoughts must have sometimes turned to the future, and in particular how much reward those many hours of Classical study might bring. For it had been demanding, work even having to be done amid the many distractions of Long Chamber. *'Just after going to bed you put your College candlestick on the top of your bedstead, and having closed your 'Plutarch's Lives' you ran over your Homer'*. [46]

The greatest award for a Colleger was signalled with the approach of 'The Speedyman' from King's. However swift his progress it got known well before his arrival what he was coming for. That was to bring news that a Fellow had either resigned or died and that therefore there was a vacancy on the Foundation. This was offered to the Senior Colleger by the Provost who would publicly *'rip'* his gown and expel him to

King's on whose bounty he might exist until the end of his days. He had though to be there within twenty days, irrespective of the Eton term.[47]

Election Saturday pretty well marked the end of the summer half and was the occasion of *'a gigantic fraud'*.[48] In order to make Long Chamber look attractive for the *'country cousins'* and give it a quite alien appearance boys spent hours rug-riding over the floor until it had a good shine, boughs were brought in to place all round the walls and to ensure that the rat skins were covered up, while shelves in the Captain's abode were filled with enough books to give an impression of a voracious and discriminating reader. Departure day saw the College filled with a wide variety of horse-drawn vehicles heading in all directions.

Those eleven years had not been without their frustrations but later he was to reflect that the benefit of a *'self-governing community'* was that *'the perfect freedom gave an inexpressible charm to Eton life'*.[49]

* * * * *

Charles Wilkinson appears to have spent his earliest Eton years in a Dame's house as the tenor of his writing suggests more than the kind of attachment to one that Tucker and other Collegers had.

Not seemingly involved in an inaugural fight himself he heard that a near relation after barely a week at Eton *'had had a fight and had two black eyes'*. *'It shows his pluck,'* he thought but a relative, presumably female, showed the letter recounting this to another, *'eyes streaming with tears'*.[50] Other mentions to do with the fighting culture then in vogue at Eton were that of a boy in a fight disdaining his second's knee between rounds and who instead *'strutted about the ring spouting Homer'*. There was also the belief that raw steak was good for a fighter.[51]

Escapades and experiments were chiefly remembered from this school phase. Electrical experiments with a Leyden jar made the hair stand on end or bring sparks from noses. A door handle was electrified to surprise the Dame, which it did. She took it in good part though making clear that once was enough. Shelley had done the same thing to Dr. Bethell in his house, in that case giving *'that slow-witted man'*[52] a sequence of violent shocks. At another time an art work on the wall seemingly produced by a red hot poker appeared to be inviting imitation. Wilkinson was mid-way through trying to depict a lion's head above the fireplace in this way when a maid came in. The result was a birching.[53]

There was another mode of entry to Long Chamber besides that of the *'exam'* faced by young boys. Eton's Statutes provided for the admission of boys into Long Chamber up and till their seventeenth birthday, if they were *'well read'*. That was a handily flexible proviso for Eton's Establishment whose well-connected members were then able to place a boy in an Oppidan house and then send him into College for a far shorter time, and at an age when he was less vulnerable.

Tucker and his peers took a dim view of these Fourth Form, Remove, or Lower Fifth boys suddenly appearing in Long Chamber, admitting to *'a strong prejudice against them'*. *'We who had borne the heat and burden of the day'* were being joined by boys from Dame's houses who had had a much easier time of it and wouldn't be tested as they had been. [54]

Tucker was an enthusiast for fagging despite himself having had a hard taskmaster (*I love the system of fagging ...it brings high and low to their bearings .... good for both'*) [55] but Wilkinson was more ambivalent about it. He gave an anecdote about Goodford, later Headmaster and Provost, when a boy Colleger.

"Hullo! You 're a new fellow ain't you ? Who's your tutor? Where do you board? What's your name?"
"Roxburgh," was the answer.
"Oh, you're a duke, ain't you?"
"Yes."
"Well, take a basin out of Lower Chamber and fill it at the pump."

That being promptly and cheerfully done Goodford told him, *'You may have my liberties'*. That meant that no-one else could fag him, an arrangement that probably suited both parties.[56] The unwisdom of standing on titular dignity was demonstrated by an Earl who disdained proffered help from a mere commoner and got himself kicked down his stairs.[57]

The darker side of fagging was a habit Wilkinson witnessed of fags on occasion being required to steal for the benefit of their masters. They might be asked to get tea, sugar, or milk for their meals, or coals and faggots for the fire. How these were obtained was of no consequence. This seeming distancing from the act was no kind of mitigation. *'They were not accessories after the fact, but sole delinquents.'* [58]

Unsurprisingly, in view of an incident in his time, he gave a full account of tossing, stressing that it was not a casually reckless affair. There were eight tossers to a blanket, each of whom had been practised in competence. *'All swayed five or six times with the tossing blanket and at the sixth 'go' all drew back with a sharp pull and the little fellow danced like a pea in the drum shouting* excelsior *until he'd had enough.'*[59] One 'little fellow', Bligh, when 9 or 10, enjoyed it so much that he came up to Long Chamber just to be tossed. There was though a gruesome accident when a corner of the blanket was not held strongly enough and Rowland Williams landed head first on the corner of a bedstead and was scalped, *'the scalp hanging down over the neck and back suspended by only a small piece of skin'*. The scalp was sewn back on and, according to Wilkinson, he didn't suffer *'either at the time or in after life'*.[60] There was no further appetite for tossing after that and the practice ceased.

Liberty nights were keenly anticipated, being *'a very Saturnalia'* [61] when all sense of rank was lost. Boys disappeared behind a blanket, an impromptu green room, emerging in various guises. Whether one was dragoon, Spanish nobleman, muffin-boy, blind-beggar or rag-seller the aim was to be so well disguised as to be unrecognisable.

It was on one such night that Wilkinson created what became something of a legend. He was present at a performance of L'Elisir d'Amore in which a mountebank appeared on stage with a horse and cart. This gave him the idea of making his appearance on a donkey at one of these 'masquerade nights'. The donkey was obtained through Picky Powell, one of the *'cads'* who hung around Eton and did business with the boys with varying degrees of scrupulousness.

On the night in question no lantern was seen coming from Keate's lane and the boys thought they were safe to proceed and, with the aid of carrots, manoeuvred the donkey into Lower Chamber. There was though a sudden warning that Keate was on his way after all.

'I just had time to throw a rug to the cad, and tell him to hold it over the beast's head, and to rub him and feed him and keep him quiet, for not a sound or movement must be heard. My younger brother was just trying on his dress (he was going as a legless, armless, blacking bottle), that is, his wicker basket, which was tight, and he could not get out of, so the boys shoved him, as he was, into another study and stood before the door. In came the doctor .... I as captain, called absence, leaving my brother to last, but when I came to 'Wilkinson, minimus,' an extraordinary answer was given from the inside of his basket, through the eye-holes.

'Here, sir.'

'Here, sir, said old Keate, 'where, sir, come out, sir,' and again that heavy sound broke out once more as if some boatswain was giving an order through his two hands at his mouth. 'What's this, sir, come out, sir,' said Keate; and, as there was no appearance, he walked up to the study-door, and there, about the size of his own little self stood the brown paper effigy, with 'Day and Martin's Blacking – greatest wonder of the age,' staring him in the face. He seized it by the cork and shook

it, crying still. 'Come out, sir, you fool, sir come out,' and my young brother, having no hands to make resistance, fell forward into the room and crept out at the bottom.'

Wilkinson major got a rocket from Keate for permitting such tomfoolery but once he'd gone the fun could begin. The donkey was pushed and pulled up the stairs and Wilkinson made a triumphal entry as Dr. Dulcimara wearing gold-braided dress, three-cornered wig and pig-tail, and dispensing wares from his saddlebags to the enthralled spectators. The memorable night ended with a picnic which the donkey shared and lusty singing. [62]

Collegers left a more tangible memento. While the usual mode of expressing displeasure with a junior was a *'stinging slap'* – and something preferred by most to the tedium of writing out lines – there was a possibly unique punishment. This was to have to write a four line witty epigram, rather a reversal of a rather common school case in which misplaced humour brought about the punishment. A book of these was kept in the Provost's Lodge. Here is one:

'Say, Dick, who wrote what Tom composed
(As wise as any Solon)
'The fire burns low – what stop goes there?'
'Why put, says Tom, a colon.' [63]

* * * * *

Looking back on the way Collegers were treated in his day Wilkinson found a good deal to condemn, echoing some of Tucker's complaints.

'When I think that we were supposed to be fed, and there was a large hall and necessary kitchens where all might have been provided, that mutton, and mutton only, was supplied from week's end to week's end though I should not have complained had there been enough of it, and we were always obliged to buy secretly of the cook; when I think that no tea or supper was provided, except a very scanty proportion of this mutton for the Sixth Form; when I think we were obliged to keep a room in town for our meals, which we had to buy for ourselves, and which ought to have been provided by the College; when I think that our parents had to pay a Dame to see to our washing and our clothes, and to offer us a room when we were on the sick list and had to stay out; when I think that the Sixth Form College bills, including all extras, really necessities for him, were within fifteen pounds of a Fifth Form Oppidan's I'm left wondering where the funds providing for the board and lodging of those on the Foundation went to in our time.' [64]

Yet despite all that, he wondered whether *'in these refined days they (Eton boys) may not have half as much fun as there was in Keate's time'.*[65]

* * * * *

Responsibility for the state of things in College lay with the Provost and Fellows. It has been suggested that intermarriages between Eton's Fellows created something rather like dynasties, and that Eton came to be run like a family business. For such as the Hawtrey's, Coleridge's, and Carter's came to look on Eton scholarships and King's Fellowships very much as their birthright. The Hawtrey's in particular had had a close connection with Eton since 1692.

Fellows were remembered as *'kindly men, conspicuous for watching over the interests of their relatives and dependents',*[66] the safeguarding of which was their primary concern and being distinctly selective in their attitude to the Statutes. For while *'the Fellows might speciously argue that the boys were treated in accordance with the Statutes these apologists of old abuses had to adopt a different line of argument if pressed as to their own position and emoluments'.*[67] They were required to provide a daily meal of mutton and a serge gown, in line with the Statutes, though these didn't stop more being added, but little was, while the Fellows ensured that they themselves had a comfortable existence. When Fellows did get involved in College affairs it was often at a trivially mundane level. Two Williams brothers, sons of a former Provost, were best remembered for their dispute as to whether potatoes should be served peeled or unpeeled.

It was at George III's insistence that Dr. Goodall was installed as Provost, crossing the wish of the Prime Minister. He was *'tall and stately'*, had a *'charming manner'*, was *'dignified without pomposity and joyous without levity'*[68] and habitually wore the costume of an Eighteenth Century church dignitary. Yet he acted according to his watchword of *'No innovation'* during his lengthy time as Provost and consequently little altered. He had a ruthless streak. When challenged over the non-observance of the Statutes he destroyed an extract from the muniments that seemed to contradict his assertions. [69]

Numerically the seventy Collegers formed only a small part of Eton. They did though have a disproportionate influence in that a number of those going on to King's returned as masters. An impression of life in one of Eton's boarding houses is given in chapter 8. According to Tucker, life there was a *'somewhat violent contrast'* to that in College.

CHAPTER TWO : KEATE

One Eton new boy was astonished by his first encounter with Keate. He recalled being '*told to go into the Upper School, heard something read, could not hear what, and on something being said afterwards, the whole school raised a yell, booing, hissing, and scraping feet. I was thunder-struck at their audacity*'.[1]

As a boy progressed through the school though Keate would come more sharply into focus. He would have seen '*a short, short-necked, short-legged man; thickset, powerful, and very active*' whose '*countenance resembled that of a bulldog*',[2] clad in silk cassock and pudding-sleeved gown, Doctor of Divinity's scarf, white bands fluttering under the chin and topped off with his tricorne hat.3 He would have become familiar with his resonant, skilfully modulated tones which though rose to a rapid-fire quacking sound when he was angry, which was often. Seen at close quarters he would have noticed the red, shaggy eyebrows which seemed to act like pointers.

Outside he carried an umbrella in all weathers which he would protrude round any corner to avoid collision with onrushing youth. He would not though permit boys to have one, saying it was more fitting for a school-girl. That prompted one of the milder protests against his authority when some boys went to Upton, took down the sign above an institution there which said 'Seminary for Young Ladies' and fixed it above the entrance to the school-yard to Keate's intense annoyance.4

Boys who had been at Eton under Keate's predecessor, the amiable, conservatively-inclined Dr. Goodall who was well liked, readily took umbrage at Keate's contrasting '*sternness of government*'.5 A taste for insurrection was formed.

In January, 1810, within a year of his appointment there was the first wave of fractious discord. Rebellion against him had been planned even before he took up his appointment, a progression from Lower Master. Sentiment was still strong against anyone thought a provocative interferer with boys' liberties. Entering Upper School he was booed all the way to his desk. This imposing structure was entered by two doors. Trying one he found it screwed up; the other proved similarly blocked. Keate got in by vaulting over it, remarking, *"I am not so old as you think"*. This manoeuvre seemed to show though that, at least in summer, nothing was worn below gown and cassock as it revealed something of an absence of anything in the pant line.[6]

More trouble followed. The boys, instead of taking their places in chapel in an orderly manner, gathered at the steps and, on Keate's belated approach, stampeded inside. To get a grip on this insurgency Keate called the Lower Fifth for an extra Absence (roll-call). No-one showed up.

When they appeared at the next one they were ordered to stay behind, and Keate began to flog them. After twenty had been dealt with the masters were summoned after Keate had been bombarded with eggs and hissed. The rest were flogged after being told they would be expelled if they refused a flogging.[7]

The King got to hear of this and expressed approval of Keate's firmness. So did the Duke of Wellington who urged him to stick to his guns and tell any disgruntled parents that they could always send their sons elsewhere.[8] It was though Wellington's eldest son, the Marquess of Douro, disguised as Keate in tricorne and gown, who one night painted his front door red, the watchmen supposing they'd been watching Keate's return and thinking Keate himself had been doing the painting, an explanation he angrily dismissed as having more to do with alcohol than observation.

* * * * *

Keate faced three serious disturbances and a fair degree of more frequent lower level disruption. Yet neither Tucker nor Wilkinson suggest he operated against a background of constant uproar. Rather it seems to have been that the generally mundane existence typical of most schools was punctuated by occasional boisterous explosions and rather more persistent mischievous subversion.

Tucker's portrait suggests a man very much in control for most of the time. He faced the boys with *'features stern; voice harsh; intolerant of the slightest mistake; rough; exacting'*.[9] Boys had to come to his division with their seventy lines of Horace or Homer learnt by heart. It was though conceded that some boys were unable to do this and their ration was ten lines. These though were said last to prevent this being a route for a quick exit.10 There was construing to be done in the pupil room before facing Keate or another master. A capable boy might produce verse of sufficient quality for it to be recommended to Keate, and the boy, *'sent up for good'*, would be called up and after slithering past a row of knees, stand beside Keate's desk while his lines were sonorously read aloud.11 Before the institution of the Newcastle Scholarships and other awards, that was the ultimate accolade. At the other end of the academic scale it was generally possible for the *'saps'* (half-idlers) and thorough idlers to get their work done by more proficient youths. There was sometimes emergency aid for a boy struggling with verse writing in the shape of *'a little round paper pellet passed with a few moderate verses done with judicious mistakes'.*12

On occasion the error could hardly be passed over as when a boy rendered Horace's *'Exegi monumentum perennius aere'* as *'I have eaten a monument harder than brass.'*

'Oh, you have, have you,' said the doctor, *'then you will stay afterwards and I'll give you something to digest it:'* 13 presumably a sharp reminder that what the Ancients wrote was meant to make some kind of sense.

Keate operated under the difficulty of the sheer size of his division which reached 198 boys which meant little focus on individuals. Having only seven or eight masters for about five hundred boys implied sizeable divisions but the uneven way they were distributed made Upper School forms huge. For Lower School masters each had about twenty boys to deal with.

The Rev. Henry Knapp, Keate's number two, operated in conditions which would have sorely tested the strongest disciplinarian. He taught in a room with tiered seating which could accommodate about 80 boys. Knapp though had 110 in his division with the result that after the initial jostling to find a seat in this cramped arena about thirty boys had to hang around the door. A boy called on to construe might appear breathlessly at Knapp's desk seeming to burst with eagerness to display his knowledge when in reality he might just have responded to a hasty summons from his fives game. Presiding over this throng Knapp was remembered as being either *'ridiculously fierce or ridiculously mild'*. His retort to a boy protesting at being singled out with *'Please, sir, I was doing nothing. I didn't speak,'* was often: *'I don't care. I will have somebody flogged'*. If the boy later approached him civilly he could be persuaded that he'd made a mistake. He was an excellent scholar, *'a good-natured little man'*, *'more humbugged, not to say bullied, than all the other masters put together'*, and popular with the boys in his own house.[14]

In Keate's division Edward Coleridge recalled being called to construe only twice in a half. Some of those sat near the back were also able to slip out unnoticed and play fives in the chapel buttresses while those who wished to play up got their chance amid the gloom in 5 o'clock winter school. The only light came from a dim chandelier and the two candlesticks on Keate's desk. A wise preliminary was to check the sconces for gunpowder before lighting the candles. From time to time there were waves of drone-like singing and a glaring Keate jiggled the candles to try to see where the noise was coming from but the boys had mastered the art of making the sound with their mouths shut. Another diversion was firing bread pellets. Keate though habitually made the tactical mistake of looking at the point of impact when one hit the oak panelling rather than seeking the shooter. Misbehaviour during daylight was riskier. One co-ordinated provocation was the dropping of stone ink bottles on the floor so that Keate *'began to wax very wrath by nine o'clock'*.15

He faced other irritations. An Eton shop keeper took to selling plaster moulds of his profile. Hoping to put a stop to that he bought up all the shop's stock, seemingly unaware that that did little good without getting hold of the mould.16 Then Windsor Fair was a handy venue for picking up toys with interesting possibilities. One such was a cuckoo toy which a boy was able to make work with his feet while displaying his innocent hands.17 Impertinently annoying too was the young nobleman who took to impersonating Keate and carrying out bogus Absences.18 Anyone identified who comprehensively overstepped the mark though got short shrift. Thus Lord Sunderland's decision to celebrate Bonfire Night on Keate's lawn, his firepower including a small cannon, was his last at Eton.19

* * * * *

The second major disturbance during Keate's time occurred in 1818 and a youth called Marriott was the cause of it. He, displeased at Keate's bringing forward the time of Absence, decided to cut it as it interfered with his racing schedule. That, and his refusal to be flogged, led to his expulsion. The following morning in school a voice boomed out, "*Where is Mariott?*" The shout was repeated amid booing. Keate took no notice and continued the lesson.[20]. Later a stone was thrown at a window of the unpopular Green's house. Emboldened by that, others threw stones until all were shattered. Yet that was not followed by any flogging and work went on as usual. What revived the ill-feeling was the action of some tutors in seeking from boys a written *'confession'* that they had had nothing to do with this *'rebellion'*. Whether Keate was behind that initiative is unclear. In the event it precipitated more serious trouble. When Keate entered the schoolroom he found his imposing desk smashed to pieces. He pretended not to notice anything amiss and proceeded as normal among the wreckage. Later though the whole school was summoned along with all the masters and six boys were singled out and expelled along with another boy who made an unwise remark.²¹ Those initially expelled were three Oppidans and two Collegers. The sixth boy, Palk, was overheard by his tutor saying 'Never', after Keate had expressed his wish that these unfortunate events would be forgotten and was overheard by his tutor, Ben Drury, who drew it to Keate's attention. It in fact did Palk little harm as after a somewhat partial account of proceedings had been given to the Duke of York's Commander in Chief, this indignant officer gave him an army commission.²²

There were conjectures as to just how Keate could have known who had smashed his desk. One explanation was that Cartwright, his servant, and also a sort of intelligence agent, had spotted boys coming up to school at an unusual hour, sledgehammer probably concealed beneath a gown, and guessed they might have mischief in mind. Getting himself to a spot on the false roof above Upper Chamber from where he was looking down directly on Keate's desk, he would have had a clear view of the wrecking.23 A variant was that he just happened to be there effecting some repair to the chandelier and so fortuitously got a clear view.

These expulsions did though have a calming effect to the relief of local inhabitants, alarmed at the riotous conduct of the boys. The College too became quieter for a while. Challenging Keate was one thing but few really wanted to be expelled.

Wilkinson had little doubt that the birch was an essential element of school life and, in true clerical style, adduced illustrations of biblical justification. It was not though, he insisted, wielded without a sense of what was appropriate. For trivial offences, the beating was often light. For one of the youngest boys, and some were only six or seven, there was *'little more than a tickling which would scarce warm him up on a cold morning'*.24 On the other hand, a boy in serious trouble might get double cuts from two birches and also have to endure a *'jawbation'*. *'He had no favourites, and flogged the son of a duke and the son of a grocer with perfect impartiality.'* 25

There was little doubt as to the frequency with which the birch was used. Tucker too was quite sure of its need. *'Nothing but a firm hand would have kept these gentry in hand.'* 26 That Eton should have found it necessary to have a rule that a boy who got flogged more than twice a day would miss his remove (form promotion) suggests a considerable number of repeat offenders. Keate's once sending away a boy who'd shown up for the third time in a day may have been forbearance to spare him that. Stories circulated. There was the case of a boy sent with a message to Keate, beaten before he could explain himself: and of the confirmation candidates, supposedly beaten as their names had been put down on a list much like the daily beating 'bill'.

Keate conducted very little of the flogging on his own account. Rather it was the daily list compiled by masters that filled the library with various offenders, a number of whom had been found wanting in class. One such was the boy who could do no better with a line of recitation than *'latos, something, something, agros'*.27 On one occasion there were a large number of such miscreants. The cause was the confidence of Fifth and Sixth form boys that a certain bit of academic laxity could be harmlessly exploited. A custom had grown up of these two forms on certain days being set work at three o'clock which was then left at a master's desk two hours later. Little notice seemed to be taken of it. This time though the master did look them through and noticed a good deal of similarity between the versions. Closer inspection showed that there appeared to have been only three or four authors of these seventy-two copies. Keate saw little point in investigation and summoned them all for a beating. *'Five (swishes) went on after five in the gentlest of fives – and the whole matter, in point of fact, was looked upon as a gigantic joke'*. It seemed that on that occasion even Keate didn't take it entirely seriously.28

Boys reacted in different ways. Some refused to show any sign of pain. Others would *'howl when they were under the rod'*.29 In some cases the howling was put on *'from sheer impudence'*.30 Sir Harry Goodriche counted aloud the number of strokes he got, his voice getting noticeably higher as the cuts went on from five to ten.31

Possibly the most impudent challenge came from a boy who was fairly certain that a beating would soon be coming his way and who, as preparation, got a local artist to paint a portrait of the Headmaster on his bottom. The birching duly happened and the art work rather painfully defiled.32

Gladstone managed to avoid the birch by what he later admitted was a somewhat specious argument. As a fourteen-year-old preposter of his form he had failed to mark down a boy coming late to school. For this he was roundly upbraided by Keate who called for a birch. *'If you please, sir,'* he argued, *'my prepostership would have been an office of trust if I had sought it of my own accord but it was forced upon me.'* Keate, inclined to give more latitude to logical challenge than candid admission, let it pass.33

One response left him temporarily stumped. His wrathful thundering at a youth looked to be heading in the inevitably painful direction when the boy stood up and said: *'You know, sir, that I have always regarded you as a father.'* It was a little while before Keate could get out his muttered response: *'Yes, I believe you do,'* and forgot the punishment.34

As to what feelings lay behind this accepted institutional practice Wilkinson thought this a burden on a master who *'had to pocket his pride and delicacy'*.35 Maxwell Lyte, doyen of Eton historians, reckoned it might have been to some degree because Keate enjoyed it.

Keate's own punishment was generally an imposition. *'Say by heart the second chapter of the Ephesians in Greek tomorrow morning in my Chambers.'* was his response to Tucker's arriving late for lock-up.36

* * * * *

Fights at Eton, as in the wider community in early decades of the Nineteenth Century, were very much a part of daily life.[37] Looking back on his schooldays there Gladstone could recall there often being two or three a day. Most were impromptu scraps but occasionally there were prize fights, bouts which continued until one of the combatants was either unable or unwilling to continue. To excel at these was to gain the kind of legendary status which would earn you a place in Eton lore. On one occasion though a fight ended in disaster. Seemingly originating in an unintended kick a quarrel broke out between Francis Ashley, aged thirteen, and Charles Wood, fourteen and bigger. A fight was arranged on the playing fields in the presence of rival supporters. It went on for two and a half hours towards the end of which *'neither combatant was capable of striking a blow. They were simply pushed together against one another in the last ten rounds or twelve when both fell though no blow had been struck. Ashley fell, and Wood falling forward at the same moment, landed on top of Ashley, striking him with his left knee on the back of the neck.'* Ashley was carried back to his house and laid on his bed. The boys with him thought his comatose state due to the influence of alcohol. Mr. Milnes Gaskell thought that he'd got through half a bottle of brandy and Wilkinson too thought brandy had been given *'with fatal effect'* though he only watched three rounds. Thomas Taunton, who acted as his second, and writing much later to refute the suggestion that a great deal had been drunk – there were rumours at the time that the best part of a bottle of brandy had been drunk between rounds – maintained that there had only been phial of brandy brought from the Christopher Inn and that the only use made of it had been to massage Ashley's bruised hands. Later when Ashley's elder brother and two Booth brothers were playing cards in the same room, Ashley major noticed that his brother's breathing had stopped. There was a panicked rush for Dr. Fergusson but all he could do was pronounce Ashley dead. Keate was set against prize fights and would stop them if he ever got wind of one. Addressing the school after this tragedy, he did not, he said, object to fighting itself; indeed he was glad to see a boy being struck at once returning the blow, but criticised the poor judgement and lack of a sense of responsibility of those present.It was thought that it could have serious repercussions as both boys' fathers, Colonel Wood and Lord Shaftesbury, were bitter enemies but Shaftesbury refused to prosecute.

* * * * *

Those approaching the end of a lengthy spell at Eton would have had ample opportunity to assess Keate. He had one particularly disagreeable trait and that was to instinctively disbelieve a boy. Whereas it was thought not the thing at Rugby to tell Arnold a lie because he always believed it Keate was only too ready to spot guilt in a boy's eye.

That though was a part of his public persona which Tucker was at pains to show was not the whole picture. *'The lesson over, his manner changed completely; he was low-voiced and courteous'*.38 This very different manner was shown in the breakfasts which he arranged for groups of Fifth and Sixth Form boys. *'Nothing could have been more courteous and genial than the host on these mornings; full of pleasant talk; full of anecdote; full of Eton allusions; and endeavours to bring out his guests. He was, apparently, not the same person. Every trait of severity had vanished.'* 39

Then any boy reaching the rarified height of the Sixth Form would appreciate that he was being taught by an accomplished Classicist, a man who had won four Browne medals and the Craven Scholarship. A particular feature was being invited to 'Play' in Keate's Chambers when he gave *'form, beauty, and intention'* to Greek choruses declaimed in sonorous tones. That though only happened for a part of the year and sometimes boys drifted away after Keate failed to show up.40 Sixth form boys had to have interleaved books with a comparative passage from another source relating to the page of the text.

Keate only had favourites in so far as he encouraged boys of ability and willingness. In part that may have been down to a certain realpolitik, an acknowledgement that only modest progress could be expected from most boys, and from some, not even that. He laboured too under the difficulty faced by other Heads then of having the greatest difficulty in disposing of incompetent staff. One way was to buy them out. At Eton there was another and that was to make such a person a Fellow. That in the end was the way in which the idle and unpopular Green and Bethel were got out of the classroom. His own practice he made a little more sensible by creating a middle Fifth Form in 1820, thus reducing his division to a hundred. [41]

A daily presence of which all would have been aware was that of him in chapel. That though was not for him an occasion of spiritual meditation but of constant watchfulness, aware that some boys had irreligious habits such as chanting very different words from those in hymnal or psalter, and ostentatiously waving an ominous notebook in the direction of the more exhibitionist. Chapel management hardly helped to foster a reverential spirit, the clergy anxious to get out as speedily as possible, but not before boys had been subjected to sermons *'mumbled and jumbled by aged men with weak, smothered voices'*.42 The building too, Tucker found, was in a *'cold, cheerless state before restoration'* [43] and before a noble lady paid for its heating. There were though moments of unintended and deliberate humour. *'My sins are more numerous than the hairs on my head,'* was the text injudiciously chosen by a Fellow *'bald as a coot'*.44 Then there was the occasion when a leading tenor of his day, John Hobbs, was well set in Handel's 'Comfort ye' when his mellifluous tones suddenly turned into a shriek. He was led out, it being assumed he'd had some kind of fit. The truth was that a young Colleger had run a pen into his calf. 45

Despite that, Tucker thought there was *'an innate religious feeling among the greater part of the boys'* noting that Sunday services got a more respectful audience than weekday ones. 46 As to the innate state of Keate and his masters one boy was not so sure. Following the melee on the chapel steps, and Keate accusing the boys involved of *'irreverence',* he reflected that he'd never thought of Keate, or indeed any other of the masters as Christian, at any rate, *'not in the ordinary sense of the word'.* 47

There were other occasions when Keate would show a more genial public persona. On the morning of June 4th he would announce a later 10.00 p.m. lock-up because he *'supposed there was a cricket match'*. This feigned ignorance of the real cause, the celebrations of that day on the out-of-bounds river, the festivities being *'not allowed, not forbidden'*, brought forth a barrage of *'booing and laughter which might have been heard through the open window half over Eton'*.[48] In class too there were occasional lighter moments as when Keate revealed his awareness of ongoing dramatics by saying "Lydia Languish, construe," and having a red-faced George Williams rising to do so. Tucker in fact claimed that Keate could have stopped the rows at the end of 'prose', so called from Keate's pronunciation of 'prayers', which had so astounded a new boy had he been minded to do so. There are other glimpses of him in less assertive mood such as watching the cricket while drinking neat brandy or laughing in a good-humoured way when passing a meeting of the Literati though perhaps cocking an ear in their direction to check they weren't venturing on to forbidden territory by discussing political events of the last fifty years. Despite that it sometimes seemed that the Catholic question was one that had dogged the Athenians too.[49]

There was a good deal of literary activity, much of it in the form of short-lived magazines. The brilliant and prolific W.M.Praed though started up the Etonian with *'refinement of idea and powers of expression rarely to be found'*.[50] Gladstone, who acquired the strange nickname of 'Merry-pebble' – probably not one that would have occurred to his future cabinet colleagues – was remembered as a most industrious editor, sitting at a desk covered in manuscripts.[51]

* * * * *

In 1832 Keate faced the most serious of the threats to his rule and, as in 1818, the immediate cause was the expulsion of a popular boy, Munro, after he'd refused to be flogged.

At the subsequent Absence, once again the occasion of tumult, Keate left his name off the list but it was loudly shouted out by the boys who then roundly booed Keate who *'stormed and threatened'* to no avail. The following day the disturbance was louder and longer. In retaliation Keate then called an extra Absence at 8.00 p.m. Only two small boys rather nervously turned up, one of whom, irrationally, and suggesting Keate had quite lost his self- control, was then seized by the collar, shaken and threatened.[52]

All masters were then summoned to attend a meeting after they'd dealt with lock-up in their houses and all met at 9.15 p.m. The classical technique of divide and rule was then decided on with boys to be brought along to Keate's study in relays. A message was sent to Wilkinson, duty Preposter of the week, for the key to the birch cupboard and for two 'holders-down' to be sent along.

Boys though still had to submit to the birch and the first two flatly refused. '*Very well,*' said Keate, *rather nervously I (Wilkinson) thought, 'then you will be expelled from the school tomorrow'*.[53] Here was perhaps a moment of as high a drama as could be likely to happen at a school. He could hardly expel eighty boys. Yet having already started down that road how could he draw back.

The next boys summoned again demurred but with less assurance and Keate, sensing this weaker opposition, brow-beat the boys, his fearsome presence being particularly alarming in a candle-lit interior until they submitted and were flogged. Boys in Knapp's house shouted '*Don't be flogged! Don't be flogged!*' [54] from the windows as convoys of boys were marched past. Keate though had now got the measure of the situation, any demur raising his ire with cuts on the head '*getting fiercer and fiercer as he found the resistance weakening*'.[55] The beatings went on till nearly 1.00 a.m. The last boy to be beaten was found to be wearing a check shirt showing that he'd been boating and therefore had been out of bounds for which he got double the number of cuts. After that Keate '*was himself again*'.[56] The two boys who had refused submitted to a flogging in Upper Chamber the next morning.

The sequel was instructive. Next day, as Keate crossed Long Walk a large crowd of boys, including many of those beaten, cheered him. That amounted to, on their part, an acknowledgement that all had been involved in something of a game, without much underlying vindictiveness on either side. It suggested too that Keate must have retained the physical strength that, as an Eton schoolboy, had him called a pocket Hercules. A predecessor, G. R. Heath, had once beaten seventy boys but suffered such aches and pains he had to retire to bed for several days.[57]

There were though occasions when Keate thought acceptance of a situation better than sustained conflict. On Ash Wednesday a Pig Fair was held in College, extra lessons being put on to keep the boys away from it. That though proved ineffective one year when a surprise was laid on for Keate. Just as he was seen emerging from his lane a signal was given and a '*jockey; a scion of a noble house... seized a pig's ears as his bridle and went roaring past him'* at such speed that Keate could catch no more than a glimpse of the porcine racer. Angrily, Keate demanded his identification but when after a while this had not been forthcoming he instead made a joke of it. *'There, there, foolish boys, I know pigs will squeal and boys will laugh; there, don't do it again.'* It was though the end of Pig Fairs in College.[58]

* * * * *

There were though those who could find little good to be said of Keate. To Gladstone he was always *'a graceless, senseless, cruel ittle martinet'*.[59] On going to see him after his retirement, when he married, he saw an altogether softer side of him in dandling a child on his knee. Others remembered the many acts of thoughtful kindness of a *'mild-mannered, good-humoured gentleman'*.[60]

There were various markers during his time. Soon after Waterloo his presence in Paris was spotted after he'd been seen eating ices in Tarloni's and a number of Old Etonian officers, including the expelled Lord Sunderland, arranged a dinner at Beauvilliers, said to be the best dining place in Paris. During this *'jovial banquet'* Keate *'paid his addresses in large bumpers of every description of wine, and towards the end of the dinner expressed his delight at finding that his pupils had not forgotten him, concluding a neat and appropriate speech with Floreat Etona!'* He was cheered and the company *'parted on excellent terms, highly gratified with the evening's entertainment'*.[61]

On retirement the boys presented him with various gifts, three pieces of plate worth £600, and £3,000 sterling. In retirement he became a canon of St. George's Chapel and a Hertfordshire vicar where Wilkinson served as his curate. He occasionally went back to Eton and was well received.

Many held him in high regard. At an anniversary dinner in 1849 he was cheered to such an extent that, rising to speak, he found himself too overcome to do so. That impressed even Gladstone. [62]

While he was altogether a different person in his private life he may have reasoned that he had little choice but to maintain a daunting public persona in order to secure any kind of order. His lasting impression was shown by graffiti representations of his tricorned figure, immediately recognisable, throughout the Empire. In A.W. Kinglake's eyes he had *'the pluck of ten battalions'*.[63]

His relationship with Gladstone was soon altered, Keate writing to him as a young M.P. for help in staving off the threatened railway.

The College made a fuss about it but succeeded only in delaying the inevitable for a few years.

Tucker and Wilkinson were boys at Eton between them for twenty of Keate's twenty-five years. Tucker read Wilkinson's memoir and disagreed with some of his views about Keate.

Both agreed that there had been a great deal of beating and did not doubt its necessity but differed as to its distribution. *'We must not hold lightly the man who has flogged half the ministers, secretaries, bishops, generals, and dukes of the present century,'* wrote Wilkinson.[64] That, argued Tucker, was too comprehensive, the great majority of those *'sent up'* being repeat offenders, usually Fourth Form boys, some getting the birch twice in a day while others went through an Eton career without a birching.[65] As to the practice, any judgement of Keate should bear in mind that *'it was a coarse age – coarse in manners; coarse in habits and tone of thought'.*[66]

As to the quality of the education offered, Tucker's judgement was as harsh as Wilkinson's quoted earlier. *'He was wholly a man of Greek and Latin. He followed : he might have led.'*[67] He did though concede that Latin and Greek were thought an essential part of a gentleman's education. To strike out on a different path against this widely accepted orthodoxy would have required something of a pioneering spirit, not generally a Headmasterly quality. A stronger criticism would seem to be that he could have introduced a better course of instruction. He might, Tucker suggested, have discarded the weak volumes of Latin and Greek prose and ensured that boys learnt some Ancient History. Altogether, it was a system based on *'lax thought'.*[68]

Wilkinson took a more positive view of Keate thinking him underestimated as a teacher and pointing to the number of awards gained in his time. The success was though based on a near monopoly of the Browne medal, with twenty-two won in twenty-six years. Other awards were gained more occasionally. In addition he noted that the College had educated twenty-eight future bishops.[69] Those facts did not though particularly impress Tucker who thought only that *'such scholars could not be held back under any system'.*[70]

In most ways Keate's rule seemed to Tucker a series of missed opportunities. After all, he was *'Lord Paramount in his time'* who had *'all at his command'.*[71] Wilkinson though was at pains to make clear that his strident criticisms were meant *'without any reflection on my old master, who was unable to make any change, being curbed by superior authority'.*[72] Opinion since has largely taken his line that Keate was only able to progress change as far as Goodall permitted which, with such a conservative character, was not very far at all. Keate's encouragement for his successor's reforms after a change of Provost would seem to support that view.

Critical as he was of Keate in many ways, Tucker had enough respect for him to show a strong dislike of anything demeaning. His tricorne hat was not some arcane survival but standard Etonian wear for Headmaster and Lower Master. Kinglake's description of him as looking like *'a cross between Napoleon and a washerwoman'* did not amuse.[73] Nor did he care for the paper-cut silhouette that showed him almost as a diminutive appendage to Goodall.

One of the virtues of a Classical course of instruction in Tucker's eyes was the strengthening of the memory. After a while he found the regular learning of set pieces came very readily, *'almost without effort'*.[74] That would seem to be exemplified by the extremely detailed acccount which he and Wilkinson were able to give of their Etonian boyhoods so many decades later when extremely elderly clergymen.

It seemed to suggest to him a sense of historical perspective too. *'England, after the manner of all dominant nations in Europe, will rise to its zenith – some day – and then decline like Rome of old, Spain in more recent times, and others.'* [75]

* * * * *

The following letter was written by an Eton boy in Keate's last year. He clearly found a good deal of enjoyment in his daily life. [76]

Eton College,
Feb. 27, 1834

Dear Uncle,
I have taken the opportunity of a half-holiday to write to you. I like Eton VERY much indeed. I am placed in the middle remove 4th form, out of which I shall take my remove on 4th of June into the upper. We have very little work not nearly as much as I had to do at Mr. HINDE 'S. Two or three times a week we have a six o 'clock lesson in the morning, then one again at 8, then again at 11, again at 3, and again at 5, but at 5 o 'clock and 11 o'clock lessons we are not in for more than 10 or 15 minutes., as we have only to say a few lines of Greek Grammar. Dr. Keate is the Head Master, the Rev. Mr. Knapp second, and there are ten assistant masters. I am very comfortable here. I have 2 oz. of tea

and 1 lb. of lump sugar allowed per week. I mess with another boy of the name of Fort. I am in the room where a boy named Eden died last year. We have fires till Easter. Mr. and Mrs Dupuis have been very kind to me; we live very well here; we often have fish and on Sunday a glass of wine. A perfumer in Windsor brought an action against the Eton fellows which has come off, but I have not heard the result. On Fair-Day all the boys went up to Windsor; some of them pelted the show-men, upon which followed a regular fight, the people joining in the fray. The Etonians got the best of it as they were armed with sticks – then came the constables, and the Mayor, from a window, called out, "I charge you in the King's name to assist," which they did and were thrashed. In the middle of all this row, up came Keate, and away they all ran! This perfumer pretended to rescue some of the boys in his shop, and then split on them to Keate. Keate let them off, but the next thing the Eton fellows did was to smash every window in his house and every thing in his shop window. I wonder if you saw an account of it in the paper. I wear a clean neck cloth every day and shirts when I happen to want them. About coming home there are two ways; one in a fly to Gerrard's Cross and be taken up by the Mail, and the other is to go by coach direct to Cheltenham, and then go by the Alert to Worcester – the latter costs half as much as the other. – My love to all, not forgetting the Right Worshipful the Mayor of Worcester.

Your Affectionate Nephew,

J.C. Dent

Image of Keate from paper-cut silhouette

CHAPTER THREE : ROUGH AND TUMBLE

WHILE MIGHTILY UNPLEASANT THINGS COULD HAPPEN TO YOU IN ETON'S LONG Chamber, and no doubt in some of its boarding houses, a gruesome initiation could await you elsewhere.

Winchester had the painful ceremony of 'tin gloves' when a junior's hand was held over a burning wood brand, supposedly to give it a readier tolerance to hot handles, pots and pans.[1] Rugby had a couple of treats in store besides the roasting familiar from 'Tom Brown's Schooldays'. 'Lamb Singing' required a new boy to sing to an assembled company. If either he or his song failed to find favour he was made to drink a mug of water crammed with salt which often resulted in prolonged illness.[2] An alternative was being stripped and hurled into a pond. A Liverpool youth, terrified, was heard to shout, "Lord, receive my soul," as he flew through the air.[3] Westminster had the brutal practice of subjecting a junior boy to 'tanning', when one foot had to be put in a basin while his backside was booted.[4] Westminster fags were too perhaps the most put upon of all, having to wear special waistcoats with enough pockets to contain anything that might satisfy a senior's need or passing fancy.[5] Nor were these rituals always merely a preliminary. At Harrow being transferred from one class to another meant having to endure the requisite number of bumps by being thrown up against the ceiling. That was followed by 'pinching', a practised assault on tender spots.[6]

A newcomer would quickly encounter alien ways and demands. The twelve-year-old Thackeray had barely arrived at Charterhouse when told by an older boy, "Come and frig me".[7] A new boarder there might experience long evenings in a closet, a sort of glory hole into which as many as twenty or thirty boys was squashed in and enjoined to silence. If voices were heard outside the door was opened and random thrashings inflicted. Yet one boy later remembered these awful sounding nights as among the happiest of his life.[8] At Winchester any new boy who'd got into the expensive habit of drinking tea at home would be advised to forget it. For while beer was compulsory tea was forbidden and tea things smashed if discovered.[9] Here too he was well advised to swat up on 'notions' Winchester's own patois, if he wanted to avoid trouble.

Common to all these schools was the Spartan state of the dormitories. The Prince Consort, walking through Westminster's Long Dormitory, found it hard to credit that a gentleman of his acquaintance should ever have slept in such rude surroundings.[10] Charles Darwin, sent to Shrewsbury at the age of nine, complained to his father about his *'bed as muck'*. The Headmaster, Dr. Butler, could only though respond that if Darwin's bedding was to be bettered so would that of all the other boys have to be with a corresponding increase in fees. His dormitory, with twenty or thirty boys, had only a single window at the end. Darwin never forgot the *'atrocious smell of that room in the morning'*. The contrast with home must have been particularly acute as he lived only a mile away and frequently ran back and forth.[11]

Washing provision too was generally meagre. Catherine, Darwin's sister, having scented an unwashed aroma exuding from him and his elder brother, Erasmus, got from him a grudging admission that he washed all over every two weeks and his feet once a month. Pretending to be sick, she rushed from the room. Things were still pretty basic at Shrewsbury in the 1870's when H.W. Nevinson recalled how *'we ran down naked from the bedrooms to sheds in the back yards, sluiced cold water over us with zinc basins, and then came dripping back to dry upstairs'*.[12] Markham's Westminster experience was similar for while in his house there was *'a long range of basins, tubs were then unknown'* and he doubted whether he *'ever got a really good over-wash in the winter months'*.[13] (In passing it might be suggested that those of us at Prep. School in the mid-Twentieth Century with its routine of weekly baths and change of clothes were probably closer to Victorian youth in terms of hygiene than to today's regularly showered pupils.)

Whiffiness though was a common feature of Victorian life. Inspecting a Brigade of Guards Queen Victoria recoiled at their powerful reek. *'That, Ma 'am,'* responded Palmerston, cracking the last of his many jokes, *'is what they call esprit de corps'*.[14] According to a gibe of Winchester boys it was best to keep some of the clergy at a distance:

The Reverend the Dean
 Is not fit to be seen,
And his son at thirty
 Will be just as dirty.[15]

In the first half of the Nineteenth Century Public Schools were volatile societies. Not all boys flourished under regimes of senior boys laying down the law and being left to do so by established custom. It was a matter of being left to sink or swim. Lord Chatham (Pitt the Elder) thought Eton fit only for boys of a *'hot and violent character'* and quite unsuited for those of *'a docile disposition'*. In his experience the school cast a widespread malign influence for he *'scarce observed a boy who was not cowed for life at Eton'*.[16] Few masters wished to be thought 'spying' on their boys and were quite content to leave most house supervision to senior boys.

The recurrent cycle of boys growing older and leaving meant frequent changes of regime and boys sometimes found one that had established a fairly congenial modus vivendi, even if it did involve a fair amount of whacking, departing and a group less well regarded taking over.

An event at Winchester in 1829 showed the underlying stress in the system when fags rose in revolt against a group of prefects who were good scholars but lacked that essential quality for boy respect - that of being good at games. The head prefect, George Ward, who had no interest in sport, attempted to enforce his authority with the cane but his efforts led to him being set upon in hall by a pack of juniors. Only his strength enabled him to escape with the loss of his coat tails. Six of the fags were expelled.[17]

'In a Public School,' wrote the Rev. Sidney Smith, of whom more later, *'every boy is alternately tyrant and slave'*.[18] With a thoughtful, good-humoured boy-master the 'slave' phase may have amounted to little more than the performance of specified duties at set times. If the fag was bright enough to do an uninterested master's construing for him then relations might be cordial. Gladstone was favourably remembered by one of his fags, John Smith Mansfield, later a Police Magistrate. *'He was not exacting, and I had an easy time of it. I cannot remember doing anything more than laying out his breakfast and tea-table, and occasionally doing an errand.'* [19] There was though scope for brutality and even sadism for those so inclined. At Eton a bully called Rowles took to drilling juniors in his house and, when that was stopped, riding them while wearing spurs and exhorting his 'horses' to impossible leaps.

Having an elder brother didn't always help. Mrs Trollope was confident that her elder son, Tom, would keep an eye on Anthony when they were both at Winchester. He did, but probably not in the way she would have meant. It was said of Winchester in the late 1820's that if you heard screams it was likely to be Trollope being beaten by his brother: once with a cricket stump.[20] Likewise, the Duke of Bedford fairly laid into his brother, Lord John Russell, at Westminster.[21] Thackeray at Charterhouse saw himself as *'abused into sulkiness and bullied into despair'* [22] but when the school roles were reversed he was recalled as a popular boy, kind to juniors.

An innate conservatism at the leading Public Schools, partially excepting Rugby, meant that in the first decade of the century there was little prospect of change. There was every confidence that the system that had evolved over time was the best and most serviceable one. As Goodford, Head and later Provost of Eton put it: *'boys can only attain to the genuine stout self-reliance which is true manliness by battling for themselves against difficulties'.* [23]

As for fagging, it was said that without it you would have bullying instead. There are though plenty of instances of oppressive fagging and bullying co-existing. Still, even if grudging admissions of fault were occasionally conceded the Public Schoolboy was claimed to be better off than the boy in a private school for whereas the latter was preparing for life the former was said to be already living it.

* * * * *

Mr. Smith, teaching at Westminster at the end of the Eighteenth Century, made frequent reference in his diaries to acts of violence as if they were a normal part of school life. A successor, Mr. Campbell, saw a very clear external cause in that *'we always act second-hand scenes among men'.*[24] The turbulence that occasionally broke through the bonds of civil society may have been exacerbated by the example of the French Revolution. Government spies were on the watch for any kind of subversive activity. So it was that the poets Wordsworth and Coleridge came under suspicion after being seen on a walk writing things down in a notebook. There were calls for strong action against *'atheistic philosophy, Jacobinism, and diabolism'.*

Maintaining order throughout the country was a major challenge. A force of Prussian soldiers was engaged to patrol East Anglia which they did without too much scruple. A man thatching his roof was deemed a sniper and shot dead.[25] The Duke of Newcastle tangled with his Newark tenants and as a consequence had the windows of his London house smashed and Nottingham Castle burnt to the ground.[26] The Habeas Corpus Act was suspended in 1817 and following Peterloo the repressive 'Six Acts', which included curtailing the freedom of the Press, were passed.

In the years after Waterloo there was a growing strain of virulent disaffection in the seven major Public Schools and in 1818 there were uprisings in all but one of them, including the Marriott affair at Eton, already noted. Yet while such scenes as Etonians parading around with a banner proclaiming *'Floreat Seditio'* might suggest participation in outside volatility the causes were all those of perceived mistreatment inside school.

At Winchester an unpopular master, 'Puffer' Williams, provoked the boys by invading their privacy and reporting their misdeeds to the Head, Dr. Gabell. In retaliation boys got the keys from the college porters, locked the servants in the lodge, gained control of the towers, and nailed up the Warden's doors. Supply let them down though as with their limited facilities they were only able to produce a ghastly soup. Twenty-seven boys were expelled as a result but it saw the departure of the hated Williams.[27]

At Shrewsbury much of the animus was directed at the Head, Samuel Butler, notorious for the severity of his punishments. These included the sensory deprivation of being put in a closed coffin-like box and, not infrequently, forgotten about for some while. One of many protests against the standard of the food was followed by placards abusing and threatening Butler and a popular and high-spirited boy, Thomas Coltman, paid the bellman to roar out satirical comments at the Headmaster's choice of prefects to bemused locals. Things took a more serious turn when farmers were threatened and ancient stained glass windows smashed. Coltman and two others were expelled but before departure were seen wandering in the Headmaster's garden at night. Knowing that some of the boys had firearms Butler locked himself in and requested armed protection from the mayor.

Butler wrote to Keate, asking advice as to how to react to such determined insubordination. The reply intimated that Keate was none too flattered to be thought an authority on such business. He wrote as well to all the parents, saying he would not have back any boy after the holidays who would not submit to his authority and for a while life at Shrewsbury became more restricted with juniors having to attend roll calls every half hour and seniors every hour. His response was at least logical. That was to say that as boys had been abusing their liberty they would have rather less of it.[28]

Dramatic though some of these revolts sound, some may have been rather enhanced in later recollection. Tucker denied that what had happened at Eton in 1818 could be called a rebellion. To him it was no more than '*a silly disturbance* '.[29] One might speculate though that some vociferous Old Etonian M.P.'s, among those who gave the weak Commons speaker, Abercrombie, such a hard time in the 1830's, had honed their heckling technique at Keate's Eton.

The last of the great Public School rebellions, that at Marlborough in 1851, could not be passed off as a disturbance. A recently established school, it had acquired the worst features of the system : huge classes with discipline maintained with *'weapons of hideous length',* large dormitories and meagre rations. To escape the miserable regime boys went off to town, got drunk, and annoyed the inhabitants. These misdemeanours resulted in the Head, Mr. Wilkinson, regularly withdrawing privileges.

There came a point when the boys, largely clergymen's sons, had had enough, and planned retaliation. Over a thousand squibs and crackers were obtained and hidden along with huge rockets and quantities of gunpowder. An appropriate date was fixed, November 5th., and a starting signal, the firing of a rocket.

'On the signal, the school appeared to blow up. The court became ablaze with fireworks, and fireworks shot from every building. Mr. Wilkinson, rushing out in extreme agitation, had a bottle full of gunpowder exploded behind his back and rushed back. The other masters were equally powerless. Chaos reigned all night. The long corridors of B House echoed to ceaseless detonations. For two long days the College reeked of gunpowder and smoke drifted through the smashed windows and broken doors. The authorities were paralysed.' [30]

The disorder lasted for a week. The upshot was that Mr. Wilkinson surrendered, agreeing to restore the boys' lost privileges. Soon after he resigned, taking up the more tranquil role of country parson.

* * * * *

Life at a Public School in the first half of the Nineteenth Century, at any rate until one attained a position of some seniority, might seem to have been an uncomfortable, sometimes even hellish experience. Yet that was not generally how a number of later writers saw it. A more common note was to wonder whether boys in the more regulated regimes that marked later Public Schools had half as much fun as they had had. Did Eton boys still have such larks as they had enjoyed under Keate, Tucker wondered. A caveat has though to be entered here in that almost all of those who wrote about their Public Schools, especially those who did so at length, had fond memories of their school, even if mixed with sharp criticism. They tended to look back on the predominantly Classical diet, off-putting to many, as nourishing literary skill and aspiration.

One feature of school life then was the amount of free time they had and the various ways in which it was used. The Rev. T.G.Bonney had happy memories of his time at Uppingham in the 1840's:

'We spent more time in country walks than many schoolboys, going in pairs. On half-holidays we had 'calling -over' but the Headmaster readily gave leave of absence to the older boys .... The result of out freedom was that several of us took an interest in natural history : some collected birds' eggs; a few, like myself, looked after fossils ... churches or other buildings in neighbouring villages often had features of interest and I have several sketches taken in these rambles.' [31]

Not all activities were so unexceptional. Poaching was regarded as a natural part of life in country schools but did sometimes lead to confrontation with keepers and landowners. The Rugby landowner, Boughton Leigh, complained strongly to Arnold following an affray in which one or more keepers were thrown in the river. Arnold asked his praeposters to identify the boys concerned but on that occasion they proved uncooperative, making little effort to find any names, and seeing this more along the traditional lines of boy solidarity against authority. Consequently the whole school was forced to parade in front of Boughton and his keepers. Five or six boys were recognised and expelled.[32]

A number of writers asserted that in their schooldays they generally went into a public house for no more than a passing pint and that sounds credible. It seems to have been dormitory sessions that tended to excess. The fifteen-year-old Charles Minet recalled sitting up all night at Winchester *'with three other fellows swigging wine and playing cards. We had three bottles and a fine ham.'* He was not too well the following morning but undeterred for soon after there was mention of *'a great bowl of punch'*.[33]

London was a rather different prospect. Charterhouse boys were able to witness the Smithfield executions, perhaps noticing the subsequent sale of bits of the hanging rope. Some may have been present at the execution of Thistlewood, leader of the Cato Street conspirators whose object had been to murder the cabinet and may have heard his last pronouncement: *'I shall soon know the last grand secret'*.[34] They would have been aware too of the abundance of pornography and prostitutes in the area.

Westminster too had an unsavoury reputation. *'Hell's Kitchen'* Dickens called it. A watch had to be kept to muster sufficient strength to repel any posse of invading youth, or 'Ski's,' as they were termed.³⁵ Harrow too had trouble with local boys especially during snowy phases of winter. Boys were forbidden to engage in snow fights so that flight was the only option, and the speedier the better, as these 'Chaws', as they were termed, often had the caddish habit of putting stones inside their snowballs. Despite the prohibition there were sometimes set-piece snowball fights on occasions such as half holidays.³⁶

It sometimes seemed to Markham that Westminster was happy with its unprepossessing milieu for *'it always seemed to me that the whole of the respectable part of the town of London was out of bounds, and all the slums were in bounds'*.³⁷ Not that that proved too much of a barrier for while an out of bounds Queen's Scholar might be too readily noticed from his dress of tail-coat, black waistcoat, black gown and mortar board, *'we town boys were always at it... skipping up town'*.³⁸ Nearby was Wright's, a small public house. *'We were not allowed to go there, but, nevertheless, the thirsty man must be refreshed'*.³⁹ Once, he and a friend were passing an inn which had a board outside saying 'NO RUM-JAM'.⁴⁰ Out of curiosity they went in to find out just what it was. It was as well to ask, for it turned out to be the overflow of the washing-up, spirits, beer, water, etc. A more cerebral practice was going to the House of Commons to hear a debate. Only Collegers were allowed in of right, so long as they were gowned but Barker, a friend of Markham's, had a relative who was a senior Commons official and they were allowed in.⁴¹ Whatever the level of debate, or interest of the subject of the moment, presence in the Commons was generally preferable to attendance in the Abbey which was often *'fearfully cold'*, and where sermons could drag on interminably. *'We dreaded Canon Wordsworth. He would preach for an hour or sometimes for an hour and a half'*. ⁴² Headmaster Liddell was though recognised as a very good preacher.

Various ways were found of enlivening school life. While it was the ambition of many to act in the school's prestigious plays, others found a rather different interest in betting on the casting. If a master left the room there was chance of a *'grease'*. ⁴³ Here two boys at opposite ends of a bench got a good purchase with their legs against the end of the desk, and squeezed all the boys in between into a heap. Then while little notice seemed to be taken of the books in the Busby library others made good targets for air rifles.

Outside there were often *'mills'* (fights) conducted with due process and with raw beef for black eyes. This sign of combat was winked at by the masters. *'Run your face against a door, I suppose.'* ⁴⁴ Amongst the various games contrived for a confined space was *'Five and a header'*. Playing this boys stood behind a line eight or ten feet from a wall against which they had to bounce and catch a ball though on the fifth throw it had to be headed. Failure resulted in the unfortunate one having to stand behind a wall corner projecting beyond this only an arm. Other boys then took aim at this seemingly disembodied limb.[45] Racquets got Markham involved in a *'fratch'* when the school captain demanded that the court be immediately given up for his use. Markham not only refused but gave him *'a good smash a tergo with my wooden racquet'*.[46] After this assault on so exalted a rump there were furious splutterings including dark threats of a tanning which after a while fizzled out.

St. David's Day was a red-letter day. A sovereign was offered any boy who could claim Welsh descent and all were free after breakfast. Many went ditch-leaping. Though the school had become increasingly hemmed in by bricks and cobbles the countryside was not far off. All went off in high spirits to tackle the most demanding leaps, perhaps hoping this time even to straddle 'Spanking Sam'. Fags welcomed the chance to be a part of the action, taking up the supportive role of 'shagfag' for the day.[47]

Life in Mr. Marshall's boarding house was enlivened by a variety of diversions. Kept hidden under Markham's bed was a springboard with the aid of which he was able to turn a somersault in the air and end up in a sitting position though some boys were able to do that without such an aid. There was a bowling catapult for playing miniature cricket, small whist cards for ready concealment, a contrived billiard table, and boxing gloves for disputes.[48]

Mr. Marshall had to endure various planned and unplanned surprises. A bolster was once dropped past his window so as to give the impression of a falling boy. Outside though he could find no sign of any calamity. Then *'one Saturday evening we had made some gas but the brew was a failure, it would not light, so we left the bottle in a dull fire and forgot all about it. ..... Marshall was in the middle of the prayers when bang went the gas, blowing our soda bottle to atoms'*.[49]

On fine summer nights Markham had the habit of climbing out on to the roof and sitting smoking with his back to a chimney. If, while gazing at the myriad chimneys of the other boarding houses he had contemplated his future he would have had little doubt where it lay for *'we were all very military in those days'*. [50]

CHAPTER FOUR : VOICES OF PROTEST

In 1802, three men met one stormy Edinburgh night. They were the Rev. Sydney Smith, Henry Brougham, and Francis Jeffrey. It was an evening of high spirits and laughter while the gale roared outside, perhaps enlivened by Brougham's famous punch mixture, a concoction of rum, sugar, lemons, marmalade, calves-foot jelly, and more rum. It was also a highly significant meeting for it was then that Sydney Smith proposed the starting of a journal which in due course emerged as The Edinburgh Review.[1]

Jeffrey was initially unenthusiastic, and with good reason. Being a lawyer, he was well aware that journalism, then a despised trade, practised in Grub Street, and the law were quite incompatible [2]

Then the liberal opinions which the journal was going to espouse would bring down further obloquy on those behind the venture. The same reservations might have applied to Brougham, also a lawyer, but he was keen on the idea, though later fell out with Smith and departed over the proposed editing of his many contributions, but returned as soon as the first issue proved a great success.[3] As for Smith, some wondered what someone with such a strong strain of freewheeling burlesque in his character was doing in holy orders at all.

Smith began as editor but it was Jeffrey who subsequently had a lengthy editorial spell. Its significance here is that both Smith and Brougham had, in their different ways, a sense of grievance about Public Schools, which both were keen to expound.

*****

The Rev. Sydney Smith's singular personality may owe something to heredity for his father, an Eastcheap merchant, had an eccentric side. In the course of getting married he began to reflect that marriage would be awfully tying. After the ceremony he announced that he was going to have to go to America at once and left his bride in tears at the church door.[4]

Returning some while later he bore his wife five children, four boys and a girl, in the course of exploring England during which, according to Sydney Smith's biographer, he *'bought, altered, spoilt, and sold a score of residences in different parts of the country'*.[5] Sydney, the second child, was sent to Winchester in 1782.

Winchester then was between rebellions. There had been three in the 1770's and there was to be another in 1792. Looking back on his schooldays there in later life he could seldom repress a shudder. Even when a celebrated wit he found little to amuse in his memories although in schoolboy terms he was quite successful becoming Prefect of Hall, a position of absolute authority likened by one writer to that of Grand Mogul of China or the captain of a man-o'-war. As prefects he and his brother were remembered as a couple of rather overbearing youths.[6]

* * * * *

Starting with a most influential article in an 1810 edition of The Edinburgh Review Smith poured scorn on Public School ways.

' *The power which the elder part of these communities exercises over the younger, is exceedingly great – very difficult to be controlled – and accompanied, not infrequently, with cruelty and caprice ……. It is not the life in miniature which he is to lead hereafter – nor does it bear any relation to it: he will never again be subjected to so much insolence and caprice; nor ever, in all probability, called upon to make so many sacrifices …. The morality of the boys is generally very imperfect, and their objects of ambition frequently absurd. The probability then is that the kind of discipline they exercise over each other will produce (when left to itself) a great deal of mischief; and yet this is the discipline to which every child at a Public School is not only necessarily exposed, but principally confined …. Submission to tyranny lays the foundations of hatred, suspicion, cunning, and a variety of odious passions.*'

This exalted status of senior boys Smith put down to an abdication of responsibility by the masters. *'This neglect is called a spirited and manly education'* but frequently led only to *'a system of premature debauchery'*. In fact, if that's all that can be done you might just as well call a forest *'a Public School for oaks and elms'*. The result was harmfully divisive. *'The towering oak that remains is admired: the saplings that perished around it are cast into the flames and forgotten'*. Nor was this altogether to the 'swell's' advantage for he often left school *'with an absurd and pernicious sense of his own importance which is with difficulty effaced by a commerce with the world'*.[7]

Henry Brougham, a Scot, had no personal experience of Public Schools and launched an attack from a different direction.

Elected as M.P. for Winchelsea in 1816 he became a member of a Select Committee to examine *'the abuses connected with the education of the poor'*. He soon became convinced that one of the abuses was the perversion of Founders' intentions in the use made of endowments, that what had been designated for the *'pauperes and indigentes'* was being used to educate the better off, or merely siphoned off for personal benefit.[8] There was plenty of supporting evidence. Berkhamsted School, which had taught 144 boys, was reduced to 10 after its Head, Forsan, refused any more boys admission.[9] The Perse School in Cambridge had reduced its roll from 100 to 15 while its Fellows paid themselves £840 p.a. [10] The practice of Eton's Fellows of rack-renting for personal gain was a particularly glaring case of dubious practice and came in for scathing comment.

Brougham, *'with his gaunt, ungainly figure, his awkward, ungraceful gestures, and his rough unamiable features'* [11] had by this time made his radical presence widely known. He opposed the income tax, was passionate for the abolition of slavery and a strong advocate of Parliamentary reform. His forays into education had attracted considerable attention with his 'Practical Observations on the Education of the People' selling 50,000 copies and going through twenty editions and he was one of the founders of the Society for the Diffusion of Useful Knowledge. His energy was prodigious – it was the number of his contributions that had led to the temporary breach with Smith – and his talent broad-based : after a paper of his on light, colour, and prisms was published he was made a Fellow of The Royal Society at the age of twenty-five.

He was only too aware of his abilities, being convinced that whatever he put his mind to, whether it be writing, reviewing, speaking, or legislating, he could undoubtedly do it better than anyone else. His defence of Queen Caroline in a celebrated case made him something of a national figure which further raised his profile and self-regard. This megalomania tipped over into jealousy when he scented a rival for his pre-eminence, as with Macaulay when he started writing for The Edinburgh Review. When the two met Brougham cut his rival dead.[12] Smith was only too aware of his churlishness. Awaiting a performance of The Messiah, and noting Brougham's arrival, he remarked to his companion, *'Here comes Counsel for the other side'*.[13]

His approach to educational reform was typically boisterous. The bill he framed had as one aim that of bringing the Public Schools under Government control. Tipped off by a disgruntled King's Fellow, Peter Hind,[14] that the Eton statutes were being wantonly disregarded from self-interest, he took up the matter of the misuse of endowments in the House of Commons in May, 1818.

'I hear it said that they (the proposed powers of the Commissioners enquiring into the education of the lower orders and 'the abuses of charities connected with the education of the poor') are inconsistent with the rights of private property. Under the flimsy pretence of great tenderness for these sacred rights, I am well aware that the authors of the outcry conceal their own dread of being themselves dragged to light as robbers of the poor, and I will tell these shameless persons, that the doctrine which they promulgate, of charitable funds in a trustee's hands being private property, is utterly repugnant to the whole law of England.'

Unsurprisingly this provoked a strong resistance. It was argued that the Government dictating the use of endowment funds would be the real betrayal of the Founder's intentions, and that Brougham was trying to bring a Scotsman's alien concept into the running of these schools. Then it was put to Brougham that any body which had visitors, governors, and overseers should be exempt from the provisions of the proposed bill.[15]

Brougham was forced to appreciate that no further progress could be made with the bill unless he agreed to exclude the Public Schools from any legislation – a concession which he later regretted and to which he attributed the continuation of abuse.

CHAPTER FIVE : DIVERSE SCHOOLINGS

Most professionals like to think that they enjoy a measure of security : ideally that moving to another post would be their choice rather than someone else's. Schoolmasters were usually well favoured in that regard, even if often miserably paid, but not everyone thought that a good thing.

Adam Smith, who provided one of those dates often remembered from schooldays ('The Wealth of Nations' – 1776) and whose statue has recently appeared in Edinburgh's Old Town, was one such. He was hostile to the whole business of endowment, thinking it gave schoolmasters over much security and that that bred an unquestioning attitude to education : that it entailed too little incentive to question the traditional curriculum and not instead to teach more useful arts.

* * * * *

An obdurate conservatism was the chief characteristic of Public and Grammar schools. Until the 1860's 'Public School' was not a term with any legal definition. Rather it had come to be used of a select number of ancient Grammar Schools. What marked out this group were their history, endowments, boarding, and Classical education. The exclusion of these six (Eton, Harrow, Rugby, Charterhouse, Winchester, and Westminster, with Shrewsbury on the margin) from Brougham's legislation showed that they had already become recognised as a distinct set.[1]

The illustrious past of these schools was though cutting little ice with many parents. Not only were the middle classes unconvinced that these schools were likely to be of benefit to their sons but they were losing their appeal to their traditional clientele. It was said that fathers lived on at Public School in their sons. Fewer were making that happen.

There were serious discouragements. A considerable one for the aspirant middle classes was the innate conservatism of the curriculum. Brought up themselves on a Classical diet, and often in the schools they went back to teach in, most masters were too imbued with this knowledge to contemplate teaching anything else. Others might see it as *'a monkish system'* [2] but to them it was the bedrock of sound education.

Then there was the polluted and unsavoury atmosphere around the London schools which had got increasingly cramped by surrounding bricks and cobbles and a degree of fetid squalor which prompted concerns about contagious disease. The Great Stink of 1858 made substantial sanitary improvement an unavoidable priority. Moberley, Winchester's Headmaster, put the drop in numbers down to the same cause.[3]

With the passing decades of the early nineteenth-century there were increasing comments about the softened tone of society, sometimes merely observational, but often with a critical suggestion that youth was being unduly indulged. Maybe quite a few fathers were not over keen to subject their sons to the harsh treatment they themselves endured while it's been suggested that mothers had a growing say. Instances of ill-treatment occasionally surfaced in the Press but many must have been talked over in the upper regions of society. Some may have got to hear of complaints such as that to the Westminster Head in 1841. *'You will grant, I am sure, that a parent has some little ground of complaint when he sees the face of a son disfigured, or his hand mutilated, or it may be his legs lamed'.*[4] Boarding was often viewed in a mercenary light as an opportunity to make a good deal more money than could be gained from the classroom. It was the part of his education that impacted most on a boy, the whole experience often leaving him ill-taught, much flogged, and hungry.

Just which factors had the most effect at each school will remain debateable. What is not in doubt is that numbers at some of these schools had fallen to a level that seemed to threaten their very existence. Particularly notable is the abruptness of their decline. Thus Charterhouse was reduced from 489 boys in 1825 to 137 in 1832 and Westminster from 300 in 1821 to 90 in 1846. There was a similar picture at Winchester, 332 boys in 1818 to 67 in 1841, and Harrow, 295 boys in 1816 to 128 in 1828 and a mere 69 in 1841. The sharpness of the decline in the 1830's can be seen from the number of starters at the eight Clarendon Schools dropping from 575 in 1830 to 412 in 1835.[5] Shrewsbury though bucked the trend, its mere 20 boys in 1798 rising to a healthy 285 in 1827.

So dire indeed were Harrow's prospects that C.J. Vaughan, applying for its Headship, was advised not to *'throw himself away on Harrow'*.[6] It had become a squalid, largely deserted school, its five privies lacking water and being a recognised health hazard. A master trying to install his own heating system succeeded only in burning down a wing. Nor could the houses run to bathrooms or even bath tubs. So unpromising did the situation seem that the school's governors contemplated *'the probable dissolution of the school'*.[7]

To some the Public Schools seemed doomed to a terminal obsolescence.

* * * * *

Grammar Schools had been established without any class basis but rather to provide an education for the youth of a district. The Taunton Commission of 1868 found that there were 792 schools offering, or purporting to offer, some form of secondary education. Many of these were Grammar Schools of ancient foundation quite a few of which had sunk into a state of dilapidation so that the Classical education they were meant to be providing, and for which there was often little desire, had lapsed. Schools which had closed awards at an Oxford or Cambridge College were often unable to take them up for lack of a pupil with sufficient Classical knowledge.[8] It was not uncommon for a new master to take over a school and find only a handful of pupils or even a vacant classroom.

In many cases endemic embezzlement drained a school of its resources. Nottingham was one particularly bad example. Here it was found that school property had been sold and endowments and other school monies diverted for such purposes as feasts.[9]

Even well run schools found two particularly intractable problems. They offered a free education to very small groups, often the sons of freemen or parishioners. The required fees were a burden to the poorest in good times and often unmeetable when there was depressed trade or a poor harvest. Then there was the statutory requirement from a school's foundation to use the endowment for the teaching of the Classics. In 1805 Leeds Grammar School went to the Chancery court to try to get a legal permission to teach other things with this money. It took ten years for Lord Eldon to give the negative ruling that any other subjects could only be regarded as 'ancillary'.[10] This was not an encouraging instance but many other schools went down the same path in an effort to broaden the curriculum, many successfully. All involved with the running of a school had though to be convinced that the time and expense of the exercise seemed worthwhile.

A number of schools managed to get themselves on a surer footing by having boarders, many coming from far afield. These boys tended to come from better off households and gave a school roll more stability. There was some doubt as to whether this was legal but here Lord Eldon took a more pragmatic view, realising that if he ruled it illegal a large number of schools would have to radically alter their ways. Manchester Grammar School was particularly well thought of, and it charged boys 60-140 guineas, the latter sum rather more than an undergraduate would need to support himself for a year at College.[11]

As has always been the case in English education the personality of the Headmaster has been a crucial factor. Thus Richmond Grammar School flourished under one Headmaster but declined under his successors.[12]

William Whewell was one Grammar School boy who rose to considerable prominence, becoming one of the leading scientists of his day, wrote a 'monumental' study of tides, invented an anemometer, was an authority on the coinage of new scientific words, and in 1841 became Master of Trinity College, Cambridge. He was deeply involved in philosophical debates and attempted to unite the history and philosophy of Science in his 'A History of Inductive Sciences'.[13]

He and the geologist, Charles Lyell, wrote to Prince Albert deploring the 'moribund state' of Cambridge's Science. He did not though at first see the introduction of a Scientific Tripos as the answer until talked round by the Prince. Deeply conservative he argued that no new theory should be taught for a hundred years to allow time for it to be properly evaluated.[14]

He showed his sense of duty in authoritarian ways, being *'arbitrary, unconciliatory, and sometimes excessively rude'*.[15] He was not to be trifled with and was quite prepared to act the part of 'bulldog' as Albert Pell recalled. During a fracas outside Trinity *'a townsman ventured the attempt of thrusting Whewell aside, whereupon that wondrous example of stature and wisdom took the rapscallion by the coat-collar into an angle of the church and pummelled him unmercifully – a warning to us undergraduates that we had better take ourselves off'*.[16] He was too capable of tactful quick thinking. Asked by Queen Victoria what all the bits of paper floating in the Cam were he answered that they were discarded examination papers, knowing full well that they were pieces of lavatory paper and a reflection of Cambridge's inadequate sewerage system. Undergraduates and Fellows saw little of this *'standoffish and astringent figure'* [17] as he contented himself with issuing occasional proclamations from the Lodge.

It can't really be argued from the case of Whewell that Grammar

Schools were facilitators of social mobility as he started with at least some advantage. His Lancaster father was a master carpenter who owned some town property. The son looked destined for the same trade until taken from the carpenter's bench by the intervention of the parish priest and sent to Heversham Grammar School where he gained an exhibition to Trinity that was in the gift of the local squire. This he was only able to take up after sufficient funds had been raised by public subscription.[18]

The replacement of awards designed for the poor with those achieved on merit did not help working class families, for that replaced one barrier with another. The requisite knowledge to shine in exams could only be had after expensive tuition, out of the question for most.

* * * * *

Education was regarded as a state matter only in so far as proscription went. The Test Act debarred Catholics from a wide range of public offices until eventually repealed in 1871. Others, such as the Nonconformists, had no wish to participate in an education with such a heavy Anglican character. In 1816 The Privy Council gave a grant to Brougham's committee to investigate the education of the lower orders. That was the first state expenditure on education since the 1650's. [19]

Central to Brougham's claim for state control over Public Schools was his assertion that, despite appearances, they were in fact Charity Schools, and that this could be shown from their statutes. The mere prospect of legislation provoked strong responses. It was asserted that a cardinal aim of the Founders had been to establish a community free from outside interference and that any notion of the State having a say in the conduct of affairs would be anathema. It followed from that that the Trustees were the sole guardians of the endowment which had to be regarded as private property. In which case, this was no business of the House of Commons as the regulation of private property was a matter for the House of Lords. Many distrusted the temper of the House of Commons suspecting it of *'a disposition to subvert and discredit institutions familiar from custom or venerable from antiquity'*. [20]

Lord Clarendon once observed that the lower orders were better educated than their masters.[21] What he had in mind was the lack of any teaching of Science or any of the other useful arts. As a generalisation that made little sense as so many got no education at all. Brougham's survey revealed that in 3,500 parishes there was no school of any kind. Then, as G. M. Young showed, statistics could give a misleading impression of the amount of practically useful education. With an average schooling of eighteen months to two years many left unable to read or write. Fewer than half of Salford's 1,800 children were able to do so.[22] The crosses in marriage registers showed that a third of men and two-thirds of women were unable to write their names.[23]

What was almost certainly the case though was that intelligent boys, especially if their abilities lay in non-Classical fields, were better off than at Public School had they the good fortune to attend a school of progressive excellence such as one of the best of the Dissenting Academies. That at Warrington achieved such a reputation as to be styled *'the Athens of the Nonconformist north'* [24] while that at Kendal had extensive scientific apparatus. Any attempt to bring these schools within the state orbit would have been doomed to failure as the prime reason for their establishment had been to escape the pervasive Anglicanism. Dissenters had in any case been greatly emboldened by such milestones as the foundation of University College, London, in 1825. When later on the introduction of compulsory state education meant some accommodation had to be found with nonconformity it was the cause of prolonged dispute and a multiplicity of court cases. Other voluntary bodies also had a strong sense of their independence.

There were pockets of innovation. A striking example was the school started up by Thomas Wright Hill at Hill Top, Birmingham, later moved to Hazelwood in 1819. It was infused with Maria Edgeworth's notion that the most effective lessons are those in which a child is doing something. Hill's philosophy was that learning is best taught by teaching. Though that sounds like the wrong way round his school was remarkably successful, not least in the subsequent careers of his five sons, the best remembered being Rowland of postage stamp fame. [25]

Application was encouraged by a school currency which had no value outside school. Just as singular was that rewards and fines were administered by a boys' court in which all could have their say. While the masters ruled in the classrooms the boys managed things outside them. Weekly staff meetings were held to discuss improvements, there were visits to canals and coal mines, and an exhibition became the main feature of Speech Day. It had a wide curriculum with great emphasis on English (including shorthand) and exceptionally well-equipped Science laboratories. Corporal punishment was unknown.[26]

Lord Ashley, later Shaftesbury, turned his attention to those who seldom got any kind of schooling by establishing the Ragged School Union, founding one school himself and sustaining this interest for thirty-nine years. He sounds initially taken aback by their pupils' appearance which was *'wild ..... the matted hair, the disgusting filth that renders necessary a closer inspection, before the flesh can be discerned from the rags that hang about it'* and noticed their *'shivering in apparel that would be thought scanty in the Tropics.'* [28] Neighbours were often far from keen at the prospect of numbers of urchins congregating in their street unless they realised that the schools were run in an orderly way with a paid teacher. He arrived to teach them in the evening, freed from his daily job while the children, if under parental control, were often required to do factory day work to help the family's finances. Many of these children had been in prison, runaways, the children of convicts, or had spent time begging. As many were itinerant, Ashley tried to secure more regularity by offering a different fifth day if four in a week had been attended. That was to give the girls instruction in needlework and the boys' tuition in tailoring and shoemaking, hoping by this means to make them useful members of society.[29] The high moral tone was reinforced on Sundays when only religion was taught. Dickens disliked that aspect of the schools though generally supportive.[30]

Between 1844 and 1881 300,000 children passed through the London schools alone. [31]

*****

The state was slowly heading towards a more active role in the nation's education. In 1838 Sir Thomas Wyse had impressed the House of Commons with his statistical demonstration of England's educational backwardness compared with other countries and narrowly failed to carry his proposal for the establishment of an English National Board.[32] Grants were being given to voluntary bodies and inspectors appointed to ensure that the money was well used. That implied a formulated set of regulations and an increasingly tight control over what went on. There was a clear direction of travel.

CHAPTER SIX : ETON AND KING'S

WILLIAM JOHNSON MADE HIS MARK AS AN OUTSTANDING SCHOLAR AT ETON, achieving the aim of intellectually ambitious Etonians by winning the Newcastle scholarship, Eton's highest award. This involved twelve papers on Divinity, Latin, and Greek along with a viva voce, conducted on this occasion by Gladstone.[1]

Newcomers to King's would have had no great sense of being Freshmen in the social sense in that most students would have been recognised as former Collegers and some of the Fellows as former Eton Masters.

Daily life was regulated by provisions made for a younger generation of students. It began with compulsory chapel at 8.00 a.m. though absence could be accepted if an epigram was submitted, a demand familiar to Etonian Collegers. By chapel time porters would presumably have shaved the students as was their prescribed duty. Later two morning lectures had to be attended, almost certainly in College as there were few University lectures at that time. Little more was asked until attendance at Hall dinner which in Johnson's day was at 4.30 p.m.[2] That was followed by a compulsory wine party which the more serious scholars, the 'University Men', could leave after an hour. Ample time was left for whatever diversions might appeal. King's had a high standing on the cricket field. With his limited vision ball games were beyond Johnson, but he took to the river with vigour, being in a King's VI which bumped an Emmanuel VIII.[3]

* * * * *

An event of 1689 had a profound effect on the future of the College. Up till then, the Crown had appointed the Provost. A vacancy arising in that year, it looked about to be filled in the usual way when the College, after various representations, and with the newly arrived monarch no doubt having more pressing matters to attend to, gained the right of appointment. This was a most unfortunate time for such a change of procedure as the Court had Newton lined up for the post while the College eventually settled on Charles Roderick, Eton's Headmaster.[4]

Had Newton become Provost the College would have had to see which persona it got: whether it was the energetic tackler of counterfeiting at the Royal Mint or the Member of Parliament whose only recorded contribution to debate was to ask for a window to be shut. He would though have brought far more lustre to the office than Roderick, a man of grave, formal manner with a schoolmasterly enthusiasm for the punishment of minor misdoings.[5]

This strengthened the bond between Eton and King's, Roderick being followed as Provost by three more of Eton's Headmasters, a procession which can hardly have been in the best interest of King's, however familiar and agreeable. Nor did Kingsmen tend to participate in wider society in the way that those at other Colleges did for King's, still marked by its founder's imprint, had very much the feel of a closed community.

Henry VI's statutes had provided for a community of seventy and that number had been kept to. That meant that there were few opportunities to join the College, and usually there were places for only three or four freshmen. The contrast with other Colleges was marked. In 1850 there were one hundred and twenty-nine freshmen at Trinity, three at King's.[6]

Fellows had an agreeable existence. Whether they led an intellectually full life or a predominantly social one was up to them. The Fellowship, and its remuneration, continued even if a holder ended up in the madhouse.[7] So attractive was the prospect of a Fellowship that attempts were made to secure one by bribing a Fellow to resign. Little changed while Provost Thackeray, a man of extremely conservative views and lengthy tenure (1814-1859), held sway. As the Provost had a veto over anything he deemed objectionable he could block any proposed reform.[8]

Some change did though occur. King's had insisted on its legal right of exclusion from University exams. Later Provost Okes, Thackeray's successor, questioned that claim, considering it based more on custom than law.[9] Consequently Kingsmen graduated without having to sit any examination and, if three years had passed since admission to King's, were granted a Fellowship. Within the College though rather more was starting to be asked. In 1829 an annual College exam was initiated then in 1836 something very like Finals – a third-year exam, success at which was essential for the award of the B.A.[10]

There had though been a difficulty over University exams. Classics were the academic life-blood of the College and a Royal Commission of 1850 had commended the quality of its teaching. Sitting for the

Classical Tripos, set up in 1824, would have been an obvious step except that it required Maths as well – hence the envied double first. Old Etonians though had either very little or no knowledge of Maths. In 1849 however Maths was dropped and Kingsmen were able to sit the Tripos.[11] A number of Fellows had long wanted the College to take University exams but had been rebuffed by Thackeray. After his death King's scholars were required to take it and later it was made compulsory for all either to take the Tripos or a more general exam. Tripos results were keenly awaited – even the porters took to betting on the results.[12]

Not all welcomed their growing importance. Some saw them as fostering a spirit of envious emulation that was at odds with true academic study, a feeling that in some quarters has persisted as a residual reservation. They did though give more focus to what was the whole business of a University, the stimulation of the intellect.

When made Chancellor of Cambridge University, Prince Albert had been taken aback by the limited range of subjects offered for study. That had been in part a consequence of its Anglican dominance and the large number of dons in holy orders, many of whom, in A.C.Benson's judgement, lacked the knowledge to have any real claim to the requisite expertise in their allotted field.

* * * * *

Physically the College had changed a good deal since Roderick's time. The need for additional accommodation had been provided for by the Gibbs building. It proved a burden to the College. The foundation stone was laid in 1723 but the debt not fully paid off until 1768. Prime Minister Walpole, a Kingsman, led the way with a donation of £500 but, compared with other colleges, it had a comparatively small field from which to solicit. Sorely pressed, even the College bells were sold.[13]

The College was better placed when further building was envisaged. It had been planned to complete the front court with a block facing the Gibbs building. However, after a competition, and a change of mind, the choice was William Wilkins' screen. This, along with the Porters' Lodge and Dining Hall, which seemed unrealistically large for such a small community, were built between 1823 and 1828. The Provost's Lodge, which had been a prominent building between the chapel and King's Parade, was knocked down and sited inside the body of the College. The Old Court, which had been the heart of King's, was sold to the University.[14] This had all been affordable despite most of the College plate disappearing in a huge burglary.[15]

The Royal Commission of 1850 had been impressed by *'the character of the college'* which, in its view, had *'never before been so eminent than during the last few years in proportion to its numbers'*.[16] This might be put down to its complement of Eton Collegers though it needs to be remembered that none of them had at that time entered Eton through any kind of properly selective exam and that these results had been obtained without the initial academic test. The Commission had though been less taken with College governance. Statute VI had exhorted members of the Foundation to a sort of conspiratorial silence in its Oath to Scholars. This injunction to secrecy, concluded the commissioners, was about the only statutory requirement rigorously observed.

Fellows were required to be resident. Many were not. They were to attend services daily. Most never went anywhere near the chapel. They could not have any substantial assets of their own.[17] That led to some attempt to disguise wealth as in the case of the Rev. Charles Simeon, a noted divine who had the practice of praying on the roof of the Gibbs building where, as he said, *'No eye but the Supreme can behold me'* and who was able to fund the building of the King's bridge.[18]

Had he been so minded, Provost Goodall could have responded to Hind's 'treacherous' briefing of Brougham in kind. Others though were to scrutinise King's statutes and practices and effect change.

*****

William Johnson's time at King's was marked by academic distinction with his being awarded a King's scholarship and the Chancellor's Medal for English Verse with his poem on Plato – though not one he really thought his best. Finally he won the coveted Craven Scholarship.

His thoughts then had to turn to his future. It had been supposed that he would take holy orders and then teach but neither part of that particularly appealed. He made up his mind that it was going to be the law and he decided on the Inner Temple, picturing the attractions of the Temple Garden, the London Library, and Westminster Cloisters. He had to put aside the idea of returning to Eton with its temptations towards *'love of money, gormandising, jealousy, intrigue, and imposture'*.[19] The Bar it was to be. Then came an invitation from Dr. Hawtrey, Keate's successor, to take up a mastership at Eton. An immediate response was asked for and Johnson swiftly decided that it was to be Eton after all. Before departing he was elected a Fellow of King's, as was the custom, and was to spend many of his vacation weeks at the College.[20]

William (Johnson) Cory

CHAPTER SEVEN: AGENTS OF CHANGE

Thomas Arnold • Samuel Butler • Edward Hawtrey

THE COMPLACENCY WHICH HAD BESET MANY INSTITUTIONS WAS CHALLENGED IN the first decades of the Century by two energising movements – Utilitarianism and Evangelicalism. One aspect of the former was its insistence on the collection of statistical data, much of which was of use to Parliamentary reformers. The tone of debate tended to shift, in G. M. Young's phrase, *'from humbug to humdrum'*.[1]

Evangelicals insisted on religion being rather more than the routine practice it had too often become, insisting on its passionate application to all aspects of daily life. Both shared a sense of urgency which meant that the sooner you got cracking the better. Thus John Stuart Mill was started on Greek at three, Latin and Arithmetic at eight, and Logic at twelve[2] while Charles Kingsley was preaching sermons from his nursery pulpit at the age of four, his outpourings being shown by his mother to the Dean of Peterborough.[3] Habits of constant application persisted. Edward White Benson, when Head of Wellington College, made a practice of reading the Old Testament in Greek while shaving.[4]

No Evangelical had a greater influence than Thomas Arnold. He too was an early starter, being given Smollett's twenty-four volume History of England at the age of three.[5] He was not particularly well placed to succeed when applying for the Headship of Rugby as he was then teaching in his brother-in-law's private school at Laleham. Yet so impressed were the governors by his testimonials that they offered him the job without interview.[6] They even agreed to his demand to have complete personal control in the management of the school. This put him in a most unusual position. Conservatively minded governing bodies were generally unwilling to cede such power.

His predecessor, Dr. Wooll, seems to have been quite well regarded but, as elsewhere, numbers had fallen away.

To Arnold though the primary task was not their increase but the spreading of zeal. Shortly before taking up his Rugby post he had been ordained chaplain and the chapel pulpit was his spiritual base. By publishing his sermons he ensured that they reached a much wider audience. The sight of Arnold preaching must have been the dominant impression that many Rugbeians went away with. In the case of those who never reached the Sixth it might have been almost the only one.

A contrast with Eton might be noted where problems of audibility stemming from the acoustics and the often idiosyncratic delivery of the elderly Fellows meant that only random phrases such as *'nine and twenty knives'* and *'shoe-strings'*, or what sounded like that to one boy, could be caught devoid of any context.[7] If Eton's services, particularly the weekday ones, could often seem little more than routine meetings devoid of any moral uplift, and its masters happy with this tokenism, no-one could have accused Arnold, who wept openly at the story of the Passion, of not being a fully committed Christian.

* * * * *

Having from the first gained autocratic control in the running of the school Arnold tended to employ his powers collaboratively.[8] He treated his staff, over whose appointment he took great care, more as colleagues than subordinates. He ensured that they were better paid, held Council meetings every three or four weeks, was prepared even to get outvoted, and put them in charge of the boarding houses, abolishing the age-old system of Dames' Houses.

Equally important in his eyes was to recast the role of prefects. They were very much his agents, and were to carry on the fight against sin on his behalf. They were to think of themselves like officers in the army or navy where *'want of moral courage would indeed be thought cowardice'*.[9] Prefects had not previously thought of themselves as agents of authority but rather as the top stratum of boy society, as rulers in their particular domains who'd tolerate only the most limited magisterial incursions.

While boyish transgressions elsewhere were usually regarded as offences and dealt with either by impositions or flogging, to Arnold even the most trivial offence involved at least a patina of moral guilt. He did though identify six sins for particular attention. These were profligacy, as seen for example in drunkenness, falsehood, cruelty and bullying, active disobedience, idleness, and a 'bond of evil' – ties of wickedness.[10] Significantly, the 'spirit of active disobedience' seemed aimed at the general unruliness of Public School life and may too have reflected Arnold's concern at what seemed the threatening turbulence among the lower orders.

Indeed, the state of boyhood itself seemed to Arnold a highly undesirable phase – a state of mind that might seem to make him unfit for schoolmastering. Boyish high spirits seemed to him *'like the gaiety of a drunken man'* or *'the shouts and gambols of a set of lunatics'*.[11] Yet only twenty years earlier, Arnold as a boy at Winchester had been involved in spirited action. One such was an invasion of his dormitory and he gave a lively account in a letter home of the affair, mentioning a locked door and smashed windows. Arnold escaped hurt but another boy was less fortunate as he *'received such a Wound in his Posteriors from a stone that he now fled howling to bed'*.[12]

As Headmaster though all he could now see when surveying a boyish assembly was an enormous reservoir of sinfulness with which he, his staff and prefects would have to do battle : and one in which success was by no means guaranteed. For life *'was no fool's or sluggard's paradise into which he had wandered by chance, but a battlefield from of old where there are no spectators, but where the youngest must take his side, and the stakes are life or death'*.[13] Or more pointedly :- *'it is quite surprising to see the wickedness of young boys, or would be, if I had not my own school experience and a good deal else to enlighten me.'*[14] He could not look at a group of boys laughing and chatting round the School House fire without *'seeing the devil in the midst of them'*.[15] Rugby boys may have thought him about to adopt more ruthless methods with them when he imported a gallows to the school but it turned out to be only for him, something of a fitness fanatic, to swing on.[16]

* * * * *

He was by no means sure that Public Schools were a good idea, a thought unlikely to have troubled contemporary Heads such as Keate, Moberley, or Butler. For having so many boys in one place meant that sin could spread, plague like, throughout the community.

Arnold's temper when roused could be formidable. An instance of this occurred in 1832 when he entered Mr. Bird's class on a routine inspection to ensure that the boys had done the set work. March, a rather sickly youth, floundered when asked to construe but then protested that they'd not been asked to look at that passage. Arnold lost his temper, shouted, *"Liar! Liar ! Liar!"* at the boy and there and then gave him eighteen strokes of the cane. That was twice the number Keate would have given for the most serious offence. March was away from school for some days after this. It turned out though that he had been right, and Arnold's remorse was profound. Apologies were made publicly and privately.[17] It reached the local Press though and five years later hostile verse alluding to *'thy rod clotted thick with an innocent's gore'* showed that the affair had not been forgotten.[18]

Arnold's ways could sometimes be boorish. He summarily expelled a boy called Marshall for resisting three prefects, refusing to be beaten, then running off with the stick. When his father went to see Arnold, involving a long stagecoach journey, he refused to see him.[19] Other parents too took umbrage at his haughty ways, preferring to meet at school functions and dine together at venues where there was no Arnold.[20]

For a year he combined his role of Rugby's Head with that of Regius Professor of History at Oxford in which he was a marked success. That though, and his time at Rugby, came to a sudden end when he died of a heart attack in June, 1842, at the end of the lengthy half, one of the two rather unequal school terms, and just as he was preparing to go off to his Lakeside retreat for a spell of holiday.

* * * * *

Barring exceptional circumstances, such as wartime, numbers are the acid test as to whether a school is prospering or declining. This wasn't to Arnold the prime consideration. Indeed, he wanted to restrict growth from the 127 boys he inherited from Dr. Wooll to 260 but under Tait, his successor, the role neared 500. By that yardstick, with the trend steadily upwards, Arnold's Rugby had been a success.

Much larger, more general claims have been made for his influence. It has been suggested by Stefan Collini that he *'transformed what had been a fair specimen of the debauched and riotous establishments known as Public Schools into the character-building, God-fearing, scholarship-winning model for the reform in the 1840's and 1850's of other schools of its type'*. [21] Arnold's influence was undoubtedly considerable but not easy to understand. He certainly did not prompt an equal enthusiasm for boys to be educated at the other leading Public Schools.

There were some general factors behind the decline, though harder to see which operated most strongly at the different schools. There was the inherited Classical curriculum which was the staple diet and whose predominance none of the schools saw any reason to question.

Increasingly though, others did. Many in the growing and aspirant Middle Class were looking rather to have their sons acquire some useful knowledge rather than being groomed in the ingredients of Classical study.

There was too what we would see as the skewed priority of running a school with the predominant aim of making money. A school of course had to make itself a financially viable concern. Yet the formula of extracting as much as possible from boys by having a number of boarding houses for Heads and masters to make money from, while keeping a strict limit on the number of staff to avoid spreading income too widely, and often leaving boys poorly provided for, was failing.

It was a procedure with a long pedigree and one who showed how lucrative it could be was Richard Busby, Westminster's long-serving Seventeenth-Century Headmaster, a man of extraordinarily wide interests reflected in the Busby library and whose independent caste of mind was mirrored in the diverse attainments of pupils such as Henry Purcell, Robert Hooke, and John Locke.[22] He became increasingly preoccupied with gaining as much money from the school as possible, his *'devilish covetousness'* [23] in Pepys's phrase, by having boarders in his own house and employing few staff – at one time there were only two. Just why he should have wanted to do that is puzzling as he was personally ascetic and spent so little on the school as to leave it in a dilapidated state. Joseph Drury at Harrow moved to a rented cottage so as to fill the Headmaster's house with boarders and is thought in his twenty years to have accumulated £80,000. [24]

Then Public Schools were harsh environments. Many thought that a good thing: that a boy needed to have his metal tested in a sufficiently challenging manner. Yet a rather different line was being taken by a number of writers in the influential periodicals who saw a rather softer tone being adopted by society. Sometimes this was purely observational, at other times critical, as suggesting rather less moral fibre. Defenders of the Public Schools often attributed deficiencies in their intake to their own difficulties in making adequate teaching progress.

There was good reason to recoil from the prospect of sending a boy away into such a maelstrom of dubious activity. Despite his dislike of Public Schools, Sydney Smith felt he couldn't stand in the way of his bright son Douglas's prospects, and accepted an offer from his elder brother Bobus to pay Westminster's fees. Unhappy at what seemed to be happening to him there he several times thought of taking him away and later put down his son's early death in part to his ill-treatment which included severe laceration by a master and nearly having an eye put out by another boy. [25]

In the third quarter of the Nineteenth century a different prospect of independent education opened up with the proliferation in the number of schools, many set in attractive country locations, with broad acres reminiscent of a country estate, and pleasingly removed from urban squalor while the spread of the railways meant that most were fairly easily accessible.

* * * * *

Arnold was rare indeed among Headmasters in propounding views which had a currency far wider than the school circle. Even Queen Victoria had a copy of his published sermons, annotated in her own hand.[27] From all he wrote and said to underpin his belief that religion should underpin politics and a good deal else it was evident that he believed strongly that an institution, be it government or school, should be infused with a strong Christian spirit. Yet he had little discernible effect on contemporary Heads, too well set in their own ways to seriously contemplate any marked shift of direction. This Evangelical phase waned with the diminishing hold of the Oxford Movement and with the sporting parson becoming the more congenial archetypal cleric, and one that meshed well with the Public School ethos of muscular Christianity that became stronger from the mid-century.

Many had been unaroused by Evangelical fervour. An old Oxford Fellow protested: *'Away with your Jerusalem. Give me wine, women and horses'*.[28] Lord Melbourne thought it was coming to something when religion was allowed to invade private life.[29] While at Rugby Arnold had his enthusiastic disciples others were less imbued with any sense of reverence. One wonders how he would have reacted had he known that some of the prayer books he'd circulated among the boarding houses were being used for footballs. At least one Old Rugbeian, W. C. Lake, looking back on his schooldays, regretted having allowed his preoccupation with religion to reduce his participation in sport and other boyish pastimes. [30]

Samuel Butler at Shrewsbury appreciated that Arnold had got the numbers up but could see little more. Gladstone insisted that Eton's religious revival, if indeed there was one, owed little to Rugby. Arnold himself though was only too well aware that his crusade against sin had been only partially successful and that many undesirable traits, such as drunkenness, had persisted. Yet despite what he would have seen as an incomplete mission J.S. Mill's argument that Arnold, despite his propagandist zeal, had more effect on practice than ideas seems convincing. [32]

Within the school he introduced a broader curriculum, one in which Classics still led the way, but insisted on intelligent study. That and a more sweeping change were noted at the Universities where Rugbeians were particularly well thought of as part of a marked alteration in manners and morals, more a revolution than a reformation it was thought. Their distinctiveness was sufficient to make them sometimes rather socially divisive with their tendency to keep their own company, form their own societies, and give them something of a reputation for priggish aloofness.

Then there was his posthumous influence in the number of his staff who became Headmasters elsewhere, men who tended to look beyond Arnold's Rugby to take their schools forward, itself suggesting a more freethinking attitude among Rugby masters than was habitual elsewhere. George Cotton at Marlborough for example highlighted organised games, in which Arnold had never shown more than a passing interest, to counteract the chronic indiscipline which had undone his predecessor.

Two books also had a considerable later effect: Dean Stanley's 'Life of Arnold' and 'Tom Brown's Schooldays', the one pious, the other showing a more robust version of school life.

* * * * *

It wasn't Arnold that later Headmasters tried to emulate though but Samuel Butler and his doings at Shrewsbury.

Like a number of highly influential Victorian Headmasters he was appointed at a young age, twenty-four in his case. That though seems less of a gamble with the school's future when its dire state is considered. Decades of mismanagement, and unhelpful involvement in a court case which had been going on for 170 years,[33] had reduced the role to twenty in 1798 when Butler took over. Yet a little more than twenty years later he was angrily petitioning Brougham's committee for exclusion from the scope of its coverage on the ground that it had a right to be viewed on the same level as the likes of Eton and Winchester, on the ground that it was a boarding school which attracted boys from as far afield as Scotland and Ireland, that it had a historic name, ample endowments, and a solid Classical curriculum. Any such claim would have been ludicrous in 1798.

Shrewsbury's transformation was solidly fashioned on the extraordinary success of its Classical teaching. In effect that meant predominantly Butler's teaching, as with poor pay and prospects few assistants stayed long enough to have any sustained influence though the practice of appointing from former Salopians ensured some continuity of practice. 50% failed to last five years and only 22% managed ten years or more. By contrast, 36% of Harrow's staff stayed for thirty years or more while in the period 1800-1859 only 2% of Shrewsbury's did.[35] Significantly too it was then the general custom for Headmasters to teach the Sixth during the most crucial phase of a scholarship seeker's education.

What happened in the lower forms mattered too. Butler introduced a system of regular examinations and of promotion on merit.[36] One master was rebuked for excessive flogging, Butler putting it to him that a boy was more likely to prosper from encouragement than from being terrorised. Another was chided for giving as an imposition nineteen pages of a Greek grammar to write out, suggesting that any disposition to succeed at Greek would be well and truly extinguished by the nineteenth page.[37] Somewhat against the temper of the age, his first response to academic lapses was not to reach for the cane. He did not though spare the feelings of a parent whose son was idling but on more than one occasion waived the fees of a promising youth when there was financial difficulty.

Throughout his time Butler's ambition was for consistent academic reward as measured by University scholarships rather than regarding them as an occasional embellishment of the school's record. In that regard he was the most successful schoolmaster of his generation. From Cambridge, Shrewsbury's honour boards list sixteen Browne medals, nine Chancellor's medals, and nineteen university scholarships in the Classical tripos. At Oxford, where contact was more occasional there were eleven firsts in Literis Humanioribus and the Ireland won every year bar one between 1827 and 1833, this including a boy, Thomas Branker, who won it while still at school beating, among others, the Oxonian Gladstone who did not take it too well.[38] The foundation for this success was Butler's inspirational teaching but he applied himself too to the examination process making regular trips to Oxford and Cambridge to confer about marking and curriculum to an extent that might be thought rather improper today. It prompted the comment from Christopher Wordsworth, Master of Trinity, that *'Dr. Butler comes here year after year just as a first-rate London milliner makes a yearly visit to Paris to get the fashions'*.[39] Butler calculated that in 1836, the year in which he left Shrewsbury to become Bishop of Lichfield, 39% of the boys at the school in his time had gone to Oxford, Cambridge, or Trinity College, Dublin.[40] That was not in itself much of a competitive achievement when so many Public School leavers took a different tack but underlines the academic ethos that Butler had instilled.

Butler's academic victors were though regarded with some reserve by the Universities and assurances sought that a new arrival would be a well-behaved individual. The Master of St. John's asked for foreknowledge of any *'sowers of sedition'* among prospective newcomers.[41] For Shrewsbury had a reputation for disruption both before and after the 1818 uprising. While Arnold had been largely successful in making prefects his agents, Butler was often at war with his Sixth Form. [42]

Behind a good deal of the truculence was Butler's refusal to delegate : in other words, to allow senior boys the degree of authority they tended to enjoy elsewhere. It could be thought that he was rather ahead of his time here, that he was more in accord with later Headmasters who became rather more like partners in the exercise of boy authority, often moderating its influence. As it was though, Butler stood accused by the boys of *'hatred, malice, and revenge'* [43] as he complained to the parents. In the aftermath of the 1818 rebellion he expelled the captain of the school, all the prefects, and the captain's successor. While things were calmer after 1818 Butler's way of conducting his relations with the boys continued to cause tension. Yet he managed the rather contrary state of having generally good relations with parents, overcoming strong initial resistance from locals to the strongly Classical direction in which he was taking the school, many seeing that as an unrewarding avenue for their sons. The governors too needed some convincing that such was the best course. Heads of Colleges were not warned if an academically promising youth might also be something of a desperado.[44]

Flogging, and there are contrary views as to the degree of severity of his practice, he saw as a correctional measure without any high moral overtones. Then while he didn't proclaim his religious beliefs there is no reason to believe him any less devout than Arnold. As to the kind of moral problem that almost inevitably kept cropping up in such a community, Butler was realistic. He knew for example that senior boys met local manufacturing girls by arrangement in the church but didn't think masters could do more than try to check it. [45]

Undoubtedly Butler's most illustrious pupil was Charles Darwin. Any claim though that the school's classical teaching had sharpened his faculties would have been strongly denied. *'Nothing could have* been worse for the development of my mind than Dr. Butler's school.'[46] Despite being generally decried, the thesis that a Classical education instils the highest transferable skills is still occasionally heard. Dr.Rae, when Headmaster of Westminster, liked to remark on the number of his pupils who took Classics to a high level and subsequently had considerable success in the city.

Butler's efforts flagged somewhat towards the end of his lengthy tenure but by the time of his departure his reputation was such as to enable him to virtually nominate his successor. This was Benjamin Hall Kennedy, one of his students and, if anything, an even more illustrious Classicist. He was also long-serving (1836-1865) and made a lasting and still continuing mark with his Latin Primer, revised by his daughters, and still in print today.

* * * * *

Strange it seems to us now that there should have been clerical and academic family dynasties, many of whom reached the highest offices, some active in both fields. The church had, for example, the Sumners and Wordsworths, the schools the Drury's, Carter's, Coleridge's, Drury's, and Hawtrey's. The Hawtrey family had had a connection with Eton since 1692. Keate's father having been for many years Master of Stamford Grammar School he himself was headed for the classroom. [47].

Edward Craven Hawtrey was described as *'the most grotesquely ugly person I have ever seen'* by Charles Kegan Paul in 1841.[48] W.C.Green qualified that, seeing him as *'the ugliest man in England, and the most agreeable'*.[49] The singularity of his appearance was a particularly prominent lower jaw which had prompted his schoolfellows to call him *'monkey Hawtrey'* and may have been the reason for his lisp. Worse, he came close to death after being set upon by some boys at Datchet. He was said to have been reluctant to sit for a portrait but nonetheless there are various depictions of him, including an oil painting in the Provost's Lodge, and a cartoon.

There was nothing though retiring in his manner. Visitors were addressed in a grand, oratorical, somewhat theatrical manner, with expansive, sweeping gestures. His dress too would have aroused attention for what with his various adornments boys reckoned he *'stood up in £700'*.

'He wore and gesticulated with a pair of gold eye-glasses; he added a velvet collar to his coat, which was tightly buttoned at the waist; he was loaded with rings and jewellery, and his handkerchief was richly perfumed.

"As one stood by him as a praeposter", said an old pupil of his to me, "while he called absence, he exhaled a strange combination of essences."' [50]

One of these would not though have been nicotine.

'A blackguard habit! – only fit for life-guardsmen! – unfits you for the society of ladies! – no gentleman ever smokes!' [51]

In the judgement of A.C. Benson this dressiness was *'hardly appropriate to his position'*.[52] He did though also see him as Eton's greatest Headmaster. To another, much later writer, the impression was of *'a mincing dandy'*. [53]

* * * * *

Hawtrey had been an Assistant Master at Eton since 1814 and was Senior Assistant when becoming Headmaster. Soon after he had a meeting with Keate at St. George's where Keate was a canon, discussing ideas for reform. He was encouraging. *'I should not have had the courage to do this myself, but I highly approve of it, and hope you may get the fullest credit for it.'*[54]

Hawtrey did succeed in getting some of his ideas past Goodall. A most significant change was the practice he began of himself teaching a division of far more manageable size than the unwieldy ones that Keate presided over. This consisted of the Sixth Form, always limited to twenty boys, ten Collegers and ten Oppidans along with the six top Collegers and Oppidans in the Fifth Form.[55] He took over what had been *'the swishing room'*, converting it into a library. This altered the dynamics of daily teaching in Upper School in that the other masters could teach without the Head's brooding presence. This gave them a greater sense of latitude in the way in which a lesson was gone about. Hawtrey though was equally anxious to ensure adequate progress, consulted Butler over examinations, and started to make Trials, the yearly exam, affect a boy's placing in a way they hadn't before while introducing other tests.[57] Another major change was to end the kind of semi-detached relation that a boy could have with the school by having his own private tutor. These were still allowed but could no longer be a boy's sole tutor.[58] More of a bond between master and boy was formed by his making a master responsible for a set of boys throughout their time at Eton. He was not though able to get Hodgson's agreement to having masters who hadn't been Kingsmen as Collegers as masters.[59]

In 1840 Provost Goodall died, his body lying in state in the Provost's Lodge, and some while later his successor was announced. He was a man of a very different stamp. Though he'd been a boy at Eton and a Fellow of King's Provost Hodgson's subsequent connection with Eton had been brief. A year's teaching there had convinced him that his future lay elsewhere. He was then elected tutor at King's during which time he became a close friend of Byron.[60] After that he followed a clerical path as vicar and archdeacon. He could therefore consider Hawtrey's proposed reforms without the uncomfortable backward glance of a former Headmaster and was an enthusiastic advocate of change. The appointment by Lord Melbourne was made on the recommendation of the Prince Consort. [61]

There had been another consideration behind his appointment. The Fellows had been hoping to do what the King's Fellows had managed in 1689 – to wrest the right of appointment from the Crown. That had been in their minds when approaching Keate who declined, not wishing either the expense or the administration and Dr. John Lonsdale agreed to take up the post.[62] The Court was though rather more involved with Eton than the more distant King's. George IV had rated Keate's sherry highly [63] and William IV had often driven over to watch the boys at sport [63] while the Prince Consort took what at times must have been a rather uncomfortable interest in the curriculum.[64] Lonsdale, growing fearful at becoming the focus of a Crown versus College dispute, turned down the offer shortly before institution and Hodgson was appointed instead, a B.D. being conferred upon him by royal mandate to satisfy statutory requirement.[65] (This being a Crown appointment led to an uncomfortable period at Eton in the 1960's when a high-ranking civil servant, Lord Caccia, was appointed and arrived full of ideas for change in a brisk, business-like programme quite at odds with Eton's way of doing things).

From the outset he was determined that something should be done about Long Chamber. *'Now, please God, I will do something for those poor boys.'* [66] Its dire state was attracting hostile report such as this in 1834. *'The inmates of a workhouse or gaol are often better lodged and better fed than the scholars of Eton.'*[67] Tucker showed that parental complaint could have a limited effect, as with beds and food, but the boys seemed to get little response from the College. *'You will be wanting gas and Turkey carpets next,'* a deputation was told in 1838 after asking for a water supply.[68] In 1841 only two boys presented themselves for admission to the College to fill the thirty-five vacancies. The only absolute qualification was being baptised and there was doubt as to whether one of them, Branwell, had been. Provost Hodgson promptly removed any doubt by calling for a basin of water and baptised him on the spot.[69] The College sometimes responded defensively. When the King of Prussia visited the College in 1842 and asked to see Long Chamber, he was told that that was not permitted, though plenty of others had been up there.[70] Nor was it a hotbed of academic luminaries but rather the contrary as one of Hawtrey's early aims was to raise the academic level of the Colleger to that of the Oppidan.

Rumours of proposed changes reached the boys and not all approved. One of those who did not was Arthur Duke Coleridge, who like others had come to Long Chamber after an earlier spell in a Dame's house, in the way disapproved of by Tucker.

'The rumour spread that Long Chamber was to be cut up into loose horse-boxes. This coming reformation of our lives and morals filled us with dismay. We might deprecate, we could not avert the impending sacrilege, so we wrote reams of lachrymose verses, by way of protest against the demolition of the sacred place. Some of us had shivered from the cold there, for the windows were usually broken, and the snow and wind found their way in beneath the heavy old shutters; but we heard whispers of intended hot-water pipes in the projected new prison, and this was an intolerable outrage'.[71]

* * * * *

In some ways Hawtrey differed markedly from his predecessor. 'Keate, as it were, felled the trees, but Hawtrey cultivated the soil,' was how his biographer put it.[72] His initial instinct was to believe a boy and to think that he was more likely to benefit from encouragement than threat. 'Very well, very good exercise,' [73] was his habitual praise after reading out a deserving boy's work. Of course teaching thirty-two boys was a rather different proposition from dealing with nearly two hundred.

Hawtrey himself, though he hadn't been a University man, just a Kingsman, had a keen interest in language, always wanting to find and learn more. He was said not to be a really accurate scholar but the range of his verse in its various forms and tongues show him to have been something of a literary polymath. When later on he was Provost, a visitor was taken aback to hear him discoursing with French, German and Italian guests with equal fluency in their respective languages.[74] He is thought to have spent about £30,000 on books, many of which later found their way into the school library which he founded.

As is not uncommon, his pupils had differing views as to his effectiveness as a teacher. Green found him *'stimulating and suggestive'*

[75] while Coleridge found it *'more picturesque than useful'*.[76] Green did though concede that too much time was spent reading the same texts which by the time a boy reached the Upper Fifth had become over familiar. Hawtrey defended this restricted usage on the ground that you can't teach too much properly. More generally, he was out of sympathy with the prevailing trend in Classical studies for more emphasis on philology, considering taste a better criterion. One boy, Sidney Walker, found the Classical aura sufficiently stimulating to apparently learn by heart the whole of Homer and Livy, according to one account, though another, perhaps more probable, restricts that to most of the Iliad. Rather solitary intellectuals tended not to fare too well in Public Schools and Walker was remorselessly bullied and died young.[77]

Hawtrey's Upper School arrangement had the advantage to masters of allowing them to teach *'in a leisurely and tranquil manner'* which must have been appreciated. The downside though was that there could be less certainty that all were concentrating hard enough on the Classical disciplines, with *'diminished rigour'* being noted. After about ten years Hawtrey was disconcerted by the comment of a Fellow that the boys' work showed less accuracy than had been the case in Keate's time and he set about attempting to revise Eton's Greek Grammar.[78]

Though himself interested in many languages, he accepted the current Public School conviction that the Classics had to be the central focus of study. In the largely unavailing hope of getting Eton to allow more scope for foreign languages the Prince Consort donated prizes.[79] It was not often though that boys were able to put themselves forward for German or Italian awards while French posed a different problem. Some of the boys were quite fluent but they tended to be boys who had French mothers or whose families had property in France, raising the question of just what part Eton had played in advancing their knowledge. Hawtrey added a different incentive by introducing an English essay prize.[80]

The most significant educational development of Hawtrey's time though was the introduction of Mathematics, distinct then from Arithmetic. The first three stages of the latter, ending with long division, were being taught by Major Hexter who had a boarding house. Hawtrey persuaded a second cousin, Stephen Hawtrey, a Cambridge Wrangler, who ran a Windsor school, St. Mark's, along practical lines, to start up Maths teaching.[81]

Maybe it was the kudos of teaching at Eton, or perhaps willingness to oblige a relative, but it didn't seem much of a deal for Stephen Hawtrey.

To start with he had to buy out Major Hexter and then build and pay for the necessary premises. These consisted of a Rotunda, later used for other events such as concerts and lectures, and some rather basic classrooms. Then while he had the status of an Assistant Master his teachers didn't, being barred from chapel. In the socio-academic world of Eton they were looked on rather as 'licensed outlaws'. Mathematics did not though become a compulsory part of the curriculum until 1851. Later, when the matter of renewal of leases came up, Hawtrey for long found the College frustratingly dilatory.

Headmaster Hawtrey's time at Eton gave rise to a number of anecdotes. A latecomer prompted the following.

Hawtrey: Why are you always so late, M.?
M.: Please, sir, I can't manage to dress quicker.
Hawtrey: But I manage to dress and get into school on time.
M.: Oh yes, sir, but then I wash.
Hawtrey: Do you mean to insinuate that I do not wash? [82]

Others tended to arrive late for early school.

'"Here comes the rising sun," the Rev. Cookesley would say when Algernon Swinburne *'appeared with a shock of red unbrushed hair, trailing shoe laces, and an avalanche of books slipping from his arm'*. [83]

Once under way, Hawtrey's lessons were prone to diversion. Toys tended to appear on desks at the time of the Windsor Fair when his attention was elsewhere. Wooden frogs, which could be made to jump two feet in the air, were a favoured choice.

'Once a cat so appeared. "Take away that cat," when it was seen. Exit cat. On goes the lesson. Up comes a kitten. "Take away that kitten." In its place rise cat and kittens. More vehemently : "Take away cat, kittens and all." Some other childish tricks were rebuked with "silly boys".' [84]

A favourite ploy was to allow for a range of things to be confiscated, placed on his desk, and then to try to get them back again. Hawtrey's manner of proceeding suggests rather more patience than clout.

Near a fireplace in the library hung a bell-pull. During a lesson a rather bored boy pulled it. In came Finmore, Hawtrey's servant, to be sent away, told that he had not been rung for. This happened a second and then a third time after which Hawtrey remarked: *'I see what it is. Someone has been perpetuating a foolish and unmannerly joke.'* He didn't though try to find out who. [85]

When the time came for a beating, a young noble played a famous prank. After the first stroke he *'executed a kind of leap he'd learnt from a mountebank and came down on all fours'*. Hawtrey, rather more solicitous towards titled boys than Keate, immediately apologised – *'touched some nerve no doubt – better go home and be quiet – better send for Dr. Ellison'*. Hawtrey might though have been suspicious that something was up from the number of boys who, forewarned, and much to his displeasure at this *'disgraceful curiosity'*, had crowded into the library to watch the proceedings. [86]

A disturbance outside his door one day turned out to be two boys fighting. He told them : "Well, boys will quarrel, and I suppose, if they do, they had better fight : but you need not do it just by my door." [87]

Holidays too yielded a story. Staying one winter holiday with an old pupil he was informed that they were all going hunting next day. His protestations that he'd never ridden a horse in his life were swept aside and he was saddled up on an Irish mare called Camilla which roared off and *'flew like a thunderbolt – the free and exulting animal hopped merrily over hedges and ditches, bringing me in triumphant and unscathed at the death of the wily animal, sly Reynolds'*. He was given the brush which he put on prominent display. [88]

* * * * *

In Johnson's opinion he was not a great organiser but one whose dealing was often *'makeshift and patch – work. Yet for all that, a hero among schoolmasters, for he was beyond his fellows candid, fearless, and bountiful'*.[89] He was also passionately opposed to cruelty, an admirer of virtue and genius, forgiving, and able cheerfully to admit of an error when finding himself in the wrong.

Some anecdotes are illustrative. Evening school commenced at 5.15 p.m. yet it was often apparent that then, and for some while afterwards, Cookesley's division was unattended, the reason being his regular custom of dining at 4.00 p.m. and being reluctant to leave his port.

Hawtrey would wait some while before sending a boy to remind Cookesley that the quarter hour had struck. [90]

There was a practice of departing Etonians giving the Headmaster a gratuity styled 'Leaving Books'. Ten pounds was the going rate. Hawtrey continued this with a little more tact than Keate, who was once noticed with his foot on a ten pound note which had fluttered loose, by turning his back on the leaving boy to shut or open a window allowing time for a discreet deposit.[91] He had a habit of putting the notes inside books so that future Etonians taking books from the library shelves sometimes found an unexpected bonus.

Like Keate he had groups of boys along for breakfast at which his literary talk was remembered as was his manner, which was *'always courteous; you felt he treated you as a gentleman'*.[92] Usually present too were his sisters, rather gracelessly nicknamed Elephantina and Rhinocerina.[93] He was always trying to do the right thing by the boys. One promised a postmastership at Merton College was disappointed after it turned out there was no vacancy. As compensation Hawtrey gave him fifty pounds.[94]

He conducted himself in some style with no great concern about cost, driving around in a *'capacious chariot'* [95] with a couple of postillions. A boy given a ride after coincidentally found to be going in the same direction to stay with relatives remembered his presence as that of *'a genial man of the world'*.[96]

* * * * *

The changes effected by Hawtrey were considerable. Perhaps the most important was the alteration to Long Chamber both in its form and nature.

Arthur Duke Coleridge must have had some relish for life in Long Chamber with such rituals as Atkins, Hawtrey's servant, thumping on the door giving fair warning of the Headmaster's nightly entrance; of Hawtrey often turning a blind eye to the unconvincingly concealed sets and props for plays ; the celebrations which often centred round a couple of Governors, substantial barrels of beer acquired from the Christopher; of having to pay Atkins a shilling to clear up the mess the following morning.[97] Despite such communal camaraderie there seems little doubt that, given a choice between the old and the new a Colleger would have opted for the latter. For now he got one of the fifteen self-contained cubicles into which the room had been partitioned or his own bedsit elsewhere. To oversee arrangements the well-regarded C.J. Abraham gave up his flourishing, over-full house to become Master in College and *'often dropped into our room for a friendly word or two'*.[98] Then the token 'exam' by which the youngest boys in the past had entered Long Chamber, really just a mask for nomination, was ended and entry made properly competitive. This bore fruit in the year when two Collegers became Newcastle Scholar and Medallist, the start of a long sequence of awards and of College gaining a sustained reputation for intellectual distinction, and of growing competition for places.[99]

The growth in numbers during his time brought about a more general expansion with the building of a number of new boarding houses. Unlike the earlier houses they tended to be purpose built and more uniform in design. One pseudonymous Etonian, James Brinsley-Richards, found the often unpredictable layout of the older houses with their unexpected recesses and oddly shaped rooms rather more interesting.[100] Their management too largely changed with masters replacing the dames who had run them though Eton, typically, kept the old name. A sanatorium was built to put the treatment of ill boys on a more regular footing.

The Christopher Inn was purchased from the Crown [101] though with so much profit made from Eton boys and their families, nine-tenths of their takings, it was not too long before another one got going.[102] At a meeting of the Masters called by Hawtrey to decide this most had agreed but a few had argued that having such a source of temptation in their midst was a bracing moral challenge. That brought forth the response from Mr. Coleridge that *'the Devil will do that without your help'*.[103]

Restoration work was carried out on the chapel with the removal of the reredos and the high boxes of pews which created space for three hundred boys. According to convention the Headmaster could preach only if invited to do so by the Fellows. When he did so, Hawtrey preached with an incisive effectiveness rarely matched by a Fellow.

Outdoors there were interventions. The most significant was possibly the building of eight Fives Courts in 1847, opened with a linguistic flourish with celebratory verses in Greek, Latin, German, French, and Italian.[104] It was one of the few sports then to have specialist equipment in that gloves were an obvious requirement. On the other hand, any heavy pair of boots would do for football, providing they didn't have nails in. On the drowning in the Thames of another boy, Charles Montagu, he set up a swimming committee to seek to prevent further tragedies.[105] Ditch leaping with poles was stopped after a boy nearly impaled himself on one [106] and the unpopular cricket fagging was also brought to an end. A little more sense was made of Bounds with the road to the castle being brought within them.

One change that took some courage was the abolition of the triennial Montem, perhaps the most bizarre ceremony, and one dating back to Tudor times, carried on by any Public School. From its origin as a nutting expedition to a nearby wood to mark the Feast of the Conversion of St. Paul it had at some point come to involve the wider community with demands for a salt tax. That though later changed into a straight demand for money. The business part of the occasion took place in the morning with boys being despatched to stop vehicles and pedestrians, those being sent to distant stations such as Gerrard's Cross being given an armed escort. Stopping a carriage with an armed escort might seem more in the nature of a hold-up but, according to Tucker, *'when Bath and Western coaches were stopped at Slough by a graceful boy in a fancy ball dress, and when a large silken bag, strongly encased in network was presented to the passengers for 'Salt', a general smile was the usual answer and coins were dropped laughingly into it'.*[107] Those who did so were then given tickets to exempt them from further demands.

At mid-day the whole extravaganza was on view with the assembly for the procession to Salt Hill, the highlight of the day displaying an array of colourful costumes, many faux-military. At twelve it set forth, two bands playing. *'Captain first, with his eight pages behind him; all dressed alike, looking like pretty little girls in pretty little boys' dresses. Then the other officered Sixths, with their pages, according to rank'.*[109] Then came the Fifth form with cocked hat, scarlet coat, sash and sword, marching in two's and behind each two lower boys in blue coats. Once at the Mount the Flag which had been worked hard at in Long Chamber, was waved in the presence of the College authorities and visitors, the final wave marking the end of the ceremonial.[110] There followed dinner for the whole school at the Salt Hill Hotel, followed by some ritual swordplay with the ceremonial staves being cut to chips and cabbages having their heads off.[111]

The weeks leading up to it were an anxious time for the School captain who doubled as Captain of Montem. For he did not want the Speedyman to come with news of a King's resignation until he was safely into the twenty-one days period of grace given to go to Cambridge. The start of that three-week period, 'Montem sure Night' was an occasion for boisterous celebration with the banging of window shutters and crashing of the half-ton bedsteads.[112] For removal to Cambridge before that that would have meant his having not only to forfeit the ceremonial prestige but a substantial sum, in its last years around a thousand pounds. All monies went to the Captain of Montem from which he had to pay for the evening dinner and for breakfast the next morning for the hundred most senior boys as well as paying for wanton damage inflicted with swords. He emerged though with enough to see him comfortably through his King's undergraduate days.

Despite the colour and spectacle, not all thought it a grand affair. Gladstone saw the whole thing as *'a wretched waste of time and money; a most ingenious contrivance to exhibit us as baboons'*[113] and Johnson viewed it as occasion for *'odious orgies'*.[114] It became more of a public spectacle than the College wished for with the advent of the railways, the *'double-barrelled assault of the iron demon'* [115] with the large number coming to see it including drunks and criminals.

Hawtrey saw it needed either to be greatly altered or stopped and after consultation with Hodgson got agreement to its ending. One fan, Queen Victoria, needed some persuading that it was for the best. So did a number of Old Etonians who liked to see it as part of the school's immutable tradition. Most though accepted that its time was past and accepted its abolition. Hawtrey gave the disappointed would-be Captain of Montem three hundred pounds by way of compensation.

The increase in numbers during his time from 444 to 777 was what gave Hawtrey the greatest pleasure, providing as it did sure confirmation that the College was well set. Like Butler, but unlike Arnold, he had no desire to spread himself beyond Eton though he did make some telling interventions outside it. Little could have been farther removed from the Etonian world than the ragged school he founded at Windsor.[115] Then while his setting The Great Exhibition as a Latin theme might seem the height of perversity,[116] he saw the possibilities of the telegraph, suggesting to the police that it be used to catch a murderer which it was, successfully.[117]

It may be significant that the more disapproving of the comments about his dress, like that quoted earlier, came from the more censorious later decades. E.D. Stone saw it differently.

'What if he affected a blue frock-coat when he went up to London, and came into school one day, his grey hairs shot with purple and green in the endeavour by aid of some marvellous hair dye to rejuvenate himself and mock the approaches of age? Such eccentricities only endeared himself to us the more. What so ingratiating as a foible?' [118]

Edward Craven Hawtrey: Headmaster

CHAPTER EIGHT : MID-CENTURY ETON

THE VICTORIANS DEVELOPED QUITE A TASTE FOR SCHOOL STORIES. IN 1998 'ERIC, or Little by Little' was on to its 26th edition, amidst a large number of similar offerings. The curiosity persisted into the Twentieth Century. Girls were packed off to their boarding schools hoping that something like a Malory Towers adventure awaited them while boys prayed that whatever they were entering would not be too much like Bunter's Greyfriars.

So what was it actually like? It would be idle to pretend that Eton was typical of very much else but it does possess much the most abundant strain of memoir. These give a lively impression of day to day existence there.

Amongst those who in later life sat down to chronicle their experiences were W.C.Green (1843-1851), James Brinsley-Richards (1857-1864) and A.C.Ainger (1853-1860?). Ainger's was more of a collaborative effort in that he roped in two contemporaries; Neville Gerald Lyttleton to write about cricket and, with John Murray, to describe life in a Dame's House, Ainger himself having been in College.

Arthur Campbell Ainger, who seems in later life always to have been referred to as A.C. Ainger, arrived at Eton from Walthamstow by stagecoach but at the end of the half was able to go home by train. Soon it would be only masters who could remember the time-consuming stagecoach.

He had though one immediate concern. He had arrived wearing a brown suit. While school wear had not become as prescriptive as later on this was an unexpected garb and there was some consultation on whether he could go on wearing it.[1] Aware of the cost in acquiring it he was relieved to be permitted to do so. Others arrived in surprising garb. Brinsley-Richards remembered a boy ' *with a coloured cravat tied in a bow*' , and another *'who for a brief calm hour cruised about College in a white beaver hat with long hairs'*.[2]

Fashions had been changing. 'Swallow-tail' coats were going out of fashion at Eton in favour of short coats though they continued to be worn at Harrow. Less popular too were the 'barn-door' trousers with pockets at the top : pockets at the side became more the thing though for some while disapproved of at Harrow which tried to insist they be sown up. 'Turndown' collars had been adopted in place of the prominent 'Gladstone' collar though a modified version of it was taken up by the 'swells' and became the first item of dress to mark social difference. Fancy waistcoats later became a particular craze with Pop. Distinctive too were the 'chimney-pot' hats which boys can be seen wearing even in sporting photos, though there were a few caps as well. Ainger also recalled being given a clean white starched shirt each day.[3] Green remembered Pop as earlier being a prestigious body but not a particularly dressy one.[4]

Brinsley-Richards recalled his arrival at this *'boy's paradise',* where he took up residence in Eliot's house. *'What a grand thing it was to have a room to myself freshly furnished, for every new fellow was treated to a new bureau, carpet, table-cloth, and to a cupboard full of new crockery, Britannia metal tea-pot etc.'* [5] He can't though have been anticipating an assault on his furniture when *'three lower boys marched solemnly into my room with three pokers and explained that they must spoil my bureau's face unless I strongly objected... this done my three friends retired after congratulating me on no longer being a blind puppy.'* [6]

He was at pains to point out that there was no bullying in his house and believed that to be generally the case : that the days when it was customary for a new fellow to be *'licked into shape'* [7] had passed and attempts to take advantage of new boys were frowned on. He mentioned a hoax when a *'very green hand'* was persuaded that, as it was his birthday, he could ask the Head for a half-holiday for the whole school, and stammeringly asked for everyone to be given ginger beer, put down on his father's account. This produced great merriment from boys and masters but it was later made clear to the perpetrator that what he had done was not very clever. To bring that home he *'felt the whole weight of his fag-master's boot'.*[8]

New boys were given a fortnight's grace to find their feet before being asked to fag. Brinsley-Richards was one of three fags who did for Hall, a 'swell' who was 'in the boats'. He was *'of indolent mood'* doing nothing that he could get others to do for him, often sent his fags out for food, was particular about his tea, faddish about coffee, and sometimes tip-toed down to the kitchen to check that his toast wasn't being made by throwing bread onto hot coals. Any transgression here and the toasting fork could double as a cane.[9] The least welcome duty though was reading out a Latin crib to a group of Upper boys preparing Homer or Horace. That required two fags: one to do the reading out and another to 'keep cave' and whistle if the tutor came into view, also giving those involved in nefarious activities such as whist or beer drinking time to put away bottles and cards, and get out books and look studious if Eliot looked in. Sometimes, after lock-up, whistlings could be heard all over the house but Eliot *'feigned not to notice'*.[10]

Being only ten Brinsley-Richards might have been put in John Hawtrey's house along with most of the Lower School boys and he wished he had. Hawtrey he saw as *'a kind-hearted, loveable man, who understood boys'* [11] but who was also firm and had as a guiding principle that whatever boys put their minds to they should do whole-heartedly. He had nothing against Eliot, *'a thorough gentleman, well-liked'* [12] whose boys were anxious to avoid giving him any offence. He did though allow young boys a great deal of liberty which was not always to their advantage.

He had two friends, characterised as Cherry and Pug, the latter a boy of highly independent spirit, a *'scoffer of all authority'* but who had a considerable knowledge of arcane topics.[13] The result of getting on the wrong side of authority was demonstrated when a small boy called Neville was punished in Lower School in the public way then in vogue. As preliminary, two boys were deputed to act as 'holders down'. *'I had pictured a rod as nothing more than a handful of twigs, but this thing was nearly five feet long ..... it appeared a horrible instrument for whipping so small a boy with'*.[14] He feared a similar fate himself when, after a jumping excursion, he and two other boys found the idea of a shandygaff at a Salt Hill hotel irresistible. Just as the quart pots were on their way though, a master, the Rev. Wolley appeared and they fled. The custom then was that a master had to physically apprehend a boy before any further action could be taken and the three soon realised that they were no match for Wolley's *'remarkable legs'* and surrendered.[15] They were though able to plead *'first offence'* to avoid the birch. These jumping parties took on ditches, streams and other watery stretches, testing nerve and athleticism, but the resultant clothing was a sore trial for the boys' maids, these, in Eliot's house, going by the names of Crab and Drab. Provision was to be had at Brown's shop, frequented by Lower School boys and where the *'little fruit tarts with cream'* were perhaps the prime attraction.[16] He became aware too of the different regimes in the various houses, going into one and finding a boy quite openly smoking a pipe and drinking port.[17]

* * * * *

The Lower School was run very differently from the Upper. Instead of huge divisions five masters coped with about a hundred and ten boys, implying regular scrutiny of a kind exceedingly difficult further up. Boys might enter as young as seven or eight and would find themselves at the foot of an academic structure which could take ten years to scale.

From the bottom up the forms were: Unplaced, First Form, Second Form, Nonsense, Sense, Lower Greek, and Upper Greek. In Nonsense the requirement was to make a scanning verse out of words you were given by the master. In Sense you had to form a verse from words translated by you from English and to mark off the quantities. Placement in either of the Greek forms depended on how much you knew. From the start boys found themselves on the foothills of classical study.[18]

A familiar figure in the Lower School was Mr. Harris, the Writing Master, *'a grey, round-headed little man'* who was adamant that as his position was enshrined in the statutes he could only be dismissed by Act of Parliament. Boys had to go to his lessons three times a week until an acceptable standard had been reached. An opponent of steel pens he was forever mending quills, often had one behind his ears, and would sometimes absent-mindedly go off home like that. Occasionally a senior boy whose writing had degenerated would be sent down in a state of high dudgeon – something that greatly amused the juniors.[19]

Brinsley-Richards found the Lower School Room, Eton's oldest, rather a depressing place. Little light filtered through the windows, covered in wire netting as protection against fives balls and *'on murky winter days the masses of old oak made it look dark as a church vault'*. Also, as compared with Upper School, it was hard to be idle. It seems he was started in the Second Form as a couple of quick removes took him up to Sense.

* * * * *

In the far brighter Upper School, the two rows of lofty windows threw light on the chandeliers, curtains, and busts. In 1855 it was decided that there was no room for any more of the latter which were not always treated with due respect – Hawtrey had to allude to unwanted pencilled epithets. Here you progressed through Fourth Form, Upper and Lower Removes, Fifth Form, and, exceptionally unless you were a Colleger, the Sixth Form. The Fourth and Fifth forms had several divisions. In Green's day 407 boys were in one or other bit of the Fifth Form, leaving not that many to be in anything else.[21] By contrast the Sixth Form was always restricted to twenty boys, ten Collegers and ten Oppidans. That meant that most Collegers would get to be in it but proportionately very few Oppidans.

Upper School had five master's desks though usually not more than three of these curtained off spaces were in use at any one time. This was by no means ideal. Later A.C. Benson recalled setting a test when the answers to the questions being asked were being loudly supplied by a master in an adjoining division. It took the Germans to come up with the model of a central assembly space with classrooms radiating from it. There were no writing facilities, and fly-leafs of text books had to be used for jotting down anything like set work. These prolonged oral sessions were a test of a master's capacity to be interesting or, if he couldn't manage that, to be an effective disciplinarian, no easy matter with such sizeable divisions.

The steel nibs, of which Mr. Harris complained, had another use for bored boys, that of forming the nose for a paper aeroplane. Stephen Hawtrey ('Stephanos' to the boys) once came angrily barging through the curtain into the adjoining set, dart stuck on the top of his head, to find the thrower.[22] There were occasional unintended affronts. Two boys, Bagge and Barrington, thought themselves alone in Upper School and started fooling about wrapping each other in sections of curtain. After a while Barrington had Bagge rolled up in the curtain and began *'smiting him enthusiastically over the head with a lexicon'*. When the curtain parted though it revealed not Bagge but a furious Rev. Wayte. Seeing Barrington so obviously taken aback by his appearance Wayte after a bit saw the funny side, smiled the one daily smile he was said to permit himself, and said no more about it.[23]

Not all classrooms added to Eton's lustre. The sole merit of Hawtrey's Maths rooms, in Ainger's eyes, was that they had fireplaces.[24] Mr. Wolley's room *'would have excited the wrath and derision of a modern School Board Inspector. .... It was a musty little place under the colonnade, where seventy boys used to be packed, but which was so dark and stuffy, that the door had to be left open in all weathers, with Wolley, often blue-nosed on cold winter days'* [25] and could often be seen *'stretching his long legs into the cloister outside.'* [26] Mr. Wayte's was another *'dreadful little room'* being a narrow loft in the tower above the library *'where the forms were so low and so close to each other that* boys sat with their knees higher than their waists; and the boys of each row rested their backs against the knees of those in the row behind'.[27] In fact, concluded Ainger, there were *'some nine or ten rooms, not one of which would stand a chance of passing a Government inspector of National Schools at the present day'. (1916)* [28] Brinsley – Richards too had thought such classrooms hardly worthy of Eton.

Entering almost any class in Eton in the 1850's and you would have found a cleric conducting matters. Vocation apart, there were practical reasons for returning from King's to Eton in holy orders. While a fair number of clerics had an upper class background many had more modest origin. Being in holy orders, and a man of god, nullified the class issue as he and his like could be seen as men apart. There could be a related later reward in the granting of one of the forty College livings, and for the select, and well-connected few, a fellowship along with it. Johnson was almost alone in being a layman but clerical predominance started to be lessened from around 1860.

Looking back on his Fourth Form days Brinsley-Richards recalled the Rev. Francis St. John Thackeray with *'his spectacles, his wandering look and nervous gait'*. His accomplishment as a scholar was not matched by an ability to handle boys. He had a habit of making jokes at which boys laughed so uproariously as to often have a praeposter sent from Mr. James's division requesting less noise. Novels were read, food eaten, loud conversation carried on, practical jokes played, and cribs blatantly used during saying lessons. At the end of the lesson the page used as crib was often pinned to the back of his gown *'out of sheer bravado'*. Any punishments given were seldom done.[29] The Rev. George Frewer was little more successful in getting very much Mathematical exertion or punishments done. Kind, patient, and dignified, *'when beginning a lesson he always flustered and threatened a good deal, as if he had suddenly repented of his leniency during past times, and meant to turn over a new leaf from that moment. He would march rapidly into the classroom, seize a piece of chalk before the fellows were fairly seated, and cry fiercely: "Humph! There shall be no more idling in this room."'* Yet he was shrewd and witty, managed his house well, and had many extra evening pupils.[30]

Brinsley-Richards candidly admitted that he'd done little but amuse himself in return for his parents' annual outlay of £200.[31]

Back in the house, the *'indolent'* Hall had left and he found himself one of a number of fags answering to 'Blazes', a nickname given for his hair. Blazes was a considerable swell, *'a hard rider, rower, and mighty beer-quaffer'*,[32] to whom fags were simply servants. He was demanding. All of his many trophies had to be kept polished and breakfast kept his many fags hard at it with his varied culinary needs which often included an awkward hot plate. No praise was ever given, yet boys much preferred to fag for Blazes than for a more subdued character who made fewer demands and always said thank you.[33] When 'staying out', putting himself on the sick list, which usually happened on full school days, he would sometimes send any lower boys also around out for Bass or claret, or both in sequence. Brinsley-Richards was once sent out twice on this perilous mission, knowing that any discovery by a master would have meant twelve cuts as Blazes must have known. Though he got rare praise, being called a 'little brick', he was careful not again to 'stay out' the same day as Blazes.[34]

* * * * *

As 12's or 4's, the time for the ending of lessons approached, there was sometimes a degree of fidgeting and on occasion a medical emergency, such as a nosebleed, that required immediate quitting of the class. Minutes later the now restored youth might have been seen haring off to try to bag one of the Fives Courts. Other schools showed little interest in trying to recreate Eton's Wall Game, but it certainly started something with Fives, Eton's version of the game being widely played in other schools. Its popularity was such that one of the terms was often called 'The Fives Half'.[35]

Football needed no special equipment, only a pair of heavy boots so long as they had no nails in. All were expected to take part, upper and lower boys alike in the same game, something Brinsley-Richards afterwards thought absurd. Younger boys often got hacked by their seniors and in frustration often ended up shinning each other. Upper boys never wanted their juniors on the same cricket field, apart from fagging for ball-retrieving, so why had football been so compulsorily inclusive? Until the mid-century there were few matches against other schools, one difficulty being that each had its own rules and an agreed set had to be determined in advance. For kickabouts the goals were often marked on trees. For the field game proper two poles without crossbar marked the goals, sticks the corners, but, if there were any touch lines they were roughly scored in the turf. This led to encroachment and rough shoving back, one of those repulsed being the spectating Prince of Wales, apology being made when the faux-pas was realised though the amused Prince laughed it off.[36]

Westminster also had two versions of the game described by Markham in some detail. All had to take part in 'Green' which was played on a field with goals about twenty yards wide, the posts being trees at the Abbey and Terrace ends. Defence of such expansive goals required a large number of goalkeepers, usually small boys, though any field player thought to be playing poorly, perhaps through being a 'funkstick' might also be put in goal. The game started with a bully when the ball was thrown in and in the course of which shinning was allowed. You could catch the ball if taken full toss or after the first bounce and run two or three paces with it. *'Of course, when running like this, the enemy tripped, shinned, charged with shoulder, got down and sat upon you – in fact might do anything short of murder to get the ball from you.'* He came to *'fearful grief'* one day getting knocked out. Match play was a little more like the later Association in that a boy bearing down on goal had to beat a single goalkeeper standing between two tall, narrow posts. Yet you could still catch and run, there were no field placings and no heading.[37] Westminster too had a strange variant of hockey, played with a football and giant hockey sticks, which had a brief vogue before being banned on grounds of danger to life and limb.

Cricket was the one game that had invited external competition, the Eton-Harrow match being well established as an annual fixture. Byron had performed modestly for Harrow with scores of 7 and 2, though considerably better in his later telling.[38] Harrow's declining numbers probably explained Eton's complete dominance in the 1820's but their recovery made for a greater challenge. 1847 was Eton's sporting 'annus mirabilis' with triumphs over Westminster, Winchester, and Harrow on land and water.[39]

Thereafter during the 1850's Eton had no success at all against Harrow's cricketers. Excuses were looked for. Harrow on its hill did not have the diversionary attraction of a river. Then there was the Lord's pitch, a *'fiery; turnpike like'* surface. There was something in that. It was a notoriously bad pitch on which a Notts batsman was killed in 1870.[40] But of course it was the same for both sides. Then individuals could be faulted. Murray blamed G.R. Dupuis for three defeats. Scores of 0, 0, 0, and 5 might be disappointing for the crack batsman but he cannot have deserved sole blame.[41] Johnson presented a cup for a cricket house competition, stipulating that all players must wear proper cricket shoes, *'white dabs'*.[42]

Many Etonians though chose to expend their energies on the river – to become 'wet-bobs'. Before being allowed to row boys had to show that they could swim to prevent further drowning tragedies. This involved the waterman rowing a punt of naked boys to a starting pole where they had to swim an approved distance for the adjudicating judges and, but hard to see why, show they could do headers rather than 'taking a gutter', doing a belly-flop.

One morning, while Brinsley-Richards was fagging with teapot and kettle, Blazes suddenly decided that he would do for a wet-bob and ordered him to take a daily swimming lesson until Wolley and Carter were able to pass him. Before he'd managed that, the draw for the tutor's sweepstake was drawn, each pairing being that of senior and junior boy, and, to his consternation, it paired him with Blazes who was not over pleased at that but took it in good part. To his relief he suddenly mastered the art of swimming, and could then take to a gig for hard rowing lessons, sometimes encouraged by a passing Blazes. When the race occurred the two principal rival boats collided, leaving Blazes and Brinsley-Richards easy winners. He pocketed two pounds as prize but more valued was Blazes saying, "Well rowed, young 'un". [43]

There was a glamour to the river shown in its elaborate dress. The Captain of Boats wore an admiral's uniform with cocked hat and gold-laced trousers, enjoying *an ephemeral though dazzling glory*.[44] The supreme glory was to captain the ten-oar 'Monarch'. In 1829 a challenge to race on the river was made to Westminster, the wording of it being unwisely left to the boat-builder, Billy Goodman, whose weirdly phrased invitation led to jibes as to the level of literacy at Eton.[45] In a race which attracted heavy betting Eton triumphed. The King was present in 1837 when Westminster won, a reverse he put down to the fact that Hawtrey had been watching.[46] The following year the race did not take place. The Eton crew was all ready for it but Westminster failed to show up, the reason subsequently discovered to have been that the Headmaster had locked them up. There was still no fixture when Markham, a dedicated oar and captain of boats, went over to Eton to try to presuade authorities there to discuss a resumption. He was given a boating outfit to change into to look the part but his plea was unsuccessful.[47]

There was a good deal else. Athletics was given encouragement with the start of the mile race (1851) and of the steeplechase (1846). 'Jumping' became more ambitious with the introduction of 'leaping poles' though Hawtrey banned them after a boy nearly impaled himself on one. Hockey had a brief vogue until deemed 'wet'. Oppidans and Collegers had their own beagles though they joined together in 1867.[48]

Afternoon diversions over, all had to be back in school for evening classes at 5.15. Those in Cookesley's division, and awaiting his often tardy arrival, must have had a degree of apprehension knowing him to be a man of uncertain temper. In action he was a stimulating and eccentric teacher but regarded by many of the boys as *'violent, even mad'*. Prizes were often offered for good work but usually foirgotten about.[49] A boy once threw a stone at him. When questioned as to why he had done it, and meeting with a denial that he had been the target, the boy was flogged not for throwing the stone but for lying. Coleridge was collared by him when on the point of leaving and asked to deal with another liar. *"You are the captain of the school. I want you to take and lick that boy to within an inch of his life."* Coleridge, deeming his time at Eton already to have come to an end, declined. He had great faith in the efficacy of the cane, his *'doctor'* with which he tried to secure order in his house.[50] The house though proved his undoing as he got into financial difficulties with it and had to leave Eton as a consequence.[51] He had an interested observer of his practice in the person of Disraeli, researching life at Eton as preparation for his fictional school in 'Coningsby'. Hawtrey though disliked the novel, thinking it reflected poorly on the standard of discipline at Eton. [52] The proximity of London with its alluring theatrical productions proved something of a temptation for the Rev. Henry Knapp and the Rev. Benjamin Drury who would often go off for the weekend, sometimes taking one or two pupils with them and marking their verses in a curricle on the way back. On one occasion, when with two young companions, things got a little out of hand and they all had to be bailed out of Bow Street Magistrates Court. An excellent sholar, Knapp enjoyed the good things of life *'and was not afraid of cracking his second or even his third bottle of claret after dinner'*. As with Cookesley, money problems overcame him, and, deeply in debt, he fled to Elba. [53] Most masters, it would probably be fair to assume, led a more humdrum existence and managed things rather better. With some there was no messing around. One such was the Rev. William Adolphus Carter who, in Ainger's estimation, *'ruled by terror; he was strict to a degree calculated to break a small boy's spirit'*. In class *'Carter sat at his desk with a victim by his side and a heap of copies before him'*. It was said that some boys with a good chance of reaching the Sixth, begged their parents to take them away from Eton rather than spending any longer in his division. Yet out of class he was *'friendly and hearty, with an infectious laugh'*. [54]

After a year of disporting himself in the Fourth Form Brinsley-Richards found life under the Rev. James a very different matter. *'His voice is* loud and peremptory, his manner hard, his speech curt. He is a neat and creaseless sort of man; his shirt collar stands high and stiff; the bow of his white necktie is broad'. After the larks of Thackeray's division the transition was sharp. *'We were like a tribe of young Bashi-Bazouks suddenly brought up under a Prussian colonel.'* Every boy in his division of seventy was made to feel that he had his eye on him. One practice of his meant boys had to have their wits about them. For whereas many masters would go round the division in a systematic way asking for some construing, so that a boy would have a pretty good idea whether or not he'd be called on, and if so to have his cribbed bit ready, James would dart around unexpectedly. For he hated idleness with a real passion and his stern challenge to boys in whom he detected it made him unpopular at first but this was later replaced by respect for his integrity.[55]

Nor was there any light relief in Maths where the Rev. Edward Hale was one of the few Mathematical masters to make any lasting impression, a well-liked man of broad interests, who taught several other subjects, and was nicknamed 'Badger' from the shading of his beard and whiskers.[56]

The Rev. James Leigh 'Jimmy' Joynes was another strong disciplinarian being recalled in action like this :

'Hannibal was now approaching the foot of the Alps – I'm looking at you Parker – when the mountain tribes assembled – write out and translate the lesson Parker.' He had other ways of crushing misbehaving boys. One such, a small boy called Coombe was picked out with *"C-o-o-o-o-mbe" (with a long intentional drawl) "go and stand in the corner, Co-o-o-o-o-mbe". Now if I were to talk to one of these fine big fellows, he would say, "Jynes, Jynes, who's Jynes?" – but as it's only Co-o-o-o-mbe, go and stand in the corner Co-o-o-o-mbe."* [57]

Nor was taking liberties with the Rev.Day a good idea with his giving out of a punishment being a sort of slow torture with the form being like this : *"write out your Homer lesson "* – the delinquent turns to go – *"and translate it"* – he moves a little way – *"twice"* – a few more steps – *"with accents"* – a few more – *"and stops"* – he reaches the door – *"before lock-up"* – he escapes at last. [58]

The Rev. F. E. Durnford got the nickame, 'Judy' on account of his high voice. A painstaking tutor and housemaster he was very popular with parents and had more than seventy boys in his house. It was said of him that he never went to bed on Wednesday nights but sat up marking his verses, the strain of such conscientious ways no doubt the cause of some irritability.[59] The Rev. George Plumptre was another well-regarded master. Boys from other divisions whose masters were away would sometimes go into his lessons, and be allowed to stay for a while, before being bidden to leave.[60]

It would be hard to criticise these masters for the harsh methods some employed to manage their divisions bearing in mind their size and the sometimes rum places in which they conducted lessons. Many had something of a reputation for good scholarship though their classical remit could lead to a blinkered outlook. The Rev. Yonge was thought to have a *'sovereign contempt for everything he did not know'* but edited Homer as did Cookesley while the Rev. Marriott was regarded as an ecclesiastical authority. Good scholarship did not though necessarily translate into effective teaching. Nor did some, like Cookesley and Day, ever strike up much of an accord with boys. [61]

* * * * *

Oscar Browning had a good deal in common with Brougham. Like him he was a larger than life character with a distinct trait of megolomania who even as a boy at Eton had decided that the worst fate in life was to be ignored. When, as a King's don, he looked out of his window on to Front Lawn one snowy morning, and saw O.B., the intials by which he was widely known, trod into the snow in giant letters, he could have been sure he'd made his mark.

In adult life he was able to indulge his passions for dining and bathing. He gave the King's kitchens a list of fifteen possible breakfasts so that what was put before him each morning should be something of a surprise.[62]

Maybe this was in part a reaction to his time at Eton. For while he was housed in the now reformed Long Chamber conditions remained pretty Spartan. Mutton was still the pretty monotonous mid-day fare with junior boys having to wait until they'd served their seniors before they could have what was left. Breakfast at nine o'clock consisted solely of bread and butter and as there was little enough time until 9.30 school to eat even that hungry boys would first go to Joe Brown's for buns and coffee. Often though he went hungry.[62]

His education had begun at a young age, starting Latin at four, Greek at eight, and developing some facility for the writing of Latin verse by thirteen.[63] He had his elder brother, William, a hunting parson who liked to drink champagne on saints' days, to thank for his preparation for Eton though gratitude may not have come too readily at the time. For William, fifteen years his senior, ran Thorpe school and was a demanding, though very successful tutor, convinced Oscar needed pushing hard. In the event he came third on the Eton list. In a subsequent year Thorpe boys took the top three places and William was able on the strength of its burgeoning reputation to considerably expand the school.[64]

Oscar did not at first win many plaudits. The Rev. Cookesley thought him out of his depth in his division and Johnson, his tutor, thought him too selective in his efforts as well as deeming him unsociable, conceited, and cross.[65] One cause of the unhappiness which he often felt was '*my social position at Eton*' [66]

Collegers, many from modest backgrounds, were very much looked down on by the wealthier boys in other houses. 'Dirty tugs' they were called while Collegers retaliated rather more tamely by calling Oppidans 'town boys'. They were distinctive, having to wear their serge gowns wherever they went, even to the sports field. If bidden to take a message to one of the other houses it was best to do it briskly before too many missiles could be thrown at their retreating backs. Then it was Collegers who had the chore of holding down miscreants during swishing. They would have been aware of the confident 'swells' parading their increasingly dressy selves around the College and of the sons of nobles, sat separately in stalls in Chapel, a distinction which continued at Cambridge where sons of nobles could wear a gold tassel on their caps.[68]

His reading was prodigious with Byron his hero. He described the literary content of his room one Sunday night in 1854. '*My room is a faint shadow of my mind. It is strewed with books. Here is a list of them. On the table – Byron's works, Plymley's Letters, Ellis's Passage of the Alps, Horatii Opera, Livy vol. 2, Spectator, vol. 5, Prior's Life of Burke, Addison's works, vol 3, Burton's Anatomy of Melancholy. On the small table, Byron's life, vol. 6, Lighter Hours, Napier's Battles and Sieges. On the water pipes Green's Life of Mahomet, Gibbon's vol. 5, Mont Blanc and Back, Students' Guide , Thucydides, various editions of Aeschylus, Gibbon's Miscellaneous Works, vol. 5, Elegant Extracts of Poetry, Byron, Blessington's Idler in Italy, Disraeli's Miscellanies of Literature. On the sofa, Arnold's History of Rome, vol. 3, and the first vol. of Cluverius' Italia Antiqua – such a wilderness in my mind.*' [69]

Though he continued to get poor reports, few of his contemporaries can have left Eton better read. He had by this time too acquired a love of music which was to stay with him. Games he played with no great aptitude but reckoned Fives easily the best. Johnson once claimed he could bowl him out but in the event was unable to do so.[70]

'*Bah! I hate Eton!*' he wrote in his journal in 1854 [71] and though there was the social cachet of election to Pop at the second attempt he never saw his Eton schooldays as anything but a painful chore. The surprise must be that he went back. One inviting vista opened up during his last days at Eton. Introduced to Lord Colchester he was taken by him to the House of Lords. This glimpse of the world of the titled Victorian movers and shakers proved alluring.[72]

* * * * *

By the 1850's William Johnson was a familiar figure at Eton and noted for his eccentricities. He was seen walking down Eton High Street with three pairs of spectacles perched on his nose and, on one occasion, chasing a hen along the road under the impression it was his hat though that was on his head. At times the boys must have wondered what to make of him. One wearing a watch chain had it pulled off and thrown into the river, no explanation being offered. The award of a Newcastle was celebrated with a successful scholar by stamping on a top hat.

Oscar Browning left Eton with a high regard for Johnson. He later wrote of *'the paradise of my tutor's room'*.[73] He described a scene in which a dozen boys were working at their Latin verse, each on a different subject while Johnson made occasional suggestions to each from his desk *'stimulating their invention and their humour'* while marking the Sixth – Form Greek Iambics and whistling to himself an air from an Italian opera.[73]

Not that things were always as placid. At times he would *'fall into great rages, or simulate them, stamping about his pupil-room'*.[74] His tongue could be cutting. A man not known later in public life for any great sensitivity never forgot the occasion when, being tardy, he tried to enter Johnson's division unnoticed and was told that such a proceeding was quite unnecessary as *"You've pretty well established your insignificance already"*. Made a Fifth-Form master in 1851 few in his division were likely to forget this *'stooping, sarcastic, energetic, caustic, and tenderly sensitive'* man.[75]

He had a gift which many schoolmasters must have coveted but fewer managed and that was an inability to be dull. Whatever he turned his unpredictable mind to he gave a particular sparkle. His intellectual level meant that some of his repartee passed his pupils by but they got enough from him to ensure practical success.[76] One famous division of his subsequently produced eighteen Firsts at Oxford and Cambridge, and that at a time when university was not the chosen next step for many leavers.[77]

View of Eton College Chapel

Rev. C.Wolley

Rev. R.Day

Rev. S.Hawtrey

Rev. E.Hale

Rev. F.E.Durnford

Rev. J.E.Yonge

W.Johnson

Rev. J.L.Joynes

The Eton Eleven of 1858

Brinsley-Richards illustrates how he challenged boys to think critically.

'He would sit with his legs crossed, and in a curled-up posture, holding his book within an inch of his spectacles, and in the middle of a lesson would break into rambling soliloquies by way of conveying his unconventional opinions upon the heroes of scripture or mythology.

"Adam – contemptible person, lays the blame of that apple business on his wife. Fancy a gentleman saying, 'This woman tempted me and I did eat'. Eve must have thought him a poor creature."

'A boy would be reading the story of Lucretia and Tarquin; "Lucretia – silly little woman; I have no patience with her. As if she couldn't simply have boxed his ears instead of making all that fuss!" [78]

He made boys think for themselves in his insistence on cutting through hypocrisy and cant. It was the opinion of A.C. Benson that *'innumerable men owe the awakening of intellectual interests entirely to his incisive and vivid talk'.*

His reputation spread beyond Eton. Palmerston seriously considered him for a history chair at Oxford but was over-ruled by the Prince Consort[79] and there were rumours that he might be off to teach History at King's. For while he was a leading classical scholar – there was even speculation as to whether he thought in Greek – his historical knowledge too was considerable, his particular interest being military and naval history.

An enduring legacy was 'The Eton Boating Song'. He did as well write much verse of real distinction. A verse from 'Academus' has a haunting quality:

'I'll borrow life, and not grow old;
And nightingales and trees
Shall keep me, though the veins be cold,
As young as Sophocles.
And when I may no longer live,
They'll say who know the truth,
He gave whate'er he had to give
To freedom and to youth.

Then there was the famous elegy 'Heraclitus':
They told me, Heraclitus, they told me you were dead,
They brought me bitter news to hear and bitter tears to shed.
I wept, as I remembered, how often you and I
Had tired the sun with talking and sent him down the sky.

While to Yonge, mathematics was *'mere vanity'* and French deserving only *'the attention of a trifler'*.[80] Johnson's attitude was quite the opposite. He knew little science but thought that a serious failing and gave much thought to what should be taught and how, crystallised in his *'On the Education of the Reasoning Faculties'*.[81]

The arduous nature of much classical study had been seen by many of its practitioners as a beneficial challenge. Johnson though could see no virtue in *'the worship of difficulty for its own sake'*. He recognised that for many, once the stage of declensions and conjugations had been passed and they were confronted with such concepts as gerunds and participles a level of linguistic difficulty had been reached that floored many willing pupils. Others made little effort, relying on the crib or the help of a brainy fag such as Stafford Northcote to see them through lessons.[82] Verse was a bugbear with many. *'I hate Latin verse'* declared Pochin, and he can't have been alone. For, as Chandos observed, few boys can write elegant verse in any language.[83] The whole classical edifice seemed designed for an intellectual elite and left many floundering, cheating, or simply apathetic, thinking they had better things to do with their time. Even with today's more thoughtfully produced Latin texts there still at some point comes the need to cope with what are for some, elusive concepts. Johnson suggested that French might be a better subject for study in that it did have a grammar of quite adequate rigour. He did his best for the existing regime by producing a series of texts, improving on what was thought to have been little changed since Malim's Tudor primer.

Provost Hodgson's death in 1853 necessitated changes and one was fairly predictable. That was the elevation of Hawtrey to replace him. The other was less so. There had been a general feeling that the Rev. Edward Coleridge, Keate's son-in-law, would be the next Head but it seems his high-church views counted against him and it was Dr. Goodford who was appointed.

Charles Old Goodford, 'Goody' or 'Cogger' in boy parlance, was an excellent scholar but thought rather a dull teacher, *'unawakening in manner'* in Green's words [85] and not much of an orator. Nor had he made a great success of his house. Yet Johnson viewed the prospect of his accession with equanimity. *'Goodford is honest, righteous, methodical, learned, brave, laconic, prudent, unmeddlesome. He is also weak in health, uninfluential, obscure, unpolished. No one admires him, everyone respects him. We shall probably be happier under him than under Coleridge.'* [86] Brinsley-Richards could later be as positive. *'Dr. Goodford was an excellent headmaster, not a genius, not a fussy autocrat setting down his foot where a little finger would do, not a stern man delighting in punishment, but equal in his rule and perfectly firm.'* [87]

On first coming to Eton he was told by 'Crab', one of the maids in Eliot's house, that once he'd seen Dr. Goodford's face he'd never forget him and found that true. *'Those who like to see signs of character in a countenance would not have complained that Dr. Goodford's lacked originality. Yet it was not a face to make boys afraid. It seemed to say nemo me impune, but there was evident kindness and geniality in it. The Doctor could enjoy a joke, and was rather disposed to view things from their humorous than from their melancholy side.'* [88]

His love of puns got Brinsley-Richards and a friend out of a tricky situation when *'mooning down Castle Hill'* and at a corner almost bumped into the Head.

"Unde? Et quo?" he asked, cocking his head as he always did when he thought he had propounded a poser.

"Ex ludo, domine, ad ludum," I answered straight out, hat in hand. The pun upon the word ludus pleased him vastly, and he condescended to laugh, telling us to continue our walk.' [89]

Within the college bounds he was always attired in *'bands black, silk cassock with a broad sash, and a D.D. silk gown with baggy sleeves. I have been there at eleven at night bearing a note from my tutor, and have found him in full academicals, seated by the fire in his study, reading 'Punch'.* So unusual was it to see him dressed in anything else that some boys wondered if he even went to bed in this garb.[90]

He was hospitable, a good horseman, and could surprise boys. Walking through College one night, as was his custom, a boy sneaked up behind his back and made derisory gestures. When he reached the door, and without turning round he remarked, *"You forgot the shadow on the wall".*[91] On another occasion he burst into a room to catch some boys playing whist, though no-one could work out how he knew that was what they were doing. [92] (Whist had been something of a passion with Provost Goodall who sometimes got distinctly huffy if anything prevented his nightly game.) [93]

In school he made a significant alteration in separating the top two Fifth Form divisions from the rest of the school and drawing up for them a new scheme of work, rather extending the change that Hawtrey had made. One introduction though must have been welcomed by tutors through gritted teeth. That was 'Sunday Questions' in which theological testers were set and had boys pestering them for enlightenment.[94]

There was no suggesstion that Goodford was anything more than a regulation flogger, though a particular one, never liking to use the same birch twice. Rather it seemed he saw it as an unavoidable part of his role. Yet his time gave rise to quite a few swishing stories.

In 1856, one youth, Morgan Thomas, defiantly refused to be flogged and was expelled, but, his father supporting him, the affair reached the correspondence columns of 'The Times'.[95] Johnson doubted whether he would have got much Etonian support as *'the squires wished, no doubt, to have their beefy brats coerced sharply'*.[96]

One boy, a future M.P., got the idea that walnut juice applied to the bottom would make a beating less painful. He didn't though anticipate it turning his bottom brown. When he was readied at the block, Goodford recoiled in horror until the accompanying praeposter, seemingly in on the wheeze, explained things whereat Goodford laughed and walked off without doing any beating.[97]

Preparing to go home before Christmas, and given permission to do so a day early as his mother, the Duchess of Montrose, was then ending her stay at Windsor, Graham was whiling away his time by catapulting marbles at railway trucks at the station. Unfortunately for him he was caught in this strongly forbidden act by the Rev. Walford who insisted on taking him back to College. The Duchess had no objection to being detained while he awaited his stinging retribution.[98]

Election Saturday, falling just before the boys' Monday departure, was an occasion of high jinks which sometimes went too far and Goodford had to put in an additional stint at the block on the Sunday evening. There was a temptation for any misbehaving leaver to ignore any summons and leave unchastised on the Monday. The downside was that they would be unable to visit again or have their initials carved as legacy.

That prompted a story that went the rounds of a boy who had left unpunished but later thought better of it. Hearing that Goodford was holidaying in Europe he chased after him with a birch, narrowly missing him as he moved from place to place until he finally came across him in the monastery of Mount St. Bernard. Here Goodford was provided with the birch and flogged him in the presence of the monks. The truth alas was more prosaic. He was told to report at the start of the ensuing Michaelmas term and given a sharp lecture. [99]

Finmore, Hawtrey's former servant, but now Goodford's doorkeeper and official rod-maker, *'a shambling old fellow whose face was covered with eruptions like grog-blossoms'*, took care to deliver the rods to the swishing room when few boys would be about. Once though, a sudden lack resulted in a mid-day delivery which, despite an attempt to conceal the contents of the cart, was ambushed with boys gleefully running off with the birches, not heeding Finmore's saying that they would all get beaten anyway.[100]

There was rather more of a poser one morning when Goodford turned up in the swishing room to find that block and birches had vanished. That was the doing of some old Etonians who, thus equipped, formed their own London club, qualifying admission to which was to have been flogged at least three times at Eton.[101]

For his last three weeks as Head Goodford put the cane aside in what must have seemed a worrying development for Finmore, no doubt hoping his successor would sustain a brisk trade.

Towards the end of his period in office Goodford made some significant changes. One was to do with beating. Following an episode in which a boy was put on the flogging list, unjustly in the view of his tutor who thought him incapable of the charged offence, a revised system was introduced. Whereas before a boy's name had merely to be put on the daily bill for him to be flogged, there had to be discussion with the boy's tutor, creating something of a filtering process in discouraging masters from over-hasty assignments, aware that some justification might be sought.[102]

Then he restricted the peculiar Etonian practice of 'shirking' by bringing Eton High Street and the road to the river within bounds. Hitherto should a master be encountered out of bounds, the practice was to 'shirk', to seek to hide, and, however unconvincingly, to make pretence of invisibility. Sixth Formers were exempt but they in turn had to be shirked by lower boys, and could make a point of it. One Eton boy. neglecting to shirk a Sixth-Former, was told to go to Long Chamber. Asking a friend what for, the answer came: *'For! to be half killed; that is getting as sound a licking as ever you had in your life'*. The river had posed practical difficulties. The way to it was out of bounds so that Staff were not supposed officially to know of anything that went on there. Keate had been anxious that the boys should keep off the Thames on an occasion when it was in flood but, keeping up the pretence of ignorance, expressed himself in such circumlocutory language as to leave himself open to wilful misunderstanding by the captain of boats.

Two occasions that had often been marked by undue excess were abolished. The Oppidan dinner had been a lengthy affair, starting at four o'clock, interrupted by having to make the 6 o'clock absence, during which Dr. Goodford kept his eyes firmly on the list so as not to notice too much, and then resumed. The last one, in 1859, was apparently a fairly restrained affair, a waiter surprised at how few bottles had been opened, but even so one of the swells in Eliot's house considerably over-indulged. He was *'so mightily drunk that it took half a dozen fellows, our tutor's butler, and two boys' maids to get him upstairs. He violently resisted our efforts to undress him, and when he had been put between sheets, he rolled out of bed, and wanted to go down-stairs in his nightshirt and shake hands with his tutor'.* Eliot though discreetly kept out of the way.[104] Ended too were 'Check Nights', rowing expeditions which were often also the cue for extravagant indulgence. To compensate for these abolitions Goodford gave permission for oarsmen to compete in the Henley Regatta, excusing them fom six o'clock absence in order to do so.[105]

The Windsor Fair was a standing invitation to break bounds, and one that a number of masters did little to prevent, some giving out double pocket money and one even making a pun of the word 'fair'. There were to be found *'Aunt Sallies, rifle-galleries, and circus of dogs and monkeys'* along with all manner of kinds of invitation to gambling, one being roulette with cads encouraging having a go by bawling, *'Now, my little lords, step this way. Yer needn't have cause to fear the masters nabbin' you there. We've a big dorg, who'd pin any parson that tried to come arter yer.'* Brinsley-Richards and his friend Croppie had been reasonably successful at the table when a cry of "Master!" was raised and they fled only to almost run into the Rev. Joynes. Racing away they were encouraged to outpace him by a hallooing crowd and got away. Although Joynes later reported them Eliot took no action, only asking how they reckoned Joynes as a racer.[106]

The proximity of Windsor Castle meant that the College was well aware of important events. For these the College often provided royal pages. These were recalled as usually being *'very pretty boys'* but their conduct was often less attractive. Millinery of those deemed lesser notables was often treated with some disdain. One boy, cashiered for rudeness, hoped that wouldn't affect his hoped for Guards' career.[107]

One such event was the wedding of the Prince of Wales for which triumphal arches and bunting decorated the streets while the boys sported wedding favours along with white gloves and new hats. A somewhat haphazard procession headed for St. George's Chapel including Gladstone who *'shambled past us in a gold-lace swallow-tail with a cocked hat like a half-moon, and a sword sticking out straight behind him'.* Excitement was such that later that day around three hundred boys burst through the police cordon to try to get another look at the now married couple at the station. All did though get an extra week's holiday.[108]

Eton High Street itself held plenty of attractions and temptations. Trouble would follow if a boy had been found to have entered any of its thirteen inns. Banned too were the toyshop and the tobacconist's, the former because it did a brisk trade in cribs though the ban only effected a reduction in business. Popular with a number of boys was Runicles' shop in which were a number of lathes which boys were allowed to use for a charge of a shilling an hour and subsequently decorated their rooms with the result, generally *'neither decorative nor useful'*.[109] Williams the stationer provided the necessary books for College and had a virtual monopoly of this business. One Towers had an Eton shop and allowed boys to his garden to shoot crossbows. When found to have been plundering Eton boys though he was sent to Botany Bay for seven years. Then there were two tailors, the deaf Tom Brown and his rival, Denman, forever promising a seldom met punctuality.[110]

The severe winter of 1860-1861 was the background to a serious confrontation. Thick ice made for excellent skating, some coming from London for it, and an array of tents being set up by purveyors of the likes of hot tea, coffee and chestnuts, much to Goodford's disapproval. More serious though was a mass snowball fight which broke out among a number of rapidly increasing participants and resolved itself into one lot defending the bridge while attackers tried to drive them off it. The defenders then being driven back the contest continued into the High Street to the alarm of the shopkeepers. One who came out to expostulate got a snowball in the eye, had his windows smashed, and fled the bombardment of his person by scrambling over a wall into his neighbour's garden. Two masters arriving on the scene ended the barrage. Two of the ringleaders were flogged and two others sent to apologise, a rather different conclusion to a similar affair in Keate's time. The shopkeeper came off worst, being without any College custom for some while.[111]

Masters may have had it in mind that something of that kind might happen in winter weather but another happening cannot have been at all anticipated. One evening Brinsley- Richard's pal, Croppie, marched into his room and displayed a golden guinea. It turned out that he had overheard a conversation between their two maids in which they'd been talking about former times when floors were sanded rather than carpeted, and how valuable coins could be found underneath. Prompted by this to do a little mining underneath the floorboards he'd quickly found a guinea, a shilling and three pennies. The two of them, with their friend, Pug, then succumbed to gold-digging fever, trying as many under-floor spaces as they could. Though trying to keep it quiet, the news of this spread around the house and into other houses. The digging mania ended only when a boy in Drury's house fell through a thin layer of plaster into the room below, startling its occupant into loud howling, he thinking the house was falling down. Thereafter thorough checks of all mining activity in the houses were made and further activity barred. [112]

* * * * *

Religious practices underwent some change in the 1850's. The need for substantial chapel restoration was recognised and the building closed for a year while this was carried out. Meanwhile the boys used a wooden structure called 'the tabernacle'. [113] By 1858 the school had grown to a size beyond the capacity of the chapel and Lower School boys started using a cemetery chapel on weekdays and St. John's on Sundays. Various premises were used before a Lower Chapel was later built.

The substantial, classical organ-loft was removed and the organ placed elsewhere. The *'hideous'* reredos was taken out along with the box pews for the College's male and female servants, and the stalls in which the nobility had been used to preen itself, *'a very absurd distinction'*.[114] Removed too was the panelling along the side walls. (The same was partially done in King's Chapel in the 1950's, an alteration which remains extremely controversial today.) It was while that was being done that some murals were uncovered. A Fellow going into the chapel while the work was under way immediately realised their significance and ordered a halt to the work. He though was over-ruled by the Provost and the murals were removed. A substantial College benefactor, a Fellow, the Rev. Wilder, gave fourteen large windows, one of many sizeable donations he made.[115] Up till then all apart from the west window had been plain. Rather more controversial, at least in the opinion of the boys, was the arrangement made for the East window. 'Lights' appeared at intervals, and on each occasion the boys had to pay a sort of 'window tax'. Completion must have been greeted with some relief.[116]

Nor did anything that took place there greatly bestir most of them. Preachers, mostly Fellows, were more remembered for their peculiarities. *'Pedestrian Peck'* who had prayed for the defeat of the Reform Bill was remembered for his *'grotesque mannerisms and Spurgeonisms'* though it was also said of him that *'a kinder and more narrow-minded ecclesiastic never lived'*.[117] Of Plumptre it was recalled that *'in the pulpit, he always held his glasses an inch or two in front of his face'*, and his wasp-swatting gestures were caricatured.[118] Hawtrey began the practice of Headmasters preaching occasionally and was capable of delivering *'orthodox and eloquent'* short sermons.[119] Broad church, he was prepared to stand by Anglo-Catholics and had little interest in the controversies generated by Newman and Arnold. His brevity must have counted in his favour. A Westminster canon preached for fifty minutes in front of the boys. Dire threats were made to his son if *'your governor preaches fifty minutes next Sunday'*.[120] The canon got the message. Confirmation though was taken a serious business, the formidable personality of the Visitor, Samuel Wilberforce, Bishop of Lincoln, ensuring it was so.[121]

The choir of St. George's came to sing briefly on Sunday afternoons before hurrying off for its own service and occasionally a choir came from Eton High School. Not till 1868 did it seem to occur to Eton that it could perfectly well form a choir on its own. Oscar Browning had got up a secular choir but had laboured to get its members to appreciate the difference between a tone and a semi-tone. Before it was able to make any kind of musical mark the chapel witnessed various performances. Robert Bridgewater's *'coarse and aggressive'* singing was disliked by Eton boys who called him *'thunderguts'*.[122] The ability of the organist was questioned when it was said that *'his right hand knoweth not what his left hand doeth'*. Nor were relations between organist and blower always harmonious. *'You can play Rogers in D if you like but I shall blow for Attwood in C,'* an affronted blower once expostulated.[123]

Eton boys generally semed *'a cold, stagnant, mute congregation'*.[124] The irreverent mood of many was indicated by the busyness of the 'master-at-desk' whose task was to secure orderliness and before the service commenced might have *'a miscellaneous collection of articles – knives, fives balls, bags of eatables, apples, even quinces, on his bookboard, which he had confiscated from impatient boys'*.

One man seemed to have his thoughts set more distantly. The chapel clerk was pleased to show people a coffin he had stored in a part of the chapel then used as a lumber room. It had been made for a boy who was drowned but had not been used. Grey, the clerk, said he was keeping it for his own burial and buried in it he was.[125]

Risen to the Fifth Form Brinsley-Richards found his circumstances very agreeably changed. He was given a sizeable room whose windows overlooked the Thames and Windsor Castle's tower and terraces. It was a room which he had previously entered with a sense of foreboding – Blazes's old room.

"Your tutor thought you would like it, sir," said Crab, the boy's maid, as she called my attention to the new paper on the walls, and to the new carpet, hearth-rug, and table-cloth. ....and please, sir, we have had your pictures hung up for you so that the room might not look bare when you came." [126] He reflected that the single pewter tankard he had won with Blazes looked slight indeed alongside the previous array of trophies and went off to buy some more pictures to fill some of the blank spaces.

He found his division, Mr. Birch's, congenial, appreciating his often straying beyond the classics into English Literature.[127] Out of school he found a new interest, the newly formed Volunteer Corps. This had been prompted by the scare of a French invasion in 1860 and its instigator, the Rev. Edmond Warre, was to be increasingly influential in Eton's affairs as well as being the only cleric on the Army List. It was a most popular act and there was no lack of boys eager to put on the uniform of *a whitey brown tunic with light blue facings edged with red cord*. Drill was at the heart of it. *'The whole corps used to drill from 8.15 to 9.15 on Monday mornings,'* and truants were rebuked or fined. Lord Elcho came to review the force dressed in civvies, rather a poor show it was felt, and a shooting team was sent to test their prowess at Wimbledon.[128]

Then came excitement with the news being conveyed to the Headmaster that the Queen and Prince Consort would review the corps with its members invited to dine at the castle afterwards. Hearing this, many other boys wanted to join the corps but its commandant, Arthur Chandos Arkwright, would only have boys who had achieved sufficient competence and stressed the importance of performing well, the Prince having been used to seeing the high standards of drill achieved in the German military schools. The review lasted about twenty minutes with various march pasts after which a long line of two rows was formed and on the order for three cheers *'we gave about three times thirty, bawling and waving our caps on our bayonets whilst Her Majesty retired'*. Then followed *'a very well-spread dinner, with champagne unlimited'* in the lavishly decorated Orangery.[129]

This review had taken place on a cold, damp November day, was the Prince's last public appearance and may have been the occasion on which he caught the chill from which he subsequently died. When school resumed after Christmas all the boys wore mourning.

In the Fifth form, Brinsley-Richards became something of a 'swell', joining Pop. As such he took his turn at the customary orating though while writing the usual subsequent summary of what he'd said wondered whether he'd added much to the stock of human knowledge. A rather different challenge was to master the art of *'the long glass'*, our *'yard of ale'*, the tricky bit managing the final tilt of the globe without having the beer splashing all over your face.[130] His dormant cricketing ambition was unexpectedly revived when he was passed a note during a lesson on Horace asking whether he would turn out for the XI against the Quidnuncs. However, a score of three and some liberties taken with his bowling ended his dream of sporting success and he consoled himself with pleasant afternoons on the river.[131]

An enforced change came about when Eliot was made a Fellow and his house came to an end, its occupants who were staying on at the school having to move elsewhere. His friend Cherry left to prepare for the army but he and Pug hit on a house with a tutor known to be more popular than strict. It did too have many Lower boys so that there were always plenty of fags around. *'I wish I could say that our fagging powers were used with discretion'*, he later reflected.[132]

At the end of his last summer half there was a series of farewell meals. There were leaving breakfasts at the White Hart and Castle Hotel, along with toasts, and farewell dinners and suppers given by tutors. Distributed too were leaving books for departing friends. In the end he returned to his room to find that Hill, the carpenter, had packed everything away into two large packing cases.

'The house is silent, and I am alone in my room with those two big packing cases, and the memories of seven years'.[133]

He regretted the abolition of Election Saturday, the half now ending on the Friday thus limiting opportunities for excess, but also taking away the final, moving chapel service, one that struck a chord even with those so far little taken with religious practice.

(Housemasters of a later period, especially during the 1960's, faced a lengthier tricky phase when exams ended some three weeks before the end of term with temptations in some quarters to experiment with drink and drugs).

There remained for Brinsley-Richards just one final ceremony, the presentation of a leaving book to the Headmaster who by this time was Dr. Balston. He greeted him with a smile and said –

"Well, your time amongst us has been a happy one, I think. "

"Yes, sir." [134]

Charles Old Goodford: Eton Headmaster and Provost

CHAPTER NINE : TROUBLE AHEAD

By 1862 some Public Schools were prospering while others were less favoured. Eton's growth continued with it amassing 840 pupils while Harrow had made an astonishing recovery under Charles Vaughan. From seemingly being on the brink of dissolution in 1844 it had a role of 481. Rugby was well favoured with 463 while Winchester had recovered from a low of boys in 1855 to 216. Their unappealing London location was one reason for the low numbers at Charterhouse and Westminster, both having only 136 boys while Shrewsbury with 140 was also in decline.

Parents had to decide what they wanted from a school and what would most benefit their sons. The growing class of successful businessmen were clearly attracted by the social cachet of Eton even if it was hard to see that what was taught would greatly advance their sons' prospects.

Not all though thought that the most important aspect. To John Walter, who had three sons at Eton, it was character that was at the heart of education. A key aim should be *'to train the mind to overcome difficulties, and to get it into shape'*. Too much knowledge could actually be a bad thing in that it could *'confuse the mind'* with the result that *'you lose power'*. He was not alone in having the idea that there was only so much knowledge that youth could comfortably digest. The result of overdoing it might well be the emergence of *'an effeminate, enfeebled bookworm'* rather than the kind of *'manly gentleman'* who could be of service to country and Empire.[1]

Yet a sound classical basis was a considerable advantage if the school syllabus was to be productive. Charles Dickens had his son, Charley, prepared by a private tutor before seeing what Eton made of him. Cookesley, *'a most excellent man in his way'*, examined him, thought him well grounded in Virgil and Herodotus, but saw a need for tuition in some verse work, recommending a Mr. Hardisty for this. *'I must not hesitate to tell you plainly that this appeared to me to be a conventional way of bestowing a little patronage,'* Dickens wrote to Charley's tutor but went along with it. He decided to have Cookesley as Charley's tutor but to place him in Evans's house. Dickens's suggestive use of *'in his way'* in his description of Cookesley suggests he may have spotted, or been told of, a certain quirkiness in his nature,[2] one trait being the over-use of his *'doctor'*,[3] his cane. Evans's house was extremely popular with a good sporting reputation, something the eight Lyttleton brothers considerably enhanced. Two years later, in July, 1851, Dickens gave an account of taking Charley and three friends down the river picnicking but becoming mighty anxious in case one of them got drunk, and he was called to account, but though *'the speech of one became thick and his eyes too like lobsters' to be comfortable'* all was well.[4]

Hard though it was for many Etonian Fellows and masters to think in terms of education in any terms but that of a classically dominated one, some had an uneasy sense that an inflexible resistance to the changed requirements of mid-nineteenth century society was growing increasingly untenable. The Dean of Christ Church, Dr. Gaisford, argued that one reason for teaching the Classics was that such study *'could lead to positions of considerable emolument'*.[5] That though could only happen if you were any good at it, and the field for such expertise was a limited one. Proof of more general competence was being demanded by the Civil Service and even the army. A need for external cramming before an army trial hardly reflected well on a school.

Realising this, Eton set up an army class. Johnson took a dim view of this, seeing it as pandering to the *'soldier pedants of the Horse Guards'*.[6] That seems rather out of character, he being a knowledgeable enthusiast for the army and navy and a good deal readier to countenance changes than most Etonians. What that seems to show is Eton's touchiness at the prospect of change, if change there had to be, being enforced from outside rather than evolving internally.

* * * * *

Matthew Higgins had a brief spell as a boy at Eton and did not in retrospect savour the experience. He aired his feelings under a pseudonym, 'Paterfamilias', in the Cornhill Magazine in May, 1860, and returned to the fray a number of times.

To him, the whole ethos of the Public School was dubious in the extreme in that they were *'for the most part, mere money speculations, in which the welfare and progress of the pupils were held altogether subservient to the pecuniary profits of the masters'*. Headmaster Goodford's annual income of £6,000 was noted. There were too few masters, the proportion of boys to masters being *'dishonestly small'* which meant little supervision, with deficiencies too readily resolved by the cane. Claims of success were often unjustified for *'it never seemed to occur to them that a boy might have thriven in spite of that lax and dishonest system and not in consequence of it'*.

Dull boys learnt little from the largely classical syllabus. Just how wanting in relevant knowledge they were was shown by the difficulties posed by army and Civil Service exams. He called for a Parliamentary Commission to put an end to the narrowly based teacher sources provided by New College and King's and to insist on the proper recognition of modern subjects such as French and Maths.[7]

Later in the same year criticism came from a rather different quarter. A tirade from a radical journalist might be shrugged off but measured criticism from an Old Etonian High Court Judge was a rather different matter. Speaking rather more in sorrow than anger in a lecture at Tiverton, he commended the influence of Eton on a boy's character and saw growing up in such a beautiful place as most beneficial. He went on though very much to echo Higgins's criticisms and added two others. The newly enriched were sending their sons to Eton solely for *'useful connections in after life'* and he thought that less time should be given to religion. His intervention was seen as highly significant. *'Sir John Coleridge has belled the cat, and it is to be hoped that now all who have an interest in Eton will discuss the matter fearlessly.'*[8]

Returning to the controversy in December, 1860, Higgins was able to cite the concurrence of this influential advocate without adding much new. Sydney Smith's powerful article fifty years ago was cited and Higgins saw his contentions as still being clearly justified.[9]

Throughout the Winter and Spring of 1860/1861 a number of journals kept up a barrage of criticism. The debate had been started by Etonians and, even when the subject was ostensibly Public Schools, Eton was the critics' almost exclusive target.

Fault was found with the teaching. Goodford had not kept to his policy of having one master for every forty boys. More masters were needed. Some of them should be teaching Modern Languages and Maths which needed much more attention. Excessive time was spent on the Classics which did little for a dull boy who saw no real incentive to try. This widespread lack of application was turning Eton into *'a castle of indolence'*.[10] Objection could also be made to a good deal of the *'impure and unholy'*[11] Classical content. Termly exams should determine standing in the school.

There were criticisms of Eton's extravagance under which parents were said *'to wince and groan'*.[12] Leaving Books was only one of a number of extras that they found themselves paying for. That is, if they were any longer able to afford having a son or sons there. One complaint was that those who considered an Eton education fitting for their sons could not manage the fees. 'Paterfamilias' had little time for Eton's masters who, in his view, had made teaching at Eton a mere *'breeches pocket question'*.[13] An Eton master drew £45 p.a. from the foundation but most were earning around £1,000 p.a. One way of boosting your earnings was to take a number of private pupils. Each private pupil would add ten or twenty guineas to a tutor's income, and some had dozens. Money too could be made from a house though incompetence here could lead to indebtedness and departure. They were too criticised for a snobbish attitude to the Oppidans. (In a way this was not altogether surprising. They themselves had been Collegers, had gone to King's, and returned as masters, the shared background breeding a somewhat exclusive mindset.)

Not all of Eton's critics blamed the masters though, one at least thinking they'd been unfairly blamed for failings, and held rather to the view that it was the system rather than the masters who were to blame.

Attention was drawn to the wealth sloshing around Eton, (it was thought then to have an annual income of about £20,000) and the questionable ways in which moneys were raised and spent. The operations of Provost and Fellows came under close scrutiny. Sir John Coleridge had seemed to encourage this line of enquiry when in his Tiverton speech he had remarked that *'the non-observance of the Eton statutes is, I must say, a most shocking thing.'* [14] That Fellows should have preferment to one of the College's thirty-seven livings was seen as *'nepotism in its most unblushing form'*.[15] Highly questionable too was the practice of rack-renting: of charging a fine on the renewal of a College lease, the money accrued being divided into nine shares, two for the Provost and one each for the other seven Fellows. *'A more gross instance of dishonesty nowhere exists.'* [16] Nor should Eton's masters *'have claim to retire as pensioners upon the bounty of the founder'*.[17]

Writing to Brougham, who though long out of office was still taking an interest in this debate, Henry Reeve, like Higgins a well-travelled man of independent means, urged him to *'keep my secret, but I have in preparation a regular mine under Eton College'* [18]. The explosive material was probably the discovered Huggett MSS in the British Museum which was a transcription of the Eton Statutes. The excitement came from the supposed breech in their secrecy. Quoted was the stipulation that Eton scholars were to swear on entering Eton that they were unable to afford £3.6s.8d. on their maintenance. From this it was argued that Eton had originally been created to serve the poorer gentry and yeomanry and that what had happened subsequently was a perversion of the founder's intentions. One reason for the removal of the Statutes from public view, Reeve suggested, was that some of its proscriptions did not accord well with the dignity of a Fellow who was *'not to frequent taverns or raree-shows, not to grow immoderately long hair or beard not to wear green, red or white breeches, not to annoy those below by urinating out of the window or emptying slops on their heads'.*[19]

In fact, what was the point of the Fellows? *'They form a perfect specimen of those comfortable bodies which our ruthless reforming age insisted on making uncomfortable, where it has not swept them away altogether.'* Especially one which had achieved a good deal of hereditary succession to add to its nepotism, mismanagement and sinecures – the Fellows did little enough for their £1000 a year. What effect they did have was often unfortunate. The Provost could obstruct the Headmaster while the general standard of the Fellows' chapel preaching was often thought deplorable [20]

'Paterfamilias' considered the standard of teaching in village schools to have greatly improved since the introduction of inspections but supposed the likes of Eton too grand to consider any such thing. A growing number of critics though reckoned matters serious enough to need the scrutiny of a Parliamentary Commission.

Another line, familiar enough today, was that far too much was made of Eton. *'Eton is held up as if it were the be-all and end-all here. To succeed at Eton was the highest aspiration anyone should indulge in.'* [21] Although its mystique made it seem something of a mystery it is in fact *'the first school in England only in the sense that the richest people send their sons there, and because it has a large and influential connection'.*[22]

The tone of debate became notably more acerbic. In March, 1861, Goodford was alleged by 'Paterfamilias' to have been the author of an article accusing the Cornhill Magazine of *'the foulest form of falsehood'*, *'egregious mendacity'*, and *'deliberate abandonment of the truth'*.[23]

Supporters of the Public Schools had plenty to say in response to criticisms. A defence of the Classics was offered in that they offered a study of humanity and politics – *'all human life is there'*.[24] Yet many were agreed that the curriculum needed reform, even to talk of *'a scandalous deficiency of mere instruction'*.[25] This, it was generally suggested, could be done through internal evolution and without a need for any radical upheaval. *'No great change in the ordinary method is needed, but only to apply it with judgement, patience, and tact.'*

Yet to many what was taught was not the over-riding reason for sending a boy to Public School. Rather was it that he would emerge well fitted to take his place in society. For *'it is in the physical and moral training of our great English Schools that their peculiar excellence consists'*. There *'egotism is checked – self-importance repressed – reserve, self-reliance, the necessity of cultivating cerain qualities, and of deferring to the claims of others are indelibly impressed'*.[26] He would in all probability emerge a well rounded, self-reliant character *'imbued with the qualities of spirit, honour, and endurance which mould and mark the character of an English gentleman'*.[27] He would be the sort of man who could do a job in the Empire and, as Wellington said, *'with two N.C.O.'s and fifteen privates get a shipload of convicts to Australia'*.[28] That kind of competence mattered more than mere knowledge.

Character must be allowed to develop without attempts at constant regulation. It was a common fallacy of the private schoolmaster to think that *'the human character is an elaborate article of manufacture to be painfully put together by certain cunning artificers who are called schoolmasters'*.[29] Moreover, this close supervision could often amount to little more than spying or bring about the picking of favourites. As a writer in the Saturday Review put it: *'the time of liberty must come; the leading strings must be broken at last'*.[30]

By contrast it was important that the Public School ethos survived. Any attempt to turn Eton into something more like a private school would be disastrous. It could even, 'The Times' noted ominously, begin to herald the downfall of the aristocracy in its implicit challenge to the hereditary principle. For it is in Public Schools that *'the fathers live there in their sons'*. In other schools *'there is not found the same self-education, the same moral unity, and lifelong associations'*.[31] While hereditary privilege had many assailants it also had its robust defenders. 'The Times' indeed was credited with having some influence in the appointment of the deeply conservative Dr. Balston as Eton's somewhat reluctant Headmaster after its advocacy: an appointment surely welcomed by Queen Victoria who is supposed to have remarked *'Dr. Balston! The handsomest ecclesiastic in my dominions!'* [32]

School novels the Quarterly Review considered deleterious in the misleading impression they often gave of school life with a *'picture of school life which is neither faithful nor edifying'*. Characters were grotesquely caricatured as with the boy Barker in 'Eric or Little by Little' who is shown as a *'monster of malignity'*. By contrast little is to be gained, as the author does, by setting up *'an exaggerated elevation'* and disgracing those who fall short of it. The novel 'Basil' by the Rev. E. Monro featured an *'academy'* which was rather more like *'a hell upon earth'* presided over by a Mr. Dobson who was *'a prodigy of pompous absurdity and time-serving imbecility'*.[33] It managed too to throw the blame for bullying and indiscipline on the parents. Little enough like the real thing too, it was suggested, was the idea of school life given in 'Geoffrey Davenant', a novel by the Rev. W.E. Heygate. Here the boys were shown as actively engaged in disputing theological points while there was the appalling notion of their making their confessions to the Headmaster. Clerical authorship of many of these books no doubt accounted for their moral preoccupation. 'Tom Brown's Schooldays' by contrast conveys more of the rough and tumble of school life though the reader is reminded of the Doctor's all-pervading presence in the background.

* * * * *

With a growing number of voices calling for a Royal Commission to investigate the running of Public Schools, some Etonians felt a particular bitterness towards criticisms of the College aired by fellow Etonians. Thus William Johnson complained of those who *'betrayed the comparative idleness of those not working for the Foundation to the enemy'*.[34] This also suggests something of a siege mentality with a consequent lashing out. That was something one Fellow, Dupuis, was prepared to do literally when he threatened to take a dog-whip to any intruder.[35]

Those Etonians who entered the journalistic lists were almost all from the College which had been the particular target of several writers. Yet it needs to be remembered that it had only seventy boys out of the school's eight hundred and that in many ways Oppidan life went on in a very different way. The Headmaster, less checked by the Provost, had a fuller control of that larger number to whom the Eton-King's connection meant far less. Oppidan leavers bound for university went off to a variety of Oxford and Cambridge colleges.

Evidence that many boys were learning very little came from a number of sources. Particularly telling was evidence such as that from an Oxford examiner given to the Clarendon Commission that of 168 candidates examined [43] were *'utterly unfit to undergo any examination whatsoever'*.[36] There was a sharp divide between those who had benefited fom a classical education and those who made little or no progress. One lad gained sufficient proficiency to engage the Head over a disputed matter in Latin. The issue was the beard he'd grown and his continued insistence that the Statutes entitled him to do so. Finally admitting defeat he bought a razor but sent the bill to the Provost.[37]

Classical knowledge and use persisted throughout adult life among its more successful students. Several of Eton's historians quoted liberally: whether as homage to their background or what they saw as the most concise way of expressing a thought. Error was quickly spotted by the cognoscenti. There was a general shudder in the Lords when Clarendon, who'd not been to Public School, tripped up with '*Sunt bona quaedam mediocra, sunt plura mala*', misplacing the last two words. For most alumni though, the Classics were surely little more than a long forgotten chore.

Some schools had curricula that ranged well beyond the classical. Stonyhurst claimed to have had the first school Chemistry laboratory in an English school (1808).[38] There was outstanding scientific teaching at the City of London School and Manchester Grammar while even the conservatively inclined Winchester made a start with Science in 1857.[39] Then while Dr. Balston saw little value in teaching French, suggesting that boys should learn it before going to Eton, it was generally taught elsewhere. At Charterhouse some Sixth Form boys learnt German while History was taught up to the reign of George III.[40] From its foundation Cheltenham College clearly saw the benefit of a broad syllabus in that it offered besides the Classics, Modern History, Hebrew, French, German, History, Geography, Drawing, Experimental Science, and Hindustani – the latter with colonial service in mind.[41] Ampleforth had a particularly strong language tradition, its curriculum including French, Italian and Spanish along with History, Geography, Botany and Ornithology.[42] Altered demand was seen in Edinburgh Academy's over-insistence on the Classics nearly bringing about its downfall.[43]

One development was seen as a cause for concern by some and that was the growing part played by games in a school's practice and ethos. The 1850's is generally held to be the decade in which games altered from being activities got up by the boys alone and came to be organised and coached by masters. Some Heads saw the benefit of channelling boyish energies into playing field competition and away from disruptive behaviour. Henry Sidgwick though hoped that at Eton '*the physical strength, gymnastic skill, and social talents, may ever yield in influence to real intellectual pre-eminence and deep earnestness of character*'.[44] Sport was though to become ever more influential.

Strong feelings were aroused and sharp words used in the course of this controversy. Yet feelings were not always as polarised as the language might suggest. 'The Times' conceded that educational deficiency could well result in *'downright ruin'.* On the other hand, Henry Reeve, he of the exploding mine, opined that *'Eton boys are early imbued with the qualities of spirit, honour, and endurance which mould and mark the character of English gentlemen'.* The Public Schools had no more inveterate opponent than Brougham yet, when asked for advice as to where his nephews might be sent, he replied – Eton.

* * * * *

When defenders of Public School practice had reluctantly to admit that there were faults to be found, two targets were offered in justification. It was claimed that as a result of their more indulgent home life, matching the *'softened tone of society at large',* [47] boys were becoming less able to rise to challenges. The other problem was the preparatory school which, it was alleged, failed to give their boys an adequate grounding. In Luxmoore's words, Public schools were much hampered by *'the defects of the raw material with which they are supplied'.*[48]

These schools were rapidly increasing during this period, from an estimated [20] in 1850 to around 400 in 1900. With some the charge of inadequate grounding seems improbable. Pupils from William Browning's two schools were able to satisfy Eton's most challenging tests. At Eagle House the Rev. Edward Wickham educated six of the country's most prominent headmasters in a school renowned for its classical excellence.[49] On occasion some of these schools may almost have done too much. Neville Lyttleton recounted how, after Geddington, he found the work in Eton's fourth form so easy that he became idle.[50] Temple Grove, at East Sheen, quickly established a sound reputation and was larger than most which tended to be small establishments of around twenty boys. Of course not all pupils at these schools would have been high achievers but they offered a prospect of academic success to the willing and able.

Sent off to the Rev. Dr. Roberts's school at Mitcham, Milnes Gaskell found this daily routine :

'The boys rose at 6.30 and translated Ovid until eight, when there was breakfast of boiled milk and bread. Until eleven they learnt twelve lines of Ovid; from eleven to one there was play. Dinner was at one, and in the afternoon they read English and did sums. At 5.45 supper was served and after prayers there was play until bedtime at eight.' [51]

Some detail has survived of Temple Grove's daily routine :

'Hands, face, and perhaps the neck, were washed daily; feet once a fortnight, heads as required; a vernal dose of brimstone and treacle purified their blood, a half-yearly dentist drew their teeth, and it was their custom under flogging to bite the Latin Grammar.' 52

Any boys unduly cosseted by a supposedly more agreeable home life must have got a rude shock at their new school, in particular the painful redress for any failing. Dr. Roberts liked to teach while wandering round his premises and had canes placed for ready use all over the place.[53] At Geddington, the Rev. Church gave boys a thorough grounding but sometimes at the cost of an ungovernable temper. One boy had his ears boxed for giving a false quantity, was then so stunned he could do nothing but repeat his error, was soundly thrashed and sent to bed. For a while he had the plan of beating any boy who'd not finished his set work by noon.[54] At Mitcham, Ainger and a fellow miscreant were in trouble for the crime of an unauthorised trip to the village and the purchase of apples. For that they were set to write out Ainsworth's dictionary, end of term bringing this bizarre punishment to a close while they were still on the 'A''s.[55] Sometimes it got too much. An unhappy boy at Mitcham with Milnes Gaskell ran away and was brought back and put in a locked room kept just for that. A story told of another school was of a headmaster so unpopular with the boys that they drew lots to find out which of them would kill him. His own son drew the lot and bashed him over the head with a poker, but he survived the assault.[56]

Despite their harshness, the schools mentioned above were serious academic concerns. And despite the omnipresent severity boys had a good deal of fun playing cricket and football, though some, like M.R. James at Temple Grove, later thought it would have been better if someone had been able to show them how to play properly, and other games such as prisoner's base. Because of the small size of these schools certain things were possible, such as keeping ponies, that were later out of the question.

Ainger was quite convinced that many others would seem to invite comparison with 'Dotheboys Hall' where any idea of an Eton scholarship was mere fantasy.

The desirability of some collaboration resulted in the setting up of the Incorporated Association of Prepartory Schools in 1892 in order to agree the vital matter of a uniform size of cricket ball. Then the introduction of Common Entrance in 1903 ensured that all boys reached a passable academic standard.[57]

CHAPTER TEN : SETTING UP THE COMMISSION

At the start of the 1860's Eton gave little sign of being on the verge of any significant change. There was still an attachment to the old ways and the teaching had not altered a great deal from the previous century.

Provosts and Fellows were seen as guardians of heritage, Provosts in particular being figures of considerable ritual significance and practical import. Eton had a succession, mostly of former Headmasters, while at King's two, Thackeray and Okes, spanned most of the Nineteenth Century (1814-1889).

When the Provost of King's visited Eton he was escorted by two Posers, and they all drove up from Slough in a yellow chariot. Arrived at Lupton's Tower, they were greeted with a Latin oration by the Captain of the School who was generally coached by a master as to content. The two Provosts were meant to greet each other with a kiss in royal fashion and boys sometimes watched with curiosity to see whether they actually did so. The task of a Poser was to examine scholarship candidates but before getting round to that he would choose some small Collegers to act as pages – to run errands and see to his meals. This was a popular assignment as it was rewarded with a guinea and often a share of the Poser's table.[1] Out of term Provosts had to attend to the wider College estate with lands and livings spread across many counties. Before the coming of the railways this involved something like a royal progress in the Provost's stagecoach.

In outward display too, the Fellows exhibited every sign of extreme conservatism. *'For instance, knee-breeches, buckles and shoes were kept to by a few. Coats and hats were also corresponding. Collars were worn, very high collars by some, and voluminous folds of neck-cloth. Frilled shirt fronts characterised a few, spotless and fine.'* [2] Their ladies sometimes used a sedan chair in progressing to an evening party within the cloisters.[3]

Relations between the Fellows were not always cordial. Dupuis, when canvassing for Provost, was rebuffed by the elderly Hunt, who always kept his coffin in his room. *'Get out of my room, you lousy son of a French sea-cook. None of your French blood in this College'.*[4] There were too occasional differences with King's. One such concerned the practice of Fellows holding College livings to which King's took objection. The Visitor, the Bishop of Lincoln, was drawn into this, and gave judgement in favour of Eton. Then, although free of classsroom duties, the Fellows were not always immune from schoolboy nuisance. One such was to knock on Plumptre's door then, urchin – like, run away. Irritated by this wheeze, and seeming to hear footsteps of pranksters ourtside his door one evening, Plumptre thrust open the door and grabbed a suspect only to find he'd arrested a sack of coal.[5]

The task of the Commission was to determine just how many of their powers it was in the interest of schools to retain and whether the formation of an altogether different kind of Governing Body might not be a better idea.

* * * * *

For those wishing for reform of the Public Schools the omens seemed favourable when a renegade Old Etonian became Home Secretary. This was Sir George Cornewall Lewis who had made his views abundantly clear in published articles in The Edinburgh Review, of which for a while he was the editor. The tenor of his attitude can be seen in such comments as that fagging was *'the only regular institution of slave labour enforced by brute force which exists in these islands'*[6] and his criticisms of regular flogging *'performed on the naked back by the Headmaster himself'.*[7] He thought solitary confinement would be a far better idea. Clearly, he was going to offer conservatives little succour.

In April, 1861, he stated in the House of Commons that as the *'Principal Class of Endowed Schools'* had been brought within the remit of Parliament and especially of the Charity Commissioners, there was a case for an enquiry into the Public Endowed Schools. He proposed to get the views of Headmasters to see whether they thought a Royal Commission the best way forward.[8]

Seeing action of some kind as being clearly on the cards one M.P., Sir W. Heathcote, tried unsuccessfully to gain an exemption for Winchester by arguing that it was legally an Oxford College.[9]

Anxious that the legislative process should this time maintain its momentum Brougham asserted in the House of Lords in June that most of the present difficulties had arisen from their having been exemptions in the 1818 Act and was anxious that that should not recur.[10] The Lord Chancellor assured him that this time there would be no exceptions and that the schools had been generally co-operative. Pressing the issue again later that month Brougham learnt that the Commission had not yet been set up but was satisfied that proceedings were under way and congratulated the schools on their co-operation.[11]

It came into being on July 18th. 1861, with Lord Clarendon as its chairman. Handsome, engaging, industrious, and with a ready turn of phrase, he had had wide-ranging diplomatic experience in St. Petersburg, Spain, and as Viceroy of Ireland at the height of the famine, where his reception of QueenVictoria on her visit made such a good impression as to leave him subsequently in favour at court, as well as holding several other offices of State before rising to Foreign Secretary shortly before the Crimean War.[12] No enthusiast for military adventures, he saw little to be gained from British involvement. *'The beastly Turks have actually declared war,'* [13] he wrote as the crisis worsened. Faced with the inevitable, he was though a steadying influence during the conflict. In 1859 though Lord John Russell decided he would be his own Foreign Secretary and Clarendon refused other proffered posts, leaving him free for this task. Oddly though, he had not himself been to Public School.

He was joined on the Commission by Sir Stafford Northcote (Eton), Lord Lyttleton (Eton), Edward Twistleton (Winchester), The Earl of Devon (Westminster), Halford Vaughan (Rugby), and William Thompson, Professor of History at Oxford University (educated privately).[14] Clarendon was less than impressed by this ensemble. *'Devon is weak, Northcote pedantic, Thompson idle, Twistleton quirky, Vaughan mad'.* He did afterwards though concede that *'they all had merits and have worked well together'*.[15] Indeed, without a good deal of effective collaboration it may be doubted whether they could ever have produced such a rigorously compendious report, the example of being *'laborious in the last degree'* no doubt set by its chairman. Anyone who has staggered into a Library Reading room under the weight of the report's volumes will appreciate that they didn't take their duty lightly.

Their task was to examine the running of nine Public Schools; Eton, Winchester, Westminster, Harrow, Rugby, Charterhouse, St. Paul's, Merchant Taylor's, and Shrewsbury. These became known as the Clarendon Schools and the term is still occasionally used today. The Commissioners were though well aware that they were investigating at a time of great Public School expansion – while they were sitting

Beaumont, Malvern, Cranleigh, and St. Edward's were all founded[16] – and took evidence from other schools as well as making comparisons with continental practice.

Reporters gained access to what seemed to some of them a bizarrely alien world. *'The evidence.'* wrote one, *'was as interesting as a book of travels in a new and unexplored country'* even though much of it was pretty mystifying to the uninitiated.[17] There was though enough oddity and hint of scandal to keep them interested.

* * * * *

To the casual newspaper reader the news that a Royal Commission was to undertake an investigation into the Public Schools may have been only of passing interest. To Provost Hawtrey though it seemed more like a threat to everything he'd ever known. For some while he'd become increasingly irritated by criticism of Eton in the periodical press, Matthew Higgins (Paterfamilias) being a particular bugbear. All the Edinburgh Review offered, he maintained, was *'a selection of facts which are worth nothing when their import is modified by the facts that are omitted'*.[18] He'd objected too to Coleridge's Tiverton speech, maintaining that the changes he wanted had already either been made or were under way. Nor did Clarendon seem at all a good choice for as someone who *'had himself a private education .... I should think utterly unfit for the duty required of him'*.[19] The notion that he might bring a more objective approach did not seem an idea even worth considering. Clarendon was certainly unlikely to offer a great deal of reassurance after reflecting on his son's progress at Harrow. *'I wish,'* he wrote to Sir George Cornewall Lewis, *'the best years of his life were not spent in forgetting French, making bad Latin verses and acquiring nothing that will fit him to be a prominent or useful member of society.'*

And where *'some reformation has been forced on them by public opinion it is always unwillingly adopted by masters who seem to be as much attached to routine as they are to dead languages'*.[20]

On December 6th, Founder's Day, Hawtrey spoke with *'with considerable vehemence'* when presiding at a dinner in Election Chamber. Trenchantly rejecting all criticism of school and college, he poured lofty scorn on a *'popular mgazine'*, presumably the Edinburgh Review, characterising Higgins as being like *'a tall bully, who lifts the head and lies'*. Suddenly *'he faltered, put his hand to his head, sat down, and was led out'*.[21] He seemed to have suffered some kind of seizure, was not seen in public again, and died soon after.

He had been the last Provost to enjoy untrammelled the authority given to that office by the Statutes. Initially supportive of reforming proposals he grew increasingly conservative, inclined to think that the measures he'd already assented to, along with those during his own term as Headmaster, were quite sufficient.

Contact with boys inevitably grew more distant. Whereas in his time as Headmaster boys had come away from his breakfasts chattering about his stories by his Provost's years his breakfasts were *'gloomy failures'* as social gatherings; the food ample, and appreciated but eaten in almost total silence.[22]

He did though retain his habit of eccentricity. On one occasion he drove over to an archery contest being staged by the Vice-Provost in elaborate costume and with his own bow and arrows which he explained as *'a Chinese bow with Indian arrows'*. He then adopted what he maintained was the correct shooting position, drawing the bow to his hip rather than to his cheek. The result was that the arrows flew up almost vertically, coming down all over the field. One though was found on the target, placed there by *'some genial spectator'* and which Hawtrey took as entire vindication of his method amongst much hilarity. [23]

In his last years he suffered a good deal from the stone and could sometimes be seen doubled up in pain in his chapel stall. To the end though he retained his good humour.

Provost Hawtrey

CHAPTER ELEVEN : ETON INVESTIGATED

The Commisioners' evidence and conclusions are given in plain text and their recommendations in italics. For the sake of clarity, the author's comments are set in parenthesis.

'THE COMMISSIONERS FOR THE PUBLIC SCHOOLS ARE DOWN HERE NOW, AND WILD is the terror they inspire.'[1] That was how Dalmeny, the future 5th Earl of Rosebery, viewed their effect in a letter home in July, 1862.

The Clarendon Commission was able either to add to or replace some of the speculation about Eton's ways with hard fact by drilling down into detail. One such was the business of the Huggett Report. It transpired that Roger Huggett, an Eton Conduct (chaplain), had illicitly obtained a copy of the Statutes, and in the opinion of the Commision, had, for whatever reason, proceeded to make certain alterations to it. They seem not to have been as secret as Reeve and others liked to think as an exact copy of them had been added to Brougham's report on the Education of the Lower Orders.

As the most trenchant criticism, most pointedly that of Sir John Coleridge, had been directed at the way the College was run, this was the Commission's starting point and Goodford and Dupuis faced exhaustive questioning on the tricky subject of College finance.[2] It found that in the period 1854-1860 the College's income was £20,569 of which £10,322 came from rents and rack rents. After deductions for expenses the annual surplus averaged £6,795.[3] That showed that the figures proclaimed in the Press had been largely accurate.

Fines on renewal of leases were regarded as without the College remit and the personal entitlement of the Provost and Fellows and that any contribution by them to College works from this source amounted to liberality on their part. (The Rev. Wilder's generous donation of £5,000 to the chapel had come with one string attached : that he was to be paid the equivalent sum of the interest on £4,000 for the rest of his days).[4]

Whether this procedure could be justified needed a little research into the *'economical usages of past times'*.[5] It did seem as though these fines had never been brought into the College accounts and that the present Provost and Fellows were following past practice.

On the expiry of leases the opportunity was often taken to get hold of valuable land and rack-rent it. A considerable increase in the College's wealth was predicted from these expiries, especially as a fair number were on valuable land near London. The Commissioners noted that the custom of the Provost making an annual tour of the College estates seemed to have fallen into disuse and thought that unfortunate.[6] It was though acknowledged that the Bursar made regular rounds of the twenty-two counties where the College had lands. Worse than unfortunate, *'evidently irregular'*, was the use made of £8,000 bequeathed by a former Provost, Godolphin, for an *'increase of scholars' commons'*.[7] No trace could be found of any of that money having been used for its prescribed purpose.

Attention then turned to the offices of Provost and Fellows, in particular to the perquisites of these positions. The excluding qualifications for the office of Provost meant that at the time of Provost Goodall's death there were thought to be only eight people from whom a subsequent choice could be made.[8] They began with the requirement to be in holy orders though in earlier times there had been men who weren't, the former ambassador Sir Henry Wotton being a notable example. As the office required only of the Provost that he preach eight times a year in chapel, clerical duties were hardly heavy. Johnson thought a layman such as *'a statesman or man of letters'* would be a better idea.[9] There was some doubt over the election process. For while in practice the Fellows nominated whoever the Crown chose they were at the same time insistent on their right of a free choice and aware that, in the event of dispute, the Crown could not legally overrule them. Johnson thought this needed resolving.[10] In practice, Fellows were former Assistant Masters, unless theoretically barred by holding too much landed property. A Fellow's ninth share of the fines was found to be worth £662. They themselves, though drawing this ample benefit, lived rent-free in their houses. When that had begun was unclear. Fellows too had the first choice of livings whose value ranged from £100 p.a. to £1,000-£1,200 p.a. If not taken up, a Fellow had the right of nomination, usually to a friend or relation, the Provost having two turns at nominating to a Fellow's one,[11] and Goodford insisting that the statutes had given the Provost the right to acquire as many benefices as he could. Johnson thought that livings could best be seen as retiring pensions for masters in holy orders.[12] As though the Fellows audited the College accounts and elected College officers from their own number, they were well placed to sustain a beneficial status quo. To ensure acquescence with the Founder's wishes the statutes were meant to be read aloud three times a year but in practice only portions were.

Noting the agreeable lifestyle of Eton's Fellows who were generally 'non-resident for three-quarters of the year while receiving a comfortable income' [13] *the Commissioners made some radical recommendations for the reshaping of the Governing Body, both in numbers and in the mode of election. Selection should no longer be exclusively in the hands of a small group of men who'd known little but Etonian and particularly College ways, and who would, in their view, tend to unconscious bias.*[14]

They made the standard stipulation that Fellows should be graduates of Oxford and Cambridge and members of the Church of England. Beyond that a wider field of selection was envisaged with the appointment of men distinguished in literature and science along with some who'd done good work in the College. A few of these Fellowships might receive 'a moderate income' while the rest should be voluntary.[15] *No difficulty was anticipated in finding unpaid Fellows. The Provost of King's should be a member of the Governing Body. As for the Provost of Eton, his extensive powers should be exercised by a broader-based body which would be able to make considered judgements less affected by 'individual peculiarities of temper or opinion'. Eton too should follow the practice of some other schools in having a School Council, of not more than fifteen members, to deliberate school issues. Then no reason could be seen why the Provost should need to be in holy orders. Nor was it thought desirable that the Provost and Fellows should hold College livings. Rather than these being used as instruments of private patronage their allocation should be left to the Governing Body.*[16]

The Commissioners' treatment of the vexed matter of fines showed its ambivalence. For while it seemed indubitable that the practice of taking money out of corporate revenue was 'not conformable to the letter and spirit and intention of the Statutes' any change should be made 'with a due regard for the interests of the Provost and Fellows'.[17] *It was recognised that they had inherited rather than devised this unsatisfactory state of affairs. (A degree of culpability might surely have been suggested for their comfortable acquiescence in the light of reforms proceeding elsewhere.) Instead it was suggested that fines be brought within the corporate account, beneficial leases stopped, and the Provost and Fellows given compensatory fixed incomes.*[18]

A statement in the Statutes that sons of those owning land worth more than five marks a year could not be considered as possible Collegers suggested to the Commissioners that the original target source had been the likes of the lower gentry and yeomanry.[19] Whether that was the case or not there was little doubt that Collegers had until the last twenty years or so been badly treated. They recalled the days when boys were locked inside the Chamber at 8.00p.m. in summer, and 5.00 p.m. in winter, were given no breakfast and a meagre suppper, had to pay a Dame to be taken in when ill, and often hired a room in Windsor. In fact they were put to almost as much expense as an Oppidan. Nor did a number of them form a part of any sort of intellectual elite. Nominated by six electors a boy simply had to construe a passage got up beforehand. As a consequence, *'very stupid boys got in who had no business to get in'*.[20] Worst was the seeming indifference of the College to their living conditions. The Statutes had ruled that Fellows and Scholars should be lodged in the same building whereas things since had been managed in such a way as to leave the boys *'improperly and culpably deprived'* of any supervision.[21] They had in fact to conclude that *'if the letter of the Statutes was adhered to, their substance was systematically violated'*.[22]

Since those dark days a considerable improvement was noted. *'Bullying and other evils are now only a matter of history and tradition.'* [23] Accommodation had been brought up to a standard where it was now *'as good as can be desired'*.[24] A reservation was though expressed about the hot water pipes, the prospect of which had aroused A.D. Coleridge's ire, thinking fireplaces might have been a better idea. Admission too was now by properly competitive examination, open to boys born in any part of the British Empire. The only exclusions were of the illegitimate, diseased, and mutilated. In practice Goodford noted that most Collegers were sons of clergymen. He wondered though if the present standard of College academic excellence might not have a disheartening effect on Oppidans though the Commissioners saw it rather as a challenge to be risen to and one which a fair number of them would accept.[25]

Things were not now altogether perfect though. *'The food supplied is ample, but the monotony of it palls.'* [26] Mutton was still the invariable dish. Then as the fags had to wait in College, although there was now an adequate number of College servants, they generally ended up with inferior joints. Scholars did still too have a number of expenses for such things as tea, sugar, washing, and attendance. Edward Coleridge, former Lower Master, thought all these things should be gratuitous.[27]

Then the Commissioners wondered about the most distinctive feature of Colleger dress – their gowns. Did these create a divisive barrier? Goodford maintained that Collegers wished to keep them. Browning though saw that as only one element in separateness. For a Colleger *'breathes a somewhat confined atmosphere; he does not drink to the full of the spirit of Eton.'*[28] Johnson made a similar point, considering that to an Oppidan a Colleger was seen as a schoolfellow rather than a playfellow. Young Collegers spoken to seemed to have a sense of living a rather enclosed life though an older witness felt that the difference disappeared at the top of the school.

The academic superiority of Collegers over Oppidans seemed to be shown by the fact that in the previous ten years fourteen of the nineteen first class Classical degrees gained by Etonians had been won by Collegers. [29]

Entry to College was now by a more realistically competitive exam with the most recent attracting fifty candidates for fifteen places.[30] More prominent advertising might though, it was suggested, attract more. The peculiar nature of this exam gave the Commissioners concern. For as boys could be admitted between the ages of eight and sixteen five sets of exam papers had to be produced to cater for this disparity. There was difficulty in making judging comparisons across these five standards. As it was a requirement of the Statutes that an older boy had to know more than all those below him a boy of sixteen needed to exhibit 'extraordinary comparative proficiency' in order to succeed. In practice the scales were heavily weighted in favour of younger boys among whom there was fierce competition of a kind that could be 'a considerable tax on strength at such a tender age'.[31] The Rev. James was aware of boys 'who have been worked up tremendously at Preparatory School'.[32] It was recommended that there should in future be just one exam sat by boys between the ages of eleven and fourteen.

More generally, the distortion of the intention in the Statutes which had seen the Fellows appropriate for their own use far more money than had been put aside for the scholars should be sharply reversed. King's Scholars should have 'a full gratuitous course of education' accompanied by 'a liberal maintenance allowance'. Small payments for such items as tea and sugar should be abolished.[33]

As was their wont, the Commissioners interviewed a thirteen – year – old King's Scholar at some length. They particularly wanted to find out how demanding fagging was. His day began at 6.30 a.m. when he was awoken by a servant in order to be able to wake his master at 7.00 a.m. Waiting at meals was the most regular duty. At dinner, for example, he had to 'take the plates round and pour out the beer'. There was too the obligation to be always on call, having to respond promptly to a shout of 'Come here!' at any hour of the day.

"Suppose you did not come?"

"Then, very likely, you would be thrashed."

Fagging at dinner and the 'Come here!' practice were the two bits of fagging most disliked, he said.

His academic life consisted of sessions in school at 7.30 a.m., 11.00 a.m., 3.00p.m., and 5.15p.m. along with a period of construing with his tutor at 9.45 a.m. on some mornings. Although a summons from older boys often interrupted lesson preparation he was not aware of boys getting into trouble with masters on that account.

Out of class he was expected to play football four times a week though thought he might be excused if he suggested an acceptable alternative. Cricket fagging was not asked for and he enjoyed Fives, playing it when able to secure a court. After all that, he was expected to be in bed by 10.00 p.m.

Before Eton he had been at Mr. Waterfield's school.

"Do you like Eton better?"

"Yes, much." [34]

College, limited by Statute and custom to seventy boys, was though only a numerically small part of Eton. In 1861 there were 730 boys in the Upper School and 99 in the Lower. Goodford saw no difficulty with further growth thinking a school of a thousand quite feasible though Edward Coleridge doubted whether a Head would be able to manage a staff of the size required for that number.[35]

Eton's academic structure was one that must at first have seemed baffling to outsiders with its mix of form, remove, and division. To confuse matters the word 'remove' was used in four senses as 1. Form 2. Subdivision of a form, 3. Promotion as in 'getting his remove' 4. Of a set of boys in the same remove.[36]

Complaint was made of the low standard of entry candidates who in many cases were unable to cope with what was described as easy translation of English into Latin in prose and verse and from Greek and Latin into English. (That anything of this kind should be thought 'easy' suggests the anticipated level of attainment). Those unable to make the grade were placed in the Lower School. There was no lower age limit but no boy was admitted after the age of fourteen.

'Trials' were taken to ensure a boy had made adequate progress to proceed from his form to the next. A bright boy could try for a 'double remove' by tackling the exams of the remove above the next. If he beat two-thirds of that form he leapfrogged his peers. On the other hand, a boy failing the not too demanding trials had to stay down. Before getting to the top a boy usually went through nine divisions.[37]

> The Commissioners were less sure that expansion to a thousand pupils woul be a good idea, maintaining that a school should not get to a size beyond which the Headmaster can have an influence on each boy.[38] As things were presently arranged, he couldn't. One reason was the differing disciplinary views taken by masters of a boy's activities. This was reflected in the varying ethos of boarding houses which tended to dissipate the authority of the Headmaster. Ideally this would mean a school of around 500 pupils but with suggested reforms the total might be 800 : 650 in Upper School and 150 in Lower.[39]
>
> In response to claims that boys were being sent to Eton poorly prepared, thus starting off 'in arrears', it was recommended that those accepted should show evidence of having been grounded in the Classics and Arithmetic while having grasped the basic elements of one foreign language.[40] A particular problem was seen with boys not ready for Upper School and being sent to Lower. The mix of 'older and more backward boys with younger and more forward ones' was 'a fruitful source of evil'.[41] Often idle, they tended to impose themselves by bullying. To counteract that, it was recommended that no boy should progress from Lower to Upper School without passing the same exam as boys coming from Preparatory schools and that no boy should be admitted to Upper School after the age of fourteen.[42] No preference should be shown. Indeed, going further, it was suggested that no boy should be allowed to remain in the school who failed to make adequate academic progress.[43]
>
> In other ways fault was found with Lower School. The comment that masters in Lower School should take their teaching just as seriously as those in Upper suggested that not all masters looked particularly assiduous. Then there was an odd situation with regard to boarders in that the Lower Master had a house with a mixture of boys from Upper and Lower School. He and other Lower School masters should in future take only Lower School boys.[44] Then the balance between work and

play was questioned when what was required of boys 'seems to us to be in excess' and to leave little time for relaxation and exercise.[45]

* * * * *

Attention turned next to the position of the Headmaster, starting with his emoluments. These comprised a yearly stipend (£16), a College sum (£219), Entrance Fees (£5.5s), and Leaving Presents from Fifth and Sixth Form Boys. Much the highest source of income though was the £6.6s. annual payment from all boys, the size of which will be realised by multiplying it by 829.

From this there were various disbursements: £50 to Senior Assistant Classical Masters, £44.2s. to other Masters, £15 for examinations, and £350 for prize books.

During the period 1856-1861 the Head averaged annual receipts of £5,744 and net receipts of £4,491.[46]

His teaching was that of the Highest Division consisting of 30-34 boys while he also had the task of setting all examination papers for Trials except for Arithmetic and Maths: this work, *'extremely inconvenient and heavy'*, it was thought could be shared.[47]

Change of this kind though needed the agreement of the Provost. The Commission noted that the control of the Provost was *'active, extensive, and minute'*,[48] and exercised over such matters as holidays, school books, and school hours. (From a Head's point of view this sounds mightily inhibiting, rather as though David Cameron was still prowling around Number Ten insisting on briefing or debriefing May or Rowan Williams was sat in the Lambeth Palace Library vetting Welby's sermons. Hawtrey's own latitude may well have largely been because Hodgson was not a former Head). The Fellows too could make their voices heard.

Views were sought as to whether the influence of Provost and Fellows was a beneficial one. Edward Coleridge thought it was, Goodford diplomatically expressed no definite opinion, while Carter, Lower Master, thought it obstructive. The strongest opinion though came from Johnson who reckoned the Headmaster *'crippled in all directions'*. In particular, *'the interference of Hawtrey, when Provost, with the Headmaster was constant'*.[49] Assistant Masters spoken too were in general agreement that the Head should have a free hand in the handling of ordinary administration but should not have uncontrolled powers.

Johnson proposed an entirely different regime by suggesting that the authority of the Provost be replaced by a body incorporating Provost and

Fellows, Headmaster, and some Senior Masters.[50] This chimed with the Commissioners' observation that other Schools had regular meetings of School Councils. E.D. Stone, Housemaster and father of Faith Compton Mackenzie, Johnson's biographer, thought a chance to express views orally *'would have been a great boon'*.[51] (Maybe the lack of this kind of oral outlet was a reason why some Eton masters developed a habit of writing letters of considerable length to each other, none possibly more prolific in that respect than Browning). The cited reason for not doing this, *'lack of time'* was one often heard at Eton.

As the proposed financial changes all involved cuts, it must be supposed that the frequent combination of salary and fees was deemed to amount to too much. Comparisons with other schools may have strongly suggested that. For example, it was found that an Eton master might well be getting five times his Shrewsbury equivalent.[52] *The Head's income should be reduced from £4,500 to £4,000 and the Lower Master's from £3,180 to £2,200 while Assistant Masters should get £300 – the latter at least would be an advance on the £40-50 offered to a new master. Stephen Hawtrey's salary of around £1,000 was to be reduced to £300 or £600 if he had no boarding house. Tarver should get another French-teaching assistant but at a cost of seeing his £1,050 reduced to £600.*

*In future there should be no additional payment for studies that form a part of a school course, an end to such incidental payments as Leaving Books, and a uniform charge for board and lodging paid into a common fund, designated as a 'Fee Fund'.*53

This proposed fund into which moneys should be paid, incomes drawn, and from which any deficiencies could be supplied, implied a significant change. This would have the effect of putting the Bursar rather than the Headmaster as the principal agent in the operation of the school's finances.

More specific notions as to what the Provost and Fellows might receive were made. £2,000 was considered an appropriate sum for the Provost and £700 for five Stipendiary Fellows. All other monetary allowances should be abolished though insignificant payments in kind, if appropriate to College tradition, could be retained.

Altogether, an estimated £3,206 would be saved by these alterations.[54]

* * * * *

A peculiarity of Eton was noted in that a boy had two mentors – his form teacher and his tutor. A good deal of a boy's time was spent in the pupil room having his work corrected before he went off to school where he would spend on average two and a half hours a day doing work which involved a good deal of repetition. It was noted that the books used consisted of extracts, mainly of Homer, Horace, and Virgil rather than whole books,[55] and some doubt was expressed as to whether the system of 'calling up' provided a sufficiently effective stimulus.[56] This method did though ensure careful and punctual marking, something not always found elsewhere.

Just how effective the dual system of tutor and form master collaborating on the same piece of work was was queried. A defence of this practice was that it put boys on their metal and helped the form master to ensure a high level of accuracy. But if this was so, why did so many boys still think it necessary go along with a crib?[57] It was noticed that masters tended to call on the quicker and cleverer boys disproportionately in order to make headway with lessons. Then as a tutor's pupil room contained boys varying in age from thirteen to eighteen he couldn't possibly offer appropriate instruction across such a wide age range but would have to give the same lesson to all.[58] Balston's and Johnson's argument that boys would read the same limited number of texts with increasing stylistic awareness, responding to a tutor's adaptive approach, was thought not likely in practice. (Browning's description of Johnson's Pupil room in which suggestions were being thrown out to boys individually while he was sat at his desk marking Greek exercises suggests that he, at least, offered more than a uniform lecture). It was also observed how limited was a boy's involvement during repetition lessons, his active participation often lasting barely five minutes.[59]

Two recommendations were made. There should be no more construing before school and repetition should be conducted in smaller subdivisions with more masters involved in order to speed things up. [60]

* * * * *

While the school determined which form a boy should be in, parents chose their son's tutor, though King's Scholars were allocated to various tutors by arrangement. A tutor required rather different reading from his pupil. He was formally paid ten guineas for this but in practice expected twenty.[61] In 1861 a tutor had an average of 37 boys with some having many more, Goodford's limit of 40 being often disregarded. This pecuniary factor induced a temptation to over-emphasise work in the Pupil Room at the cost of that done in school. Johnson saw that as a reason for the decline in Oppidan standards, suggested an increased stipend, though Carter argued that this kept a man more competitive than a fixed income.[62]

This dual function of a master meant that school life was more onerous for an Assistant Master than, say, at Winchester. Asked just how long they worked Masters responded with estimates ranging from nine to fourteen hours a day. When though it was put to Balston that the demands made on his masters might be excessive he disagreed, holding that they made them give proper attention to their work.[63]

An Eton Master did though have an ample sense of security as no record could be found of a Master ever having been removed. He might though after appointment have little beyond the Head's 42 guineas until he'd been able to establish himself. Usually a Classical master would get a house after about three years and would be able to charge his boys, theoretically limited to thirty, £120 p.a.[64] A full house would give him an average income estimated by the Rev. James at £1,145 though he cited a maximum figure of £1,845.[65]

Just who might be appointed was considered, the field having just been widened with the selection of the first Oppidan master. Carter was against any further broadening of the source arguing that only Etonians really understood Eton's ways. Coleridge disagreed, thinking a limitation to Etonians *'unwise and prejudicial'*.[66] So too did Johnson, maintaining that as Collegers had participated in Eton's social life to only a limited extent they were not that well versed even in Eton's ways; suggesting that Masters, even a Headmaster from other schools might be a good idea; and pointing out that the Maths Masters, none of them Etonians, didn't seem to find any great difficulty in getting to grips with Eton's ways. [67]

* * * * *

Interestingly, it seems to have been parental complaints that boys had first to go to the elderly Hexter rather than to Wrangler Hawtrey or one of his Assistants that prompted his being pensioned off. Hawtrey though found continual problems with staff recruitment and retention.

Maths Masters were very much treated as an inferior caste and were very conscious of it despite one or two belated concessions such as being allowed to wear gowns, even, from 1861, in chapel.[68] They had no authority out of school. It was more like five years before they could normally get a boarding house, and then generally only one of the lesser ones. Worst was limited income, made up chiefly from private pupils. Balston saw nothing amiss with their being paid less than Classical

Staff as they did less work while Goodford seemed to think their lower status justified as they were not Etonians.⁶⁹ Hale ('Badger') who taught Maths amongst other things, took a different line, suggesting that Maths Masters could be tutors.⁷⁰

A boy spent about three hours a week on Mathematical study. In the course of it he read Colenso's Algebra and four books of Euclid. Some studied trigonometry while a very few progressed to conic sections and analytic geometry.⁷¹ During 1860 about a hundred boys were getting extra tuition with the question being put as to whether some of this didn't simply result from boys making insufficient effort in class.⁷²

The teaching of other subjects was patchy.

While boys in the Lower School were taught some modern history and those in the Upper School some Ancient History there was no regular teaching of either History or Geography. Most Assistant Masters wished for regular teaching of both.⁷³

H. Tarver, French master, whose French father had held the same post before him, had no recognised position as French had no part in the syllabus, and described himself as *'a mere objet de luxe'*, and who had been taught French as an adult in France, had constant staffing problems. Hawtrey had foisted on Tarver a Signor Sinibaldi whose *'unpleasant accent'* and other traits had reduced numbers from 100-60. Since then there had been four assistants as well as his brother. The number of pupils had reached 130 but had slumped back to 75. He found difficulty in countering the rival attraction of play-time and the disadvantage of cost which resulted in frequent non-attendance. Complaints to the Head or tutors about that had proved unavailing. The situation, in short, was *'very unsatisfactory indeed'*. He had managed to get one concession from Goodford, that boys should be allowed to sit a French paper in their exams for a few extra marks though Balston stopped it, unwilling to countenance anything that reduced time for Classical study. This state of affairs must have been particularly frustrating for a man who clearly took his work seriously – he compiled a French dictionary – and most Assistant Masters felt there should be some French teaching.⁷⁴

There were no Natural Science lessons but a broad range of occasional lectures. Music was not taught but a number of boys had private lessons. Stephen Hawtrey had the idea of introducing fifteen minutes of music into his Maths lessons but was not allowed to do so. There was also a good drawing master who had about thirty-five pupils.⁷⁵

Concern over fitness for the army exam had led to the formation of the Army Class in 1856. Boys were allowed to drop three Classical lessons in order to do more Maths and also to study more History and Geography. Before long though two-thirds of the Assistant Masters had complained about this class, arguing that the dispensation to spend less time on Classics was just leading to idleness, especially after admittance was widened beyond the Fifth Form, and the substitution of Maths was stopped. That clearly lessened its attraction, probably too its usefulness, so that when the Commissioners came across it there were only three boys in it.[76]

* * * * *

While the higher regard for Classical as opposed to Mathematical masters was explicable in terms of their relative longevity no justification could be seen for it. All masters should henceforth be regarded as of equal status.

The Commissioners noted that while there had been some introduction of Modern Studies there had been little attempt to harmonise them satisfactorily with the Classical syllabus. They were insistent that time be found for Modern Languages and Natural Science. [77] *To show what they had in mind it was suggested that lesson time should be allocated like this:* [78]

    Classics 12 hours
    Maths 3 hours
    Modern Languages 2 hours
    Natural Science 2 hours

In addition each boy should have the opportunity to learn either music or drawing with these, along with French, being added to the syllabus. With these additions a boy would spend twenty-one hours in school which, along with the twenty-three spent with his tutor, would give him a forty-four hour working week.[79]

By the time an Oppidan reached the Upper Division of the Fifth Form he might find little to urge him on. For whereas at this point a Colleger would face a fairly stiff exam preparatory to moving up to the Sixth the Oppidan would reach a point where he was no longer examined. This was thought the cause of 'the acknowledged want of energy among the Oppidans in the upper part of the school'. A better idea was thought to be to split the Upper Fifth into two divisions with promotion based on exam performance and to encourage academic ambition by having more boys in the Sixth Form. In addition boys who had reached this point might be given a wider variety of subject choice with their future careers in mind though that should not be taken as an excuse for idleness.[80]

Goodford saw an inherent problem in getting Oppidans to fully apply themselves. 'As a body the Oppidans are boys who have not to work for their bread, and many of their parents tell them so.' [81] (Yet that could not have been predominantly so. Johnson once calculated that of forty-two boys in his division only thirteen stood to inherit landed property and the fuss about the army class showed an active concern about future prospects.)

Sir John Coleridge strongly urged that the proceeds of two or three suppressed Fellowships should be used to create a number of Oppidan exhibitions worth fifty pounds a year and the Commissioners took the same line, suggesting between twenty and forty of these be inaugurated.[82] A little more publicity of academic achievement might also provide a stimulus: publishing in the school list the names of those who reached the 'select' stage of the Newcastle was suggested. [83]

* * * * *

One suspects that the formation of the Army Class was an unenthusiastic response to pressures over competitive entry and that the authorities did not need much persuading to restrict its operation. Over other matters though the Assistant Masters often made little headway.

The Commissioners noted a good deal of irregularity in the school timetable. There were three whole schooldays and altogether the boys were in school for fourteen or fifteen hours a week. This routine was though disrupted by Saints' Days which were holidays while the preceding Eve was a half-holiday.[84] This prompted Johnson to 'particularly desire and earnestly advise the complete reconstruction of our timetable, with a view to greater regularity, and in the number of school hours, particularly in the summer months'.[85]

A number of masters expressed disquiet over one feature of Classical method. Boys were regularly set to learn by heart eighty lines of Homer and sixty of another author. That though was often only partially learnt with boys relying on being able to guess their bit. They thought there was a good case for less repetition and more translation. Balston though was keen on boys going on learning that set amount.[86]

There must have been a good deal of frustration behind the un-Etonian like formation of a Committee of Assistant Masters to urge on the Provost the case for re-editing and changing school books. It drew a hostile response with the Provost refusing to acknowledge this body, whose existence was clearly seen as an affront. The Masters were told that they could, should they wish, make representations to the Head who, if he saw fit, might take them to the Provost. In practice, the committee did not get any kind of encouragement from either Goodford or Balston during their time as Heads. *'This is the state at which the matter stands at present; a Committee has been nominated, and has held a few meetings, but has neither power nor responsibility,'* averred the formidable Rev. James. [87]

* * * * *

It was noted that there seemed less incentive to work than at other schools. This, it was thought, had a good deal to do with exams and promotion. The standard of 'trials' was very moderate and a boy had to be *'very stupid who is kept down long'*. [88] Of the two removes he got in a year one was automatic. There was another exam, 'Collections', which tested work done during the term but that too was judged easy to pass. The result was that a boy's increase in knowledge did not always keep pace with his rise up the school. In fact when an Oppidan reached the Upper Fifth he faced no further exams but rose solely by seniority while King's Scholars faced a fairly stiff exam to determine their standing in College. [89] The Commissioners wished to impose their own exam in order impartially to assess levels of attainment but that was not allowed.

Prizes could foster the *'spur of emulation'*.[90] At Eton there must have been quite a few of these judging from the sum set aside for them, (£350), but little was made of the awards. For, as Browning said, *'they are decided by the Headmaster and nobody knows who gets them'*. [91] He thought Oppidan parents keen for their boys to get on. Johnson thought the answer was to create Oppidan scholarships at both Universities and some at school too. Sir John Coleridge was similarly minded, suggesting suppressing some Fellowships in order to fund forty Oppidan exhibitions.[92]

As to subsequent careers, the Commission calculated that about 40% of Etonians went on to University where there was a wide range of scholarships.[93] Half of all Oxonians though went to either Christ Church or University College with it being noted that *'the wealthiest, and therefore on the whole the idlest, go to Christ Church'*.[94] About seventeen a year went to Woolwich for the start of an army career, not all passing muster, while a very few went to Sandhurst where they were uniformly successful.[95]

A suggestion of any kind of failing in Eton's educational practice was often met with the response that boys too often arrived ill-prepared. The Rev. Birch, whose house was often favoured by the nobility, his brother having been a tutor to the Prince of Wales perhaps having something to do with it, though he was not over-impressed by title, held that parents set too little store by Classsical proficiency at home. A number of those who failed the entrance exam were sent to Lower School where they often caused problems. Being too old for their form they were often *'the greatest bullies and set the worst example'*.[96] (This wide age range was noticeable too in the Upper School. In the highest division of the Fifth Form the youngest was 13.9 and the oldest 16.11 while a Fourth Form had a spread from 12.7 to 17).[97] Johnson wanted no boy leaving Lower School aged over fourteen without first being examined while the industrious Durnford ('Judy') thought Lower School might serve a better purpose as a receptacle for backward boys.

There were found to be 140 boys in the Lower School, recovered from its nadir of 11 in the 1830's. The Rev. Carter, Lower Master, had four Assistants who taught classes varying in size from 13 to 31. The long hours of work were noted : 7 a.m. to 6 p.m. in summer and 7 a.m. to 4 p.m. in winter. Not until these had been worked were the boys allowed any play.[98]

The report then made fairly brief mentions of several other aspects of Etonian life though some, such as chapel, were more fully considered when it came to recommendations.

The College's religious practices were thought highly unsatisfactory. Provost Goodford assured the Commissioners that the custom of taking singers from St. George's for a Sunday service had been going on for at least three hundred years but that was not thought adequate justification. The Statutes had provided for a choir and while other now rather arcane provisions had been allowed to fall into desuetude there was no reason why the College could not provide its own choir.[99]

The cathedral model could perfectly well be followed with 'singing boys' and 'singing men' being engaged, the College taking full charge of the boys, though not apparently to the extent of educating them, but given a sum from College funds and then apprenticed to a trade.[100] (If that sounds rather a cold attitude it was then generally accepted that that was the limit of a clerical body's educational responsibility. Before the advent of choir schools in the latter part of the century the education of choristers was often difficult – many schools unwilling to have boys regularly nipping off for practices and services).

Then there was the nature of chapel observance. While Sunday services were treated with reasonable respect, the weekday ones often were not. Asked whether they were 'productive of any reverential feeling' Browning's response was direct. 'I should say not; the boys' only object is certainly to get out as soon as they can'. [101]

Recommendations were that the daily service should not exceed fifteen minutes, that it always include music, and that others besides the Fellows should preach.

The role of the Sixth Former in maintaining discipline through impositions and 'licking' was noted. So too was the fact that there was in practice little beating. *'It is not thought the thing'*, as *'there is a sort of feeling against it'*. [102] Eton did not operate the kind of monitorial system seen in other schools which delegated formal powers but seemed none the worse for doing things rather differently. Sixth Formers and some of the Fifth had the right to fag junior boys.

As for the Headmaster's role in maintaining discipline, Goodford claimed that there had been less flogging since tutors had been consulted. Yet he still admitted to five or six weekly sessions during his time. One witness, Mr. R.A.H. Mitchell who had left Eton three and a half years ago, that was while Goodford had been Headmaster, questioned whether tutors were in practice often consulted. *'He (Goodford) considers himself a machine, and seldom takes any excuse, observing that what had failed to satisfy the complainant cannot satisfy him.'* [103] Nor was he aware of any reduction in the number of beatings during his time.

'Shirking' was a practice that most Assistant Masters wished to see the end of. There seemed little sense in encouraging a boy to run away when he might need to be spoken to.[104] Nor were masters consistent in their attitude to it. Another idiosyncrasy concerned drink. This was tolerated at 'The Tap' and 'The Christopher', unlike the other Public Houses, so long as a boy was not seen going in. No sign of excess drinking was observed but a warning note sounded about the possible development of bad habits.[105]

Edmond Warre saw one of the virtues of games activity as the discouragement of extravagant habits such as drinking. The Commissioners were more inclined to put this kind of excess down to parents giving their sons too much money. They noted too the time a boy who had hopes of making the cricket eleven would spend practising: at least two hours a day on whole schooldays and five on half-holidays.[107]

Whether or not a boy had a happy and productive time at Eton depended a good deal on the house he was put in and where he spent a good deal of his time. While there seems no reason not to suppose that most boys had as pleasant a time as Brinsley-Richards there were exceptions and one, with unfortunate timing for Eton, had attracted some publicity. It concerned the fourteen-year-old son of Lybbe Powis Lybbe, M.P. who, he alleged, had ben grievously mistreated in Mr. Wolley's house. Signs of this were *'certain marks about the legs'* and having been hit on the head by another boy while lying in bed with measles, along with other instances from which Lybbe claimed that there was no order in Wolley's house and, further, that the house captain must have known of this ill-treatment. A doctor friend, Mr. Stocker, claimed to see a big difference in the boy since his going to Eton, that he always had *'a scowl about his countenance'* and advised taking the boy away. That was done, weight being given the doctor's opinion, though neither father nor son really wished it. *'He did not want to leave Eton ; no boy would.'* Wolley strongly refuted accusations of disorder.[108]

As with so much at Eton the overgrown thickets of practice needed pruning back to get a clear view of the thirty houses. Most (17) were run by Classical Masters, and others by Maths Masters, gentlemen unconnected with the school, Ladies, and one by the Drawing Master. They contained between 5 and 49 boys. No Classical Master could have more than 30 while there was no restriction in Dame's houses and boys paid less in a Maths Master's or Dame's house. The custom was for boys to have their own rooms though brothers shared.[109]

A house, so long as it was not one of the smallest ones could be a profitable concern and there was *'a regular scramble for any house that falls vacant'*. There was though an initial expense to be faced, put at £1,500 – £2,000, though the Rev. James thought he'd spent between £3,000 – £6,000, an estimate of some latitude, on the rebuilding he deemed necessary.[110] In return, a tutor got from each boy a basic charge and a sum for extras estimated by Eliot to total £175 p.a.

The situation was complicated by the College not having retained ownership of these houses but let out on leases of varying length. Tenants who had spent a good deal on their houses expected recognition of that and, as a result, *'a multitude of complicated and uncertain claims have sprung up'* usually asserted when a house was being left.[111]

Particular mention was made of Evans's house. Run by a gentleman with no other connection with the school it was judged to have *'a merited reputation for judicious management'*.[112]

Although complimenary of the way Evans ran his house this was not thought a good model. While Evans argued that he could devote more time than a tutor to the running of the house the perceived disadvantage was that a parent then had to deal with two people rather than one in getting an assessment of a boy's progress.[113] The recruitment of a number of young masters was suggested with a house being offered only when they'd proved themselves.[114] The complicated tangle of vested interests and tenancies had though brought about a situation that could not be too readily altered.[115]

CHAPTER TWELVE : THE OTHER CLARENDON EIGHT

THE COMMISSIONERS DELVED DEEP INTO THE ORIGINS OF THEIR SELECTED SCHOOLS and with good reason, for in most cases the founding Statutes had constricted their development. It was instructive to evaluate a school's present in the light of its Founder's intent. Deviation from the letter of the Statutes was not necessarily seen as a fault provided it could be seen as a remodelling of the school's essential character. Predominantly this was seen as preserving its classical curriculum, something occasionally challenged by middle class parents with Foundation rights who had more utilitarian ideas as to what their sons should be taught. These and other conflicts of interest it fell to a school's Governing Body to resolve and the Commissioners gave a good deal of time to examining their composition and effectiveness.

Winchester's founding statutes of 1382 are thought to have been the model for Eton's and the stipulations for the governance of both bodies are very similar. A Warden and ten Fellows bore the administrative responsibility for running the College, appointing both the Headmaster and Second Master. To check all was well the Warden and two Fellows conducted an annual 'scrutiny'. This involved questioning seven senior and seven junior boys as to aspects of their daily life. Beyond the school the Warden and Fellows had to manage endowments worth a healthy average of £15,494 in the seven years prior to 1860. Extensive lands were owned in Hampshire, Wiltshire and throughout the South-West with leases being run down to increase income. It also had thirteen livings, each yielding between £100 and £500 p.a.[1]

While it seems always to have had virtually a full complement of the 70 scholars provided for in the Statutes it had not though been notably successful in getting admissions from Commoners. In 1858 there had been only 68, though that had increased to 131 three years later. George Moberley, Headmaster since 1835, and before that a boy at the school during the 1818 disturbances of which he always maintained that the rebels had been right, put that down to *'a reputation of bad health'*.[2] A major change came to the College fortuitously. Winchester had as close a connection with New College as Eton had with King's and it was that that brought it within the scope of the Oxford University Commission of 1857 which insisted on open competition for all awards and meant an end to the system of scholars being nominated by electors, without any competition, these being the two Wardens and two New College Fellows. Moberley had strong initial doubts, fearing it would lead to the College having to accept *'very undesirable members of our community'*. It wasn't long though before he changed his mind. *'This open competition brings boys from all parts of the country, and so spread our connection very widely'*.[3] It also had a stimulating competitive effect, an open scholarshp coming to be seen as more prestigious than a closed one. Unlike Eton, scholars and commoners viewed each other on socially equal terms. This much wider interest in the College prompted the building of a new boarding house with an anticipation of increasing the school role to around 300 boys.[4] Winchester too had a piece of inherited good fortune. A former Head, Dr. Goddard, left a substantial legacy for the payment of all costs of salaries and instruction. All a scholar had to pay was £1.10 to the French master. The College was maintaining a choir, the choristers recently relieved of the chore of bedmaking and having an apprenticeship paid for on leaving the choir.

Evidence of long-established custom was found. Dinner was eaten off wooden trenchers. Boys slept in small chambers lit at night by 'half-faggots' on oaken bedsteads more than two hundred years old.[6]

One custom seems to have been unique to Winchester and that was the institution of boy tutors. Each of the ten senior boys was given charge of a number of juniors with the idea of helping with lessons and general conduct in return for which they were given two guineas by each parent. Moberley was strongly in favour of tuition as addition to class work.[7]

The right to fag was a privilege given to the eighteen prefects. This generally consisted of being sent on various errands but fags could be called on to take a share of the heartily disliked cricket fagging, though that was limited to two hours.[8]

A boy in trouble might be asked to do a written imposition though requiring learning by heart had become a more regular punishment. If the offence was serious he might be sent to Moberley for a flogging though he insisted that only happened ten to twenty times a year. When it did he had to make use of the 'vinem quadrifidium', an implement said to have been invented by a Fifteenth-Century Warden. *'It consists of four strong twigs of an apple tree, about three feet long, at the end of a long handle.'* With this ancient implement a boy might get lucky for *'it is chance whether he is always hit'*. Moberley would have preferred a birch but felt bound by custom. It was a public event.[9]

The Commissioners had the same kind of doubts as to the effectiveness of Winchester's Governing Body as it had expressed about Eton's. The 1857 Oxford University measure had introduced one change. The ten Fellows were to be reduced to six, no replacements for any dying or resigning until that figure had been reached. A wider change was though thought desirable with an increased and broader based body. This, it was proposed, should consist of the Warden and eleven Fellows of whom though only four would be stipendiary on £700 p. a. These alone should have to be resident for at least a part of the year.[10]

As at Eton, there had developed a practice of selective application of the Statutes. Some provisions clearly had to be allowed to lapse as appropriate only to much earlier times, such as that the Fellows should sleep three to a room. That consideration had though encouraged the insidious habit of highly selective application of the Statutes, self-interest rather than appropriateness being the touchstone. Among the dubious practices was that of the Fellows dividing up fines among themselves. This amounted to £6,598 in 1860.[11]

Relations between the Warden and Headmaster seem to have been a good deal less demanding than those between Eton's corresponding pair with the Warden content to take a less intrusive approach. Moberley had the view that his authority existed over the whole school while that of the Warden was restricted to the management of the scholars. That being put to the Warden, he disagreed, seeing his as a wider remit. Moberley saw no reason though why this or any other difference of view would not be settled by amicable discussion. Indeed, the Fellows impinged on Moberley so little that he remarked that, 'I really do not feel their presence at all'.[13] That raised the question as to whether they were really serving any useful purpose as a Governing Body.

The connection with New College was thought beneficial, though with reservations. Money saved from the reduction in the number of stipendiary Fellows should be used to create thirty Winchester scholarships tenable at New College.[14] On the other hand, when it came to selection of Winchester Fellows, New College's should be shown no preference. Moberley, himself *a Balliol man, saw the supply of masters from New College as a limiting factor and wanted them more widely recruited.*15

Pointedly, the report commented that the College's sound position as regarding the payment of salaries and tuition costs was wholly down to Goddard's legacy and owed nothing to any measures that the College itself had put in place.

The future of the London schools was a key issue for the Commissioners. The number they were educating was modest. Westminster, which in 1825 had around 300 boys had only 136 in 1861. Charterhouse, which had had 480 boys in 1826 was reduced to 136 in 1861. St. Paul's and Merchant Taylors had retained a constant number throughout that period, 153 and around 260 respectively. Key questions were why the rolls were so low, whether a school should be wholly or predominantly day or boarding, and if a move away from an existing site might be beneficial.

Westminster was not well placed to take any kind of costly initiative, having no external assets of its own and being entirely dependent on revenue. From that £3,235 had to be found to pay the Head and his seven assistants, more than half of that going to the Head.[16] Thus the Clarendon Commission was told that any kind of further expansion would be difficult. Its boarding houses were limited to thirty-five boys, some of whom were half-boarders and others home boarders, but all 'Town Boys'.[17]

Appointments and admission were dealt with in a rather arcane manner. The Head and Under Masters were appointed alternately by the Dean of Christ Church and the Master of Trinity though the choice had to be approved by the Dean of Westminster.[18] College admission involved emerging triumphant from a system of challenges. A boy had to challenge another over a prepared text. If he did so successfully he went on to another such contest. The whole thing could take six to eight weeks, the Head acting as Moderator and the older boys as helpers.[19]

Conditions in the Long Dormitory in which the forty Queens Scholars slept had grown rather more civilised with its division into *'forty distinct sleeping places'* divided by partitions eight feet high and curtained off from the central passage though whether it was adequately warmed was questioned. No complaints were heard of the food though it was noted there was not usually much left for supper.[20]

Fags were much put upon. They had to rise as early as 4.a.m. in order to start preparations for their masters and beyond that could be called upon at any time.[21] It was though the treatment of junior boys in College that left other Heads and reporters present at the Clarendon sessions aghast. They heard of the practice of 'tanning' in which a boy *'puts one leg in a certain sink and ... one authorised boy takes a run at you, and kicks you as hard as ever he can'*. Equally objectionable was the practice of 'buckhorsing', not explained but guessable.[22]

This ill-treatment was not quickly forgotten. Mr. Meyrick had a son at Westminster but, while he was up at King's, urged him to write to the Commissioners detailing his unhappy experiences at Westminster. Meyrick jr. had started in a boarding house but had been transferred to College and it was there that he experienced excessive fagging, capricious and extensive punishment, and general bullying. Mr. Meyrick wanted his son to be allowed to go back to the boarding house but this the Head, the Rev. Scott, refused. The boy was then taken away from the school.[23]

As to sport, it was said that *'rowing is regarded with special interest by all Westminsters'*. [24]

'No boy should ever be kicked.' That was the first of the Commissioners' recommendations, reflecting the strength of feeling against established practices that amounted to little more than licensed savagery. The Headmaster told the Commission that he had given instructions forbidding kicking, restricting the time fags had on call, and ending the custom which required juniors to go around carrying such things as pens and papers for the use of seniors. He was nonetheless given a thoroughly uncomfortable session. It was thought too that the system which entrusted the four Head Boys on the Foundation with the maintenance of discipline was one that *'requires watching'*.[25] Altogether the punishment regime was one in need of reform *'to prevent the tyrannical exercise of power on the part of seniors over juniors'*.[26]

The Commissioners recommended starting a rather broader method of entry. It also saw a need for additional funding to teach more subjects with Town Boys being asked for an additional £1. 15/- while the Chapter, encouraged to have some lay representation, should take on the cost of the Scholars' tuition.[27] Beyond that, the transfer of some part of the Abbey estate for the school's support was suggested.[28] Arguments could be made for and against Westminster's moving to the country but while it remained in London it was considered more likely to appeal to *'day-scholars'* than boarders.[29] To ensure that these important issues were discussed in all their implications the addition of several lay members to the Governing Body was proposed.

Charterhouse from its foundation in the reign of James 1st had had the dual function of Free Grammar School and hospital.[30] Annual income from its estates, being such as houses, farms, rents, and timber, brought in an average of £22,747 in the years 1853-1860 of which around £8,000 was being spent on the school. Though its numbers had picked up somewhat from a low point of 94 in 1835 they were far short of a fairly recent 480 (1825). The Head was paid £1,100 p.a. and there were six Assistant Masters, all of whom taught both Classics and Mathematics. Whether the Head had any authority to dismiss them was unclear.[32]

There were three categories of boys: Foundation Scholars, Boarders, and Day Boys. A boy became a Foundation Scholar by the increasingly discredited method of being nominated by the Governors and then having only to face an exam of a most elementary kind. At the end of his time at school he could be put in for an exam that could secure him an exhibition worth £80 at any Oxford or Cambridge College.[33]

In the event of a routine fault such as lateness a boy's name was entered in a book. Three entries meant being sent up for a flogging though that could happen straight away for more serious offences. Fags were not required to perform any *'menial services'* the Headmaster, Dr. Elwyn, observed. That did not though accord with the discovery of boys charged with looking after fires and dealing with the lavatory. Fags were being asked to servants' work.[34]

It played a good range of games: cricket, football, hockey, and fives played with bats.[35]

No need was seen for any radical change in the composition of the Governing Body which included many men who had 'distinguished themselves in different professions', only the addition of four Governors with some knowledge of Modern Studies to add to the Classical expertise.[36] *Objection though was taken to the procedure for admitting Foundation Scholars, entry via 'unrestricted competition' for boys aged 11-14 being seen as far preferable.*[37] *Similarly the leaving exhibition should be open to all boys. Looking at the school's future it was thought that if it saw its future predominantly as a boarding school it would probably thrive better if it moved to the country.*[38]

Unlike Westminster, St. Paul's had no connection with the cathedral. It was run by the Mercers Company which appointed members of the Governing Body, called the Court of Assistants, and all the Masters. It stressed its authority in a rather heavy handed way by putting all the masters up for re-election every year – though this seems to have become only a formality. This body had a degree of flexibility as the Statutes contained a provision for their modification.[39] The roll though had been a consistent 153, that being the provision of Dean Colet, the school's Sixteenth-Century founder, citing the draught of fishes in St. John's Gospel.[40] It was comfortably endowed, a problem being seen as knowing what best to do with the surplus (£2,500) from the Coletine Estates.[41]

There was no distinction between the boys. All were regarded as scholars and educated free of charge. Each member of the Court of Assistants took a turn in nominating a boy for admission.[42] About an eighth of the boys were boarders.[43]

Masters were not allowed to beat but could give up to six blows of the cane on the hand and the use of the rod was unknown. A mild form of the monitorial system was exercised in ways such as making a misbehaving boy stand in a particular place to draw him to a master's attention.[44]

A disadvantage of its site was the lack of a playground. Boys were though allowed to use part of the Kennington Oval during the cricket season.[45]

No fault was found with the ethos of the Court of Assistants which had managed property solely in the best interest of the school and shown itself a 'pure and diligent administration'.[46] *It was though deemed to be too large and unwieldy a group to be an effective Governing Body.*[47]

Strong arguments were seen for the school's removal from its St. Paul's Churchyard site, including traffic noise and health risks. This alternative position need not necessarily be in the city. In any case, St. Paul's should start to think in much more enterprising terms, forget the artificial 153 number, and think rather of a school around the 500 mark.[48] *If it was going to continue to have boarders then they should be looked after properly and a boarding house built.*

The Headmaster, Dr. Kynaston, felt that the school offered too many scholarships and exhibitions, that 'no school in relation to its size is better endowed that St. Paul's' and the Commissioners sensed a sort of academic languor, of being in a school without a sharp competitive edge.[49] *This seemed to be reflected in its University record which was respectable but without very much 'first-rate attainment'.*[50]

Merchant Taylors had been founded as a school for 250 boys and seems always to have had about that number : in 1861 it had 262.[51] The company considered itself to be in total control of the school, one important power being that to appoint and dismiss masters, of whom there were six, all teaching both Classics and Mathematics.[52] It had dealt with the school *'in a liberal and generous spirit'* recently having spent £20,000 on improvements to the buildings.[53]

Boys were admitted on a system of nomination by rotation by members of the company and had to pay a fixed charge.[54]

Flogging was rare, *'not once in three years'*, though masters used the cane. The task of a monitor was to *'assist in the work of the school'* for which he was given a small fee.[55]

The condition of the buildings was judged good but more were needed, in particular some better class rooms. A playground too was thought desirable. Some recreation was had at the Oval Cricket Ground for which a rent of £20 p. a. was paid.[56]

Members of the corporation were urged to surrender their right of nomination of entrants and instead adopt the practice of merely putting forward candidates.[57]

Then the staff of six Classical masters was thought too scant and the appointment of another two was urged. Maybe too some arrangement for lunch on the premises might be made.[58]

Reconciling the Founder's intentions with its later development proved particularly difficult in the case of Harrow. Founded by John Lyon in 1571 he left an endowment for the school and the road estate, the latter a common bequest at the time. A financial quirk had increased the road endowment far more than the school's so that in 1861 the road estate was worth £3,500 and the school's only £1,100. A change there could only be effected by Act of Parliament.[59]

The Founder had envisaged local boys being educated free while 'foreigners' paid. The qualification for being local was living in the parish. That had had the effect of bringing families to live at Harrow in order to claim Foundationer status – widowed ladies in reduced circumstances being one group mentioned.[60] A school not by any means that well off hardly wanted a number of parents claiming fee exemptions or reductions. Nor was there a deal of logic in favouring local inhabitants when the school had a national reputation and was getting boys from all parts of the country and Empire. Vaughan when Headmaster had set up an 'English Class' for the sons of local residents to try to get round this difficulty which had another aspect. To some parents a curriculum with some rather more utilitarian elements had more appeal than excessive hours of the Classics and this the 'English Class' went some way to address.[61]

Its revived popularity was fairly recent. As noted earlier the 'Keepers' or Governors had had so little confidence that Harrow had any future that they were mooting its closure. Yet in another illustration of the extraordinary volatility of school rolls in the early and mid-Nineteenth Century the number of boys leapt from 79 in 1844 to 314 in 1847, and by 1862 had reached 481. The spurt was due to its having the outstanding C.J. Vaughan as Headmaster followed by the equally capable Montagu Butler.

The Headmaster's main income came from boys' entrance payments and the profit he got from keeping a large boarding house of 63 boys.[62] The 14 Classical Masters likewise boosted their income of £150 p.a. with boarding house profits in the region of £15-29 per boy.[63] The houses varied in size, the smaller being the more expensive to run, and usually had rooms holding two-five boys though there were some single rooms. All money that came into the school went direct to the Headmaster from which he made disbursements so that what appeared a fairly staggering income of more than £11,000 was in practice a good deal less than that, especially as both Vaughan and Butler had been 'liberal to the point of munificence'.[64]

It was the Headmaster who conducted the entrance exam in Latin and Greek, Maths having once featured but been dropped. This had to happen before the boy turned fifteen.[65] There were a large number of prizes keenly competed for, including two John Lyon Scholarships, tenable for four years at any College.

Flogging was rare with about twenty beatings in a school year. For minor offences written impositions and learning by heart were the norm, though disadvantages were seen in both. Overlong impositions could lead to slovenly handwriting while learning took time to hear. Maybe as a result Harrow came up with 'extra work' on half-holidays, a forerunner of the deadly detention.[66]

The Head Boy was a formidable figure. In the case of a *'very gross offence'* it was he who administered a *'public whopping'*. He was also responsible for the games money, the management of football, as well as being captain of the Rifle Corps, the latter popular with the boys when it involved shooting but less so when being drilled. The first fifteen boys in seniority also had a good deal of authority being entitled to beat anyone up to the second division of the Fifth Form.[67]

Around 250 boys were liable for fagging though you were allowed to call a halt after three years. This included being available for service at breakfast, tea, cricket, and racquets. He was required to play football unless unfit or excused by a monitor.[68]

While its recent rapid revival was clearly to be welcomed this should not become uncontrolled and an upper limit of 500 boys was suggested, very close to the point then reached.[70]

The extinction of the Foundationer class was suggested though without penalising those already on the Foundation. Nor should the John Lyon Scholarships have any kind of local connection. The 'English Class' should develop into a school with a suitable building. That way it could more readily adapt to the kind of curriculum better fitted to local youth.[72] *(This later happened in 1876 when the John Lyon School was founded.)*

A more professional method of handling money was thought desirable than that of having it all go direct to the Headmaster. No criticism could be made of the way in which Vaughan and Butler had dealt with the revenue but such a loose method was liable to store up future trouble. One saving was identified: the abolition of the office of Lower Master which had just become a sinecure.[71]

The premises needeed a good deal of attention. The older schoolrooms were found very unsatisfactory; being 'obviously deficient in ventilation'.[72] *To get a grip on such problems the Governors needed to have more direct control. Their number should be increased from 6 to 12 with three of them having some qualification in Literature and Science.*[73] *Butler had said that all matters of administration were left to him. That perhaps was better than incessant probing but by no means ideal.*

Shrewsbury owed everything to the Reformation. Founded by King Edward VI and Queen Elizabeth it was given the estates of dissolved collegiate churches. Consequent on that nearly all of its endowment income came fom tithe rent charges (£12,714) with a mere £306 from other sources.[74]

It had been set up as wholly or largely a day school offering free education at a time when Shrewsbury was an important provincial centre. An Act of 1798 had though restricted that to the sons of burgesses while also setting up exhibitions for local boys at the universities. An Act of 1853 opened these up to wider competition.[75]

There was though still a notable local connection. Of the 60 day-boys 22 were sons of burgesses and educated free while, despite the 1853 measure, many exhibitions at the universities still gave preference to sons of burgesses or natives of Shropshire.[76]

There were two boarding houses, one for seniors and one for juniors, both run by the Headmaster and both in poor condition. A few boarded at houses kept by other masters, though that needed the Head's permission while some others boarded out in town.[77]

Despite having some boys boarding in town Shrewsbury kept itself as separate from the town as possible, memories of ructions in Butler's time perhaps being still fresh. Boys were not allowed into town and day boys could only wear their caps in school.

In 1861 the school had a modest role of 131 boys, a substantial decline from its total of 295 in 1832. There seem to have been several reasons for this. There was the dilapidated, off-putting state of the school buildings which could be compared unfavourably with the pristine condition of the rapidly increasing number of proprietary schools.[78] The nature of the education the school offered though was a contentious matter for some and could be contrasted with wider curricula elsewhere.

The Headmaster, B.H. Kennedy, was perhaps the leading Classical teacher of his generation and author of the ubiquitous grammar. He had a staff of eight, all only modestly remunerated with Kennedy himself thought to get about £2,000 p.a.[79] He and his staff usually met weekly for consultation. Under his regime and with his distinctive method the school had been remarkably successful in its own Classical terms. Able boys were promoted to the Sixth Form soon after arriving at the school while competitiveness was fostered with the award of about twenty prizes with a few 'merit money' prizes given for such things as punctuality and good exercises.[80] Shrewsbury scholars were notably successful at the universities, especially Cambridge, with 35% of boys leaving for one or the other.[81] The influence of many of them came to be long-lasting with the number of Fellowships gained.

That's all very well, reasoned some Shrewsbury worthies in a memorandum to the Commission but what we really want is a broadening of the curriculum with much greater prominence given to subjects more likely to be of value to the middle class. Kennedy had gone some way in this direction by setting up what was termed a 'Non-Collegiate Class' in which Greek was dropped.[82]

Discipline was sustained in a rather bureaucratic fashion by the master who had the title of 'Secretary of Discipline'. He kept a book with two pages for each boy for 'merit marks and penal marks'. Four merit marks earned a half-holiday while penal marks resulted in impositions with the penal sheet being shown to Kennedy. Flogging occurred *'perhaps half a dozen times in a half year'* and expulsion was rare.[83]

Authority around the school was invested in twelve Praeposters. Something of Roman practice was recreated in that these boys were urged to look on themselves rather as Roman Senators and to be prepared to put forward as a basis for negotiation with Kennedy any ideas they might have for the betterment of the school. Of the Clarendon schools Shrewsbury alone forbade the Praeposters to beat. There was very little fagging.[84]

Day boys lived a very different life from the boarders going home promptly after school though Kennedy thought they might have profited from a *'more active life by more sociality and more play at school'*.[85] (If he really believed that one wonders why he and his staff hadn't managed to bring that about.) Kennedy had hardly helped to bridge the divide by hiring a cricket ground for the boarders and being reluctant to let the day boys play on it.

The Statutes provided for *'shooting the long bow, chess play, running, wrestling, and leaping'*. These had become cricket, football, boating, swimming, and gymnastic exercise. Impromptu recreation was hardly possible though, the playground being an inconvenient three-quarters of a mile away.

The Commissioners saw a need for considerable change and an important first step was to have a Governing Body capable of effecting it. The existing body was thought quite unsatisfactory. The Headmaster was appointed by St. John's but the College was not represented on it. Then the Mayor was a member but only for his Mayoral year. The appointment of four extra governors by the Crown and Corporation was thought desirable.[87]

An improvement in the condition of the school buildings was seen as an urgent requirement along with the erection of new ones. It was suggested that some of the funding committed to exhibitions might be diverted to this work.[88]

Despite its meagre roll it was thought best that the school should continue as a largely Classical boarding school with all local preferences removed. It was though prepared to allow a generous transition period with compensation for a lost right with the idea that forty free scholarships be created for sons of burgesses for *'a limited period'*. However, all particular rights to free education *'shall expire after twenty-five years'*.[89] It was thought desirable too that awards should no longer be linked to a particular college though it was conceded that such an alteration would need Parliamentary sanction.

The *'non-Collegiate Class'* was seen as acceptable so long as it didn't heighten the demand for a middle class educational format to the point at which it became irresistible.[90] It did though need careful watching in view of perceptions that it had come to be seen as 'a refuge from work'. Boys in it should pay the same as scholars (20 guineas) and the Governing Body needed 'to watch its working narrowly'. The Trustees too were uneasy about it, seeing it as perhaps the first step on a downward path to Shrewsbury becoming a commercial school.[91]

Feeling that all boys should be within the orbit of school authority it was thought profoundly unsatisfactory to have some boys boarding out in town. Also, the start of the school day would be more convenient for these and for day boys if it began a little later. Nor could any good reason be found to stop day boys wearing their caps out of school.[92]

A most comprehensive study of its history showed the Commissioners just how far Rugby had developed in a way not foreseen by its founder, Sir Lawrence Sheriff, in 1567, and just why certain apparent archaisms still mattered. Much more briefly, this was the substance.

The school had been set up to educate *'the children of Rugby and Brownsover chiefly'*.[93] At that time Rugby was a small market town and Brownsover an even smaller settlement. By the 1860's though Rugby had become important as a centre of the Midland Railway with a hugely increased population. Its growth had come to be reflected in the outlook of a school advertising itself as '*a great English school educating boys from all parts of the British dominions'*. Brownsover meanwhile had remained a settlement of modest size which sent no boys to Rugby.[94]

The difficulty was that the Statutes gave those living in Rugby the right to have their boys educated free of charge. It was suspected, as had been found to be happening elsewhere, that some parents had moved to Rugby in order to take advantage of that. When the Commissioners visited Rugby 67 of its 463 boys were found to be Foundationers.[95]

Appreciating that this had become a considerable problem the Trustees imposed a residential qualification, first of two years, then increased to four. There was too the tricky matter of eligibility, the Statutes having vaguely included boys *'from places adjoining'*.[96] The Trustees had used their initiative to decree that the provision should extend ten miles into Warwickshire and five miles into the other contiguous counties.[97]

Then there was the disparity between what was originally offered and what these boys were receiving. The school's curriculum had expanded well beyond Latin and Greek and Foundationers in practice got all these other subjects free too.[98] Rugby was far less well endowed than it had been when it owned valuable London property in the Conduit Close area of Gray's Inn Fields. Its worth had declined with it becoming a less popular residential area and a deterioration in the condition of the buildings.[99] It could barely afford this level of liberality. Land it did own had increased in value quite disproportionately, that in Warwickshire and Lancashire yielding just 1 /46th of that in Middlesex.[100] The latter looked a bit like an afterthought, being put down in a codicil in the Founder's will. This seemed rather bizarre. *'The national and metropolitan site of the property bestows all and receives nothing; the provincial site bestows comparatively nothing and receives all.'* In the seven years ending in 1861 Rugby's income had averaged £5,653, a substantial decline from the sum of £43,221 reached in 1807.[101] Though getting along well enough it could do without unproductive demands on its resources.

The Commissioners found Rugby an enterprising school, more receptive to changing educational ideas than the other Clarendon schools. In part that may have been down to not having had an Old Rugbeian as Headmaster since 1777,[102] thus avoiding what often became an ingrained resistance to any but the most modest change as well as generating its own initiatives. Arnold of course had raised the school's profile in public consciousness and its religious lustre in particular was sustained by his two successors, Dr. Tait and Dr. Temple, both of whom went on to become Archbishops.

Headmasters were answerable to a board of twelve Trustees which had absolute authority over such matters as numbers, ages, charges, and exhibitions. In practice though it left the day to day running of the school in the hands of the Headmaster.[103] In 1861 Dr. Temple presided over a team of eighteen Assistant Masters and 463 boys. He had considerable authority, being empowered to dismiss any but the seven most senior Classical masters. His salary was made up of a stipend, fixed by law, boarding fees, and school instruction fees all amounting to £2, 957, as well as having a handsome residence, a good garden, and four acres of pasture.[104]

The Assistant Masters divided the sum of £17,396 pounds between them which gave an average income of £966. This was a generous income though lessened somewhat as personal income by the practice which had developed of donating some of it to school improvements. A part of it though was questionable, and again the problem was to do with Foundationers. Masters got a stipend of £120 for teaching them.[105] An alteration in practice saw Foundationers being charged the same as the other boys. That though was not charged to the parents but taken out of revenue. In effect the masters were getting a double payment which meant that the instruction cost for a Foundationer of 31 guineas was twice that for the other boys. Masters taxed the school's resources in another way. An Act of George IV required that after ten years service a master leaving Rugby was entitled to draw a retiring stipend of between £100 and £300 p.a., and style himself a Fellow.[106]

Income from a boarding house boosted a master's income. There were eight of these, the Headmaster's with 73 boys being the largest. Dormitories held between two and sixteen boys with every boy in Upper School having his own study for which he had to provide his own furniture, usually acquiring his predecessor's.[107]

Discipline imposed by masters involved learning by heart and impositions and occasional floggings, said to occur only about eight times a year, the sixth Form being exempt by law. Boys in the Lower School were though sometimes put in solitary confinement to reflect on the error of their ways.[108]

Praeposters were a key feature of the system in sustaining an orderly regime. Boys found guilty of *'frequenting public houses, turbulent conduct, drinking or smoking'* could be given impositions or, if deemed appropriate, five or six strokes of a cane on the shoulders. Use of the fist was forbidden. A danger with the system was that of a monitor getting an excessive sense of self-importance but it was generally seen as effective with little sign of *'excess or abuse'*.[109]

Sixth Formers alone could use fags. That involved sweeping and dusting Sixth Form studies, attending the Sixth at supper, playing football, occasional fielding at cricket, and taking part in such other sporting activities as 'runs', 'brook-leaping', and 'hounds', the latter usually over a course of five or six miles. In fact fagging seemed to have largely evolved into a regime of compulsory games. The school close of thirteen acres, on which a number of games could often be seen going on at the same time, was seen as a valuable recreational asset. Games were managed by boys from Upper School who imposed a 'Big Side Levee' tax for that purpose.[110]

All boys attended chapel on Sundays when the Headmaster preached and strong participation by the boys was noted. The Commissioners got a favourable sense of the school's moral tone. *'Smoking is generally considered an affectation, drinking bravado'*.[111] (Of course, in the comparatively short time they were there they couldn't be sure just how many boys practised such precepts).

Unusually there were only two holidays in the year, Christmas and Mid-Summer. Additionally boys were allowed two and a half days leave once each half-year on parental request.[112] These must have brought a welcome change from the routine of getting up in time for the first lesson at 7.00 a.m.

A major change thought desirable was in the composition of the Board of Trustees. No fault could be found with them on an individual level as affairs had been conducted with 'a scrupulous personal integrity'.[113] The difficulty was that this was a self-selecting body which had come to be made up mainly of neighbouring landowners whose outlook had come to have 'a uniform and exclusive quality'. To broaden their perspective and at the same time be able to make a more direct contribution to the school it was suggested that four of the Trustees should be elected with the aim of bringing in men versed in scientific and literary pursuits.[114]

They needed to settle the business of the Foundationers. Simply giving privileges to boys who happened to live in Rugby did the school little good.[115] While it was acknowledged that Rugby had deservedly established a high reputation it was in danger of being outpaced by schools such as Eton and Winchester with their competitive entry scholarships. High-achieving boys won awards at the Universities and a reputation for academic excellence was likely to attract the best qualified masters and be more inviting to parents. Rugby should immediately set up twelve scholarships in the Classics and twenty-four exhibitions for each of the school's subsidiary subjects.[116] Funding for these could come in large part from the abolition of the retired master's stipend and from the elimination of Foundationers. It was though suggested that the rights of existing and prospective Foundationers should be treated 'with some tenderness' and a fairly lengthy process of change submitted. There should be only twenty-five Foundationers after ten years and none after twenty.[117]

A number of other financial changes were recommended. The practice of relying on the liberality of masters donating some of their income for the school's benefit was thought unsatisfactory. While masters were likely to be committed to projects which they had funded, in whole or in part, this was not a proceeding with any kind of central direction. It was 'wide and loose .... being based on uncertainty '.[118] The Trustees should manage all this kind of business. An instance of a need for channelling of a substantial fund into a major project was Dr. Temple's desire for additional building. Rugby had been built for 320 boys and then had considerably more. A main aim was for each form to have its own room. That induced reflective speculation as to both need and desirability.

Boys spent a lot less time in their schoolroom than they had in the past. Then while the increasing tendency for classes to be educated in a more secluded manner than having a number taught simultaneously in a large hall was noted, whether this was necessarily a good thing was queried. After all, if boys were to go on to become barristers or Members of Parliament they would need to be able to work efficiently against a very considerable ambient noise.[119]

Then while the inappropriateness of the retired masters stipend had been acknowledged with its restriction to special cases there was no clear sense of what that meant and complete abolition was advised. It was simply 'an anachronism and anomaly'.[120] *Also the double payment masters had been getting for teaching Foundationers should cease with the ending of the stipend.*[121] *Moreover the stipulation that they could draw a stipend after ten years work at Rugby, and style themselves Fellows, was deemed inappropriate. Little justification could be seen for the use of a Collegiate title in a school which had never had any kind of Collegiate connection.*[122]

The value of the Close for games was acknowledged to the extent that the suggestion was made that it might at some point expand into the Headmaster's sizeable garden.

CHAPTER THIRTEEN : JUST WHAT GOT LEARNT ?

THE COMMISSIONERS HAD NO DOUBT THAT THE CLASSICS SHOULD REMAIN AT THE heart of education. While in part they hold their place through '*custom and habit*'[1] it was also because of their '*intrinsic excellence*' in that they provide '*the finest and most serviceable mould we have for the study of language*'.[2]

Looking back at that era with the benefit of very substantial hindsight, it is very clear how educationally divisive the insistence on the supremacy of the Classics was. For so much time was devoted to it that proficiency or lack of it largely determined a boy's form placing and must to a large degree have often shaped his general attitude to school work. A successful Classicist was more likely to approach other subjects with a degree of confidence, or, if not greatly interested or apt at them, with the knowledge that they counted for less than what he was good at. A failing Classicist would find that, for example, comparative Mathematical ability would not see him much advanced in form seniority or general academic esteem.

At Harrow, for instance Classics was weighted at 4-1 against Maths and 9-1 against Modern Languages.[3] At Charterhouse a boy's Maths marks were added to his Classical marks to determine his ranking in the Classical school while no account was taken of French.[4] Rugby's calculations, though having the Classics at the core, were unusually broad, intent on working out a boy's 'aggregate proficiency' and including even music and drawing. Even so, it ranked Modern Languages as worth only 8/100 marks.[5]

The insistence on the Classics as the dominant educational influence was becoming an increasingly archaic practice. Whereas this had been widespread in Europe in the Eighteenth Century the emphasis had very much turned to the use of the national language as a medium of instruction. This involved a more varied set of activities than predominantly turning words into other words. A heightened linguistic consciousness was an important element in the Nationalist uprisings of the mid-Nineteenth Century. By contrast English barely featured in the Public School curriculum. That could be partially justified by saying that they learnt all necessary grammar from Latin but it gave them little acquaintance with English literature. In part that was because a good deal of contemporary English literature was viewed with a degree of suspicion for its radical tendencies. Boys were urged to read uncontroversial works such as the historical novels of Sir Walter Scott.

* * * * *

Rugby greatly impressed the Commissioners, who judged its *'teaching of the literae humaniores to be absolutely unsurpassed'* [6] and gave a full account of its Classical method. The main ingredients were construing or oral translation and learning by heart. Construing had three modes: word for word, sentence by sentence, and free translation. Written translation from English into Latin was done almost throughout the school while translation into Greek began in the Middle School. No original composition was asked for below the Upper Division of the Fifth Form. During the last thirty years a good deal more time had come to be spent on translation than original composition, a trend approved of by the Old Rugbeians spoken to.[7] Unlike Eton, where a boy might advance to a new form but still meet the same books, new books were encountered on promotion. It was noted too that the Assistant Masters had considerable latitude as to which books were used.

Dr. Arnold had always insisted on an intelligent approach to the Classics, seeing it as an essential grounding in the appreciation of historical truths and of politics. Merchant Taylors was also complimented on its intelligent approach [8] while a strong tradition at St. Paul's was noted: boys who reached the Sixth Form could give up Greek but few did.[9] Harrow was urged to do less original composition and more translation.[10] Despite that advice the report suggested that original composition was more of a stimulus to the imagination than translation. Recitation was seen as a useful aid to accuracy and memory while there was a warning against allowing repetition becoming slovenly.[11]

It was felt with several of these schools that the number of masters employed had not kept pace with the increase in their rolls. Particularly did that seem to be the case at Winchester and Harrow.[12] At Charterhouse and Merchant Taylors masters were expected to be all-rounders, to teach Mathematics as well as Classics.[13] Arnold had had his Rugby Masters teaching Classics, Maths and French, justifying the latter by thinking it improbable that boys could ever attain any conversational fluency so that it might as well just be taught grammatically. Dr. Tait, his successor, instead engaged men with specific abilities.[14]

Mathematics had begun in these schools at various times and was made compulsory at Harrow in 1837. Harrow's Headmaster, Dr. Butler, who had been a Senior Wrangler, was a vigorous advocate of the subject, ensuring that all boys above the Fourth Form spent three hours a week on it. Each year there was a voluntary exam for four Maths prizes which included a gold medal worth ten guineas. To ensure proper respect for the subject Mathematical masters were given equal status with their Classical colleagues.[15] Elsewhere it was generally being taken seriously. A boy in the top division at Winchester might give seven or eight hours a week to it while Merchant Taylors was thought to be rather overdoing it by having Mathematics every afternoon.[16] The subject was thought valuable as *'an instrument of mental discipline'* if less interesting than the Classics.[17]

While the Clarendon investigations were under way Dr. Butler was considering a major structural change: that of having a separate Modern Department distinct from the Classical side. Though strictly beyond its brief, the Commissioners visited a number of the newer schools. One of them, Cheltenham, had setup a Modern Department and its Head, Dr. Bradley, had found it *'most valuable'*.[18] However, the Commissioners were largely unconvinced, seeing this kind of parallel development as a source of confusion.

Harrow had a highly effective French master, Mr. Ruault, who had disproved the widely held belief that a Frenchman cannot keep order. Every boy below the Fifth Form learnt French and was permitted to start German if by then he'd learnt sufficient.[19] Winchester and Rugby too had the practice of learning both in succession. Rugby had experimented with a Conversation Class but been unable to make that work effectively and had changed it into a session of French reading or translation in which only French was spoken.[20] Shrewsbury allowed boys to drop French in order to spend longer on Classics.[21] The Universities had not particularly encouraged the study of Modern Languages by not examining them. While it acknowledged that both Mathematics and Modern Languages had come to be taken more seriously both were judged to need more teaching time and more commitment as both were *'worth doing well'*.[22]

History and Geography were very much treated as minor subjects, an hour a week being typically devoted to them. Winchester saw a difficulty in making it a subject for study, Moberley making the sometimes quoted remark that he would not know how to go about teaching it in set lessons. The Commissioners too didn't think you could teach it to any great extent. Rugby had no such inhibition, teaching a course that ran from the Greeks to the present, though it was thought that such a comprehensive course allocated such scanty time must be rather superficial.[23] Harrow's Upper Sixth boys got an hour's history a week as well as being set occasional holiday tasks.[24]

English appeared only on the fringes of the curriculum. Winchester had a tradition of public recitation with renderings that were ' *almost always Shakespeare or Milton'*.[25] At Rugby boys learnt poetry by heart, wrote English essays, and went in for an English Essay prize.[26] None of that though had any effect on a boy's form placing. Other schools were urged to include some English in their practice. Other unusual features were the teaching of Hebrew at Merchant Taylors [27] and the lack of any music or drawing at St Paul's, though in the other schools only a minority of boys did either.[28]

There was though what was considered a glaring omission in all but one of the schools, and that was the teaching of Science. It was one thing to host occasional lectures but another to make it a curriculum subject. The exception was Rugby which built a laboratory at a cost of over a thousand pounds and then asked boys to choose between Modern Languages and Natural Philosophy, as it termed it. A disincentive was that Science cost an extra six guineas. A more limiting factor was that the 'lecturer', as he was styled, was basically a Mathematics teacher and gave only a quarter of his teaching time to Science. While he was lecturing another group of boys was busy in the laboratory with a prize awarded for the best Practical Chemistry analyst. While the initiative was applauded it was felt that results so far had not matched expenditure. To progress the subject properly the school needed two full time Scientific teachers and an end to the six guinea payment.[29] Lower School boys too might benefit from Science, by finding it '*a more wholesome and agreeable relief to the learning and application of Grammar Rules and to the technical working of arithmetic'*.[30]

* * * * *

Six forms had become the norm though Merchant Taylors had seven and St. Paul's eight. Within that structure a more involved system of divisions, removes, and sets had developed. The ideal class size was seen as about thirty and the suggestion that boys found being taught in larger classes more stimulating was judged doubtful. At Harrow a boy was faced with fourteen ascending divisions. Fitness to progress was rigorously tested with boys being put through three exams a year as well as having weekly or fortnightly placings in what was deemed *'a good and effective system'*.[31] Rugby had a system of rather baffling complexity to an outsider, though no doubt those in it understood it well enough, involving promotions not only upwards but sideways too into 'parallel forms' [32] as well as having alternative form structures for Mathematics and Modern Languages. These contained 27 Maths and 19 Modern Language sets.[33]

Promotion was generally given on a basis of seniority and merit. The consequence was that boys progressed at different rates and a form would often contain boys of widely diverging ages. Older boys did not always look encouragingly on their younger, brighter classroom companions, a situation that in the worst cases led to bullying. Over rapid promotion could also have the unsettling effect of boys having too little time to accustom themselves to a form master's ways.[34] Rugby had a policy that a boy had to make adequate progress or leave, though in practice exceptions were made. The Commissioners were of a similar mind. *'No boy should be allowed to remain at any school who fails to make sufficient progress in it'* even though they conceded there were other reasons for being at Public School.[35]

The attitude of the Commissioners towards failure in the Classics was possibly coloured somewhat by their own expertise. The general cause of failure was thought not to be *'ineptitude'* but a boy's *'slovenly and inefficient way of working'*.[36] They were though men who generally showed a broad-minded outlook during their enquiries and elsewhere another rather different sentiment was expressed with the acknowledgement that a boy might hit the buffers through *'the continual teaching of a subject in which he cannot advance'*. Another difficulty was seen as that of *'ineffective teaching'*.[37] The question perhaps was in what degree these factors, individually and corporately, resulted in failure. They did not though have any time for idleness. If a boy felt no great interest in what he was being asked to learn, a sense of duty should ensure he got down to it properly. Should a boy wish to give up a subject, say Latin for Maths in order to prepare for the army exam, that should happen only after careful consultation and subsequent monitoring to ensure it wasn't just a *'cover for idleness'*.[38]

Doubt was expressed as to the truth of the occasionally heard maxim that *'a boy's head will hold no more than a certain quantity of knowledge'*. It was important that every boy *'should be taught, and taught effectively, every branch of the school's regular course of study'*.[39] The often expressed Middle Class wish for less of the Classics was countered with the assertion that education should be more than the *'calculation of direct and immediate utility'*.[40]

Utility was a part of the Commissioners' thinking in a rather different way. For they were clear that such Classical exercises as the writing of Latin verse were not ends in themselves but a means to gaining greater facility in the use of English.[41] Altogether the education offered by these schools was judged *'sound and valuable in its main elements, but wanting in breadth and flexibility'*. [42]

All these schools had systems in place, sometimes quite elaborate and seeming to owe something to the statistical bent of the era, for assessing a boy's progress. The shadow over all the Commissioners' investigations though was the growing realisation that a considerable number of boys seemed to be learning very little indeed. At the outset their plan had been to set an exam to be taken by a proportion of boys in the nine schools. They had not though allowed that. Observation led to the conclusion that *'of the time spent by nine boys out of ten much is wasted'* and that often the opportunity for progress is *'absolutely thrown away'*.[43]

About a third of the boys from these schools went to either university though Eton, with around 40% was a bit higher and Merchant Taylors with 8% much lower. A large number of undergraduates came from a few schools, with three-quarters of Oxford's in 1862 from Eton, Harrow, or Rugby.[44] A fair number of these went to Christ Church which in 1861 had 77 Etonians, 28 Harrovians, and 21 Wykhamists.[45] Many of these had little academic interest. It was said that *'the wealthiest, it is true, and therefore the idlest go to Christ Church'*.

In 1862 a third of Christ Church candidates failed matriculation and the Dean offered this bleak assessment. *'Very few can construe with accuracy a piece they profess to have read. We never try them with an unseen passage. It would be useless to do so as the answers we get to simple grammatical questions are very inaccurate.'* Some improvement in Arithmetic had been noted but *'it would be useless to try them with Euclid or Algebra'*.[46] In similar vein the Rev. O. Ogle, a late Responsions examiner, had found 43 of 168 candidates *'utterly unfit to undergo any examination whatever'*.[47] Other Colleges too found the setting of an unseen test a pointless exercise. Those who failed were asked to read with a tutor for six months, a process of catching up on neglected school work that tutors disliked but found unavoidable.[48] There was though a degree of collusion in the acceptance of low standards in that some of the smaller Colleges were more interested in securing funding than academic prowess. It was much the same at Cambridge, the Provost of King's declaring himself quite satisfied with the Honours men but *'the ignorance of the pass men'* was a different matter.[49] Some were able to make up the lost ground. Professor Price, Sedleian Professor of Natural Science, found most who came up *'sadly deficient'* at Mathematics. Consequently none had ever won the junior Science scholarship but a number had won the senior.[50]

With many attitude was the main problem, boys going up with formed habits of idleness and little intention of aplying themselves. *'They are grossly ignorant, and have contracted slovenly habits of mind.'* [51]

The Commissioners, in a devastating passage, outlined the extent of this ignorance.

'If a youth after four or five years spent at School, quits at nineteen, unable to construe an easy piece of Latin or Greek without the help of a dictionary or to write Latin grammatically, almost ignorant of Geography and of the History of his own country, unacquainted with any modern language but his own, and hardly competent to write English correctly, do a simple sum or stumble through an easy proposition of Euclid, a total stranger to the laws which govern the physical world, and to its structure, with an eye and hand unpractised in drawing, and without knowing a note of music, with an uncultivated mind and no taste for reading or observation, his intellectual education must certainly be accounted a failure, though there may be no fault to find with his principles, character, or manners.' [52]

Any school nowadays receiving a report of this severity could expect to be put into special measures. Then though there was after all an Empire to be run and having a sound character counted for a good deal. On that score the report adopted a very different tone referring to *'their discipline and moral training of which we have been able to speak with high praise'*.[53]

* * * * *

Just who was to blame for this state of affairs and what was to be done about it? Fingers were pointed in two directions. The report thought parents largely to blame though without saying very clearly why. Maybe they had in mind Gladstone's line that the increased taste for luxury and self-indulgence acted against academic motivations. Or perhaps they recalled Goodford telling them that Eton's Oppidan parents told their sons that their future was secure and they had no real need to bother with school work. Most of the others were presumably going, to greater or lesser extent, to have to direct their own futures. Blame was also cast on Preparatory Schools which were said to prepare boys inadequately for Public Schools. Here there must have been the kind of variation inevitable in an age when anyone with adequate funds could set up a school. The two alleged causes of failure may in some cases have been linked, parents sometimes choosing schools largely on non-academic grounds.

As has been seen, the Commissioners made a number of structural suggestions for improving academic performance. In addition such things as making rather more of the awarding of prizes and the publishing of school lists as stimulus and goad were advocated. But if in the end a boy simply could not be made to work properly, he should be asked to leave.

CHAPTER FOURTEEN : DEBATE RESUMED

Mr. Grant Duff, M.P. for Elgin, earlier a strong advocate of the setting up of a body of enquiry, reminded the House of Commons that *'its immediate occasion, though not its cause, was the controversy which had arisen in the periodical press about the state of Eton'*.[1] That was put more strongly by a writer in Fraser's Magazine who saw the process as *'the late great impeachment of Eton'*.[2]

The same writer though acknowledged something of a paradox in that *'at the very time that it is the foremost object of attack, its numbers are rising enormously '*[3] with Provost Goodford contemplating a school of a thousand boys. In part this was reflection of the boom in independent education then well under way. More specifically, reprehensible as the alleged shortcomings of Eton's Fellows were, they only marginally affected the education and daily life of boys. Opponents of the Public Schools who hoped that the report would send shock waves through the system had instead to witness a rather perverse effect. The singling out of these schools as a group actually enhanced their prestige. Even today, the expression 'Clarendon Schools' can sometimes be seen in the Press.

What the report did was to largely switch the focus of debate from management to the quality of education offered. The chief governance issue was seen as the role of the Headmaster with strong objection being taken by some to his having his authority diluted by a School Council, although a number of these schools already had such a body. His authority should be *'absolute'*: *'the government of a* school *should be a pure monarchy"*.[4]

* * * * *

Broadly, there were three types of response to the report. The Commissioners' contention that the Classics should remain the dominant study but with more time spent on other subjects was fairly widely accepted. A more conservative sentiment though was unwilling to admit of any great inroad into Classical teaching time. On the other pole, there were those who considered that the Classics had had their day and it was time to recast the curriculum afresh.

Positive response from politicians was essential if legislative amendment was to follow. Initial responses seemed encouraging. Grant Duff, speaking in the House of Commons, welcomed the general tone of the report. Classics, he maintained should *'hold their pride of place'* but thought that Geography, History and English Literature might also be profitably taught while French should perhaps be made obligatory along with consideration of German or Italian as a second foreign language. Earl Stanhope, speaking in the House of Lords, justified the teaching of Latin as being *'coeval with the very foundation of these schools, and formed a necessary part of their studies'*.[5] He too though was for a wider curriculum, insisting Eton should teach a foreign language and noting Balston's admission that Eton only taught English through the ancient languages. Both Duff and Stanhope wanted Natural Science taught. Clarendon, speaking in the same debate, offered a primarily literary defence. *'Modern literature is not fully intelligible, except to those who have studied the Classics.'* [6] He did though allow, rather less guardedly than had been done in the report, that boys who showed little aptitude for the Classics should be able to study other subjects while aiming a blow at Eton for having *'obstinately refused'* to teach French.[7] The Chancellor of the Exchequer, Sir Stafford Northcote, was against any Parliamentary interference in the management of the schools but proposed another commission to consult with Governing Bodies in order to revise the Statutes and abolish unwanted restrictions.[8]

H.E. Luxmoore, writing in The Quarterly Review, held strongly conservative views. He saw Eton as starting off with the handicap of having boys arriving with *'habits of idleness'* formed at Preparatory Schools and as a result knowing little. Consequently, until *'a thorough conviction of the magnitude of the evil'* was understood, and a considerable change had been effected in attitude *'nothing is gained by multiplying the denominations of study, nor is there any room left for a further range of subjects'*. Indeed, the value of Latin as a mental discipline was in danger of being lost if it was suggested to *'a self-willed idler that... he shall in time be allowed to cut and carve his subjects for himself'* . He was against making Mathematics a part of an entrance exam as boys' capacity for mathematical reasoning developed at different rates. Nor without adequate teaching did the subject make a great deal of sense to a lively boy *'who thinks it as absurd to multiply x by y, as to divide class by bible, or multiply candlestick by extinguisher'*. Neither should modern languages play any part in the entrance examination while Natural Science should be introduced *'tentatively and cautiously'*. Yet, while wary as to just where all this might lead – would it be a prelude to the appointment of a 'Minister of Public Instruction'? – he found the report valuable as *'a survey of English education from first to last'*.[9]

A less temperate response came from the Eton bookseller, E.P. Willliams, who questioned whether Clarendon had been impartial. He opposed having a Headmaster drawn from outside Eton, was against any tampering with the Statutes, thought the Commission had no business to be discussing fees, and denied many charges of corruption. On learning, he challenged the Dean of Christ Church's testimony by asserting that Etonians did well enough at Trinity and insisted that more subjects would result in mere superficial learning. In any case, there was a broader test to a good education than scholarship.[10]

The argument that there was little point in talking about a broader curriculum until more boys had got to be in the habit of working satisfactorily accorded with the conservative instinct to delay, and maybe avoid radical change. Many, including some with little connection with the schools, saw proper working habits as the foundation of all else. Thus while he held that the teaching of more Science was desirable the Astronomer-Royal had no wish *'to encourage the breed of Scientific dabblers'*.[11] The argument that boys' heads could only hold so much was aired again, as by Stanhope and Northcote.[12] Then it was said that expanding the teaching hours would cut down time for games. The report had not made much of what with some, such as Browning, was becoming a major cause of concern with the growing participation of masters and hours spent on the field, five or six a day at cricket according to Grant Duff.[13]

Although there were dissenting voices arguing strongly that the Classics had had their day, with the widespread agreement that it should remain the central study, it continued to be the subject most wished to discuss. Consequently debate centred around the relative merits of its aspects: original composition, recitation, translation, and grammar. Original composition could be seen as a stimulating exercise but to others, too much time was spent it. *'It is absurd to expect a boy to compose either prose or verse in a dead language before he has any thoughts to express, or any facility for expressing them, in his own.'* [14] Then while recitation was defended as an excellent way of training the memory others saw little point in it. ' *What is gained by making a boy* say, for example, the Alcestis of Euripedes from beginning to end?'[15] Translation many considered a more worthwhile activity. A need was seen too for a new grammar.

The Edinburgh Review, that long-term critic of the Public Schools, saw a need for a more radical reshaping of the curriculum than that proposed by the report. For it seemed that there were now in existence *'two competing systems of education – one belonging to the Sixteenth Century, the other to the Nineteenth'*. The argument that the Classics should be studied because Latin was in vogue when a school was founded cut no ice. This was merely a historical accident with little relevance to a boy's current needs and certainly couldn't be used to justify *'the expenditure of a large amount of a boy's time, and the waste of a large amount of his energies, in writing bad Greek iambics'*. Altogether there was need to rid the present system of *'mere prejudice, looseness of thought, and mystical fantasies'*. One such it saw as the notion that *'a disagreeable and profitless exercise of the mental powers must be more invigorating than one which is more pleasant'*. Then too the average Classical master was more likely to be *'an unsleeping gerund grinder than a cultivated man'*, and no Kennedy. In fact, *'if timely measures are not taken, we shall have the spectacle of an ignorant gentry at the head of an eduated people'*.[16]

The Westminster Review pointed to the expense of an Etonian education – between £150 and £200 p.a. as compared with the £36 p.a. required of a student at a French lyceum and quoted the report's assertion that *'the expensive school is all the more likely to be a bad school'*. And for this substantial sum he was put to study a subject which many were unable to progress beyond a certain point. In any case, it was fine if you were born with means, planned to go the Bar, or into the Church, but otherwise there would be little profit. Morally too, the Classics were dubious. *'No-one can read them without being instructed and amused and, we must add, not infrequently disgusted and indignant.'* Other subjects should replace them as the principal study. That certain pedagogic attitudes needed to change was suggested by Moberley's denigration of Science in his statement that *'a scientific fact, either as conveyed by a lecturer or as reproduced in examination, is a fact which produces nothing in a boy's mind'*. As to possible remedial action it was doubtful. *'There will certainly be a decent showing of doing something.'* However, *'the tone adopted by the Press, and by our public men, does not lead us to hope for too much'*. It also queried why no mention had been made in the report of Manchester Grammar School.[17] (That seems a bit hard as the Commissioners often went beyond their brief of the nine schools to talk with a few of the more recently founded ones and not infrequently adduced continental examples).

A number of the periodicals noted the improvement in boys' moral standards as testified by the Commissioners and by University witnesses. The Master of Balliol was one who saw *'very marked improvement .... in the moral training and character of the young men'*.[18] Some concerns remained. There was, for example, outrage at the barbarism of senior boys still extant at Westminster, and some controversy as to just how much beating was going on at Eton, but there was general acceptance of the report's line that old abuses had been checked or, where still evident, were in the process of being so, and matters such as fagging and the scope of monitorial powers were aired more calmly than earlier.

Many though were shocked by the revelation of widespread habits of school idleness. Reform though was a tricky matter for the Public Schools with many insisting it had to be internally generated. If not, all could be lost, for the essential character of a Public School could be destroyed. *'If they cannot be reformed from within, they are without hope, for they certainly cannot be reformed from without.'*[19] Then proper attention should be given to the good they were doing, insisted Stafford Northcote, who was satisfied that they were performing well *'the work of rearing the English gentleman'*.[20]

Reform anyway, reflected Trollope, was an awkward business for the English. *'Very slowly, very tenderly do we touch our rotten wood '*.[21]

CHAPTER FIFTEEN : THE PUBLIC SCHOOL ACT 1868

MOST SIGNIFICANTLY, THE PUBLIC SCHOOLS BILL, 1865, ALONG WITH ITS successors, was introduced into the House of Lords and was not to reach the Commons until 1868.[1] No longer as defensive as they had been at the height of the Higgins controversy the Lords found plenty of reasons to object to many aspects of Clarendon's report. A full frontal attack of the kind launched by E.P. Williams was not attempted: the report was seen to be far too meticulously researched for any such direct assault to be credible. Rather the idea was modification and delay – perhaps with the hope that nothing much after all would come of it.

Both the report and the Lords saw the role of the Governing Body as vital, though in rather different ways. In the 1865 bill the new Governing Bodies were to be set up based on the old and inheriting their powers but with the addition of members nominated by the Crown and Oxford and Cambridge.[2] Eton was to have fourteen Fellows (nine honorary), and Winchester eleven (seven honorary).[3] They were all though to have sweeping powers that gave them a say over almost every aspect of school life from deciding how many boys a school should have to which church services should be attended.

There were many objections to the bill. The Universities were unhappy at losing their power to appoint headmasters and to award scholarships. Headmasters objected on the ground of having to work with what would almost inevitably have been a constantly interfering body as opposed to the intermittently occasional intrusion that had been the way with several schools : Harrow's quarterly meetings had often had to be abandoned as inquorate. Then the Governing Bodies themselves were not too happy with the proposed additional appointments.[4]

The Clarendon report had seen deliberations and decisions about the curriculum as a key function. One of the many functions given new Governing Bodies was to decide which subjects were taught. To do this in a manner consonant with progressive educational practice the addition of men with sufficient scientific and literary expertise was proposed. Scientists though were often not welcomed. It was argued, rather unconvincingly, that such a presence could distort the curriculum, as though a lone scientist could bend a bunch of Classicists to his will.[5] Really it reflected the underlining conservative attitude that Classics was the practice of the Upper Classes and Science was an alien and obscurely threatening business: a demeaning one too as it was linked with trade.

When introduced into the Lords there was, as noted earlier, a full debate on educational content. From then on though the focus was entirely on management and Clarendon's wide-reaching educational recommendations were simply ignored. From the first the report had had a lukewarm reception, only three members of the Lords speaking in its favour, and those three being Clarendon, Devon, and Lyttleton.[6]

What to be done about the Foundation Boys was another matter to be settled. The report had suggested that one category of these boys to be encouraged was the sons of distressed gentlefolk. This though was taken up more emphatically in the Lords as by the Bishop of London who saw that it could *'open a means of education at moderate expense for such persons'*.[7] Separate schools might be set up for local youth who'd previously attended.

Eton petitioned against the bill and asked for the setting up of an Executive Commission. This followed the appointment of a Select Committee in May, 1865. The argument was made that the schools needed rather longer to reform themselves. In that they had the support of Lord Derby, Prime Minister, who put it that *'they could not alter in a few months things which had been going on for 300 years'*.[8] Parliament then becoming increasingly occupied by talk of its own reform, there seemed a good chance that the progress of the bill could be indefinitely delayed and that under the cover of this agitation amendments favourable to the schools could be inserted. Merchant Taylors got itself excluded on the ground that it was not an endowed school and the Mercers Company also managed to get St. Paul's withdrawn over the legal status of its endowments, so that the provisions of the bill would relate to only seven schools.[9]

The 1865 bill lapsed at the end of the session as did the successive 1866 and 1867 bills. The 1865 bill was significant in that little changed thereafter.

When it did finally reach the Commons in 1868 different concerns were aired. There was mention of Eton and Winchester's financial dealings. One M.P., Neate, suggested that Eton's surplus funds might be used to set up a university in the North of England.[10] Grant Duff had earlier made a similar suggestion – that of using Eton's endowmnents to fund secondary education in the north.[11] Another M.P., Ayrton, objected to the whole tenor of the bill which seemed to have as its aim solely to *'maintain a kind of fashionable education for the fashionable classes'*.[12] A radical element got the whole business given to a Select Committee.

It seems very probable that, had the bill been first introduced into the Commons, a very different Act might have resulted. As it was, the radical interest in the bill started to make delay seem less of a good idea. After years of prevarication, matters were in the end hurried to a conclusion with W.E. Forster threatening that, unless the Public School bill was expedited, other endowed school legislation would be held up.[13]

The Act of 1868 did not in the end make any specific provision for the government of each school but created a commission to discuss appropriate arrangements for each school. The largely Public School element of this commission the schools found reassuring, as must have been too the substantial Etonian membership of the House of Lords.

Foundation rights were to continue for the time being but to be phased out and replaced by competitive exams. This turned out to be another way of removing local youth which seldom got the early education to enable them to compete for this prize.[14]

There was no definite curricular provision. What was taught was to be left to individual schools. Advocates of Science, Mathematics, and Modern Languages thus faced a continuing struggle to compete for class time with the still dominant Classics. Later Acts extended the time for the settlement of outstanding issues until 1874.[15]

Education in England had never been a level playing field. Some schools taught better, some charged more. What the Clarendon Commission did was to make more explicit the hierarchical nature of secondary education with Eton and the other Clarendon schools at the peak and the technical schools wallowing in the troughs. With the Lords being principally concerned to save Eton from a legislative straightjacket the opportunity for a wider focus on educational issues was lost.

Clarendon found the sequel to the report depressing, objecting to key clauses being struck out of the Bill and seeing no good reason for prevarication. *'If the Government had been in earnest on the subject... there would have been no insurmountable difficulty in passing it last year'*.[16] He died before the slimmed down Act was finally passed. Grant Duff too considered little had been gained from the exercise and that the opportunity to ensure these schools offered a good education had been lost.[17]

Edmond Warre. Circa 1858

CHAPTER SIXTEEN: DEPARTURES

THE WARRE NAME IS STILL VISIBLE TODAY ON BOTTLES OF THE APPROPRIATELY pricy 'Warre's Port', a foundation of the family fortune after extensive vineyards were acquired in the mid-Eighteenth Century.[1] It is remembered at Eton for that of Edmond Warre's long and influential connection with the College.

Put in Vidal's house, he made a rumbustious start by kicking down a wall. For the frail Mrs Vidal this sort of racketing around was more than she could bear and he was moved to Marriott's.[2] He quickly showed though that he had no wish to be one of those Oppidans who drifted idly along but who believed from an early age that life's opportunities had to be made the most of. Never beaten he was *'sent up for good or for play nineteen times'*.[3] The reward for this assiduity was a Newcastle award at the age of seventeen.[4] By then he'd developed a passion for rowing and been elected to Pop.[5]

The list of his rowing triumphs while up at Balliol is so extensive as to suggest little time or interest for anything else. Warre though was always definite that academic work was the top priority and in the weeks preceding 'Greats' gave up rowing, gaining a first to add to his earlier first in Moderations.[6]

A fellow undergraduate observed an aspect of his character which was that of his being *'aggressively moral'*. One of his habitual sayings was that *'black is black and white is white'*, leaving little room for consideration of those trickier moral shadings.[7]

Noticeable too was his energetic participation with causes he deemed worthwhile and he was a forceful presence behind the revival of the Oxford University Royal Volunteer Corps. At that time, 1859, there was mounting alarm at the prospect of a French invasion and Sir Charles Napier, commander of the Baltic Fleet during the Crimean War, travelled around the country warning of imminent danger while Palmerston thought a French invasion could conceivably be attempted with a force conveyed in only a few steamships.[8] The revived Oxford force was given a constitution in Warre's Broad Street rooms. The compulsory commitment was to *'one hour's drill every morning, and every afternoon the practice ground is to be opened up for instruction in musketry'*.[9] Additionally, a musketry course was arranged for the Long Vacation, one of the volunteers for that being Charles Dodgson.[10] Government backing, along with Warre's efforts, overcame the University's earlier opposition to any kind of Volunteer Force, while nationally there were 160,000 civilians in arms.[11]

Like others who eventually found their way back to Eton, he thought himself set for the Bar but returned to the College on a temporary basis. During his summer holiday in the Lake District Marriott had fallen ill, and Thackeray had been put in temporary charge of the house.[12] That that was not a great success would not have come as any great surprise to Brinsley-Richards and his pals though in fairness one should say that he was still a comparatively inexperienced master in his mid-twenties. Warre though was invited to return to sort things out and found himself taking charge of a house *'not far from pandemonium'*.

He was able to restore order through force of personality rather than reliance on the cane. Boys came to think that *'to be talked to seriously by Warre'* was worse than a flogging by the Headmaster for *'he made you feel such an infinitesimal worm'*.[13] His success resulted in the offer of a permanent post which, as he found he enjoyed teaching, he readily accepted. His father provided the funds for a new boarding house to which he gave the motto 'Together', reflecting his suspicion of *'the spirit of emulation'* that could attach to individual ambition and his greater emphasis on collective achievement.[14] He filled it with boys from Balston's house when the latter became a Fellow.

Boys were encouraged to work hard and play hard. Warre himself gave a strenuous lead, not completing a day's work until exercises had been marked in the small hours. Few Warre boys were ever *'ploughed'* in exams.[15] In the house, his notions as to what was fitting verged on the Spartan. Armchairs were banned but he smiled when he found cushioned baths being used as a substitute. The sight of boys engaged in idle chatter he viewed with the same sort of distaste as Arnold but made no attempt to take boys by surprise, tramping heavily along corridors.[16]

In class he was a conscientious if at times rather too discursive master being insistent on how the boys went about their lessons. Each was to have a notebook and quarter the pages in a prescribed manner.[17] Out of class he brought his expertise to the river. No master had previously been involved with the boats and his ready acceptance was acknowledgement of his expertise and of his tactful approach. The Eton Corps was another strong concern. After taking holy orders, he was the only cleric on the Army List.

* * * * *

In 1863, when the Public School Commissioners were still continuing their investigations into their nine selected Public Schools William Johnson was sufficiently confident of his standing at Eton to write in manuscript 'Hints for Eton Masters' though there is some doubt as to whether it was ever circulated. This was highly unusual in that it advocated an uncommon degree of thoughtfulness in dealings with boys. A stammering boy should not be scolded: a boy's work should be looked over in such a way as to make him feel you are giving more than a service: repeatedly giving a boy the same punishment was pointless: and don't bring 'sin' into any of his misdemeanours. Many of his notions were to become part of later educational practice.[18]

He had by this time earned an enduring reputation as an inspiring teacher, one whose authority to formulate such precepts rested on acknowledged excellence as a Classical scholar as compared with one or two contemporaries who were thought to have shallower claims to scholarship. His presence and manner were though what left enduring impressions. *'Nothing that he taught could ever, for a moment, be dull, while he taught it'*, reflected Herbert Paul in later years.[19] To Reginald Brett it seemed that *'Johnson's sway…created a spirit that stole into every nook and cranny of Eton, unrecognised but none the less powerful'*.[20] Arthur Coleridge, an Etonian Classicist, told Brett's father that Johnson was the wisest master who had ever been at Eton.[21] Other colleagues valued his *'sage, epigrammatic and fascinating talk'*.[22] Not all though regarded him affectionately for his cutting tongue, evident in and out of the classroom, made him enemies.

Holidays Johnson filled with varied activities. Weeks were spent at Halsdon, the substantial Devon house inherited by his brother and rented from him. This he used for reading parties of Eton boys and as a base for exploratory Devon rambles. On one such jaunt, he and H.E. Luxmoore, a young Eton master, walked across Dartmoor, crossed the Taw near its source, and came upon three nearly parallel streams *'with beautiful deep, ferny, heathery banks'*.[23] At other times he ranged more widely. At Glasgow en route to Ireland he bought a compass to be sure of his bearings, noticed well-dressed maidens waiting to be hired as servants, saw two shoeless boys quarrelling over a game, then set sail down the Clyde. Another Irish trip was occasion for angling with his brother, again to marvel at natural beauty, *'scenery in full dress'*.[24] In northern parts he noted the chattery native pride of two ladies as the stagecoach in which all were travelling crossed the boundary from Lancashire to their Cumbrian homeland, while at St. Andrews he was struck by the purposefulness of the undergraduates, in contrast to the indifference to academic result too often shown by many Oxford and Cambridge men.

There were social spells, many with an Etonian connection. He stayed with the Gladstone's at their Dumfries house where he advised on the education of son John, was enchanted by the singing of a daughter, but reflected just how regrettably scanty her education seemed to be.[25] Time was spent too at Hickleton, home of Sir Charles Wood, at that time Secretary of State for India, whose two boys, Charles and Frederick, were at Eton.[26] Elsewhere he was welcome for his talk and for being able to arrive without the encumbrance of a wife. In Rome with *'the budding bibliophile'* Dalmeny, the future Earl of Rosebery, they hunted for books having to do with his Primrose ancestors, strolled through its antiquities before Dalmeny was despatched to meet the Pope, *'the old woman of Rome'*.[27] Frances Elliott, whose parents were overseas, was another boy with whom Johnson spent a good deal of holiday time. A diary entry records their presence at the Hotel Univers in Tours where *'in the armchair by my side sits a lad of seventeen, with lightish hair and a grey coat, reading Cranford, waiting till the shower passes'*.[28]

He frequently returned to King's, being given the 'noble' room to which he was entitled and spending hours in agreeable conversation which touched on, among other things, Tennyson, Newman's Apologia, and Pilgrim's Progress, the latter *'wretched stuff'* in Johnson's view. Henry Bradshaw, the popular University Librarian, was once met in a state of high excitement having just come across a copy of 'Alice in Wonderland' parts of which he insisted on reading aloud.[29]

* * * * *

William Johnson's time at Eton came to an abrupt end during the Easter half of 1872. *'One day he was with us, and the next he was not.'* [30] That was the start of *'a deep and mysterious silence'* [31] and to speculation as to what had taken place that brought about such a sudden departure and which has never been resolved. Johnson liked to suggest that his immediate resignation had been his idea. Back at Halsdon he wrote to a friend that *'I am gone ... I have just resigned'*, adding that *'I could hardly have lived through the summer half, knowing all the while it was to be my last'.*[32]

The facts though suggest that he did not have such latitude. He left in such haste as to leave behind almost all his belongings in his lodging known as 'the Trap' and these were later recovered for him by Reginald Brett, then up at Trinity College, Cambridge, and extremely solicitous on his behalf.

The generally acknowledged cause was a letter from a parent though what it contained is surmise. A probable explanation is that one of the over-affectionate letters that Johnson was wont to write to boys in his immediate circle had fallen into a parent's hands and aroused deep suspicion.

At any event, it was apparently a letter that Dr. Hornby, Eton's Headmaster, *'dared not ignore'*. Others doubted whether it should necessarily have led to Johnson's departure and that *'under a wise and strong Headmaster so great a loss to the school might have been averted'.*[33]

It was not unknown for masters to devote more attention to some boys than others, to the extent of forming like-minded coteries. A master with real Classical enthusiasms was more likely to wish to spend time with boys who shared that passion rather than with those lacking any interest and with any academic successes conferring a sense of achievement. Increasingly in the second half of the century masters with keen athletic interests sought out those with some sporting talent. That Johnson's relations with some of his chosen boys had though reached an undesirable level of intensity was strongly suspected and his letters to boys and diary entries show a strong romantic attachment. That was combined with a shrewd insight into their personalities.

Of Dalmeny he wrote that he had *'the finest combination of qualities I have ever seen ... I am doing all I can to make him an orator, and if not a poet, such a man as poets will delight in'*[34] though at the same time suspecting limited wish for involvement in the hurly-burly of life by saying that he wanted *'the palm without the dust'*. On occasion though his tone could be more like that of a jilted lover. *'You cut me for four days,'* he wrote to Dalmeny, and consequently that *'I have been unhappy for a week without you'*. Things were put right though when *'you came in and began to romp'.*[35] None got higher praise than Frances Elliott. *'The more I think of him the more sure I am that his Eton life has been unique, incomparable, a spring of happiness, and he himself the flame of boyhood, the glory of Eton, the ideal and quintessence of virtue.'* [36] And more. *'I envy you being kissed by him,'* he wrote to Brett. *'I kissed his dear foot last Tuesday on the grass at Ankerwyke'*.[37] Of Frederick Wood he later wrote that *'his mind is in beautiful order, a fair product of education and inheritance'* while he assured Reginald Brett that *'mentally I kiss your dear face and throat'*.[39] There were emotionally charged friendships among some of these boys. Charles Williamson (known as Chat for his talkative ways) seemed to possess a particular allure. Brett described the evening before his departure from Eton when he and Chat lay together on the sofa. *'My head has just left his shoulder, my lips his hair, my hand from clasping his, and so the last evening is passing, the last for ever in these relations, in the free love of so many days.'* [40] The infatuation persisted after Brett left when meeting up again at Halsdon. *'Chat is young as ever; bright as ever and brilliant. Gay, original, perfectly rapturously lovely'*.[41] It may be that being indulged by fond parents and almost fetished at Eton did Williamson little good for, unlike the high achievers most of Johnson's circle went on to become, he made little of himself, converting to Rome and then finding he had no vocation, becoming in later life occasionally reliant on Brett for his subsistence. Whether or not he participated, Johnson was clearly present at some of these amours as he made clear in a journal entry of 1868. *'I have seen young lovers interlacing like honeysuckle, rose and jessamine, romantic chivalrous friendships forming under my eye, to which I am almost admitted as a partner.'* [42]

* * * * *

Assuming, as I think we must, that the letter from a parent concerned Johnson's relations with a boy, it could hardly have come at a worse time for him.

Early in 1872 a boy called Probyn had been expelled along with four of his over enthusiastic admirers. Then a number of choristers had been found to have been carrying on clandestine affairs. Another boy, Reggie Herbert, faced uncomfortable questioning after the discovery of a foolish letter written to a contemporary. [43] School authorities seem to have been little concerned with homosexuality earlier in the century. Doubt arises from the coded way in which this was written about, even long after 1869 when the term was first coined. It could have been an aspect of bullying or *'viciousness'*. It was clearly though not a major concern. Masters habitually were more concerned with such matters as stopping their boys drinking, gambling, chasing loose girls, and, though often rather half-heartedly, to get slackers to do some work. Sex though later became a serious matter, obsession almost in some schools, and some eccentric supposedly preventative measures were tried. The Clifton Head, Percival, thought that boys seeing each others knees when dressed in sporting attire was far too exciting and had them wear kit that covered them : for which bizarre act he got the merited sobriquet of 'Knees Percival'.[44] Or the remedy could be drastic. In 1892 Brighton College closed down an entire house thought to be incorrigibly infected with this virus.[45]

In a letter to Brett, Johnson seemed to be acknowledging that he was out of tune with many at Eton when he wrote: *'How little do the wiseacres know that this sentiment (love) is part of the staple of life at a school.'* [46] Few masters wished to be associated with such sentiment, among them some piqued by Johnson's asperity. Nor had he always endeared himself to parents with the candour with which he categorised a boy's idle ways in class.

Yet if he was to be dismissed, that was now an undisputed function of the Headmaster. For the Public Schools Act of 1868 had made it clear that he had this previously rather uncertain power. It seems probable too that Warre had a considerable say in what happened. For Hornby had a reputation as something of a hermit and Warre seems to have been his only close confidant. They'd been long time friends with a number of shared interests, particularly sport. During the comparatively short time he'd been at Eton Warre had made such a considerable mark that there had even been talk of his succeeding Balston. Then whereas Hornby was often irresolute it was, in Provost Okes's view, *'Warre's strong and resolute will that gave just the backing that the more placid Head required'*.[47]

Eton subsequently made a Soviet-like attempt to erase all memory of Johnson from the collective consciousness. His name was removed from copies of the text books he'd written though the books themselves went on being used for decades afterwards. Johnson too acted with equal finality. He changed his name by deed poll to 'Cory' and resigned his King's Fellowship, though urged by a number of Fellows not to do so.

Such formal gestures though could not obliterate or transform the past. Eton went on singing its 'Boating Song' which he wrote, he said, with thoughts of Etonians in such distant places as Indian hill-forts and which Rosebery gave orders was to be played on his death-bed, as indeed it was.[48] Johnson went off to Halsdon with photographs of the boys whose company he'd cherished and had a number of them to stay at Halsdon, much to Eton's displeasure.

'And when I may no longer live,
They'll say , who know the truth,
He gave whate'er he had to give
To freedom and to youth.' [49]
(from 'Academus' 1858)

* * * * *

"Damn," remarked Oscar Browning, while gazing out of his King's window and hearing the news shouted up from below that he'd come fourth in the Classical tripos. As the three above him had all been bracketed equal first that meant he'd narrowly failed to gain the highest honour.[50] His sparsely documented time at King's suggests that, though he kept up his reading, averaging about four hours a day, in the course of it becoming strongly influenced by the humanitarian philosophy of John Stuart Mill, he seems to have shown more enthusiasm for speaking. To the chagrin of his fellow Etonian scholars, he took to speaking at the Union, after a while becoming its President.[51] Unsure what to do after King's, he had thoughts of the Bar, an ambition which was to stay with him for a good while even after going back to Eton. The invitation to return came from the Headmaster, Dr. Goodford, while he was teaching briefly at Liverpool, and back he went.[52] The year, 1860, was, coincidentally, that also of Warre's return.

Anyone who accepts a post at an institution and then makes clear he has a strong desire to alter much within it must expect a rocky ride and one ending triumphantly if rewarded with success or an uncertain future if not. So it was to be with Browning who saw himself very much up against Eton's Old School. Yet looking at what he did it seems not so much that he had a radical programme for reform but rather more that he had an insistence on doing things his own way.

He had no wish to lessen the predominance of the Classics but saw its prime value as an educationally humanitarian influence, seeing them as *'the bedrock of morality, citizenship, culture'* [53] and wished less time spent on such drier aspects as Grammar and saying lessons. Yet it was also essential for the future statesmen and men of affairs as he saw many Etonians becoming that they also acquired a knowledge of foreign languages and modern history. There should be a place for English culture too and he started getting boys to learn verse by heart though that brought him a reproving note from the Headmaster. He had little sympathy with those who pointed to Scientific ignorance. *'All Science consisted in looking through a very small hole for a very long time.'* [54] Mathematics had even less appeal. He was though very much a pragmatist, prepared to adopt other contradictory ideas if that seemed a better way. So although he had the deepest misgivings about Science, he would rather a boy who could get little or nothing from the Classics should have a go at Science rather than leave Eton without any kind of academic interest. *'No boy is stupid'*, was one of his pronouncements from which came the conclusion that effort was needed to find out what boys could be good at rather than invariably imposing on them, and then judging them by, a uniform series of requirements. He was to do more than talk about such ideas, equipping his Eton house at his own expense with the necessary apparatus for boys to study Science.[55]

That required a good deal of talking to boys and here too he was unusual in that he liked engaging boys in serious discussions, perhaps to some extent mimicking those he'd had at Cambridge with the likes of Arthur Sidgwick and Richard Jebb, and to sustain a tone with them that was more conversational than hectoring. That he much preferred to the marking of exercises, not being one of those Eton masters who sat up half the night doing so.

That was part of a wider cultural engagement he had with the boys in his house which he ran co-operatively with his formidable mother and sister, Malvina. He had no truck with Warre's Spartan notions, wanting boys early on to get a taste for artistic excellence. To this end he had works of art on the walls, Morris curtains framing the windows, and bronzes, marbles and plaster casts in the corridors. He occasionally turned the dining room into a theatre for boy productions, had a house debating society, and started up an inter-house singing competition. Sometimes London professionals came to give concerts while he encouraged an interest in little known composers such as Brahms.[56]

He showed concern for their material welfare too. Mindful of his experience of the inadequate College diet he was particular in seeing that his boys were well fed. He also employed an unusually high number of servants which meant that fagging was cut to a minimum. These developments were not greatly welcomed by those other housemasters who served up more meagre fare and faced critical comparison.

On one matter he was not prepared to consider alternative views and that was games, or more particularly masters' participation in the conduct of them. He was himself an enthusiastic athlete, regularly swimming, tricycling around the country and being one of the earliest members of the Alpine Club while at Eton he would join in games of football with the boys in his house. But he saw it as a delinquent tendency in a master to become associated with the running of games. That was no part of their role. *'Boys will always admire the body. It is the duty of the schoolmaster to make them admire the mind.'*[57] He felt so strongly about it that most of his two-hundred page submission to the Public School Commisioners elaborated his protest. [58]

Here though he was battling in vain against the growing athletic cult which became almost obsessive in some quarters, its preoccupations even entering clerical discourse, to the extent that Ince, sub-rector of Exeter College, remonstrated with his under-achieving rowers by informing them that their lack of success was displeasing to God.[59]

The Public School Comissioners expressed some concern that games should not become an over-riding preoccupation and were generally supportive of existing practices but weren't unduly exercised about the matter. In other ways though their views chimed with Browning's. Modern Languages should be a part of the curriculum. Less time should be spent on learning of Latin and Greek poets by rote. Pupil room construing prior to Division lessons should be ended. Chapel services were criticised. On another matter, Browning supported their view that a Headmaster should have unfettered power in the selection and dismissal of masters, an opinion he later had good cause to rue.[60]

A good deal seemed to be going Browning's way. Of the subjects added to the curriculum in the wake of the Clarendon Report his Modern History classes which covered excitingly radical events such as The French Revolution were the most popular. He'd shown it was quite possible to successfully run a house without being fiercely authoritarian and here he stood in some contrast to Warre. *"Good Lord, how that man frightens me,"* a Lower boy is thought to have said of him. That would not have been said of Browning whose kindness sometimes overcame sterner demands. One boy, A.C. Trench, after sculling hurried back for absence but found time for a quick glass of beer at The Tap. Coming out he ran into Browning's arms and was invited to see him the following morning.

"I suppose you know the penalty?"

"Yes, but I think it is very hard. I had been rowing for more than two hours, and I had one small glass of beer for which I shall be swished."

"You are quite right. Go away and don't run into a master again when you come out." [61]

Life at Eton had its rewards. Despite the liberality with which he treated the boys in his house he had ample funds for a good deal else. He was able to spend £300 a year on his library, maintain a fine wine cellar, and travel extensively with a servant during the holidays. Yet he was sometimes restless, wondering whether he might not have made more of himself at the Bar and unsure whether he wanted to remain at Eton for the rest of his working life as so many Eton masters did. Circumstances were to ensure that he wouldn't.

*****

Browning's breezy, often off-hand ways with colleagues were always likely to be irritating. When a boy was transferred from Marriott's house to Browning's it was seen as a case of 'filching' and Marriott was sufficiently exercised by the matter to write him four letters in two days about the matter.[62] Wolley-Dod understandably complained at Browning's boys firing catapults from their windows at his opposite house, bombarding the drawing room windows and breaking panes in the greenhouse. Browning not seeming able to stop this he reported it to Hornby.[63] Warre and Browning quickly appreciated that they had markedly different approaches to the business of schoolmastering, particularly over the place of athletics and corresponded about their often opposing views mixing the general and the personal. Warre on one occasion wrote that *'you are so satisfied with your own opinions as to make it appear in voice and manner that you hold in contempt all who differ from you'*. On a later occasion, after a *'pleasant walk together'* Warre expressed their divergence in broader terms writing that he preferred *'liberty and think that fraternity is best preserved when that liberty is respected and recognised by all, and that equality though not seen at present will come in the long run and cannot be established by enactment. You, on the other hand .... '* He concluded though with the concession that *'I certainly see your drift now, which I did not before'* . The correspondence was candid but not altogether unfriendly.[64]

Relations with Hornby began well enough with Browning writing to Henry Sidgwick that he *'promises to be a great success. We shall now be governed on the principles that universally obtain in human society'.*[65] The two were in agreement on the reform of the Classics, Hornby even taking his side against Warre whose pamphlet on the subject was deemed *'very shallow'* while being given charge of the history teaching had most effectively broadened Browning's scope. His opinions on school matters were welcomed, even his views on staff appointments.

That though didn't last long. Hornby began to judge that Browning was not inculcating the exactness of Classical discipline that he wished for and Browning's letters, often with some criticism of others, became an irritant. How could he possibly find time for such reading if all forty-four of his Assistants wrote him so many long letters? [66] Then there was a more general suspicion that Browning's mind was not altogether on his Eton work. How could it be when he was often at concerts and private views in London, externally examined, lectured on Italian literature, attended George Eliot's salon and found time for London's other political and social interests.

Hornby's time at Eton was marked by a number of controversies which semed mundane, even footling in origin, but because of the interplay of personality, came to assume a portentous aspect. One such was the question of boarding house fees. Masters approached the Governing Body for an increase to keep up with the cost of living but this was refused. Hornby then on his own authority sent out a demand for an additional four pounds a term. Unsurprisingly the Governing Body took a dim view of this and censured him. Awkwardly, the fuss reached The Times and letters appeared expressing parental indignation at the increase.

Later an increase of six pounds was sanctioned. Browning on this occasion suported Hornby, drawing up a draft memorial in his favour. The unwise, rash decision to ignore the Governing Body rather than seek some accommodation with them seemed prompted in part by exasperation with the constant interference of Provost Goodford.[67]

Browning's memorial, signed by some but not all staff, was appreciated by Hornby but it was not long before suspicions returned. Doubts as to whether Browning was really keeping on top of his Division work, and doing so in an approved manner, prompted Hornby to ask for all the exercises from the Divisions to be collected with the freely admitted intent of catching Browning out. They were returned with the comment that they had not been corrected, Browning responding that they would have been had they not been taken away.[68]

Something of a crisis developed over Browning's History teaching. This acquired a considerable reputation with masters from other schools such as Farrar at Marlborough and Bowen at Harrow wanting to learn more of his method.[69] It didn't though appeal to Hornby who preferred the subject matter taken from the distant past rather than from the reign of Queen Anne or The French Revolution under cover of which he suspected Browning of postulating radical notions. Above all, nothing recently added to the curriculum should be allowed to diminish the sway of the Classics. To remedy this, Hornby considered appointing a specialist History teacher, thus ending Browning's part in it. This prompted a most forceful, lengthy response from A.C. Ainger who wrote to Hornby that *'a rumour has reached us that you intend to make a change in the history teaching by appointing a special master for the purpose of what has hitherto been done by Browning….. It would be most improbable that the teacher would approach the present teacher either in historical attainments, power of imparting knowledge, or influence over the boys forming the class. That seems so obvious to so many us who have had pupils in Browning's History class …. Nothing of late years has been more successful'*. He ended with a strong encomium. *'We younger masters here ….. feel that we cannot do better than follow the example Browning has set us …. for he is by far your most valuable Assistant'*.[70] Hornby ignored this, informing Browning that he would shortly be replaced, the idea only being withdrawn with bad grace after protest from a number of other masters, but not before Browning, deeply offended, had contemplated leaving Eton.

A different but serious dispute was occasioned by another complaint fom Wolley-Dod to the Headmaster. This concerned George Nathaniel Curzon, a bright young boy in his house who had been getting what he deemed undue attention from Browning of a kind likely in his opinion to make him vain and spoilt. Browning had given himself the moral scope to deal with boys in houses other than his own should he see benefit in so doing. His rationale for this was that as it was common practice for masters to take an interest in boys from various houses for sporting purposes there was no reason why he should not do the same to promote intellectual and literary interests in those in whom he sawsome promising inclination. Wolley-Dod's three accusations were answered. Objections had been taken to his sending a letter to Curzon in the post ; an invitation to breakfast had been unintentionally posted: to his taking Curzon out for drives without leave ; leave had been given at a time when Curzon was incapacitated after getting a cricket ball in the eye : he had been helped with his iambics ; once only, and little aid.

Hornby sent for Browning and his opening mark seemed to show that he'd been listening to wagging tongues.

"So I hear Mr. Wolley-Dod has a good-looking pupil."

"Do you mean to say," was Browning's retort, "that you have allowed any master to tell you that I took notice of a boy because he was good looking?"

"I don't know, I'm sure," was the unenlightening response.[71]

Wolley-Dods subsequently wrote to Browning saying that he hadn't meant to give Hornby the impression he seemed to have got but Hornby clearly by now had a conviction that Browning was a malign influence. An increasingly brittle correspondence which had the Headmaster initially writing that he did not *'wish to impute any motives to you, only to point out that in a Public School appearances must be taken into account"* moved on to his prohibiting any further contact with Curzon and behaving more discreetly with other boys.[72]

Some of Browning's friends advised against giving any assurance of the kind Hornby was seeking. Probing, Hornby was asked if that even meant he could not greet Curzon in the street. No, was the response. There was to be no contact of any kind. Browning suggested getting the view of Curzon's father, Lord Scarsdale. That was rejected as inappropriate.

Browning then acted extremely unwisely by writing to Wolley-Dod, in a letter marked 'Private' to see if he would permit Curzon coming to tea. This though was sent directly to the Head and confirmed him in his belief that Browning was not only malign but untrustworthy. It may have marked the moment at which Hornby resolved on getting either Browning's resignation or his dismissal. Browning considered resignation but to do so in such circumstances would be awkwardly unpleasant. Curzon, greatly affronted when he found himself argued over in this way, had little doubt whose side he was on.[73] *'I can't say,'* he wrote to Browning, *'how distressed I am to think that I am prevented from seeing you, and all through the unkind, ungentlemanly and obstinate conduct of my tutor, whom I detest the more I see him.'* However, he concluded, there could be nothing to stop them seeing each other during the holidays, something which Scarsdale was happy enough with.[74] A friendship between the two lasted for the next fifty years with the future Viceroy once telling his wife that *'whatever I am, I owe it all to Mr. Browning'*.[75]

This business was not though, as sometimes assumed, the immediate cause of Browning's departure from Eton, though that, and Hornby's other accumulated grievances provided the context. More causes of complaint were found. The boarding fee of a boy had been unpaid as Browning thought he'd left, but forgotten about once he returned and a demand was made that the money be paid in to the bank *'without further delay or evasion'*. Then Browning was reproved for missing his classes by going up to London for a meeting about the Hawtrey memorial though his rejoinder was that as his lessons had been taken by the Mathematical master on that day he had not missed any class time at all. Even Wolley-Dod, very much Browning's nemesis, could only see a sort of *'monomania'* in Hornby's attitude.[76]

The last act in this drama arose over what would normally have been only a routine matter, resolved without difficulty. But heightened emotion brought every rift to a crisis. The point at issue here was that of boarding house numbers. Housemasters were allowed to have forty boys though that could be forty-three with permission. Browning's house was one of those found to have too many. Here was ammunition for Hornby. Browning was asked to *'state at once in writing'* whether he was prepared to comply with the regulation.[77] The Governing Body made clear it would not sanction an increase in numbers from masters who asked for retrospective permission to do so. So matters stood as Browning went off for his summer holidays.

Returning he was still unhappy at the loss of income by his having three vacant rooms and went to see Hornby about it. The conversation seems to have begun quite amicably with chat about the holidays but when the question of the forty limit was raised Hornby suddenly lost his temper.

'You are the greatest shuffler I have ever met. You shuffle in everything you do. Your character is known to the Governing Body. You neglect your work. Why don't you read Madvig's Latin Grammar? You lecture to ladies; you examine here and there; you give musical parties on Saturday evenings. Why don't you stick to your work? No-one ever treated me in a straightforward manner who did not find me straightforward.'

Browning's protestation that he had always been candid produced an explosion. *'Why, you are a liar,'* charged Hornby, now white with rage. *'You told me a lie two years ago. I wish I had dismissed you for it then.'* Suggesting that Hornby make complaint to the Governing Body, Browning then made to leave but was called back. The affair of the bills was revived, Hornby then saying that there could be no further relations between them. Browning countered with a refusal to resign and complained of the *'constant persecution'* he'd met with from Hornby. Over the matter of boarding numbers Browning felt particularly aggrieved that other transgressing masters had not been called to account in the same way.

After this stormy scene the two then talked in more measured tones about Browning's three Collegers who had also been a related issue. Browning had wanted to give them up but was told: *'if you do that I shall dismiss you. No, you shall not give them up.'* Hornby then laid down restrictions on the hours at which the three could go out in the evening to counter what he saw as the habits of idleness inculcated by Browning. The interview ended in a calmer mode.[78] Barely two hours later Hornby wrote to James, another housemaster, giving him permission to do just what he'd hotly denied Browning.

That, Browning must have thought, was that, at any rate for the time being. But no. The next day a letter arrived informing him that *'I've carried forbearance, in your case, beyond the limit which I ought to have observed in strict duty to the school ..... and after our conversation of yesterday, it is not possible for me to feel that confidence in you which is absolutely necessary to our working together ..... I must therefore give you notice that your mastership will terminate at the end of this school-time'*.[79]

News of this shock Browning shared with only a few friends for a while, getting messages of sympathy and support. A question was raised as to whether Hornby had the authority to do this. For while the Public Schools Act of 1868 had explicitly given a Head that power, whether it could apply to someone like Browning, appointed before it became embedded in Eton's 1871 statutes, was debatable.[80] In October Browning wrote to all masters, putting them in the picture. The ensuing agitation resulted in the calling of a masters' meeting to see what should be done.

There were those, headed by Warre, who were less favourable to Browning's cause, and they got a postponement of the meeting for a day. Ardour cooled somewhat during this interval and in the end they settled for sending Hornby a letter deploring his action.[81] While there were a number of masters happy to see the back of the irascible Browning, others saw his loss as a self-inflicted deprivation. Views were made clear outside the College too. Arriving for lecture at Eton, Ruskin showed Browning an ostentatious friendliness.[82]

Knatchbull-Hugessen, a person of some substance, being Chairman of the South-Eastern Railway, and M.P., who had marginally been involved in the numbers row by having a son enter Browning's house just then, took it upon himself to find out just what had happened. On the boy's admission to Browning's house, Hornby had given no sense that his tenure was about to cease, so, unless Hornby had been particularly obtuse, something must have happened in the intervening ten days. What was it? The response that *'any impartial person who knew the facts'* would approve his action brought the rejoinder that those were what no-one seemed to know. Just what was it that Browning had done in these ten days to merit dismissal? Hornby backtracked after that conceding that his actions had been based on *'moral disapprobation'*. To which Knatchbull-

Hugessen responded that others without Hornby's prejudice might have taken quite a different view of the case. Going further, he threatened to raise the matter in the House of Commons as an amendment to the Public Schools Act 21. *'All this could do no good to Eton and would be very disagreeable'*. Hornby's riposte that *'if Browning and his friends really think there was anything frightful which needs disclosure, they should not desire to have it made'*, was deemed nonsensical. For without some enlightenment on Hornby's part no-one could judge whether or not there was *'anything frightful'* behind all this.[83]

That left only an appeal to the Governing Body which asked Hornby for an account of his actions and then drew up a statement which Browning was not permitted to see.[84] The whole business then entered Press comment with the papers taking sides. Behind the Press debate there was also a good deal of gossip, the ostensible reason for Browning's dismissal seeming so trivial as to suggest rather more lay behind it. His friends thought one way of disproving such tittle-tattle was for Browning to be given a pension and, though this had the unanimous support of the masters, was curtly rejected by Hornby.[85]

* * * * *

Eton was in an unsettled mood in the years after the publication of the Clarendon report. The Old School was unhappy at some of the admissions and criticisms made by younger colleagues and contained in it. The febrile artmosphere was fertile ground for factionalism, very much evident in the downfall of Browning. An assured Headmaster with an outgoing personality might have drawn the sting from such discontents by being accommodating and impartial in his dealings.

Hornby though was not such a man. For some years after his appointment he'd been unhappy with the close attention given to his performance by Provost Goodford. He, having for many years having had Hawtrey breathing down his neck was disinclined to adopt a more distant role himself. This may well have come as a most unwelcome shock to Hornby. The Public Schools Commission report had given a distinct sense of a more distant relationship at Winchester between Warden and Headmaster than Eton's equivalent pair, of matters not discussed for a while but of a confidence that they could be amicably dealt with should need arise. As former Second Master, Hornby must have known this. His relationship with Goodford reached a point at which he protested against constant interference, a protest which had been supported by Browning. By 1875 though, when the Browning affair erupted, matters were a good deal improved. During these years however he had not helped himself to take a firm grip on Eton's business by failing to get to grips with much of the detail of its daily routines. Then his unhappy domestic circumstances may have had something to do with his tetchinesss.

Whereas a parental complaint seems to have triggered Johnson's demise, opposite forces were aroused by Browning's treatment. Anyone going about their work in radically unexpected ways is bound to incur some doubt and this Browning did. Fitzjames Stephen, whose son was in Browning's house, had heard a rumour that Browning had lent a boy a copy of Gautier's 'Mlle De Maupin', which he averred was *'nothing more than a mass of obscenity'* and could Browning assure him that was false. It turned out to be a baseless story that had emerged from drawing room gossip but was nevertheless indicative of a certain mistrust.[86] That though was more than outweighed by the reputation of Browning and his house with some parents even putting their sons down for it at birth. The news that it was to cease was not well received. Lord Portsmouth, with three sons in his house, threatened to lead a delegation of parents in procession over Windsor bridge to confront the Headmaster. This did not though happen and instead a petition was sent asking Hornby to change his mind. That however left him unmoved. Parents were then forced to look ahead and to accept that unless they could get their sons into another house their Eton schooling might come to an end and to realise that excessive agitation on Browning's behalf might not help them to do that.[87]

For a while Browning thought of legal action. Advice of friends and his own lack of money dissuaded him from that course. Knatchbull-Hugessen did raise the issue in the House of Commons in the form of a proposed amendment to the part of the Public Schools Act giving Headmasters an uncontested right of dismissing masters but it was not put to a vote. Browning had to accept that the breach was final.[88]

He never let go of the bitterness he felt about his dismissal. Though he did later have a civil meeting with Hornby he wrote to a former colleague in 1920 that he had *'never in my life met a man of more despicable and contemptible a character'*. Hornby had had a potent ally for *'Warre, who was the real cause of my dismissal, continued his vindictive jealousy till the day of his death'*.[89]

Unlike Johnson, who had promptly resigned his King's Fellowship, Browning took up permanent residence and was to remain there until 1908.

INSPECTION THREATENS THE VICTORIAN PUBLIC SCHOOL

James John Hornby: Eton Headmaster and Provost

William Cory with Rosa and Andrew in Madeira

CHAPTER SEVENTEEN : AFTER LIVES

Though the most substantial man in his Halsdon neighbourhood, William Cory, as he's best referred to from now on, was never going to impose himself. He was too shy for that. He did though get to know the villagers by giving them lifts in his cart, taking them flowers and herbs, and wishing that he could give them music. All of which made him well liked. At a more formal level he became a J.P. and endured hours of sewage and sanitation on the Torrington bench.

Practical work around the house occupied him a good deal, presumably as he wished it so, for he had a gardener. There were such routine tasks as weeding, hacking at brambles, and pumping. Husbandry was carried on in a rather idiosyncratic manner with hens on the front lawn, grooming of pigs, tame goats being permitted to jump up and knock him down, and lavish attention to his favourite donkey, Grizel, often used for taking panniers of sand to the spot where a new path was being made. A more substantial project was for the widening and levelling of a road out of the estate which involved the demolition of a high bank reducing it from 1:7 to 1:10, though oddly only for the convenience of walkers. He seems to have inherited something of his father's enthusiasm for road works.[1]

There was one assurance to his life at Halsdon. *'I am rich enough to live here, quietly, but so as to receive guests staying here'*.[2] These guests were numerous. If, as rumoured, Eton disapproved of its boys going to Halsdon it was singularly ineffective. Frederick Wood was invited to stay at *'the prettiest place in the world'*.[3] The intermittently communicative Francis Elliott, by then in the diplomatic service, turned up after a damp six mile walk.[4] The Lyttleton brothers, Albert Grey, Reginald Brett, Charles Williamson (Chat), Edward Bickersteth,[5] and, of an earlier generation, A.D. Coleridge, were among his guests. Three former colleagues, Ainger, Luxmoore, and Stone also came to stay.[6]

Some of these relationships were still intense, especially that with the '*extremely sweet, gay, sage, cosy*' 7 Chat who'd made himself enough at home at Halsdon to have a boat there. It was though to end unhappily. Cory took Chat and his friend Edward Bickersteth on an Alpine holiday in the course of which Bickersteth contracted a seemingly minor illness but which killed him. The doctor assured Cory that he was in no way to blame but the incident long haunted him.8 Troubling too was the break with Chat. Having decided against the military future which his parents had had in mind, he saw his future within the Catholic Church and joined the Oratory of St. Philip of Neri. After this he concluded that future relations with Cory would be inappropriate and sent him a formal note saying so. Though there was a brief spurt of jealousy when he heard he was still in touch with Brett, Cory accepted the change and cleared out his belongings such as photographs, writings, shirt and dressing gown but kept a locket which had Chat's and Bickerstheth's intertwined hair.9

* * * * *

The six years Cory spent at Halsdon were largely congenial. Beyond estate occupations the Devon countryside had endless charms and there were visits abroad. Travelling to Egypt, he left Brett and Grey behind at Halsdon to carry out some practical work and follow a prescribed course of philosophy and history, but then found himself thrown around by a four-hour hurricane in the Bay of Biscay, the situation made more dire by a broken tiller. The storm over, Cory, at the urging of fellow passengers wrote a letter of thanks to the captain, praising his seamanship for preserving them. Ashore, he took a dislike to Cairo but joined Lady Winchilsea and her two sons for a trip down the Nile.[10] On other occasions he travelled widely in the Middle East but strangely never got to Greece despite his expressed longing to meet real Greeks. France though was his favourite destination.

'*Love of France is my ruling passion now.*' he wrote.[11] Particularly attractive was the French ideal of liberty which he saw as bound up with its republicanism and suggested it might be a good thing if the British monarchy passed away after Victoria's death. While at Eton he'd been a fervent supporter of Victoria, reacting sharply if he heard adverse comment, he was now sufficiently disillusioned with her to suggest that she might be more appropriately gazetted as Mrs Brown.

At times though he felt the lack of any real intellectual stimulus. He was a man of opinions, often controversial, which he relished brandishing in argument. There was, for example, his view that quite a few of Shakespeare's plays were no more than *'his make-shifts, his fill-up, his shoddy'*. Some of these could not be compared with 'The Tempest' or 'Julius Caesar', both truly noble works.[12] In general *'as a poet Shakespeare moves me, as a dramatist less'*. Tennyson's play, 'Queen Mary', though it had its merits, and Irving in the cast when he saw it, suffered from not having a fine character in its script.

Of Jane Austen's works, he rated highly only 'Persuasion' while the then fashionable George Eliot, despite being *'a very noble, wise, sublime writer'* did not infuse her characters with human warmth. George Meredith though he held in the highest regard, *'the greatest genius we have next to Tennyson'*, and far superior to Thackeray and Trollope.[13] Shelley might have made a decent M.P. but as a writer was merely *'a schoolboy broken off'*.[14] Did he at times regret giving up his King's Fellowship with its intellectual challenge and the ethos to debate such opinions ? *'It is hard to live without the help of men that could teach me something,'* he lamented.[15]

He was not though done with education. He had noted the patchy quality of female education as shown in the small number of schools catering for girls' secondary education. At Eton he had made an experimental trial of a series of lessons on the humanities for local ladies but this had not been a success and left him doubting whether he could profitably do this. Now though, he tried again, first with a friend's three daughters. Hopelessly inattentive, they were nonetheless charming company and he managed to get the eldest interested in Charlotte Bronte's 'Shirley'. Mrs Guille, wife of the vicar of Little Torrington, persuaded Cory to take this further and was the instigator of classes, first consisting of six young girls, at Torrington. Whatever they got from these classes they enjoyed the sequel of a chaperoned trip to Halsdon and a river trip followed by a feast, they and their host in the highest spirits. Meetings with the Guille family led to Cory's meeting with Rosa, the sixth of her eleven children, little seen so far as she was away for a number of her teenage years at school in Bedford.[16]

* * * * *

Returned to King's, O.B., as Browning was always known by this time, and is best so referred to from now on, thought to put the past behind him. *'I wish to hear nothing of Eton.'* [17] There was little chance of that though while his mother continued living at Windsor, keeping him up to date with Eton gossip. Nor was it in his nature to let go of such a strongly felt grievance. Besides, the ties that bound Eton and

Cambridge meant that former adversaries and friends were likely to be met in Cambridge's streets and colleges. One such encounter afforded occasion to cut Warre in Trinity Street.

He had a notion of himself leading a rather ascetic existence preoccupied with historical scholarly work. This would have tallied with the drastic change in his financial position. Whereas at Eton he'd been earning around £3,000 p.a. the agricultural depression had much reduced Fellows' stipends : O.B. calculated that after eighteen years at King's his yearly average had been £133. 6. 8d.[18] In practice though that made little difference to his bank balance as what he had he spent, his mother often accusing him of extravagance. One deterrent to any legal action against Eton, though probably not the main one, was that he'd left there without any money.

He was not though slow to rediscover the delights offered by Cambridge's social life and, with far more time for an expansive social calendar than he'd had at Eton, and with financial help from friends, in particular Lord Latymer,[19] he was able to put aside such inconveniences as stopped cheques, and live life with the eccentric gusto that made him one of Cambridge's best remembered dons. He could be many things, but not an ascetic.

* * * * *

A good deal changed at King's in the second half of the century. The lengthy process of opening it up to a more socially mixed group of entrants began with the new constitution of 1861 which made provision for 46 Fellows and 48 scholars, the latter to be divided equally between Eton and other schools, and ended the automatic succession to scholarships from Eton. Nor did junior members any longer automatically succeed to Fellowships. It broke new ground too with the decision to admit 'pensioners', fee-paying undergraduates, the first of whom arrived in 1865.[20]

The College though had second thoughts about the last of these provisions and in 1873 took the decision to admit only Honours men.[21] That involved some financial loss but emphasised the College's commitment to raising academic standards. To O.B.'s calculations of his stipend might be added the more general ones of a College Historian who estimated that Fellows' earnings sunk from £280-300 in the early 1870's to a mere £80 by 1895.[22]

Reforming matters were often on the agenda in the 1880's by which time O.B. was active on the reforming side. In 1877 he distributed a memorandum. His opening observation, prompted by the College's being then in the process of framing new statutes was to assert that little can be accomplished by legislation unless what is stipulated reflects a shared vision for the future. His was for a College of about 150, all Honours men, provided with the best teaching, and flourishing in a civilised, supportive society. That was very much the way in which King's developed.[23] The way in which a Fellow was elected was a matter which O.B. took up, joining with other advocates for a dissertation rather than tripos result as the basis for selection.[24] That was agreed, and was to enable the future selection of Rupert Brooke and the musicologist Edward Dent, among others,[25] and in more recent times, made it possible for Philip Radcliffe to give up his only moderately successful Classical studies in favour of a far more productive musical future.

The role of the Provost, and in particular his emoluments, also came under scrutiny. O.B. saw the Provost as really only a lightly occupied figurehead whereas it was the tutors who did all the work. The ample salary would be justified were the College bringing in from outside a man of real distinction in Science or Literature but not if the College was merely promoting from within. A rather more frequent change of Provost must have seemed advisable to O.B. and others advocating a ten-year tenure. While that failed to get agreement some check on the salary was made with its being linked to the equivalent of four Fellowships. Of greater importance, he had by this time lost his power of veto.[26]

In 1882 a highly significant measure was passed, limiting a Fellow's tenure to six years unless he held either a College post or one of a few specified University positions. This in effect made it possible to ease out any Fellow not seen to be beneficially employed in the College's interest or to ensure that a promising start did not degenerate into a complacently cosseted tenure. A hazard with this rigour was though that of losing an outstanding scholar who'd neither been offered nor shown any interest in any form of College lecturing or administration.

*****

Provost Okes, a *'shortish, rather thick-set man with white hair'* [27] had been in office for twenty-six years when Browning reappeared at the College. (This length of service with continuance into extreme old age, was not unusual then. Dr. Corrie of Jesus perished at the age of 92, supposedly after falling out of an apple tree. Dr. Atkinson presided over Clare for 59 years while the Mastership of St. Catherine's was held for 48 years by Dr. Robinson with the assistance of a vote once cast by him for himself.)[28] Okes was a man of conservative instinct but rather more liberal practice. Himself preferring Etonians at the College, he was content to welcome others, and during the latter part of his time markedly fewer Etonian freshmen were admitted.

Nor on one occasion was the Lord Chief Justice when a servant entered with a card. After reading it Okes told the servant that *"the Provost is not prepared to see him"*. Asking a small boy, a relative who happened to be with him in the Lodge, what he supposed the Lord Chief Justice to be like, and getting the suggestion of *'a very clever man'*, he agreed. *"Yes : he is a very clever man, but not at all a good man. And that is the reason you heard me say that I am not prepared to see him."* [29]

At times he must have wished that some turbulent souls could have been dealt with so summarily at College meetings. For a number of years he arrived at these with a folded sheet of paper to be in readiness should an exceedingly virulent character called Bendyshe, whose language when coxing the King's boat had become legendary, appear. The folded sheet contained a reprimand from the Visitor for writing a profane letter to the Dean.[30] Some of those present had a good deal to say. Browning's style was marked by *'the prolixity, the quarrelsomeness, the relentless plying of the grindstone for his particular axe'*.[31] Dean Nixon, a distinctive figure with a single arm and eye, who raced around on a specially built tricycle which occasionally spilled him, was another who insisted on being heard even if sometimes he was not too clear what his view was. *"Yes, a thousand times yes – or rather, No, a thousand times no,"* was a reported interjection. These were frequent. *"Nixon just up for the 43rd time,"* was a shouted comment from a College window during the course of one meeting. He was somewhat accident prone, falling from the triforium in Westminster Abbey during the 1887 Jubilee celebrations and having a bee hive upset in his rooms. Yet he was well-liked and in later life mellowed considerably with fewer strong protests.[32] All the heat generated at College meetings did not always produce much light. *"We had a morning of display and got no further with the real question than we had at the beginning,"* Provost Okes had once to conclude.[33]

According to M.R. James, elected to a Fellowship in 1887, the contentiousness could at times be *'lacerating'*.[34] Some though kept a sense of detachment. *"Funny feller, Browning,"*,[35] was the laconic comment of the genial Fred Whitting after one meeting.

Pedantic byways sometimes beckoned. Nixon's request for dozens *more* chairs for chapel services was criticised by one Fellow who insisted that the correct usage was for so many *additional* chairs. The issue was not dropped after the meeting but Nixon's views reaffirmed in a hecktograph or jellygraph in which he questioned whether a well-known hymn should be rewritten – *'A few additional years shall roll, a few additional seasons come'* [36] His punctilious loquacity did though carry him to the Gresham chair of Rhetoric.[37]

It was though the work of Augustus Austen Leigh, in his various roles as Tutor, Dean, Vice-Provost, and finally Provost that effected major changes. In a quiet way he set about trying to make King's a teaching College. As late as 1877 only ten of the College's Fellows taught while thirty were non-resident. When those based in London were required to come up to King's in a body a special carriage was added to a London – Cambridge train.

Until then serious scholars had needed the services of a crammer to make sufficient headway. By 1904, his last year as Provost, there were thirty-five resident Fellows, most of whom did some teaching while the undergraduate corpus of 21 in 1869 had grown to 146. Some lectureships he funded himself.[38]

Before the effect of the agricultural depression began to make deep inroads into the College's income, a phase of expansive building was begun. It nearly took what would subsequently surely have been a wrong turn with the proposed demolition of the Wilkins screen, deemed by one Fellow *'a masterpiece of extravagance and bad taste'.*[39] That, like the proposed gothicisation of the Gibbs building, was though put aside. Instead, additional accommodation was provided by building further down King's Parade. (1873) A proposal for a merger between King's and St. Catherine's reached quite an advanced stage before negotiations fell through.[40] The Choir School was built in 1876 and Chetwynde Court and Bodley Court followed later. A good deal of the money needed for all this came from Fellows generously foregoing much of their dividend. [41]

* * * * *

In 1877 Reginald Brett, then 26, was told by his father, Sir Baliol, that after being up at Cambridge for seven years, it was time to get a job. The length of this undergraduate period is accounted for by his embarking on a second degree course, that of law, in order to please his father, a Judge. His heart though was not in it but it did give him a reason to linger in convivial Cambridge surroundings.[42]

It was his father's influence that got him started on the political path he was to pursue for the rest of his life for it was a word in the right place that had him appointed as private secretary to Lord Hartington, then Leader of the Opposition in the House of Commons. Hartington was one of the country's more detached politicians, greatly preferring hunting, bridge, and indulging his mistresses to the grind of political work. That left something of a vacuum which Brett was more than happy to fill and in which habit Hartington, recognising his ability, good-naturedly acquiesced. Brett happily composed the address that Hartington was to deliver to Edinburgh University on being elected Rector, consulting Cory as to content. Before long matters on which Hartington had expressed no opinion had one supplied for him by Brett, a growing habit which Sir Charles Dilke noted even to the extent of *'representing Hartington's conscience when it would not otherwise have moved'*.[43]

The prospect of war in Afghanistan was a matter on which Hartington did have an opinion which was for opposition though he kept it to himself not wishing to cause the government difficulty. Joseph Chamberlain was less restrained and Brett too thought invasion justified to keep the Russians at bay, but publicly stood by his master's stance. He asked Cory what he thought. The response from Madeira was that *'occupying Kabul would be like squatting on an ant's nest when aiming at a target'*.[44] A sense of being at the centre of affairs of State was a heady cocktail and one which Brett was determined to savour.

Cory was also consulted over his proposed marriage. On a visit to New Lodge in Windsor Forest, home of Madame van de Weyer, widow of Sylvain, Belgian minister at the Court of St. James, Brett had been greatly struck by Eleanor, the youngest of her four daughters. He also reflected that at the age of twenty-six it was time for him to find a wife. Her tender age, seventeen, did not seem a bar. He could not have done better. She was well-educated, tolerant, and musical, thought the world of Brett, but not to the extent of suppressing her own views. They spent an enjoyable two month honeymoon in Paris confounding Curzon's forecast of boredom, reading together, Nellie playing the piano, and bumping into Gladstone in an antique shop wearing a terrible hat to try and look poor.

Back in England they settled into a house in Tilney Street, Mayfair. Here Nellie quickly settled into a domestic routine full of tea and babies while having little liking for the social round though ready to accompany Brett if really necessary.[45]

There was another presence in their relationship of which she became aware and was able to tolerate and that was Brett's tendency to infatuation with male youth. While at Oxford he had had occasion in his father's company to run into Ernle Johnson, son of the Dean of Wells at the Bishop's Palace and was immediately smitten by this small, rather delicate youth. For the next seven years he carried on an intimate friendship, taking him out of Malvern School and making assignations to meet in Westminster Abbey.[46] Brett entrusted Johnson with his innermost thoughts such as confiding in him his belief that he was losing Chat and his faith and getting in return the advice to *'cling to the last chance for Chat, marry him if you possibly can; scheme; intrigue; practise on his emotions'*.[47] Transference to Christ Church did not greatly alter things for then Johnson slept with Brett's letters under his pillow and wished they could sleep in the same room. After Brett's marriage the stricken Johnson started to fade from Brett's consciousness. There would though be others.

The formation of a Liberal government in April, 1880, saw Hartington give way to Gladstone who became Premier for the second time. Hartington took the India Office where Brett went with him. His status though was now an altered one in that he had been elected as Member of Parliament for Penryn and Falmouth and thus able to give wider currency to his views, none too inhibited either by Liberal Party policy or his role at the India Office.[48] Britain's role in the east exercised him a good deal. He'd been struck by John Stuart Mill's views on oppression and wondered whether the time wouldn't come when India's protest at British occupation would not become unstoppable. His maiden speech supported British withdrawal from Kandahar thinking it unlikely that Russia would be tempted into any power vacuum. This was one of those occasions when he seemed either to change his mind or hold two seemingly contrary views at the same time, a trait which other sometimes found puzzling.[49]

In December, 1882, Hartington moved to the War Office and again Brett went with him. This brought Brett into close contact with the key figures in the Egyptian crisis. The badly dressed, chain-smoking figure of the Sudanese General Gordon, of insignificant appearance apart from his steely blue eyes, was a frequent visitor to the Tilney Street home. He urged Brett and other young men to get out to the East and see for themselves what needed to be done rather than spending time in the sort of society engagement which he loathed : not though advice Brett followed. Britain's increasing involvement in Egypt's turbulent affairs escalated to a unilateral invasion in 1882, France and Italy having declined participation. This Gordon saw as a mistake, with undue emphasis being put on the Nile trading route rather than the *'grand route'* round the Cape.[50]

Gordon could talk of the East from wide experience. Taking part in the capture of Peking in 1860 he'd gone on to win thirty-three battles for the Chinese Government while subsequently in the Sudan abolishing the slave trade and bringing order to huge areas. When the Government decided on withdrawal from the Sudan, he seemed the man to do to it.

What followed marked perhaps the lowest point of any Liberal Victorian administration and of Gladstone's personal standing with the public. Despatched to the Sudan with orders to evacuate Khartoum Gordon decided to do the opposite – to reinforce it for resistance. That put the government on the spot, creating a situation that required urgent action, either to get Gordon to obey his instruction, or to send him reinforcements. Instead there was dither, Gladstone at the time being more preoccupied with the Redistribution Bill. Belatedly an ill-equipped force was sent under General Wolseley but a relieving force did not reach Khartoum until two days after its storming and capture. Had there not been a three day delay in sailing steamboats up the Nile Khartoum would have been reached before that.[51] *'Khartoum has fallen. Gordon is dead,'* Queen Victoria blurted out arriving unannounced at the Ponsonby's Osborne cottage before spending hours in tears.[52]

Wolseley found Brett's missives more informative than any from the War Office. Like his friend Gordon he had an unshakeable belief in his own convictions underpinned by a religious fervour and little patience with opposition. He saw a need for wholesale army reorganisation ideally starting with the Duke of Cambridge, a man full of titles but little else. His views could though be startling, Brett being taken aback by his opinion that Britain should clear out of Egypt and the Sudan and go to war with Russia. Subsequently he raved to Brett over what he saw as the government's incompetence that had led to Gordon's death. Throughout the operation Brett kept W.T.Stead, editor of The Pall Mall Gazette, well briefed, occasionally leaning on him to try to ensure the news that what was published reflected Brett's focus.[53]

Wishing to have a freer hand in the House of Commons Brett left the War Office though in practice he'd already been expressing his views without much inhibition. He spoke in favour of abandoning the Sudan but concentrating on holding the Upper Nile against the French and Germans. This phase was though brief as he lost his Cornish seat in the 1885 election which returned a Conservative government. With his Liberal ideas on land reform he'd not been a natural fit in feudal Cornwall. By then he'd established a growing reputation in Parliament as a forceful if not brilliant speaker but decided that his future lay outside it. [54]

* * * * *

'Where did you get the gift of such ascendancy over the minds of your friends ? wondered his Etonian contemporary, Howard Sturgis, suggesting that *'you must often wish to get rid of it.*[55] Brett though clearly had no wish to do anything of the kind. As James Lees-Milne put it, he was *'a natural busybody',*[56] eager to know the business of others, especially where politics was concerned. With his confident, unhurried manner, and sober habit, having only the occasional glass of wine, he gained the trust of men in high places as a confidant. Morley, Harcourt, and Rosebery all sought his advice as to whether they should accept posts offered in the Gladstonian government after Lord Salisbury's brief first premiership. Rosebery went further and when out walking with Brett asked for his advice as to choice of private secretary.[57] He was close enough to Randolph Churchill to realise that he'd resigned the Chancellorship in a fit of pique, wrongly assuming that he would be thought indispensable and his resignation refused.[58]

Cory on occasion received letters in Madeira from Old Etonians asking him to put in a word for them with Brett when seeking a position, something Cory did only with reluctance, preferring men to make their own way without that kind of boost.[59] A characteristic trait of Brett's was loyalty to friends who encountered difficult times. He stood by Dilke after the calamitous divorce case which effectively ended his career [60] and kept in touch with Lord Arthur Somerset after he fled abroad in the wake of the Cleveland House brothel scandal.[61]

Out of Parliament he kept his views known by writing frequent letters to The Times. Buckle, the editor, puzzled over his attitude to the Irish question in which Brett seemed to think that the continued dominance of Imperial rule and Home Rule could be compatible. *'I don't see what you're driving at.'* Still, he published the letter.[62] Awareness of his growing influence prompted wariness in some and outright hostility in others. Harcourt received a letter alleging that Brett was regularly sending confidential information to Buckle at The Times and to Stead at the Pall Mall Gazette.

* * * * *

While his public persona seemed to exude a sort of stable assurance his private life had developed in a distinctly unusual way. He sent his two sons to Eton, but developed a relationship of great intimacy with Maurice, the younger, which he never had with Oliver. He imparted to his son the kind of confidences with which fathers don't usually burden their sons and in exchange wanted to know all about any affairs Maurice might be having. *'Anyone captured your heart yet, my Fatty?'* he asked the then thirteen-year-old whom he alternatively addressed as 'Molly'.[63] He could make little of his two daughters : *'queer things girls ….. very tiresome things until they are grown up …. a couple of spit-cats'*.[64] Pretty young actresses charmed him and he regularly appeared back stage to take one of them out to dinner. A more consequential affair was the long-running relationship with Millicent, Duchess of Sutherland, which, though platonic, was sustained in a continuous stream of letters.[65]

An older passion resurfaced in his craving for the company of the fifteen-year-old Etonian Edward Seymour and for a while Brett's diaries were full of mentions of him even of his sending him to sleep *'by combing his hair with my hand'*.

His almost reckless urge for Seymour's company led to him haunting Eton where his presence must have been noted by masters and older boys. On other occasions he tried unobtrusively to get a glimpse of Maurice through a bathroom window. The dedication of Brett's first book 'Footprints of Statesmen' to 'Teddie Seymour a.e.t.' aroused gossipy comment.[66] Nellie though was quite happy to treat Edward Seymour as a sort of honorary son but was warier of the relationship with Millie. In any case she invariably deferred to her husband assuming he always knew best, an attitude not always in her children's best interest. News of Chat Brett found unsettling as faith and young gondoliers in the persons of Salvatore and Marco vied for his attention and he drifted from place to place, unwilling to share Brett's enthusiasm for Seymour.[67]

Another impulsive element in his generally staid public persona was his attraction to racing. This had got rather out of hand being largely responsible for an overdraft of a thousand pounds and debts twice that. Both these sums his father paid off, telling him he would say no more about it. Brett was embarrassedly grateful and as a consequence gave up racing and betting and confined himself to breeding horses. His finances are something of a puzzle for so much of what he did seemed to bring in little income.[68]

He was though able to afford another house. This was Orchard Lea on the edge of Windsor Great Park and built to Brett's own design. Full of Tudor features it has a rather haphazard look with gables, oriels, and latticed windows not quite blending. More impressive was the tasteful interior with wood panelling, tapestries, and choice furniture. Highly significant was its location on the edge of Windor Great Park and about three miles from the castle. This proximity helped to bring Brett within the royal orbit.[69]

* * * * *

It was no surprise that Cory should have been attracted by Rosa as her high spirits endeared her to many. What he could not have imagined was that she would be so strongly drawn to him. *'I had a love letter today from a girl of twenty,'* he wrote to Brett. In it she told him that she had always wanted to marry an older man and that *'You are the man !'* [70]

The disparity in their ages, he 56, she 20, understandably prompted a cautious response from her parents. When though she persisted, they began to give it serious thought. They knew William well and that there was no question of his having barged his way into her affections. Entranced by her, *'wholesome as a milkmaid, as merry as an actress, as stylish as a maid of honour'*,[71] he was nonetheless level-headed enough to write her a letter in two parts, one giving reasons for the match, the other arguments against. When Mrs Guille returned home after a spell away, but kept in touch with the situation by post, and found Rosa still of the same mind, consent was given.

When that point was reached though William was out of the country. There had been times at Eton when he'd been ordered away for the good of his health and his doctor had now decreed that what he needed was a warmer climate and so he decided to take himself off to Madeira. While installed in a pleasant hotel, and finding agreeable company, he heard the welcome decision about Rosa and in July, 1877, a wedding party, including his brother Wellington, who was fascinated by the local flora, but not her ailing father, arrived on the island. Marriage was followed by a decree from William. Henceforth Rosa was to be known as 'Madame', not 'Mrs', the sound of which he disliked.[72]

In the five years spent there, they had three houses.[73] First William took a house in the hill country round Funchal, then a property for the milder climate at sea level, and finally a sizeable seventeen-room house at a median height about half an hour's walk from town. This last had a profusion of trees, camellia, pepper, orange, and custard apple along with a huge weeping willow. Amongst the plants were vines and the wild belladonna with the whole garden enclosed by a bamboo hedge. He would sometimes doze on the croquet lawn while nearby Rosa and the nurse indulged in gossip.

Very pleased with the house, William was soon engaged in familiar activities, teaching a solicitor and a clergyman and reading 'Tom Sawyer' to four ladies.[74] There was a considerable correspondence, especially with Brett and the Coleridge's. In addition he set himself a more substantial task in starting to write 'A Guide to English History'.[75] Elsewhere, Madeiran custom interested him. He noted the way boys washed their feet before going to bed, the regular bible reading, how huge loads were carried on the head even when a wheelbarrow was provided, and how different Portuguese cookery was to Britain's.[76]

Rosa's liveliness brought popularity and the pleasure that others clearly took in her company greatly gratified William. She had a sweet singing voice though with a tendency to go flat. An enthusiastic dancer, she introduced the 'Liverpool Lurch' to the island. William was all for her dancing, seeing how important it was she had her own amusement. On occasion she would come back at night and dance with William on the moonlit lawn. Once she went to a dance at the grandest island house, staying away the night, an adventure he heartily condoned.

By December, 1878, Rosa was clearly pregnant and the following June she gave birth to a boy they called Andrew, chosen for its plainness and because no Pope had ever been called Andrew.[77]

* * * * *

O.B.'s ambitions within King's quickly suffered a reality check. The office of Vice-Provost becoming vacant some months after he arrived, he put himself forward, thinking he had a good chance. In the event his candidature was barely considered. He came closer when challenging the long-serving and saintly Churtin for the Deanship but failed as well to gain a College History post. When that of Assistant College lecturer was created for him three years later he took it breezily in his stride, thereafter working in not always cordial harmony with the scholarly and productive George Prothero, and seeing it as an initial step toward higher office. In fact he was to hold no other College post during his lengthy residency.[78]

His light official duties left him plenty of time to pursue another of his aims, which was to get to know as many undergraduates as possible. This initial encounter could not always have been welcome to those invited to join him for a walk, for during it he would frequently revert to the unjustness of his dismissal from Eton, a matter of little interest to most undergraduates. M.R.James indeed found his harangues against Hornby thoroughly distasteful, observing that we were fonder of Eton and Hornby than we were of him.[79] Invited to join him for dinner in Hall, an occasion for which he always dressed in due style, conversation tended to begin with a question as to what his fellow diner had been up to. This after a while brought the comment, *'very interesting'* which was then followed by a lengthy monologue. These social shortcomings were though generally outweighed by an appreciation of his kindness and generosity.[80]

The number of clubs which he joined, helped to run, or founded, did indeed bring him into contact with large numbers of undergraduates. He became President of the Footlights, Treasurer of the Union, President of the University Bicycling Club, as well as being a member of others, such as the 'Ghost Club' which reflected the late Victorian interest in psychic phenomena. His most enduring legacy was the formation of the Political Society, formed particularly to explore issues on a historical basis, of which he was President for more than thirty years.[81] Physically he was active too, bathing in the Cam, playing hockey with gusto, and going for long tricycling rides. Even boating, the subject of such contention at Eton with Warre, got his interest with plaudits for the infrequent successes of the King's boat.[82] As a dancing partner he could trot briskly through the lancers and the foxtrot but was best avoided for the waltz.

He was always ready to widen his experience. An Apostle, he also became a Mason, not seeing that as in any way in conflict with his Anglicanism. Nor did he see that as any kind of bar to a keen interest in Christian Science. Religion was a potent force in his life and one devoid of any sectarianism. Rather he saw the different forms of religion as being various ways of reaching out to God.[83] When devised, Esperanto intrigued him, and he set himself to add it to the forty languages he already knew.[84] Then, always an enthusiastic bather, he tried the Turkish baths.

Music was perhaps his greatest passion and one he shared in his chamber music sessions. To add to the ensemble he had a couple of obeophones. His energetic but often inaccurate piano playing had not always appealed to his mother when they were at Eton. On occasion she wished he and Parry *'would not thump so'*.[85] As a duettist he invariably took the top line while his partner was well advised to conduct operations well below middle C to avoid finger clashes. In later life he preferred solo playing and was still having lessons at the age of eighty-three. With the opening of Bayreuth, he was given tickets for the Ring cycle but it seems to have left only an ephemeral impression, Wagner never seen as any kind of serious rival to Mozart or Beethoven.[86]

Life at Cambridge had run to an agreeable pattern. His mother was not sure that it was the right one though. *'I fear you will become a gouty, a gourmet, and cease to care for the simplicity with which your university career began.'* [87] One consequence of his indulgence in Epicurean pleasures was increasing girth. He was though reassured in that respect by the advice of a doctor *'not to mind too much about being stout and to let nature take its course'*.[88]

* * * * *

Thinking to burnish his academic credentials somewhat, O.B. put himself forward for the award of a Litt. D. That though was refused on the ground that none of his work involved any original research. By that time though he'd made a very different kind of mark.

Education was not to him a process to be undergone in a purely formal way, with little concern beyond one's own progress. He put his finger on one blind spot, that being that few Headmasters were too likely to find any great fault with a system that had produced them. Something of the same often applied to masters who inherited a kind of institutional myopia. To O.B. education should be regarded as a Science with lessons drawn from Continental practice. One such was the perception that the German schoolboy was much better off than his British counterpart for he could be educated at a far more modest cost. As in many ways Germany was scientifically ahead of Britain as, for instance, in the production of electricity and synthetic dyes, Britain would soon start to lag behind if unable to institute a similarly effective system of secondary education. Occasional instances of boys succeeding from the humblest background could not be used as a valid justification for the existing situation. Rather consider *'the tens who have failed rather than the units who have succeeded, and of the ore that lies buried rather than of the bright coins which circulate from hand to hand'*.[89]

These views went down well in a speech to the Birmingham Social Science Congress in 1884 as did his plan for a far more extensive system of secondary education with teachers who'd undergone compulsory training and a regular system of inspection. Overall, he told the delegates *'the mass of our nation needs a great intellectual lift'*.[90]

He was though no believer in free education, rather for a good deal more of it. The part he saw Cambridge playing was that of educating potential elementary teachers in the arts of teaching while they pursued a degree course. Objection was made that they couldn't do both : one or the other was bound to suffer.

His persistence though paid off with the formation of a Day Training Centre with O.B. as a thoroughly autocratic Principal, not averse to taking issue with the Board of Education.[91] He was something of a pioneer in his use of the seminar and took a keen interest in the fortunes of his former students.

* * * * *

To Cory, with his comprehensive knowledge of military and naval history, and strong interest in the progress of affairs, the defeat of British arms at the battle of Majuba in March, 1881, came as a rude shock. Worse still in his view was the Government's craven armistice with the Boers. It was all *'disgraceful and disheartening'*.[92] A sense of weighty unresolved issues at home prompted a desire to be more in the thick of it than a distant spectator. There was another reason. He'd begun to believe that Rosa's bouts of fever had to do with the climate while he, though fitter, had grown very thin. So the cause of their being in Madeira had now become a reason to go back home as soon as William had finished his historical work.

There had been other reminders of home. Naval vessels were often moored in Funchal harbour. They'd both been invited to a ball aboard H.M.S. Encounter and the following day invited by the captain to return to the ship. Then there were occasional, but too rare, visits from friends while news from Devon rekindled a fondness for their native county. Rising stars of the next generation caught his eye amongst whom he thought *'young Asquith'* [93] would do very well at the Bar. He was indeed soon one of the most successful barristers of his time and entered politics at some financial cost.

Decided to return to England the question was where that should be. After a while Hampstead was decided on as being something of a compromise between town and country.

Brett undertook the negotiations for the lease of the Hampstead House with its owner, Baron von Hugel. First though they went to Switzerland hoping that the newly fashionable Alpine cure would have a beneficial effect on Rosa's lungs. Though that was then thought to be the trouble it was never clear just what was wrong with her.

Rosa herself took the gloomiest view of her future, hoping to live for two years, all of which gave William the gravest concern.[94]

Back in England Rosa and Andrew were sent back to their Devon family while William busied himself getting the house into shape, spending hours in Maples and other stores, making careful selections, then ensuring that, starting with the carpets, all the chosen furnishings arrived in the right order. His efforts were greeted rapturously by Rosa who was enchanted with the house. Both were glad to be back in England, he for a renewal of the social contacts which had rather fallen into abeyance, she for the opportunities that London offered. They were to stay in the house for nine years, the longest time they had together in any of their homes.

*****

Torrington had given William some experience in teaching ladies but at Hampstead this became a more considerable occupation. A leading light behind this was Mary Coleridge, Arthur's daughter, now in her early twenties but whom William had first met as a girl of thirteen at Halsdon. Herself a bright student, she encouraged her friends to go along. After a while William had fourteen girls and ladies with ages ranging from fifteen to thirty as well as a few correspondence pupils. Some came from a distance, Margaret Cornish from Eton and Ada Prideaux from Barnes. They were of two types: ladies already in a comfortable situation in life who wanted a degree of mental stimulation and younger girls who hoped to learn enough for their own advancement. Successes in the latter group gave William particular pleasure as when Gwendoline Graham won a Newnham scholarship.

These were rigorous sessions. The programme for one of the four sets into which William had divided his students was on one occasion *'ninety minutes Plato, then tea, then eighty minutes Sophocles'*. Some found the going demanding at times. *'I have been doing some Antigone and find it very hard,'* Margaret Cornish wrote to him. Then female sensibility could be disconcerting. A girl asked to read what he deemed an innocent piece of Catullus suddenly hid her face and wept though another girl, *'a glory'*, took it up quite unconcernedly.[95] A point was made of getting to the Hampstead house on the dot even if it meant trudging up a snowbound hill to be greeted by William at the door with a reviving glass of brandy and put in front of a roaring fire.

Edith Sichel, one of his pupils, later writing of his table talk, introduced them by remarking his posture *'as with a kind of fierce but timid abruptness, he uttered the words here recorded, sitting deep in his armchair, his head, so like that of Cicero, bent forward, his hand over his eyes – a habit of his due as much to shyness as short sight – until, warmed by his subject, he would suddenly raise them and an unforgettable flash of intellect electrified and enlightened his companions'*.[96]

When discussion turned to political matters it was to William revelatory for the level of debate was carried on *'with such spirit and sense as I never saw in women'*.[97] That presumably was because he'd not previously really had the opportunity. When these students' elders suggested payment he flatly refused, saying that teaching was its own reward.

He took a pride in his 'Grecian ladies' , once reading aloud Mary Coleridge's account of the death of Apodemus of Megara with some emotion,[98] and glad to have given them the opportunity to show that they were capable of far more than playing the conventional female domestic role.

It might be noted how, contrarily, O.B. maintained that the cleverest girl could never outpace the dimmest boy. Whether he really believed that, or if it was just one of his struck attitudes, his conduct here was positively deleterious. As an examiner he was sometimes given ladies' scripts to assess which he did in such a cursory manner as to once rouse protest from a College Head. There was another difference. Unlike O.B. William had no wish to perpetuate any kind of feud with Eton. Visited by two Etonian nephews he judged that *'from these two samples, Eton the school is happy and wise'*.

* * * * *

William had long realised that whatever benefits Rosa might have got from her Bedford schooling the fostering of an intellectual interest was not one of them. She was *'domesticated – clever, not intellectual'*. He still wanted her to feel a part of the scholastic company by leaving the door ajar while she did other things in the adjoining room, occasionally appearing with tea and cakes. That was really as much contact with the 'Grecian ladies' as she wanted for she found them rather intimidating. There were though individual friendships. From the first she got on well with Janet Bartrum, one of William's first pupils, and was always welcome in the Bartrum household where she could be herself without reserve. Later she found Ada Prideaux good company.[99] These friendships were reassuring as she'd not always found the ready acceptance in certain reaches of English society that she'd found in Madeira, at times conscious of being cold-shouldered.

She did though have a variety of other interests, some of which she pursued until reaching considerable proficiency. After taking lessons in dress-making she made dresses for friends and servants and became a useful member of the Kensington School of Art and Needlework. Embroidery was a craft at which she became sufficiently skilled to give instruction. She experimented with the then nascent beauty culture, making various face creams, though this could have been the cause of a later disaster. Cats were another strong interest and she bred Blue Persians, exhibiting them at Crystal Palace shows.[100] She was keen to learn more about cookery and for a while there was talk of her going on a course but that fell through. Nor did talk of her going on the stage, suggested to her on account of her lively presence and being occasionally mistaken for a well-known actress, Mary Anderson, and which for a while she was quite keen on, come to anything, William warning of the possibly fatal draughts to which she would be subject backstage though the real reason may have been his unwillingness to have her away for such long periods. Out she went though on a different mission, to Whitechapel, brightly dressed as she thought that was what was liked, as a member of a league for befriending poor girls, and once brought home by a smiling policeman.[101]

* * * * *

On July 29th, 1884, Edmond Warre was appointed Headmaster of Eton College, receiving nine of the eleven available Governing Body votes. Later he was duly presented with the seal of office, a birch wrapped in blue ribbons, and had an accumulating pile of letters of congratulation, finally numbering 398.[102]

One, and probably the first, was that from the recently installed Provost Hornby who generously acknowledged that during his time *'your support and help and work have been invaluable'* and looked forward to the school *'making a fresh start with a new and better stroke'*.[103]

As well as being the confidant of Hornby and an effective division master, Warre had made a success of his house as evidenced by the number of families who continue to patronise it. John Walter, Chief Proprietor of The Times, for example, sent all his four sons there.[104]

Warre as Headmaster in 1905

They would have grown familiar with a man who *'never lost his temper but when he was angry he was terrible'* and who *'constantly spoke to his boys with fun and good humour, but never with sarcasm'*.[105] He had too what presumably was then the highly unusual habit of calling his boys by their Christian names or nicknames.

There were significant achievements at work and play. In 1867 his house achieved the unprecedented feat of winning the House Fours, the Cricket and Football cups, the last won on a snow-covered ground, while also in that year one boy was in the Newcastle Select and another won the Tomline Maths prize. In 1873 the house had four boys in the Sixth Form.[106] There are though always boys who prefer to set themselves unexpected targets. Thus Tom Farrer became known for having the whole of Bradshaw's Railway Guide by heart.[107]

* * * * *

Browning's biographer, H.E. Wortham, accounted Dr. Hornby *'a wretched disciplinarian'*. That though is questionable. Indiscipline there certainly was at times and one of his pupils, M.R. James, gives examples. There was the triumphal arch of quill pens designed so as to collapse on to the master's table, a caricature portrait of the presiding master inserted into a picture frame, and a boy dropping pistol cartridges into the fire behind the master with disturbing consequences. These escapades though happened only when Hornby's place was being taken by another. According to James, Hornby himself had the valuable schoolmasterly attribute of being able to interest boys in their work and was well liked.

In the view of some of the Sixth Form Warre did not compare favourably with Hornby. Used to the *'graceful and polished scholarship of Hornby's lessons'*, seasoned with delicate quips, Warre's method seemed laboured and they exhibited their disdain with yawning and other signs of rudeness. This prolonged disaffection got him down to the extent that one night he sat down and wrote the Provost a letter of resignation though wisely decided to sleep on it. Later he tore it up, resolving not to be beaten *'by a pack of boys'*.[108]

During his already lengthy time at Eton, and especially during Hornby's Headmastership, Warre had had ample opportunity to consider the desirability of any changes and he set about implementing three reforms. Fairly modest though these now seem, they were sufficient to arouse opposition, some of it even abusive, from those Old Etonians who saw them as an interference with tradition.

First was the creation of a school office set up as a clearing house for staff and boys. This must have been such an undoubted aid to the efficient running of the school that it's hard to see how a school of Eton's size could have operated effectively without one. Routine matters could now be more simply dealt with. For example, with a list of boys away from school being submitted to the office there was no longer any need for a praeposter to wander round a house's corridors to try to discover why Norris mi. was not in school. Its workload quickly became so heavy as to prompt its first occupant, Sergeant Osborn, to seriously consider resignation.

Then Trials became New Trials for all but the top one hundred boys. The differences were that they happened at the end of each half rather than annually and that whereas before the only person who had seen the papers was the Headmaster, Division Masters were now to be fully involved in the process, setting and marking the papers. The aim was to ensure a fuller check on a boy's progress and this it must have done though with the disadvantage that the brighter boys had gained more from the superseded Collections. Mainstream advancement was though always Warre's guiding ethos.

If he was to be less directly involved with Trials than his predecessor, Warre ensured that he had a good sense of the quality of the work going on in the Divisions by making surprise visits. These intrusions could be as alarming to masters as to boys. One was seen mopping his fevered brow with screwed up bits of blotting paper as the inquisition proceeded. A cannier colleague had a neat stratagem. Whatever the subject matter of the text being studied it took only a few diversionary remarks about ancient shipping to set Warre off on his favourite Classical hobby horse and avert scrutiny. Entering another Division Warre found a boy standing with ASS chalked on his back. "Sit down. Some silly fellow has been writing his name on your back." The 'silly fellow' was the master who turned scarlet with the boys barely able to suppress their glee. Looking to stride out of another Division Warre mistook the door and marched into a tall cupboard.[109]

Behind criticisms of Warre's reforms was a sense that the school was being reshaped along somewhat military lines. The office seemed a bit like an orderly office while his emphasis on togetherness seemed a rather regimental trait.

Perhaps too there was a fear that these would be the first of a lengthy series of measures that would transform the school and that some warning protest was needed.

In the post-Clarendon era Dr. Hornby had been conscious of the need to allow more time for Modern Languages, Mathematics, and Science though doing so with little enthusiasm and little sense that these changes would do much good. When pushed Classicists such as he could always point to the Clarendon Report's insistence that the Classics should remain the central study.

A reminder of the sight in Warre's time of *'Inky Parker and poor George Scott struggling helplessly with their verses in your pupil-room on Tuesday Long-Schools'* 110 would also suggest that little had changed in terms of academic priority. Indeed it puts Eton on the conservative edge of Greek-teaching schools for by now there was even among them an acknowledgement that few boys gained from verse work and that prose translation was a better idea.

Warre was an unapologetic advocate for the pre-eminence of the Classics. He defended it on two principal grounds : that it posed real difficulties to a student and presented him with the most sublime thoughts ever conceived. In 1887 a paper was being circulated, signed by three leading Headmasters, arguing for a reduction in the amount of Greek taught in Public Schools.[111] Warre could never have put his name to it. He denied that boys who had been allowed to give up Greek in other schools showed any general improvement in their knowledge of History, French, or Mathematics, though one wonders how he could have been sure of that.

He found fault with The Public Schools Latin Primer and compiled an Eton Latin Grammar, taking great pains with such details as size and type and the assignation of any profits, though alas there were none for it was elbowed aside by Kennedy's Revised Primer.[112]

As with many who took 'Greats' graduation was regarded as no more than a milepost along a lifetime's travel. For Classical masters the first priority had to be the effective use of their knowledge in class. Within the constraint of the discipline, Masters gave it their own emphasis. Warre had little interest in the lexicographical trend, drew parallels between Classical and more recent events in order to suggest relevance, and made occasional forays into Physical Geography, Astronomy, Mechanics, and Hydrostatics. Many though sustained an interest in Classical study for its own sake and remained practitioners. Warre's great interest was ancient shipping about which he wrote articles later included in the Encyclopaedia Britannica and had plans for a fuller work on Ancient Ships and their naval tactics. Throughout his life he regularly penned Latin and Greek verse, often as part of a letter, generally taking as subject matter an incident from his or a friend's life, often in witty vein. He corresponded with Gladstone, taking issue with his theory that Homer was colour blind by maintaining that few of the ancients gave any very clear impression of colour. Gladstone, at the age of 84, was planning a big book on Olympian religion.[113]

Rosebery wrote to Warre arguing the need *'for Science and more Modern Languages, and to work harder. I have long thought that we cannot face the competition of the world on Latin and Greek; but I am afraid this is heresy to you'*.[114] A.F.Walter took a different view, claiming that *'the majority do not know the difference between education and the sophistical knowledge of a few facts learnt from books. I believe that the old Eton education was the best that ever existed, or ever will exist ….'* .[115] Another of the strong defences of the Classics came from Warre's friend, Prof. Ramsay of Glasgow University, who saw the wish to do less Greek as *'really a demand for easier subjects and less work'*, modern subjects merely weakening the national culture.[116] With that view Warre entirely concurred.

Classicists by and large still found the old arguments in defence of their subject serviceable. One was the notion that the predominant reason for not wanting to study them was the quest for an easier life. Maybe that was so in some cases. But it seemed myopic not to be able or willing to appreciate that other subjects, if pursued seriously, make their own challenging demands. Allied to that was the belief that there was merit in something being difficult. Johnson had strongly contested that view, insisting that the real test should be whether or not the labour was beneficial to the boy and that, if he could make speedier progress through the foothills of another subject, that was no reason to disparage it. There was as well the idea, still prevalent in some quarters, that a boy's head can only contain so much and to a Classicist thinking like that, over much other learning was undesirable.

Science had though been making inroads into the curriculum. In 1873 the Governing Body ordered that Physical Science be taught and the Rev. E. Hale, who'd been employed as a Mathematical Master since 1850, was redeployed.[117] At his prompting before his time as Headmaster Warre got built and equipped at his own expense a School of Practical Mechanics largely with the intention of teaching boys likely to go to the colonies the sort of skills likely to be of use in the management of large estates. Opened in 1879, it failed to attract sufficient interest from the boys to be viable and struggled along until 1899 when the installation of electric lathes brought about popularity and use. The appointment of T.H. Huxley to the Governing Body in 1879 was a significant boon to the teaching of Science. He was particularly keen on the teaching of Physics and Human Physiology, stressing the need only to cover as much as could be taught thoroughly.[118]

In former times little change could be made to the running of the school unless either instigated by the Provost or given his assent. Now more voices had to be heard. The Governing Body had been given responsibility for shaping the curriculum though some members still thought overmuch real authority still remained with the Provost and thought themselves not greatly heeded.

It was Warre's practice before each Governing Body meeting to compile a list of subjects for its consideration.[119] Among those listed from an early stage were the desirability of smaller Divisions (not more than thirty); new cricket grounds; a new physical laboratory; a retiring and pension scheme for masters; more staff; better provision against fire; and lengthening of French and Mathematical schools to an hour. He got approval for five new appointments, two German, two French, and one Classical Master, the 'long schools', and an end to pupil room construing. He was not though always successful as in his attempt to link College entry to means, the contrary and prevailing view being that it should be an examination of intellectual ability only.[120] He wished too to start up a Navy Class but that never got off the ground while his attempt to end what seemed to him the ineffective army class was foiled by the War Office.[121]

Eton's system worked smoothly enough when the Governing Body and Headmaster were of like mind and competent masters could be found to implement any proposed change. That sense of accord was still though more likely to be there when Classical practice was under discussion. Still, whatever the imperfection of the system it seemed to Warre vastly preferable to that of his gloomiest prognostication – a curriculum imposed by legislation.

* * * * *

Well aware of Warre's sporting enthusiasms a number of junior boys had hopes of rather more time to be given to games. What they got instead were some rather longer lessons.

There was also an announcement of some import about his flogging policy. *"I shall flog for lying and I shall flog for smoking."* [122] He didn't in fact use the birch as much as his predecessors and when he did the preceding ceremonial was rather worse than the light touch execution. The news being conveyed by Warre to a duty prefect that a boy was to be flogged he enrolled two 'holders-down'. The three then waited outside Warre's study while he interviewed the victim. Then a solemn procession of Headmaster, two prefects, holders-down, and Headmaster's clerk made its way to the Sixth Form Room where the clerk gave a birch to one of the prefects, who gave it to the Headmaster. *'The victim then made the necessary adjustments to his clothes, the holders-down held down, and the ceremony was consummated.'* [123] Nor was there afterwards the dreaded homily or pi-jaw. Elsewhere Old Etonian meetings of The Block Club continued to celebrate the capture of the flogging block in Goodford's time with it taking pride of place at their dinners.

A Sixth Former of a later generation than his first (he must have been mightily relieved when after two years his recalcitrant pupils moved on) wrote a sketch of him:

'He had what is called a 'presence' to the highest degree. We thought him an enormous man, though actually he was not far above middle height. When he sailed into a room, with his head thrown back and a crunching stride, with flowing gown and a very broad silk band round his middle, he seemed hardly mortal in his bigness. His voice too was tremendous, it came out of the depths of him and vibrated'. Yet there was another side to him. *'All this awe-inspiring voice and presence, when combined (as it was) with great gentleness and warm-heartedness, was a combination well calculated to attract boys, and whatever the secret of it was, we certainly thought well of him.'* [124]

Like the boys, masters too wondered just what Warre's accession would bring. The radical master, Henry Salt, could not countenance the idea of working for Warre and promptly resigned.[125] Another had no great hopes. *'I distinctly feared Warre's accession. I feared the dominance of athletics, his own autocratic ways ....'* but there was *'a delightful surprise – it was like a fresh wind from the sea blowing into the place. Being now acknowledged Master of us all, Warre became accessible, kindly, interested, indulgent, and to anyone who applied in a difficult case, he was prodigal of advice'.*[126]

They were to find that, far from having any wish to run the school like some overweening C.O., his aim was to act as consensually as possible. Before submitting his list of topics for the Governing Body's consideration it was circulated among a number of his masters, giving him the assurance that, when he was asked to withdraw from a Governing Body session for his proposals to be considered, his had not been a lone voice.[127] He continued this approach long after it was generally thought he'd achieved such a degree of moral authority as to have virtually a free hand if he wanted it. To some, he was not autocratic enough.

Excerpts from a 'Private and Confidential Letter' to colleagues in May, 1888, argue against complacency.

'It all looks well, numbers increasing, more work done by the majority of boys, moral tone outwardly better, every outward reason to congratulate ourselves. Yes; but is this only show? Is the work really thorough? Are our morals really better? It is our duty to ask ourselves these questions and to quicken our observation. I rejoice in the greater freedom of intercourse between masters and boys, both in games and in leisure hours, but I urge discretion in talk about subjects other than work ….. There are some 300 boys who now, in this summer half, may be getting neither games nor rowing; do we know what they are doing? I don't want any **espionage** *or prying, but I do want you all to realise that a master is never off duty; the rules as to 'bounds' must be kept up, undesirable strangers seen talking to boys should be noticed; the increase of steam launches, trains, small villas near Eton (especially at Datchet) make vigilance necessary …. Finally, my brethren, do be punctual in school.'* [128] By December, 1884, he'd already drawn up a list of undesirable people near Eton whom boys were not to visit with a reason given in each case.

He would have been keenly aware of the sometimes bitter controversy about Eton that had flared up in the Press from time to time, particularly in the 1860's, and had no wish to see a recurrence, still less to be a participant. Where Arnold or Thring would have challenged, Warre sought a calming. While lacking their robust self-assurance, he was readier to listen to criticism.

Unlike most predecessors he had a free hand in the appointment and dismissal of his masters. An additional reform enabling him to sack a master in his first two years without having to give a reason – in effect a probationary period – strengthened his hand further. When though he became aware that a master was not doing the school any great service he asked him to move on only with the greatest reluctance, inclining to mercy. The situation within Eton though was less clear with Warre wanting more control over appointments to houses and of their entrants arguing that so long as they carried on in a semi-autonomous way there was little rigour in testing a boy's academic level, a situation that bothered the Provost of King's who thought that a far higher overall standard of Oppidan entry should be set, reasoning that as there was such demand for places at Eton that could easily be done without loss of income.[129] One change had been made at a time when College finance was still being rationalised from its rather archaic past, and that was that Oppidan entrance money was now to be paid direct to the College rather than to the Headmaster, a change that cost Warre about a thousand pounds.[130] His successor was the first to be paid a stipend. Another matter raised with Warre by a colleague was the way in which houses had been run and in effect possessed by a master so that when the master left, the house often disappeared, as seen earlier with Eliot's, something of a contrast with the enduring permanence of Eton.

*****

O.B's biographer, H.E. Wortham, biographer underlines how a mere description of his activities falls short of the mark unless it can also convey *'the vitality, the enormous fund of good humour, the frankness of speech, the idiosyncrasies of vanity, the enthusiasm, the magnanimity, the vindictiveness, all the strange jumble of qualities which went to lift Oscar Browning into a personality with that touch of absurdity which constitutes a character'*.[131] Much of this had been recognised soon after he took up residence from his relentless socialising. Among those staying with him was *'Oscar Wylde (sic), an Oxford man, also called after the King of Sweden'*.[132] A few years later he came again, unbidden, but still welcome. Particularly well remembered among his many social gatherings was the open house kept during Tripos Week when *'cream cheeses, lettuces, great round cakes and hock'* fortified the examinees.[133] Then in the season he was in regular demand in London requiring a deal of afternoon and early morning rail travel. At times he was genuinely surprised by the notice taken of him, as when, invited to a function at Downing College, the undergraduates started calling his name.[134] Notice though, of whatever kind, was his lifeblood. When a short-lived paper called 'The Whirlwind' offered a prize for the ugliest man who could be found, some undergraduates, thinking to annoy him, put O.B. in for it. When though he was judged the winner and was awarded a silver snuff box, he took pleasure in displaying it and telling how it had been won.

Socially, his activities covered a wide spectrum. On a red-letter day he hosted Princess Mary and her husband in a carriage drive round Cambridge, at one point all abandoning protocol by joining a hurdy-gurdy player in singing a popular song.[135] On another occasion he was seen solicitously talking to a crying boy in the street while he encouraged local youth to become naval cadets, on occasion going down to Portsmouth to see how they were getting on.[136] This same vein of humanity had him wondering whether the College couldn't do a little more for its Barton estate tenants than merely take rent. [137]

Foreign travel, usually to Italy and with an undergraduate in tow had its moments. Approaching Milan by train he suddenly noticed that his pocket-book, which contained their tickets, was missing. Panic latter gave way to amusement at the reaction of the station authority which wanted only to know the name of his father and when he had died and write that down in a big book. He informed as much of the Italian Press as he could along with a short story featuring Victor Hugo and himself and was amusedly gratified with later coverage. A visit to a merry-go-round had him whirling round on an ostrich shouting out, "I say, ain't this awfully jolly ?" An argument over a monstrous lodgings bill in Rome had O.B.'s extensive wardrobe, including twelve pairs of braces, flung out of the door and having to be collected up by Fay, his undergraduate companion.[138]

Striking images stuck in the minds of his contemporaries : of his remarkably circular, porpoise-like body plunging into the Cam ; of his conducting business in his King's Rooms while draped in two large bath towels ; of how he *slept inspiringly under a red handkerchief while Phillips and I read out our essays*;[139] and of his ready conversational wit such as his response to a grumbler that his wife was dull as a deal board to beware in case he found someone a deal bawdier.

With advancing age his egomania increased along with probably quite a conscious sense of self parody. Yet after all O.B. had created the legend so he might as well live up to it, even burnish it somewhat.

* * * * *

A certain restlessness and a sense that he was not perhaps making enough of himself led him to look at other opportunities. He stood for Parliament in a number of seats where he stood little chance and without success. Had he been wealthier he could probably have got a safe seat. A lifelong Liberal, his motley political views would not have endeared him to a whip. A home-ruler, he had no enthusiasm for free trade, while seeing the House of Lords as *'a fine democratic instrument'*.[140] A strong supporter of Empire where he saw beneficial work being done, such as by Curzon in India and Cromer in Egypt he became strongly pro-Boer and an admirer of Kruger. As to the tangled pre-war international situation his opinion was that a continuance of the Tsarist Government was the best option – nothing else looked like doing any better – while he strongly protested his support for Kaiser Wilhelm with outrage at disparaging comment from parts of the Press. An admirer of Napoleon, whose bust he had, he had a firm belief in the potency of a strong ruler, or at least of a ruler in a powerful position, to make a difference.[141]

He put in for the History chair at Glasgow, again without success. This may have been prompted by his perennial grumble about the meagre funding of History at King's which he contrasted with the lavish expenditure with which the College indulged its *'pampered'* Classical students.[142] Then he found himself under criticism at the Day Training Centre. Earlier it had been difficult to get members of the Governing Body to attend meetings at all regularly, but when they started to they were often critical, especially of O.B's erratic financial procedures. On a day when he was ill and unable to attend a meeting a number of resolutions were passed which subsequently caused him to protest in the strongest terms. Instead of satisfaction, he got a letter from the Vice-Chancellor inviting him to resign which after a while he did.[143] By then though his time at King's was drawing to an end.

* * * * *

In June, 1891, Cory moved across Hampstead from Cannon Place to Pilgrim's Lane, the reason for the upheaval seeming to be economics, for they would then be paying £16 p.a. in rent rather than the £125 p.a. that their Cannon Place home had been costing him. The property was described as a 'maisonette' or 'houselet'. No modern estate agent would use either term in describing the house, for a photo shows what looks like a fairly substantial Victorian villa. For Victorians of a certain standing, a downsized house still had to have beside the family rooms – and William was determined that Rosa would have her own cheerful upstairs bedroom complete with bath and cazinka – kitchen, scullery, larder, store-room, cellar, and rooms for maids and servants. Two bow windows fronted the street, one of which William had bricked up in the interest of snugness. Rosa liked the house, began to think what uses the small, attractive garden might be put to and to make plans for a cattery by the coal cellar.[144]

William had soon resumed his earlier routine with his Pilgrims, as they now thought of themselves – two hours of Electra, two hours of Homer – though Mary Coleridge was less enamoured of the new house. Two things at this time brought him back into the public consciousness.

'Ionica', a reprint of a collection of his verse was reprinted and though the edition was a shoddy affair, it sold well. To make amends, George Allen, the publisher, printed a second batch of a thousand copies, this time with only a single error.[145] Then he sat for a portrait by his nephew, the twenty-three-year-old Charles Furse. That involved being placed on a hard chair for seventy hours, passing the time by whistling tunes. When exhibited though it was received with acclaim and was later judged his best work.[146]

During their Hampstead years they'd kept up a variety of social contact. Christmas Day in 1886 had been spent at Abbey Garden, Westminster, his brother Wellington then being a Cathedral canon.[147] Returning home the snow had proved too much for the horses when they reached the hill and they had to walk up it. William took Rosa to Cambridge where they met Provost Austen Leigh and other, to William, familiar faces. They went to Spa to take the waters in the days before it had become fashionable. The north country beckoned too. A stay near Cockermouth produced a longing to cross the Solway and venture into Nithisdale. A later holiday in Seascale, their last, in August, 1891, where he read the 22nd book of Livy, persuaded William that Cumberland was the equal of Nithisdale and that Seascale *'was decidedly the best seaside place I have ever seen'*.[148]

Among the visitors to Hampstead were Reginald Brett, Frederick Wood, Albert Grey, and Charles Williamson (Chat) in his later manifestation as Father David, then a well-liked Venetian cleric.

* * * * *

Rosa seems to have become rather obsessively manic. After becoming involved with a church with a strong sense of mission she had a three week spell of going to church twice a day. Suddenly she then became a Catholic, something William accepted with equanimity but after that he and Andrew had to go to church on their own. Her health again became a matter of serious concern. She came under the care of a 'doctoress' who ordered long spells of lying down. No particular diagnosis could be offered. Consumption and cancer were ruled out and her lungs pronounced sound so that the best suggestion was 'chronic internal inflammation'. The situation was judged sufficiently grave for her to be sent to a nursing home where she lingered for thirty-five expensive days, visited by William every morning.[149]

William had been a good deal exercised by the thought of how Rosa and Andrew would get on without him. To give Andrew some security he'd made Rosa his guardian and, in the event of her not being able to act, her brother Hubert.[150] By the time they were at Pilgrim's Lane, Andrew was on to his fifth school, though William's biographer gives no hint as to how he'd got through so many. William took a pride in his son, seeing him as truthful, sociable, and a budding naturalist though uncivilised. As he doubted whether Andrew would ever read any of the books left him by 'uncivilised' he may have meant a lack of any literary interest. It was a pride that was though tested with recurrent bouts of truculence when he was with both parents. When William was otherwise engaged he and Rosa enjoyed riding round on the tops of buses. William foresaw a naval future but Rosa was less keen on that.[151]

Future provision took on more urgency as William's own health declined. Heart trouble meant that out walking he had to stop every fifty yards or so, once prompting a well-meaning member of the public to ask if he was all right. In May, 1892, he declined an invitation from Mrs Drummond, considering it *'unmannerly to drop down dead in another man's house'* and so *'wish to say now, in good spirits, good-bye to you and your husband'*.[152] He had little doubt that his end was near. When he wrote to Charles Wood, then become Lord Halifax, he signed off with *'I am yours till death (not long)'*. [153]

Lessons for his Pilgrims continued throughout the Spring until Mary Coleridge had a card calling a lesson off. Visiting, she found him in bed but still anxious to talk about two new books he'd come across. He died a fortnight later devotedly nursed until the end by Rosa.

* * * * *

At the time of his death William had extensive plans for additions to the back of the Pilgrim's Lane House with the idea of making it a good property for Andrew to inherit. The plans had been worked out in considerable and sometimes eccentric detail including a turret for Andrew. After the house had been transferred to Rosa she gave instructions for this work to begin. William had as well been in negotiations for the small cottage next door and this Rosa bought.[154]

After two years the house had changed into a larger but less harmonious building. The cost of the work must have been considerable and the result was to give Rosa a far larger property than she needed or was able to sustain. Early on in their married life William had given her her own bank book to encourage confidence in handling financial affairs. It would seem though that her sense of feeling obliged to follow William's wishes, seeing they had nearly reached execution before his death, proved disastrous. For she got into difficulties with the mortgage and after a few years had to give up the properties.

She then took up her beauty interest by investing in a hat and beauty parlour in Bond Street. For a while she did well. The business was though fatally undermined by some dreadful publicity. It seems that one of her staff made a mistake with a face cream formula which resulted in a famous beauty having her face scarred with acid burns. There was a court case with heavy damages.

She went off to Paris, and little is known of what she did there beyond that she was poor and that rumour had her married to a Frenchman. She fell seriously ill and, as she lay dying, a brother and sister managed to get to her and be with her at the last.

'That is the end of Rosa, faithful wife of William Cory.'[155]

* * * * *

Rosebery's premiership got under way with a distinct handicap. As a peer he was reliant on the leader of the party in the House of Commons for active co-operation in the presentation of policy. In the person of his Chancellor, Sir William Harcourt, that could never be guaranteed. Indeed, Harcourt could seldom bring himself even to mention Rosebery in the Commons. Resentful at being passed over for the Premiership, the consequence of his being a high-handed, overbearing minister in his dealing with his cabinet colleagues, he suspected dark intrigue by the Rosebery faction though Gladstone would not have recommended him. So did many of the public, unaware of Westminster tensions, to whom Harcourt seemed the natural choice.[156]

Rosebery's public speeches sometimes betrayed a lack of awareness of the crucial significance of the minutiae of political utterance on fraught issues. Early on he blundered badly by asserting that before Ireland was given Home Rule the Imperial Parliament, that is *'England as the predominant member of the Three Kingdoms would need to be convinced of its justice and equity'*.[157] The apparent implication that recent efforts seemed to have counted for little aroused a storm in the House of Commons. In a subsequent speech in Edinburgh he managed to put it rather differently but many were left questioning his Liberal credentials. His actions too were often ill-judged. As a former Foreign Secretary he had useful contacts. He overplayed his hand though by conducting negotiations with King Leopold with the aim of keeping the Belgians out of the Sudan without letting the cabinet know what he was up to and similarly of entering into secret negotiations with the French through the British Ambassador. Harcourt was not sufficiently interested in foreign affairs to make the most of these rather Palmerstonian attitudes but on discovering what Rosebery had been up to, gave full vent to an anger for once fully justified.[158]

Harcourt had a striking success with his budget which for the first time introduced the principle of death duties.

Rosebery, a great landowner, queried its effect on the great estates with their possible break-up and dissolution of art collections. Harcourt chose to take this as an attack on the budget as a whole and saw little point in dealing with Rosebery's memorandum in any way except to *'treat it with the contempt which it deserves'*.[159] An ironic consequence of his budget was that he himself later suffered acutely from its provisions and ended his days in some financial difficulty. During his fraught period of office Rosebery had one rather different kind of triumph by winning the Derby, the first Prime Minister to do so, and in repeating the feat the following year. Even this triumph though was sullied in that it roused the wrath of anti-gambling and anti-betting nonconformists.

* * * * *

Rosebery and Brett had been at Eton at the same time but with Rosebery being five years older they'd had little to do with each other though enough for Brett to hero-worship him. He would too have heard Cory's assessment of him as the wisest and wittiest boy who ever lived.[160] He certainly had high hopes of his future, telling a companion when a young man that his ambition was to become Prime Minister, win the Derby, and marry an heiress, all three ambitions later achieved. Politics brought Rosebery and Brett together. As a confidant Brett had the advantage of being out of Parliament and thus in a relatively dispassionate position and found himself frequently summoned to Downing Street. It soon became apparent that Rosebery did not enjoy being Prime Minister. He spoke to Stead of being *'crucified to his post as P.M.'* while wearing *'a crown of thorns'*.[161] Brett was inclined to be dismissive of what seemed at times like megalomaniac self-pity. He enjoyed the confidences and responded with lengthy letters though these often got only the curtest reply. However his role was not entirely submissive and on occasion he urged Rosebery to a more active political role.

Any impression that Rosebery was exaggerating the strain on his health by being Prime Minister was heavily qualified when Brett was summoned to The Durdans, Rosebery's Surrey residence. Here he found a worried Dr. Broadbent who could find only the faintest trace of a pulse and thought him on the verge of mental collapse. The real problem had been lack of sleep. After lying awake, he'd taken to going out for drives during the night.[162] Now he had influenza and was still coming to terms with the recent death of his wife, Hannah de Rothschild, a wealthy heiress who brought him Mentmore.

Rumours swept Newmarket to the effect that Rosebery never had influenza but that his illness was terror at being exposed as implicated in the Wilde scandal. His private life had had moments he would not have wanted exhumed such as the Marquess of Queensberry's threat to horsewhip him for the 'offence' of getting his youngest son a peerage in the House of Lords. It took the Prince of Wales to dissuade him from doing so. There may have been other worries.[163]

* * * * *

Brett admired Rosebery's patrician hauteur but it was not a quality that went down too well with his cabinet colleagues. Too often they would try to see him but find he'd either gone off to The Durdans or to his Dalmeny seat. At other times he would summon them at such short notice that it conflicted with their already made plans. Life in the House of Lords had distanced him from much of the rougher side of politics and he'd had little sense of the ferocity of Harcourt's inter-departmental dealings. Harcourt though sometimes went too far and his displays of huffy bad temper brought some sympathy for Rosebery from his often fractious cabinet. Relations with the Queen were not always easy. She strongly objected to his plans for House of Lords reform as did most of the cabinet. Rosebery here though was more realistic than his critics, arguing that a House which nodded through Conservative measures but which subjected Liberal bills to the closest scrutiny could not continue unchanged for much longer. Yet cabinet blocked any such move.[164]

Rosebery drafted a lengthy statement in which he asserted that with the number of forces ranged against him he might as well be a prisoner in the Tower for all the headway he was able to make. In his boldest move he took his cabinet colleagues aback by threatening to resign and gained a temporary respite from hostility. Rancour soon resurfaced and various bills proved contentious as did any proposed action in the wake of the Armenian massacres. The flash point though was the singularly ill-timed proposal for a statue of Oliver Cromwell in the precincts of the Palace of Westminster which, with its reminders of Drogheda and Wexford, was bound to inflame the Irish Home Rulers.[165] With the Government struggling on other measures, ministers had had enough.

Few British Governments can have imploded quite so utterly. With talk of dissolution and resignation in the air Tom Ellis, the Government whip, urged delay as the Party was not ready for a General Election. But they were, in Robert Rhodes James's words, *'to a man, sick of office'*.[166] After a two-hour cabinet meeting Rosebery went to Windsor to inform the Queen that, with half the Parliamentary session still to run, the cabinet had chosen to resign. The Queen had little choice but to send for Lord Salisbury and usher in a ten-year period of Conservative rule.

On June 24th, 1895, Rosebery dined for the last time in Downing street in the company of the Gladstone's. It was, Mary Gladstone wrote, *'a delightful evening, the late and present Prime Ministers being merry as boys out of school'*. When Brett went round for lunch the following day he found Rosebery packing up the family portraits and making claret cup.

On the 28th the Queen invested him with the Thistle and then it was *'To London – free'* as he wrote in his diary.[167]

It was said of Rosebery that what he really wanted was power without the politics, something of an echo of Cory's observation that he wanted the palm without the dust. Nor did his thin-skinned response to criticism help him make a balanced assessment of appropriate courses of action. Towards the end of his time as P.M. he was criticised for making a number of odd crown appointments, some seeming almost capricious. Brett had been offered and turned down several jobs but accepted that of Secretary of the Office of Works. That invited criticism on the different ground of Whiggery, Rosebery appointing a wealthy friend to serve under Herbert Gladstone, the Prime Minister's younger son.[168]

* * * * *

Out of term Warre led an altogether more bucolic existence. Most of it was spent at Baron's Down, near Dulverton, a comfortable house high up above the Upper Exe. Here along with his family, he became very much a Somerset farmer. After the morning ritual of Psalm and New Testament reading he would on some days put on his wellies for the 'cutting and clearing' operation which, requiring as it did abundant vigour, seems to have been his favourite task, the luxuriant vegetation inviting such regular hacking. His energy was also productive. He excavated and levelled land sufficient for a large tennis court, also used for single wicket cricket, and cut down trees to make a rock garden.

Running the farm took up a good deal of his time and made financial inroads and he seems to have run things at a loss. *'I am a Somerset farmer and am already being ruined by buying stock and implements,'* [169] he wrote to his daughter. It was a substantial business for with the produce of his farm, the vegetable garden, his flock of sheep, as well as what could be obtained from river and woods, Baron's Down was almost self-supporting. He had though to face the same hazards as his neighbours. Wild deer occasionally invaded the farm and ate his turnips while in 1887 a dog killed seven of his sheep.

Visitors noticed how he seemed very much more at ease in the company of Somerset folk than he ever did with Eton masters or boys. He entered fully into the spirit of country life, speaking the dialect well, reading the lesson in the village church, watching the staghound meets, shooting – he was a good shot with a gun, less so with rifle – and enjoying the time-honoured harvest rites such as 'crying the neck' when the last sheaf was gathered. He had too the keenest interest in his natural surroundings, claiming to be able to identify a bird from its song and seemed to have an instinctive accord with domestic animals.

He got around a good deal too. Among his trips there were visits to friends in Keswick, Wells, and Torquay while every Summer he headed north for the shooting. Destinations were Invereshie in Strathspey, Gualin, the remote shooting lodge of the Austen-Leigh's fifteen miles from Cape Wrath, and Inverewe, where he struck up a friendship with Osgood Mackenzie whose 'A Hundred Years in the Highlands' graced Highland bookstalls for several recent decades with memories of a distant age when golden eagles were so common – you could see a dozen in the sky at any one time – that they were culled. With a hefty bag of grouse, snipe, and wood pigeon, Warre reckoned that Mackenzie had given him the best day's shooting he'd ever had. There was also a yachting excursion aboard W.H. Smith's 'Pandora' to have a close look at the British and German fleets. Then there was a trip to Lisbon to see how cousin George and his own second son were getting on with their Douro vineyards.[170]

Behind all this activity it is doubtful whether Eton was ever too far from his thoughts. Baron's Down had many visitors from the College, Edward Austen-Leigh being particularly regular and welcome, and a good deal of Eton business was conducted with schemes being drawn up. A letter from Luxmoore remarks on a serious and confidential discussion with the Head. Nor could he ever forget for long his vocation as teacher. *'Little Francis'*, a grandson, was sat down and taught *'some Greek, his letters, and a few words'*. [171]

* * * * *

While Eton had attracted much hostile criticism in the 1860's it also had plenty of support as shown by the spurt in Upper School numbers during that decade – from 600 boys in 1861 to 770 in 1868. The increase continued until it got near the thousand that the Public School Commissioners had thought too unwieldy.

As Headmaster Hornby had been conscious of the need for additional building to adequately accommodate this number of boys but had been deterred from active insistence by the Governing Body's asking where the money was to come from. Warre though was not going to be so easily deflected.

He straightaway listed what he saw as urgent needs. These were for more schoolrooms, a room large enough to hold the whole school, a new Lower Chapel, a staying-out room for Collegers, and a new Headmaster's house. He was to get all of these but it was to take a considerable time.

Now wearing his Provost's hat Hornby tended to take the line of those who, like the Provost of King's, jibbed at the cost of all this building. There was also concern as to what it would do to the College. In 1885 rumours began to circulate that Savile House and Weston's were to be pulled down and that Upper School was to have its panelling stripped before being converted into a library. None of that in fact happened, the only destruction being that of the 'old' School Library, only built in 1844, the 'gaunt pile' known as 'Wolley-Dods' which few were sorry to see go, and the more attractive Drury's.[172]

Criticism has been made of the aesthetic quality of features of Warre's considerable building : of such aspects as the choice of harsh yellow brick for the new schoolrooms, the unconvincing Gothic decoration on the Lower Chapel, and the way in which the new buildings did not always harmonise well with the older ones or with each other.[173] Warre's over-riding concern though was to get things built quickly ; he saw no time for lengthy lingering over architect's plans. The tendency of the Governing Body to plump for the lowest estimate also did not always make for architectural finesse.

Warre was helped a good deal by the support of the influential Sir William Anson, who joined the Governing Body the same year as Warre became Headmaster and who clearly had much sympathy with his former tutor. Following a dispute on the Governing Body in which it had been suggested that there was a good deal of cramping with so many boys, Warre robustly insisting that his 1000 boys had more space than Hornby's 800 when there had been boys having to share rooms, Anson afterwards wrote to him saying that *'We **ought** to give you more rooms if you want them; the money will always be forthcoming, if by no other means, than by raising school fees'*.[174]

The risk of proceeding too rapidly was brought home with the Lower Chapel where a failure to appreciate the strength of the subterranean Thames in flood resulted in 1891 in a good deal of costly underpinning.[175] Adjoining it were the new classrooms inaugurated by Queen Victoria in 1889. Later laboratories and a museum were added while the racquet-courts were transformed into a music room. To these Warre added at his own expense a large lecture room. There was too a steady addition of new houses over the design of which he had little say.

He was for long reluctant to move into the Cloisters thinking it removed him too far from the centre of Eton's affairs. Eventually though he agreed to have the new Headmaster's house there and had three of the former and then empty Fellows' abodes adapted for the purpose by the resident architect of Windsor Castle. Three impressive rooms were created in dining room, drawing room, and study, along with a fine oaken staircase, though visitors sometimes found the interior layout a little baffling. [176]

The desirability of a room large enough to hold the entire school was insistently urged by Warre and actually approved by the Governing Body in 1885 though not acted upon until 1901. A feeling that the school should offer a worthy memorial to those who had lost their lives in the Boer War arose before the war's end. One was an Eton boy who absconded to South Africa to fight in the war with fatal consequences. Warre got the support of Lord Roberts for a Memorial Hall and new School Library and strong backing after giving one of his best speeches at the Mansion House, Eton then fortuitously having its first Old Etonian Lord Mayor of London for over a century. An executive committee and a committee of taste were set up, the foundation stone was laid in 1905 and the Hall opened by King Edward in 1908. [177]

Warre didn't always get his way. His plan for a new sanatorium with the old one being converted into a choir school never came to fruition. Neither did his idea of a small quadrangle in Brewhouse Yard. [178]

Looking further afield Warre and others were alarmed at the steady growth of Slough and of its seeming imminent encroachment on Eton. Awareness that a length of the Slough road frontage had been bought by speculators to be sold for building lots prompted action. Masters made generous contributions to a purchase fund, one promising a thousand pounds, and, with help from the College, the land was secured. This served two purposes. It provided in Agar's Plough and other nearby land the additional ground for football and cricket matches which Warre had long been seeking. It also helped to secure Eton as an enclave. [179]

Not everything though could be planned for. In the winter of 1894 severe flooding immersed the ground floors of four houses and the school had to be sent home early for Christmas.[180] In 1903 two boys lost their lives in a fire.[181] This possibility had long troubled Warre who in 1899 asked for advice from The London Fire Brigade but seems to have got only a perfunctory response. Only months before the fire the Governing Body asked Housemasters, whose charge they seem to have thought it to be, to make proper provision for fire practice. Then a survey of the drains showed most to be in an unsatisfactory state.

* * * * *

Unsurprisingly, in his position, Warre had many influential acquaintances including the royal family. He had a formal role at Windsor being honorary chaplain to Queen Victoria, the Prince of Wales, and Prince George. The Queen's Jubilee he celebrated with a torchlight procession which delighted the Queen who asked for the boys to be thanked and later had Warre to dine. There was a repeat ten years later.

King Edward had a strong sense of affinity with Eton, throwing open Home Park for the fourth of June festivities and embracing the school's aquatic enthusiasm by once travelling from Windsor to Eton in a gorgeously decorated state barge.[182] A rather more tiresome presence was that of the young German Kaiser who, when staying at the Castle, would often run down to the school and expect to be taken for a walk or engaged in convesation. Warre saw enough of him to write to his sister that *'the young Kaiser will cause a European war if he does not take care'*.[183]

Among his many acquaintances were Tennyson, who once read out San Graal in manuscript form in Warre's garden, Archbishop Benson who was a regular visitor to Baron's Down, Gladstone who in old age twice gave talks at Eton, and Benjamin Jowett, Master of Balliol, who proffered the curious advice to Warre to always be a reformer but not to be caught doing it : he though never had any wish to disguise his activity.

Within the Public School community his influence had steadily grown. His advice had been sought over the selection of Headmaster at Sedbergh and later at Winchester.[184] He became increasingly active at the Headmaster's Conference and in 1892 was elected chairman.[185] That was not at all what Thring and others had had in mind in getting the body started when its initial purpose was to act as something of a counterweight to the influence of the big cheeses by getting unity of purpose among the less heralded schools. Now they had in effect taken it over.

The range of his correspondence was in itself testimony to the spread of Eton's influence throughout the world. From William Carter, then Bishop of Zululand, came fearfulness about colonial administration. *'Colonials only exploit natives; the Imperial Government cares for them.'* [186] From the Rev. A. Polhill in Peking in 1898 came news that *'the Emperor was reported to be putting on foreign dress and cutting off his pigtail'* before abdicating. In 1899 Major Fitton, writing from Omdurman, saw signs of revival in the country and that *'by the end of this year I hope that we shall have put a stop to Mahdism for ever'*.[187] In St.Petersburg Lord Cranley noted the country *'getting deeper and deeper into the mire every day. When I went on leave three months ago the prospects of any active revolt against the so-called Government seemed very remote; now that has greatly changed.'* A month later he noted that *'the fall of Port Arthur has ben accepted with astonishing resignation by the people here'*.[188] A reminder of Eton's educational sway came in a letter from W. Runciman, living in a remote spot in New Zealand, who asked that *'a Greek Testament and a Scott and Liddell'* be sent to him.[189] Warre's old house provided three Indian Governors.

There was also the unexpected correspondence. A Japanese student, assuming Eton to be a college in the more usual sense of the word, and wishing to study law, begins in some trepidation : *'Dear Sir, I have a horror to write to you'*.[190] A postcard from Switzerland asked for a prospectus but wanted to know *'Is there any unnecessary fagging or bullying ? If so my son would be taken away at once. Please put right amount of stamps on.'* [191] The Headmaster of a Negro School in Jamaica asked if Warre could supply cricketing equipment almost unobtainable there and evidently met with a generous response.[192] A friend, Auberon Herbert, wrote to him about *'the attractive yet truly terrible idea that thought lives outside the brain as well as in it'*.[193]

* * * * *

Disaster was narrowly avoided in the Brett household one November night in 1894 when Nellie returned alone to their Tilney Street House.

Most fortunately, she failed to notice a bomb on the doorstep and went straight in. Less than a minute later while she was sitting on a hall chair eating a grape there was a terrific explosion which broke the windows, twisted the railings, and blew the top stone step into the street. The blast going outward, Nellie and the servants were unhurt.

It was thought the bomb had been intended for Mr. Justice Hawkins, a few doors down, who'd recently sentenced some anarchists.[194]

No further alarm on this scale, Brett was able to consider what demands the Office of Works might be making. That he'd accepted this post was a surprise to his friends who thought that from the degree of influence he'd achieved something rather more prestigious might have come his way. The post for him though had two attractions. Being a crown post it was non-political so would not cease with a change of government. Then the nature of the work was bound to bring him within the ambit of the Royal Family.

A good deal happened under his watch. The Mall was transformed, the South Kensington Museum rehoused, the new War Office and Ministry of Health buildings begun while his brief extended abroad with improvements in the Paris Embassy. There was too an abundance of smaller scale work to do with such items as the placing and style of telephone kiosks and lamp posts.[195]

A major part of his work was the maintenance of the Royal Palaces and his term of office saw a complete overhaul. One of his first tasks was to fit a lift for the Queen at Windsor Castle and he thereafter conducted a thorough survey, delving into parts of the palaces overlooked by his predecessors. He found the royal vaults at Windsor in a dreadful state and got the Queen's agreement to have them renovated. The royal remains at Holyrood were in an even more jumbled state and, when told of this, a horrified Queen asked Brett to oversee a more orderly arrangement.[196]

From the first Queen Victoria found him an agreeable presence with his instinctive sense that while tact had to be the default mode in their relationship she also liked flashes of a little more audacity. A book he wrote, 'The Yoke of Empire', a study of her Prime Ministers, managed the diplomatic feat of being approved both by her and her bete-noir, Gladstone, largely by lauding the Queen with lavish praise throughout.[197]

His office brought responsibility for managing the events involved in the Diamond Jubilee. That required the closest co-operation with the Prince of Wales who insisted on being consulted over the smallest details such as where the children's stands should be put on Constitution Hill. To accommodate the numerous suites attending the event Brett installed a large marquee in the Buckingham Palace Gardens. Unfortunately no thought had been given to ventilation and on that stiflingly hot day people started fainting. Appealed to to do something, Brett drew his court dress rapier and made a number of slits in the canvas. A piercing yell though met one of his thrusts as he unwittingly stabbed a housemaid on the other side. In view of the assembled company, perhaps it was as well it was only a housemaid. The event though enhanced Brett's Court approval rating. A huge torchlight tattoo in front of the Palace and a service in St. Paul's both went off without a hitch and earned him a C.B.[198] Already house guests of the Prince of Wales at Sandringham the Brett's in 1898 were invited for the first of several occasions to dine with the Queen.

Another hugely significant event, Gladstone's funeral, proved contentious. For the Prince of Wales insisted on being a pall bearer, much to the Queen's displeasure. Her attitude was succinctly put. *'I never liked him and will say nothing about him.'* [199] Brett was later lightly rebuked for endowing the funeral with overmuch ceremonial. A very different event was an Eton dinner celebrating Curzon's appointment as Viceroy of India.

Some of the frustrations of his post such as having to deal with the often irritable Joseph Chamberlain or the number of pleas for the then fashionable but costly gilding in all manner of Government buildings prompted thoughts of resignation though Rosebery dissuaded him. There was some talk of his going to the War Office and to the Cape as Governor: the last though would have taken him too far away from Maurice. As it was he received the KCVO, the last of Victoria's awards and soon after had responsibility for her funeral.[200]

*****

On retirement as Master of the Rolls Sir William Brett had been created a Viscount though he'd hoped for an Earldom, and took the title of Viscount Esher. On his death in May, 1899, the title passed to his son who became the Second Viscount Esher though here he'll go on being Brett apart from references to the Esher Committee.

By the time of his accession King Edward had established a close working relationship with Brett who'd come to be seen as indispensable. *'For God's sake, don't give up your appointment. You must never leave my service.'* [201]

Brett had been fascinated by the atmosphere of the late Victorian court writing of *'the hushed reverence'* with which *'eminent statesmen and humbler folk alike moved through the corridors of Windsor as though through a shrine'* and which *'made men half afraid to speak above a whisper'*. King Edward conducted matters with less formality. Those summoned entered the room unannounced and, with a parting bow to the King, left when they chose. Brett told Maurice that *'the sanctity of the throne has disappeared'* and could not altogether approve these breezier ways.[202] Sandringham was run without any kind of ceremonial.[203] Edward was though insistent on his need to be consulted over government policy and took an inappropriate level of interest in military detail, once annoyed at not being consulted over a proposed change to the shape of the bayonet. That Brett thought silly, but, having seen how ministers bypassed the elderly Queen, was keen for them to properly recognise the King's constitutional role.

There was a good deal to be done in 1901. As well as planning for the coronation and the less immediate need for consideration of an apt monument to Victoria the King set in train a thorough survey of the royal palaces. His own knowledge of them was rather patchy and it emerged that he'd never properly seen Hampton Court before. He disclaimed any knowledge of art but saw arrangement as a proper royal concern and insisted on being briefed on the detail of ongoing works. To facilitate these works, Brett moved his office to Buckingham Palace.

Royal demand started to become burdensome. The regular summonses to Windsor involved not just the business of the day but the social round of dinner and bridge with the consequence that he was seldom home before 2 a.m. There was another difficulty in that royal service was taking him away from the Office of Works where there was a good deal of other business to see to and Brett made complaint of this to the King. His assiduity though was recognised in his appointment as Deputy Constable and Lieutenant-Governor of Windsor Castle with the medieval right of *'pit and gallows'*.[204]

The King's incessant demands on his time may have been the cause of what seems like a little restlessness. No doubt hoping to enhance his financial position he took up a partnership in Sir Ernest Cassel's financial house. This though was not a success, Brett soon realising he had little aptitude for high finance and he gave it up after two years.[205] The King had been put out at this change of course but relations soon resumed their former geniality with Brett remaining the closest royal confidant. His considerable knowledge of military affairs gave the King another idea – to make him Secretary for War. After wisely asking for time to consider, Brett declined. This appointment would have plunged him into the heart of Salisbury's Conservative administration while its manner would have been bound to have aroused criticism. Above all it would have ended his now cherished independent political role. Again the King accepted Brett's decision with equanimity.

His official involvement in military matters came about in a different way. The South African War had been scrutinised by the Elgin Commission and it had some scathing criticisms. One was the unsatisfactory nature of the relations between the army in the field and the Government and War office at home and it was this state of affairs that Prime Minister Balfour sought to address by setting up a small committee. Esher was asked to chair it and so it bore his name. The other members were Admiral Fisher and Sir George Clark who, described as *'insensitive, clumsy, uncouth, and infinitely boring'* [206] hardly sounds a congenial associate though a strong supporter of Brett's principles. When its report led to a number of dismissals there was considerable resentment but from its deliberations re-emerged the Committee of Imperial Defence and this later became a standing committee. Having himself turned down the War Office Brett was influential in getting appointed the effective Haldane who wasted little time in highlighting the threat to Britain's naval power.[207]

The extent of Brett's backstage influence on affairs was though growing contentious and gave rise to questions both in the Press and in Parliament. 'The Standard' alleged he'd acquired *'to some extent, an executive power without any sense of responsibility'*. Brett strongly denied that that could be the case as his role was purely advisory and that it was up to ministers to take decisions. Though strongly defended by Haldane in the Commons, Brett was badly stung by the unwanted notoriety of this row.[208]

Just how considerable his influence had become at the heart of government was shown in the dying days of the Conservative administration. To discuss the future chain of political events Balfour had a meeting with the King from which the monarch emerged baffled and confided to Brett that he could make little sense of what the Prime Minister had been saying. It was Brett who then arranged a second session between the pair. Further afield, relations between Curzon and Kitchener in India had sunk to such a low pitch that both men habitually assumed the other was lying and a dispute over a comparatively minor matter, as to who should hold the new office of Military Supply Member erupted into a furious quarrel. Both men though were in correspondence with Brett.[209] Balfour was such a close friend that Brett on occasion sat chatting on his bed or having lengthy talks about books. He also witnessed Balfour's jubilation, similar to Rosebery's a decade earlier, on being released from the burden of office. This was the high point of his influence on the nation's affairs.

* * * * *

The Bretts' life acquired a new dimension with the acquisition of a house at Callander, an area of which they'd grown fond. An old hunting lodge of the Dukes of Perth, it was called the Roman Camp or more familiarly 'Pinkie' from its pink roughcast exterior. 30,000 neighbouring acres were also obtained for walks and rough shooting. It soon became their favourite house.[210]

At its heart was Brett's private library and its most treasured section that of the bound volumes, eventually adding up to thirty-nine, of Maurice's letters. Towards the end of his time at Eton Maurice became less the passive recipient of all this affection but instead used it to his advantage by ordering Brett to do things, such as taking him out to the theatre. Later, when Maurice started to date the actress, Zena Dare, whom Brett too fancied in a way described by Oliver as *'the second incest',*[211] he was full of advice on how to go about wooing her, offering the highest praise a girl could get from him, that she was very like a boy. The affair dragged on for six years, she reluctant to give up the stage as was going to be required, Brett once giving her a good talking to about trifling with his son's affections, and Maurice understandably wanting him to back off. Eventually they married in secret. [212]

While Maurice was at Eton Lewis (Loulou) Harcourt, Sir William's lascivious son and secretary, made a pass at him and did the same with Dorothy, leaving her with a deep-seated aversion to men. When left alone at Orchard Lea she developed a crush on a neighbour, Margaret Brooke, taking it to the extent of suddenly popping out from odd corners of her Greyfriars home to surprise her. It was reciprocated only to the extent of seeing if her son, Vyner, fancied her. When it was clear he didn't she had little time for her. After a while Dorothy left home and fell in with the Bloomsbury crowd. Vyner, later the last white Rajah of Sarawak, had though had much more feeling for her sister, Sylvia, whom he later married.[213]

Brett had made a number of attempts to find a job for Edward Seymour but these had been unsuccessful. When though he learnt he had syphilis he lost interest in the youth. Later his place was taken by Laurence Burgis, 'Thrushy', whose ostensible role was to act as a rather speedier secretary.

Maurice, probably jealous, disliked the relationship but it greatly helped Burgis to later success in the army and the cabinet office. [214]

* * * * *

Fundamental changes greatly altered the character of King's in the second half of the century. The abolition of the University Test Act in 1871 meant that non-Anglicans could take up appointments. Keynes and Boris Ord were among a number of highly influential nonconformists who subsequently brought real distinction to the College. The ending of the ban on married Fellows brought academia more into line with society and curbed some of the eccentricity.

With the departure of Provost Austen Leigh a reassessment of College priorities, which had been the subject of debate for some while, became a hotter topic. There had been a growing feeling that overmuch stress had been placed on King's being a teaching College to the detriment of research : that while this emphasis might have been justified in the past to badger undergraduates into taking learning with at least a little seriousness, that that had been rather an Etonian approach, and those days had gone. The advent of Professorial Fellowships strengthened the bond with research.

The College's increased social inclusiveness did not come about without some bitter controversy. An inner ring of Etonians, led by A.C.Benson, considered itself the arbiter of good form and took on 'the bounders'. An ugly consequence of this was the ducking in the fountain of the Canadian freshman Robbie Ross, friend of Oscar Wilde, after exception was taken to an article he'd written in Granta. While he left the College after a breakdown, a conniving Etonian Assistant Tutor, Arthur Tilley, had his office terminated. M.R. James, hitherto very much one of the 'best set', called a meeting to persuade all undergraduates that this bitter divisiveness should stop. 'Hearties' and 'Aesthetes' had rather different ideas about College life but increasingly showed more mutual tolerance. [215]

When elected Provost in 1905, Dr. James was regarded as one of the three or four topmost world experts on the study of manuscripts. He was a quietly effective committee chairman though he heartily disliked being one and at times felt submerged beneath the welter of College business. Always approachable, he was well-liked and sustained friendships longer than most. His instincts were though all for trying to preserve a conservative harmony in the College. He didn't welcome the kind of challenge thrown down by Keynes who, soon after arriving at King's, judged the place *'pretty inefficient'*.[216] Nor did he wish for the kind of expansion being urged by some Fellows. It was said of him that he hated arguments and that has been seen as a weakness for constructive argument has to be the essence of academic life. He could though be firm where he saw cause.

* * * * *

The building of the Choir School involved the College in education at a very different level, albeit at one stage removed.

The building of choir schools with a boarding capacity brought about a revolutionary change in both the education and selection of choristers. The Chapel Royal had recruited boys from any church or cathedral choir when a boy of some talent had been spotted and had had royal authority to do so. When that practice lapsed local youth had to be relied on. Now again recruitment could be from a far wider geographical area, this time on a voluntary basis, at least as far as the parents were concerned. For the boys being adjudicated the most alarming moment was often being taken into the Combination Room and asked to read aloud, usually psalm 49, to a dauntingly gowned group of dons, something a few of them could only manage between sobs. After that, singing in chapel was something of a release.[217]

It also of course implied an obligation to educate the choristers, something which had been only patchily provided up till then. This had been held back, first, by the general assumption that bodies that engaged boys to sing had no broader kind of obligation towards them and that most would end up in trade. The report of the Cathedral Commissioners in 1855 insisted that more be done, *'that there should be connected with every cathedral a school in which the choristers should receive a sound, religious and useful education'*.[218] Further, it urged the selection of boys with the kind of intelligence that might take them beyond trade. Where such schools existed they were though too dependent on the calibre of the cleric giving the boys instruction, standards varying from the competent to the abysmal, while the preference for the Henrician Grammar School shown by the former monastic foundations had the choristers in a disadvantaged position with the time they had to spend out of school with practices and services, especially where both mattins and evensong were sung daily. They were in effect part-timers.

King's boys had to serve in Hall, which unsurprisingly they didn't always do too well, and at other times annoyed the Fellows with noise around the College. One of them, Henry Case, later wrote of how at the end of their time at King's boys were given 'box money' – the amount depending on the length of their time in the choir – to help them get apprenticeships. [219]

The school brought about occasional contact with some of the Fellows, as with the cricket match. The vagaries of the Fellows' bowling had some overs running to fourteen balls while all were not always quite on the same wavelength. M.R. James recalled how, after straining every sinew to try to make a catch but being unable to cling on, his effort brought not a 'hard luck' but a rebuke from the master, the intimidating Benjamin Benham. *"The boys don't care about being allowed to win the match, you know."* [220]

(A match at King's Choir School at this time gave rise to an anecdote which sometimes appears in garbled form, the gist of it being that King's won a cricket match without scoring a run. This was true. What happened was that the boys of the Trinity choir were bowled out for 0 after which a no-ball was sent down.)

The College provided periodic pleasures. Before the Feast with singing in the Hall Vice-Provost Fred Whitting had the boys in his rooms, offering cakes, tea, and roulette (!), while inviting new choristers to have a go at the pandemonium harp which consisted of a number of metal tubes protruding from a cigar box. A blow into the mouthpiece spurted concealed water into the chorister's eyes amid much mirth.[221] Chapel though, then as now, provided the central focus of the year in its Christmas Eve service with its introductory 'Once in Royal David's City', the first verse then sung by all the boys.[222] The evening was for some while rounded off with a gathering in M.R.James's rooms all waiting patiently until he appeared from his bedroom. Blowing out all the candles but one, he'd then start reading his latest ghost story. [223]

* * * * *

One of Dr. James's first tasks as Provost in 1905 was to inform O.B. that his lectureship was being renewed only for three years rather than the customary seven and that at the end of that period he would probably be required to leave King's.[224] Though by the end of a seven year term he would have been over seventy, the usual age for superannuation to be thought appropriate, O.B. was by no means in a mood to accept that. James had insisted that O.B. be given a pension and had threatened to resign were that withheld but got scant gratitude from its querulous beneficiary. O.B. protested that he was still in good health and with much yet to offer the College. That though was unavailing, and he had to depart with as strong a sense of grievance, of Fellows conspiring against him, as he'd had with Eton.

He retired to Bexhill, to live in a house near his sister's. Here he was a prolix hindrance on the golf course and had to endure various indignities such as the dreaded cold Sunday salad supper. He still had though a strong sense of mission. God had told him to write – saying, "You have done enough teaching. You must give up and write".[225] God's instructions seemed to coincide handily with his own inclination. Write he did in the early mornings, penning 400,000 words for his 'A History of the Modern World' in sixteen months and a total of two million after seven years. At that point God spoke again. "You must give up writing and only read and think."[226]

The outbreak of the World War found him in the Apennines from where he moved to Rome where he was to live out the rest of his life. Here he was active in a number of societies ; reading, talking, lecturing, presiding, and quarrelling – all in habitual vein. He carried on a wide-ranging correspondence, Hilaire Belloc and H.G.Wells being two of many participants while there was a regular exchange with Curzon. Sometimes there were letters from the top drawer. Queen Mary wrote to tell him good news *'about her boy'* while he had a letter from the Pope framed and hung up.[227]

The French Government had earlier recognised his distinction and given him a decoration and eventually, just three months before his death, the British Government awarded him an O.B.E. for which he was profoundly grateful.[228] By then his long-term benefactor, Lord Latymer, had commissioned a portrait of him which was hung at Eton, so, in his eyes, ending a long feud.[229] Death he regarded as a mere translation from one sphere to another, but was naturally fearful of the process. Burial he thought repugnant and was relieved by the knowledge that his ashes would join those of other Fellows in King's Chapel.

* * * * *

Brett's relations with Asquith were a good deal more formal than those with Balfour but he made it clear that he wished Brett to continue with his military work.

Asquith would have known of Brett's regular contacts with key personnel and would presumably have known of Brett's bold rebuke to Arnold-Foster at the War Office over his scheme for military reorganisation; of his difference of opinion with Haldane over his plans for a reduction in army numbers; and of his insistence that to meet any potential threat of invasion the number of troops abroad at any one time should be strictly limited.

Rising international tensions bred a sense that the peace would not hold for much longer. Admiral Fisher, for whom Brett had a great respect, was growing ever more convinced of the inevitability of war with Germany. Cassel too could see no other outcome. To Rosebery it was the signing of the Anglo-French agreement that was almost bound to turn Germany into an active enemy. The mood was exacerbated by the Kaiser's manic ranting against England as in his outburst in a box at the Berlin opera, conduct so far outside usual diplomatic constraint as to prompt Sir Edward Grey to suggest that he needed to be put under restraint.[230]

The composition of the army was a matter which continued to exercise Brett. The King and Lord Roberts favoured a conscripted army, the latter pointing out that this was continental practice. Brett though demurred, seeing it as being against British liberal values and something that should only be considered in the direst emergency. Seeing the potential of aircraft, he proposed the formation of a Corps of Aviation, later the Royal Flying Corps. In particular he was anxious that the Committee of Imperial Defence should be taken seriously, get fully briefed over naval plans, and not, as seemed to be the trend, simply be tolerated as a relatively harmless body. He went so far as to threaten resignation were it not to be given proper official recognition.

An altogether different enterprise saw him collaborating with A.C. Benson on an edition of Queen Victoria's journal. They decided on publication only of those letters preceding Albert's death, as many subsequent ones did not show her in the best light. Brett's habit of leaving most of the spadework to Benson may have coloured his reflection that Brett was *'essentially secret and indolent, greedy of reputation, wealth and power, but afraid of real responsibility'*. Few men though could match Benson's prolific literary productivity.

* * * * *

A change of monarch is invariably a time of some apprehension for a courtier and Brett must have been relieved that King George wished to retain his services. One difference between father and son he soon noticed. For whereas Edward would generally listen to advice and then make up his mind on any point George was more prone to indecision. He was too given to outbursts of strong feeling, such as when expressing his dislike of Admiral Fisher, a tendency that Brett viewed with some alarm. He was however immensely serious, rising at 5.00 a.m. to make notes on the day's scheduled events.

Fraught though the international scene was, events at home commanded immediate attention. Manoeuvrings over the Parliament Bill placed the Crown in a tricky constitutional position with the King being given conflicting advice on whether or not to allow Asquith to dissolve Parliament. It took the threat of the creation of many new Liberally inclined peers, with a draft list of 250 drawn up, to get the bill through.[232] The King was subsequently angry at the way the situation had been presented to him by his secretary, Francis Knollys, and he was later eased out of the royal service. Brett sympathised with the King on the poor advice he said he'd been given by ministers. [233]

The combination of Brett's continuing membership of the C.I.D., and his habit of writing about military matters to the Press, plunged him into serious controversy. Noting that the Territorial Force was not enlisting the desired number of recruits, he advocated the case for limited conscription while maintaining that the general practice should continue to be that of voluntary recruitment. Forcibly advocated in an edition of 'The National Review' his writing aroused a torrent of criticism. The periodical, 'The World', attacked him as an 'eminence grise', and part of the King's unconstitutional cabal of advisors. 'The cabal must go!' it demanded. Haldane saw it as an attack on the War Office and Admiralty and both the King and Asquith thought the writing of such articles unwise. The point was also made that from his known closeness to the monarch views expressed by Brett might be taken for the King's. Balfour though could see little amiss with what had been written. Brett apologised for the trouble caused, saying he could always retire if not trusted, but held to his expressed view.[234]

The Agadir crisis, when the Kaiser's gunboat, Panther, was seen off the Moroccan coast, again raised the international temperature. Brett doubted war was imminent, though aware that one might start as a result of nervous precipitation rather than direct intent but saw an absolute need to be ready for some ultimate conflict. Diplomatically he advocated an increasingly improbable alliance between Britain, France, and Germany.

Preoccupied though he generally was with military matters along orthodox lines a pamphlet with a quite different approach to them caught his eye. Written by Norman Angell, and called 'The Great Illusion' it sold 10,000 copies. Addressed to the Kaiser, its message was that armed aggression would never benefit a country. Brett was sufficiently struck by it to set up the Garton Foundation for the study of international polity with himself as chairman and Maurice as secretary.[235] It prompted the comment that Brett seemed to be running both with the hare and the hounds.

From being seemingly intractable, the position in Ireland seemed to be getting graver and sliding towards civil war. The King, deeply worried, for a week summoned Brett for an hour's talk about the situation.[236] Lying awake worrying about it by night, by day the King filled seven exercise books with notes. Curzon and Brett were for settling the unrest by force though after the Curragh Mutiny, when officers resigned their commissions rather than have to face firing on fellow Protestants, that would have been fraught with risk, and Brett later changed his mind.

* * * * *

By the turn of the century Warre was showing signs of old age and ill health. He'd had spasms of heart trouble for some while along with the insidiously debilitating Parkinson's. Such habits as falling asleep during meetings suggested to his colleagues that he couldn't stay in post for very much longer. Anson told him bluntly in the summer of 1904 that the proposed changes being considered seemed beyond his strength to implement and Warre admitted that these were best left to his successor.[237] He had too been facing growing criticism. The Senior Assistant Master, writing to Warre in 1901, gloomily reflected that *'I had always hoped that the strain and stress of the year of war would have made the English more business-like and strenuous in their work as in their games ...... how long is it since we had a first in Mods?....* He advocated *'peremptory interference'* with Pop, unpopular though that would be with O.E.'S to whose sentiments he thought Warre gave undue weight. *'As long as the supreme influence of a purely athletic body is acquiesced in it sets a fashion for the school that we can't stem.'*[238] He also considered too much time given to leave and holidays, too little to lessons. By others Warre was often accused of being a mechanical disciplinarian, of adopting a militaristic mode. This he refuted, arguing that it was rather the case that the need for adequate discipline was, in both army and school, the fundamental basis for effective operation.

When he did resign, in July, 1905, his time at Eton was viewed much more positively.

'Warre changed the conception of a schoolmaster by putting away the buckram and the mask, and the shy and pretentious aloofness of earlier Heads, and by coming among us as he really was.' [239]

And here is the observation of a former Bursar, who had not known him as a boy : *'he had that helpful gift of the born administrator, the faculty of discarding the irrelevant. Moreover, his confidence, once given, was given entirely, and you simply had to live up to it.* [239]

Of the honours that came his way two that meant a good deal to him were his elections as Prebendary of Wells Cathedral and, especially, as Fellow of Balliol.

At both he delivered the occasional sermon. While he had his moments as a preacher – his sermon on St. Paul as a Christian gentleman was deemed memorable – he was for the most part a painstaking but largely uninspiring preacher. The 170 sermons later found showed many instances of sermons written out again for a repeat delivery where only minor alterations had been made to the original. Many of his school sermons harped on sin *'with a big S'.* [240] Another recurrent and complementary theme was the trials of the early church and of lessons to be drawn from them. He was deeply interested in missionary work though Eton's own mission at Hackney Wick was not particularly successful.

As is often the case the incidental anecdote is remembered long after the prepared utterance. So it was when Warre, whose pronunciation had its vagaries, seemed to be warning boys tempted to bet or gamble that *'Dere's an evil elephant (element) in de room'.*[241]

Eton was presented with Sargent's portrait of Dr. Warre for which 1,500 Etonians had subscribed. He himself was given a replica of the Ladies' Plate and an illuminated address in a beautifully bound book. After that there was still £1,400 left over and that was given to him.

* * * * *

Two years before resigning Warre gave up Baron's Down and moved to Finchampstead.[242] With his family now dispersed he may have found the property larger that needed though he left the West Country with a heavy heart. Though he had a comfortable enough house at 'Finch', as he always called it, he was never as settled there as he had been at Baron's Down. There were practical difficulties with stove and water wheel, and maids who disarranged his books, but garden in a state of chaos was a challenge to be welcomed.

His life was regularly punctuated by functions. At various times he was presenting prizes, attending dinners, opening bazaars, preaching, and unveiling monuments. The acquisition of a car, his 'blue lion', helped him to get around, doing some 4,000 – 5,000 miles a year, though with his rather inexpert chauffeur it required a good deal of servicing. All being well it could make Eton in half an hour and Balliol in two. Once at Eton he went into the Memorial Hall, reflecting that he was *'rather in doubt as to whether I like it or not'*.[243] He also found that none of the boys recognised him. Less publicly, he also visited the sick in his neighbourhood and prayed for them.

Retirement gave more time for reflection on events beyond Eton. He must presumably have heard quite a bit about Suffragette agitation but was nonetheless shocked at the sight of 30,000 of them noisily assembled in Hyde Park.[244] Then Bleriot's Cross-Channel flight he saw less as a technological wonder and more as a threat. For now England was *'no longer guarded by the inviolate sea'*, and to counter this threat he saw a need for the creation of *'an army fleet'*.[245]

Contact with Eton was kept up with the regular visits of masters and some not always discreet conversation on school affairs. Warre had been very keen for the Lower Master, F.H.Rawlins, to succeed him but Edward Lyttleton was the Governing Body's choice. Discourse that gave Warre some sense of the temper of the masters under the new regime was probably useful preparation for his return to Eton as Provost in December, 1909. Received by the school captain with a Latin address in the new pronunciation Warre responded uncompromisingly in the old.[246] He found considerable difficulty in responding to the 229 congratulatory letters and telegrams as he *'cannot form my letters'*, presumably a Parkinson's symptom.[247]

He was distinctly unimpressed by the Provost's Lodge, *'a queer and gloomy pace facing north and east and hardly seeing the sun, staircases and passages a regular jungle'*.[248] He engaged his fourth son, who'd had architectural training, to make his desired alterations. These took a year during which he lodged in other houses. Five Tudor fireplaces were uncovered by the work, one of the occasional reminders of Eton's antiquity. Another, a little later, was the discovery by M.R. James, on his return to Eton as Provost, of a dust-covered Tudor songbook. More controversially, there was the opening of the coffin of Henry VI in St. George's Chapel to see if it did contain his bones – the verdict was that it probably did.[249] A little less ancient was the centenary of Pop in 1911.

* * * * *

It's been suggested that Warre's scholarship has been under-estimated. Whether or not that has been so, he was without doubt a serious Classicist with an outlook profoundly shaped by his reading. That could not have been said of his successor whose qualities did not include scholarly accomplishment. His failure to correct a boy who'd construed 'Pheras' as a king rather than a place, then offering the explanation that he was *'one of those old Macedonian kings'* spread embarrassingly widely.[250] That was a significant change.

Eton had been founded to provide its boys with a Classical education and to bring them up in accordance with Christian principles. Awards at Colleges, mainly for Classical excellence, encouraged ambitious study. As the practice had developed of the Sixth Form being taken by the Headmaster it was important that he be a good scholar as well as demonstrating schoolmasterly qualities. Butler and Kennedy were examples of men who brought their schools considerable kudos through their teaching and reinforced the connection with the Universities at a time when some of the gentry needed to be convinced of the point of further study.

Yet to the many boys pursuing the Classics in little more than a desultory fashion and seeing religious observance as tedious formality, the core purposes of the foundation meant little. There was something of a void in these intense communities which were fertile breeding grounds for some form of corporate enthusiasm. This had taken the form of religious zeal at Arnold's Rugby. Later the more Philistine obsession with games shaped schools' outlook and practice. It was said that at Eton only a strong athlete was not thought the worse of for reading.

Earlier a boy who spent too much time playing cricket might have been deemed idle. By Warre's time that situation had rather reversed, and the shirking cricketer was the idler.

Browning's campaign against the increasing dominance of sport, and masters' participation in it, had left no mark. With boys, masters, and parents strongly supporting athleticism the ethos of a school tended to be one in which 'bloods' tended to be prefects and to throw their weight around. Sporting photos show the change of mood. In the earliest the members of the eleven or eight stand, sit, or lounge about in a variety of garb, some looking rather bored with the business. In the later ones there is a collective, drilled eagerness, the only variations in dress being those marking gradations of athletic prowess.

This also matched the desire of Headmasters for boys to spend most of their time in some form of organised, prescribed activity. Warre's

1888 letter to his masters showed his concern that there should be some three hundred boys not actively engaged in sport with the barely concealed inference that they might be getting up to no good. He urged against espionage while insisting on vigilance. But where was the line to be drawn? Which was Warre's own demand that any boys found loitering in Thames backwaters be reported to him? Just how intrusive housemasters were must have depended to a large extent on their own inclination.

Along with this urge for conformity went a distrust of originality which to many masters seemed akin to rebelliousness. Warre had no difficulty in coping with the dense boy but was often baffled by the 'strange' boy.

He was though quite in tune with the prevailing Public School ethos in which uniform standards were seen as highly desirable. The surprise was that even Eton, where traditional liberties had been so highly prized, should have submitted to such a structured regime.

* * * * *

The outbreak of The Great War for a while sidelined the Irish issue. As President of the London Territorial Association Brett's first role was the encouragement of volunteers. Within a year 122,000 had been recruited.[251]

He was though to spend much of the war in France as liaison officer between the two civil and military commands. A fluent French speaker, he had enough insight into the French psyche to know that you were far more likely to get a positive response by appealing to friendship and sentiment than by haggling. Used unofficially at first, his usefulness in the role soon had it confirmed officially.

A constant theme running through his deliberations was the need for an effective command structure, and one that worked well within Britain and between the Allies. Acquainted with the personalities of the leading lights he was only too conscious of the harm that discordant relationships might do. Kitchener and Brett had both doubted the strategic sense of sending an expeditionary force to France, Brett fearing it might be cut off should the Germans seize the Channel ports and even open the way to an invasion of Norfolk.[252] At the head of this force was Sir John French, touchy, quick to sense a slight, and on bad terms with Kitchener whom he suspected of trying to upstage him by appearing in Field Marshal's uniform, though at that time a cabinet minister. He complained of Kitchener's writing to ministers behind

French's back and of interfering with his plans. Trying to maintain some measure of harmony between the pair became one of Brett's functions.

The reality of modern warfare hit home to Brett when he saw how badly wounded soldiers were being treated in a makeshift hospital, one overworked RAMC orderly having to to cope single-handedly. This contrasted markedly with the care being provided by the Americans who, though not yet in the war, had arranged far better medical care. Back in England he was shocked at the general casualness towards the war effort as though this was not anything too different from the Boer War. As to its outcome, he was gloomy. *'We are going to lose this war,'* he wrote to Chat in January, 1915.[253]

The revelation of a serious shell shortage, deemed a scandal by the Press, led to a campaign against Kitchener, judged responsible. Fuel had almost certainly been given to the flames by some of French's aides while French himself spoke to The Times's Colonel Repington. Badly rattled by this roasting Kitchener talked of giving up though the King wouldn't hear of it. To his cabinet colleagues the departure of this overbearing, garrulous man might not have come amiss with Kitchener complaining that Asquith was the only friend he had in the cabinet. Restoring any kind of proper working relationship between French and Kitchener after all that would have been beyond most men but Brett managed to get a letter of apology from French to Kitchener. [254]

There was friction too between Sir John and the French command when Marshal Joffre refused to accept his proposals and Brett was summoned to try to broker an agreement. The cause of the trouble he saw as the lack of an agreed unified command. The establishment of an Inter-Allied Council he saw as at least a step in the right direction.[255] At this fraught juncture in the war Brett was being regularly sent for by the King and Kitchener while Haig asked to see him and one of French's aides thought him in dire need of counsel.

Recruitment having reduced to a trickle on a voluntary basis, both Brett and Kitchener favoured conscription, later given Parliamentary approval. It was he too who had to mollify the Prince of Wales, angry at being taken away from the front and sent to Egypt.[256] Brett thought Gallipoli could have worked if Kitchener had been given a free hand.[257] Then when confidence in Sir John French had finally drained away it was Brett who was sent to tell him that he was to be replaced.[258]

Asquith making it clear to Brett that he wished him to continue with his liaison work in France, he continued to do so in an uncertain situation along with a good deal of work for the Red Cross. He saw a real possibility that France might pull out of the war following the colossal losses at Verdun.

At the same time he wanted the French to be aware of British losses, urging the Foreign Office to release all over France films showing British troops in action. A constant obstacle was the British Ambassador in Paris, Lord Bertie, hostile to Brett from the first, seeing him as an unauthorised interloper on his diplomatic preserve but whom Brett judged to be hopelessly ineffective.[259]

While in Paris for Bastille Day Brett received an urgent message from Haig telling him that a concentrated attack had begun and asking him to tell President Poincare, which he did during the course of the parade.[260] The offensive was the start of the battle of the Somme. Haig soon became seriously alarmed at the scale of the losses but Brett never lost confidence in him, convinced German resistance would fold, and arguing that the scale of the losses would increase morale among the surviving troops. He visited Haig fortnightly, writing back home about feats of British arms.

He was though also looking ahead, aware that the conflict must at some time come to an end, aware too that the French had been considering post-war policies and claims. Encountering Lloyd George on a secret mission to France he asked him about Britain's peace objectives and was told that they hadn't been thought about. From General Robertson he got the understandable response that he was too busy trying to win the war to concern himself with what might come after.

While unimpressed by Lloyd George as an individual, *'a phenomenal little cad'*,[261] he recognised that he was a man who got things done, and that was reason enough to have him as Prime Minister. He instituted one change, and one Brett had recommended two years ago, that the War Cabinet should be a body of five men, all Secretaries of State. This was far more effective than the War Council had been, Asquith finding its meetings a convenient time to compose love letters to Venetia Stanley.

The matter of ultimate command arose again when General Nivelle appointed himself Generalissimo, or so it was at first thought. It transpired though that this was something Lloyd George had authorised without consultation with the British staff and a deliberate slight to Haig. Relations between Lloyd George and his generals, and between the generals, reached a low point with the Prime Minister openly criticising Haig and Robertson, with the latter saying Lloyd George was impossible to work with and faulting Haig. Brett found all this deplorable and a sign of decadence, again seeing the root cause being no settled agreement as to where ultimate power lay.

Brett faced periodic criticism for the role that he, as an unelected individual, had come to play in the nation's affairs and was thought to be trying to legitimise it by going around in colonel's uniform. His rank had been acquired unconventionally but was legitimate in that before the war he'd accepted the Honorary Colonelcy of the 5th Battalion of the Royal Fusiliers.[262] The strain of his war work took its toll and when he became unwell Nellie took him off to Biarritz to recover.

By 1918 Brett was sick of the war, nauseated by the sight of columns of young men singing while marching along to their probable death. He doubted whether he could any longer serve a useful purpose in France though Haig was anxious for him to remain, in particular to deal with the Americans with whom there was certainly diplomatic work to be done, not least to try to dissuade President Wilson from equating German militarism and British naval power. Also, he wanted to get back to Scotland. When he and Nellie returned to England in February, 1918, Haig kept his cipher open.[263]

Nellie had made a substantial contribution to the war in her role as the Founder President of the Territorial Branch of the St. John Ambulance. In France she ran a unit of canteen workers and about eighteen ambulances as well as making regular visits to the twenty-five hospitals for which she had some responsibility.[264] Both of their sons had been kept out of the trenches, Oliver working in intelligence and Maurice as Assistant Provost-Marshal based in Paris.

Back in England after two years in France the Brett's were dismayed by the depressing atmosphere. There was a fear of air raids, no taxi cabs, the royal parks being used to house Government huts or to grow vegetables, tasteless and rationed food, and over much of the country striking workers. This latter practice he put down to Bolshevik influence and suggested to the Palace that a rather more proletarian way of running the household might be advisable, especially in view of widespread critical comments about the monarchy.[265] In deciding to give up alcohol though Brett thought the King was just being silly and enforcing the same bar on his guests made dinner purgatory for the likes of Asquith and Rosebery.

In the final phase of the war Brett had a letter from Haig expressing great anxiety at the German offensive, was relieved when Lord Bertie was finally replaced, and shocked at the murder of the Tsar and Tsarina for which he thought both Government and Court bore a good deal of responsibility.

Peace finally made, he doubted that any subsequent international negotiations would bring about lasting peace. *'War is a tragedy. Peace Congress the farce that follows'*.[266] He did though hope that only Germany would be dealt with severely and lenience shown to the Central Powers.

*****

Being asked to give up the Keepership of the Archives was a signal that Brett was henceforth going to be rather less of a presence at Court.[267] That seemed a little hard as it was he who had created the post and was one from which he drew no pay. He was though to continue as Lieutenant-Governor of Windsor Castle. Despite his altered role the King's servants still regularly consulted him over tricky matters such as what increase in the Civil List to ask Parliament for or whether or not to call a halt to royal pageantry.

More than many of his generation, Brett realised that the war had brought about a profound social change. *'The days of evening dress and solitaire diamond studs are over,'* he wrote.[268] The Victory Ball, with its inevitable ostentation seemed a particularly bad idea. The King was put out by this and other similar sentiments, seeing no reason why previously accepted standards of dress and cleanliness should lapse and asked his secretary, Stamfordham, to have words with his old mentor. Up at the Roman Camp Brett found his own circumstances harder with food and coal expensive and scarce and petrol also costly. He was though still able to afford improvements to both house and garden.

He was not though done with calls to public duty. Haig entrusted him with his notes on the workings of the CQG and GHQ which he read then sealed and passed to the British Museum giving 1940 as the date until they were to be kept secret : Haig had left the year to Brett's discretion.[269] He accepted the Presidency of the Army in India Committee [270] and in June, 1921, agreed on the Prime Minister's request to serve as British delegate on a League of Nations Armaments Commission, his last appointment before retiring to a private life. [271]

The partiality of favour towards his family continued. He got Maurice demobilised speedily from the army to put him at the head of the queue of those seeking public office. With the aid of Lewis Harcourt he got him the post of Assistant Keeper at the British Museum. It was not well paid and Maurice, growing increasingly argumentative, often asked him for money. Relations with Oliver were hampered by his marriage to Antoinette, an American girl of a wealthy family, for whom neither of the Brett's much cared. She had got into their bad books by initialling breaking off the engagement, apparently calling Brett *'a court flunkey'*,[272] and later giving birth to a girl. More significantly for them though it was a happy marriage. Dorothy continued her Bohemian life as an artist, inviting numbers of her associates to share the family's Tilney Street accommodation, some sleeping rough to the horror of the servants. She too was often asking Brett for money and often in such a caustic way as to annoy but he nonetheless encouraged her artistic work. Seeing no attractive future in England she went to New Mexico to be near D.H. Lawrence and Frieda. Rajah of Sarawak might sound a pleasing title but its holder seemed to Brett *'a perfect loony of a husband'* [273] and his daughter Sylvia not much better. The only grandchildren he had any time for were Maurice's and Zena's, in particular lavishing attention on Tony and paying his Stowe School fees.

Reading and writing occupied much of his time, often sharing his views with Chat. Meredith and Hardy he put in the front rank of novelists while recommending the poetry of Brooke and Sassoon. Lytton Strachey's 'Queen Victoria' he found insightful, despite its faults, and he added an introductory essay to the first volume of Sir Philip Lee's 'Life of King Edward VII'. He wrote 'Cloud-Capp'd Towers', an account of life in the great houses and of their illustrious occupants and, more controversially, 'The Tragedy of Lord Kitchener' in which he wrote rather more that did not embellish the reputation of a man still widely regarded as a national icon than some wished to read. [274]

Still, he could never sink entirely into private life. Maurice Hankey wrote to him asking for his views on the ideal cabinet composition and division of function, he had letters from Haig, and the informal relation he'd long had with the Queen and Prince of Wales continued. The prospect of a Labour Government he found worrying primarily in view of Ramsay MacDonald's lack of ministerial experience though later he and his daughter Ishbel stayed at the Roman Camp. He thought little of Baldwin's handling of The General Strike and became disillusioned with him.[275]

The end came suddenly when, staying with Nellie at Tilney Street, he suddenly dropped dead in his dressing room. An unbelieving Nellie rang Sylvia who was then in London to come and see if he were merely unconscious. Convinced he was dead she reflected that *'You will never be able to hurt me any more. I had no feeling of loss or sorrow because I had never really loved him.'* [276] By contrast Chat was distraught at the news. A telegram of commiseration reached Nellie from Sandringham along with a cable and letter from the Prince of Wales in South Africa.

Maurice edited the first two volumes of his letters and journals, a task which Nellie saw through to completion after Maurice's own death in 1934. Oliver then edited volumes three and four. Of the many comments after his death that of Harold Nicholson seems particularly apt. *'No man has ever had his finger in so many pies .... He was the most perfect of all lubricants.'* [277]

GLADSTONE'S TABLE TALK

(A.C.Benson, in his 'Fasti Etonenses' (1899) recalled dining with Gladstone)

In the summer of 1897 I was staying at Hawarden, and dined at the castle; I sate (sic) on Mr. Gladstone's right hand. He began to talk to me at once about Eton, and the numbers of the school. He tried to recollect the names of the masters of his own time, but could recollect only two or three – Drury and Heath, I think : I said, "Was not Knapp one ?" He turned round to me with a smile and said, "I ought to have remembered him, he was my tutor." He then described his being complained of by Heath. He said, "Three boys got round me, and persuaded me not to mark them out of school; – it was a momentary lapse of morality – had I had time to reflect, I should have said, No, but they took advantage of a very rare impulse of warm-heartedness. Heath was very angry, and to bring the enormity of my offence home to me said, "Praeposter, put yourself in the Bill -- and now, where can I find a trusty boy (with a stern look at me) to carry the Bill to the Headmaster ?" I was flogged – the only time.

There was a poor, stupid, worthy boy in my division, B – by name, whom Heath disliked. Heath came in one afternoon – very much excited, as he often was – and said to the Praeposter, "Put down B – in the Bill for breaking my windows." B – started up, "I have done nothing of the kind, Sir." "Put down B – in the Bill for lying and breaking my windows." The boy lost control of himself and said, "On my honour, Sir, I have done nothing of the kind." "Put down B – in the Bill for swearing, lying, and breaking my windows!"...

Mr. Gladstone spoke of Keate a good deal, and said that Keate ruled by 'terror without cruelty'. He seemed much interested to hear of my Eton book and said, "Put in all you can about Keate." I said that I had been struck with the fact that Keate was more humane than often supposed. He laughed and said, "I don't know about that — where did you get that from ?" There was not much humanity about him. I knew that other people were sometimes in a passion, but Keate, I thought as a boy, was always in a passion." He went on to describe Keate's reading of Blair's sermons — then his addressing the School, giving out notices, and the boys *booing* Keate — a humming noise with lips closed (he illustrated this by booing loudly) — so that Keate could never detect the offenders; "a truly British national thing that — I fear it has died out ?" "Yes," I said. "I am sorry," he replied, "that booing has died out — it gave us a sense of our national privilege of disagreeing with constituted authority." ....

Religion was then non-existent at Eton. I told my father that I did not wish to be confirmed at Eton, but the fiat went out that I was to be included among the candidates. The order was given us all for a book of sermons — but we never got it, though our parents paid for it, and Pote had the money. We were never asked if we read it — I went three times to Knapp, my tutor. He came out of his study — took up a volume of Sinclair's sermons — there was not an ounce of Christianity in them — read a couple of pages, shut the book up with a snap — said "you can go", and walked out. Three times that happened, and never another word of advice. ....

He said that Bishop Pelham of Lincoln in his address to candidates for confirmation at Eton, after a list of things to avoid, added, "and let me urge you to maintain the practice of piety, without lukewarmness, and above all, without enthusiasm !" ......

Someone at the table said they were content with the system that could produce such results. Mr. Gladstone said, "Eh!" then smiled, shook his head and said, "No, no, the system was without merit." He was silent for a moment, still shaking his head, then he said, "I will tell you a story about Hamilton — Hamilton arrived in the middle of a Half on a Saturday, and had to go into 3 o'clock church. He took a prayer book and was called 'Methodist', because it was not the custom to carry prayer-books on week-days. The next day, Sunday, he was determined to do as others did — he was a timid, sensitive boy — and took no prayer-book — but it was the convention for boys to do so on Sundays, so he was called 'Atheist'. It was mere convention — no sense in it."

He was silent for a moment, then resumed, "It is a wonder there was any religion among the boys at all, considering what masters were. A — was a profligate fellow, he used to make periodical visits to London.

B – was little better. C – often came to school drunk. I daresay they had little heart to speak to us about religion, considering what they practised themselves."

"The three great reformers of Eton to whom she owes most are Hawtrey, G.A.Selwyn as private tutor, and the Duke of Newcastle, who compelled the study of Divinity by his scholarship. The Greek Testament in our day was merely construed – not a word of comment. Till Hawtrey's time no one had any misgivings that they were on the wrong track – such is the deadening influence of monopoly on the human mind."

He spoke very warmly of Hawtrey, and said, "Hawtrey sent me up in the Fourth Form. I was heartily surprised, not only at the fact, but that Hawtrey should take so much interest in me. He was a great man and first inspired me with a desire to know and to do – but he had a sad lack of business capacity."

He spoke of Milnes Gaskell and his love for politics. "Milnes Gaskell's whole career was spoilt by his never having any wholesome advice to do anything he disliked. Milnes Gaskell had a cult for Mr.Canning (Gladstone always spoke of *Mr.* Canning and *Mr.* Pitt), and inoculated us all with a love for politics. He was very anxious to join the Eton Society, and bribed all the members with presents of *fruit*. I was awakened one morning by the bed maker, or whatever she was called, staggering into my room with a dish of fruit – a present from Milnes Gaskell, But we ought rather to have bribed him, for he saved the Society by keeping the Journal so well. We were not Liberals or Tories in those days – we were Canning or non-Canning." ....

The Dean of Lincoln, who was present, asked whether there were any Liberals in their Debating Society : "Why no," said Mr. Gladstone, "but we were restricted to debate no political event within fifty years. There was indeed one poor, miserable, misguided fellow, a Colleger, who was thought to be a Liberal. In one of his speeches he was reduced to saying that the *Bible* was a *Tory* book ! But (smiling) I am unable to agree with him."

He went on :

"Milnes Gaskell was put up to make a speech on duelling, and I had to second him. A curious choice – for I never met anyone but Milnes Gaskell who was more deficient in physical courage than myself. He made a fiery speech. 'Will you tell me that Mr. Pitt was less of a patriot because he fought a duel with Tierney – or that Mr. Canning was less of a Christian because he fought a duel with Lord Castlereagh ?' " This sentence Mr. Gladstone spoke high and loud, and made magnificent gestures at me with his hand, holding it high in the air and sweeping it to the ground. The name of Simeon was mentioned, whereupon Mr. Gladstone said, "I saw Simeon in 1815, my parents took me to Cambridge – we went to his rooms ; he was very precisely dressed like a high dignitary of the Church, not a mere College fellow – he had very courtly manners." ……..

As we left the dining-room, Mr. Gladstone said : Talking of Keate's popularity, in 1842 I was at Election Dinner, and sat next to Lord Carlisle. The Queen's health was drunk with only a few cheers, as she was suspected of Liberal tendencies. Queen Adelaide was cheered more loudly as a Tory – but it was *Keate* we cheered : he sate with his head bowed to the storm, and when it ceased, rose and stammered a few words out and sate down – it was more eloquent than any rhetoric – we were all profoundly moved – and yet we had all professed to hate him."

A few days after, I received the following autograph letter from him : -

Hawarden,
Aug. 26, 97

Dear Mr. Benson,

When you gave us the pleasure of your company at dinner on Tuesday, and indicated an intention of writing on the Keatian period, you made me very talkative, but there were two things I omitted to state.

1. One was that Eton Masters of my day, to whatever criticisms they might be open, had a great deal to do, and may, I think, be justly considered as hard workers.

2. The other was that while the teaching may be considered as narrow and as affording no proper aids to the pupil, in one point it was admirable, I mean its rigid, inflexible, and relentless accuracy. This property I think invaluable and indispensable. It has been my habit to say that at Eton in my day a boy if he chose might learn something, or might if he chose learn nothing, but that one thing he could not do, and that was to learn anything inaccurately.

Yours most faithfully,

W.E. Gladstone

CHAPTER NINETEEN : BENSON'S VIEW

A.C. BENSON WAS AN ETON MASTER FROM 1885 – 1903, A PERIOD CORRESPONDING almost exactly to Warre's rule. From a later vantage point as Fellow of Magdalene College, Cambridge, he reflected in some of his many essays on the state of Public School education. There he was in a position to judge of the effects of the system. His pessimistic tone has more than a passing resemblance to that of Wilkinson, a century earlier, quoted at the opening of this book. That is seen in some excerpts from 'Education', one of the chapters in 'From a College Window'.

'I said that I was a public-school master for nearly twenty years ; and now that it is over I sometimes sit and wonder, rather sadly, I am afraid, what we were all about.

We were a strictly classical school ; that is to say, all the boys in the school were practically specialists in classics, whether they had any aptitude for them or not. We shoved and rammed in a good many other subjects into the tightly packed budget we called the curriculum…….'

'The whole thing whizzed, banged, grumbled and hummed like a factory ; but very little education was the result. It used to go to my heart to see a sparkling stream of bright, keen, lively little boys arrive, half after half, ready to work, full of interest, ready to listen breathlessly to anything that struck their fancy, ready to ask questions – such excellent material, I used to think. At the other end used to depart a slow river of cheerful and conventional boys, well-dressed, well-mannered, thoroughly nice, reasonable, sensible, and good-humoured creatures, but knowing next to nothing, without intellectual interests, and, indeed, honestly despising them….. It is a melancholy picture, but the result was that intellectual cynicism was the note of the place.'

So what was going wrong ?
'To provide a classical education for the best boys, everything else was sacrificed. The boys were taught classics, not on the literary method, but

on the academic method, as if they were all to enter for triposes and scholarships, and to end by becoming professors. Instead of simply reading away at interesting and beautiful books, and trying to cover some ground, a great quantity of pedantic grammar was taught; and time wasted trying to make boys compose in both Latin and Greek, when they had no vocabulary, and no knowledge of the languages. It was like setting children of six and seven to write English in the style of Milton and Carlyle.'......

'The reason why cynicism sets in, is because the boys, as they go on, feel that that they have mastered nothing. They have been set to compose in Greek and Latin and French ; the result is that they have no power of composing in any of these languages, when they might have learnt to compose in one. Meanwhile, they have not had time to read any English to speak of, or to be practised in writing it. They know nothing of their own history or of modern geography ; and the blame is not with them if they find all knowledge unattractive.'

Supporters of traditional methods of teaching the classics had rather different ideas.
'The idealist says, "Never mind the use ; get the best educational instrument for the training of the mind, and, when you have finished your work, the mind will be bright and strong, and capable of discharging any labour." That is a beautiful theory but it is not borne out by results. ….. These theorists continue to talk of classics as a splendid gymnastic, but in their hands it becomes a rack ; instead of leaving the limbs supple and well knit, they are strained, disjointed, and feeble……. And if that is true of average boys educated on this system, what is it that classical teachers profess to have given them ? They will say grip, vigour, the fortified mind. But where is the proof of it ? If I saw classically educated boys flinging themselves afterwards with energy and ardour into modern literature, history, philosophy, science I should be the first to concur in the value of the system. But I see, instead, intellectual cynicism, intellectual apathy, an absorbing love of physical exercise, an appetite for material pleasures, a distaste for books and thought.'

There was another aspect to this.
'What our teachers fail in – and the most enthusiastic often fail most hopelessly – is in sympathy and imagination. They cannot conceive that what moves, touches, and inspires themselves may have no meaning for boys with a different type of mind.'

The outcome of this education can be seen at university.

'Many of them are fine, vigorous fellows ; but they often tend to look upon their work as a disagreeable necessity, which they do conscientiously, expecting nothing from it. They play games ardently, and fill their hours of leisure with talk of them. Yet one discerns in mind after mind the germs of intellectual things, undeveloped and bewildered.' ....

'The classics are retained as a subject in which all must qualify ; and the education provided for the ordinary passman is of a contemptible, smattering kind ; it is really no education at all. .... The truth is that the intellectual education of the average Englishman is sacrificed to an antiquated humanist system, administered by unimaginative and pedantic people…..'

'And the only way in which we stifle mental revolt is by leaving our victim in such a condition of mental abjectness and intellectual humility, that it does not even occur to them to complain of how unjustly they have been treated. After all, we have interfered with them so little that they have contrived to have a good time at University. They have made friends, played games, and lived a healthy life enough ; they resolve that their boys shall have a good time too, if possible ; and so the poor educational farce is played on from generation to generation.'

'Whether anything can be done to help us out of the poor tangle in which we are involved, I do not know. I fear not. I do not think that the time is ripe.'

* * * * *

He did though have some more positive ideas.

'The staple of education should be French, easy mathematics, history, geography, and popular science. I would not even begin Latin and Greek at first. Then, when the first stages were over, I would have every boy with a special gift put to a single subject, in which he would try to make real progress, but so that there would be time to keep up the simpler subjects as well. .... And if the result was only that a school sent out boys who could read French easily, and write simple French grammatically, who knew something of modern history and geography, could work out sums in arithmetic, and had some conception of elementary science – well, they would, I believe, be fairly educated boys.'

'I would try all sorts of experiments. I would make boys do easy précis-writing ; to give a set of boys a simple printed correspondence and tell them to analyse it, would be a task in which the dullest would find some amusement. I should read a story aloud, or a short episode of history, and *require them to retell it in their own words. Or I would relate a simple incident, and make them write it in French ; make them write letters in French.'…*

'At present each of the roads – Latin, Greek, mathematics, science – leads off in a separate direction, and seems to lead nowhere in particular.'

'The truth is that the present results are so poor that any experiments are justified. The one quality which you can depend upon in boys is interest, and interest is ruthlessly sacrificed.'

Two other factors helped to perpetuate the status quo.
'Classical proficiency is still liberally rewarded by scholarships and fellowships ; and while the classical tradition remains in our schools, there are a good many men, who intend to be teachers, who enter for classical examinations. But where we fail grievously is in our provision for average men ; they are provided with feeble examinations in desultory and diffuse subjects, in which a high standard is not required.'

As for these prospective teachers :
'Masters, at all but a very few public schools, are still so poorly paid that it is impossible for the best men to adopt the profession, unless they have an enthusiasm which causes them to put considerations of personal comfort aside. It is only too melancholy to observe at the University that the men of vigour and force tend to choose the Civil Service or the Bar in preference to educational work. I cannot wonder at it.'

A fundamental problem was that *'we do not know what we are aiming at'.* …. *'At present, education as conducted in our public school and university system appears to me to be neither utilitarian nor intellectual. It aims at being intellectual first and utilitarian afterwards, and it misses both.'*

'I say, quite honestly, that I had rather have the old system of classics pure and simple, taught with relentless accuracy, than the present hotchpotch. But I earnestly hope myself that the pressure of the demand for modern subjects is too strong to be resisted.'

He concludes the chapter putting this more strongly by declaring that *'if the subject continues to be shelved, if our educational authorities refuse to consider the question of reform …. I would rather have a revolution, with all its destructive agencies, than an unintelligent and oppressive tyranny.'*

CHAPTER TWENTY : AFTERWORD

Boys left their Public Schools with very mixed emotions The fourth Lord Lyttleton, sat in a railway carriage taking one last look at the school, experienced *'one of the heaviest and deadliest feelings I ever knew, to find that I was no longer a boy'*.[1] Another Etonian, leaving in 1865, could *'hardly believe it'* ,[2] sensing the pulsing energies of school life being replaced by what seemed a fathomless void. By contrast Charles Merivale thought himself scarred for life *'by the sense of social inferiority which was impressed on me at Harrow'*.[3] Trollope too had little reason to remember his time as a charity boy at Harrow kindly after having to leave Winchester through his father's financial difficulty and where he saw himself *'as a wretched farmer's boy, reeking of a dunghill'*[4] and publicly rebuked for his shabbiness by the Head. Thackeray emerged from Charterhouse with a broken nose, sustained in an epic fight with one Venables with whom nonetheless he remained on lifelong good terms, with a sense of having been *'abused into sulkiness and bullied into despair'*.[5]

Most boys leaving in the 1860's would have been aware, to a greater or lesser degree, of the controversy swirling in the Press about the character of these schools and a central feature : that there seemed little connection between the classical education they received and the huge changes transforming Victorian society which were starkly apparent to others. Telegraph and railways revolutionised communications, the latter thrusting deep into the countryside : even the horsiest squire could not be unaware of *'the iron chimeras fed with fire'*.[6] Then Eton and other schools were, in varying degrees, out of kilter with the growing mood of the time for appointment to be made on the basis of merit rather than personal acquaintance. The somewhat incestuous practices of Eton and Winchester seemed more like a Whig anachronism.

Strong feelings were aroused and sharp words used in the war of words that covered so many periodical pages. Yet feelings were not always as polarised as some of the language suggested. Although 'The Times' conceded that the educational deficiency could result in *'downright ruin'* [7] it was nonetheless anxious that things should go on much as before, in particular not wanting disturbance of the hereditary pattern. Then Henry Reeve, one of the sharpest critics, yet conceded that *'Eton boys are early imbued with the qualities of spirit, honour, and endurance which mould and mark the character of English gentlemen'*[8]

A.C. Benson concluded his 'Fasti Etonenses in similarly lyrical mood, no doubt thinking a celebratory volume of Eton's past not the place for his misgivings when he wrote that *'in the face of so much change, the essential spirit of the place is somehow the same ; the spirit of reasonable liberty is paramount'*.[9] This he clearly deemed not the place for the kind of observation he put in his diary after a visit to see Warre at Baron's Down.

'After tea he unfolded to me his scheme, with red and blue pencils, drawn very clumsily on blotting paper. It was no scheme at all. He said, "We mustn't have a modern school. We must say boldly that we give a good classical education" ... In fact his scheme is to keep the present scheme intact and specialise a little more – and call it reform. He really is hopeless I fear.'[10] He did though note the force of his presence and called him *'a great man'*.

Much of Eton's well-being he put down to the Clarendon Commission. *'The Act of Parliament, which made law of their recommendations, reconstituted the government of the School. The Act proceeded with a somewhat ruthless regard for ancient traditions, but on the whole the results were salutary. The school ceased to be medieval, and became modern.'* [11]

He had no sympathy with the pre-Clarendon Fellows whose altered status he reckoned they had brought on themselves. In one regard though he wondered whether reform had gone far enough, whether retaining the office of Provost had been altogether wise, harking back to the difficulties Goodall and Hawtrey had caused and thinking it highly unlikely that any of the newer schools would create a situation in which someone with a rather undefined role was put in a superior position to the Headmaster.

More generally, the idea that the 1868 Act had at a stroke transformed Eton and other schools from medieval to modern institutions is surely over-stating its effect. As seen earlier only some of the report's recommendations made it into law and others only patchily into practice.

The fears of Warre and others that the Government would introduce an over-arching programme of legislative reform were not borne out. In any case, legislation could only require a minimum compliance. It could not of itself ensure productive science laboratories or proficient modern linguists. That needed energy and commitment from the school. Enabling the possibility of managerial and curricular change by making both the clear responsibility of the Governing Body was the most potent legacy. Yet while there remained a strongly conservative inclination with the hold of the Classics proving tenacious – as late as the 1960's 'O' level Latin was a general University admission requirement – fundamental change was more a latent possibility than an observable trend.

At its outset the Clarendon Commission had been traumatic for those deeply ensconced in a traditional role, like Edward Hawtrey, and alarming for classical masters who saw their raison d'etre under threat. Others viewed it rather more with equanimity, approbation, and sometimes enthusiasm. Transformative change was to come about in instalments, step by step, rather than through any single event. Whether the Clarendon Report did any more than deliver a sharp jolt to the system is questionable.

Notes

PREFACE

1. Wilkinson, Rev. Charles Allix, *Reminiscences of Eton,* page v 1888
2. Norman, Capt. F.M. *At School and at Sea,* page 12. 1899
3. ibid. page 14
4. ibid. page 16
5. ibid. page 17
6. ibid. page 17
7. Markham, Capt. F. *Recollections of a Town boy at Westminster,* page 31. 1903
8. Report of the Public Schools Commission. 1864. Vol.1, page 12
9. ibid. vol. 1, page 31.
10. Markham. op. cit. page 57
11. Tucker, Rev. W.H., *Eton of Old; or Eighty Years since 1811 to 1822,* page 162. 1892
12. Shrosbee Colin, *Public Schools and Private Education,* page 57. 1988
13. Thackeray, W.M. *Irish Sketch Book.* 1842
14. Shrosbee. op. cit. page 53
15. Westminster Review. July, 1825
16. Browne, Janet. *Charles Darwin,* page 34. 1995
17. Turner, David. *The Old Boys,* page 69. 2016
18. Browne. op. cit. page 24
19. Lamb G. F. *The Happiest Days,* chapter 8. 1959
20. Tucker. op. cit. page 177
21. Markham. op.cit. page 68
22. ibid. page 11
23. Norman. op.cit. page 10
24. ibid. page 11
25. ibid. page 1
26. ibid. page 32
27. Chandos John. *Boys Together,* page 227. 1985
28. Tucker. op. cit. page 198
29. ibid. page 28. 2016
30. Norman. op. cit. pages 33-34
31. ibid. page 31

CHAPTER ONE : ETON'S LONG CHAMBER

1. Compton Mackenzie, Faith. *William Cory,* page 1. 1950
2. ibid. page 5
3. Ainger, A.C. *Eton Sixty Years Ago,* page 25. 1917
4. Tucker W.H. *Eton of Old; or Eighty Years since 1811-1822,* page 14
5. ibid. page 14
6. ibid. page 1
7. ibid. page 43
8. ibid. page 19
9. ibid. page 17
10. Tucker. op. cit.
11. Gathorne-Hardy, Jonathan. *The Public School Phenomenon,* page 62. 1977
12. Tucker. op. cit. page 31
13. ibid. page 38
14. ibid. page 31
15. ibid. page 32
16. ibid. page 44
17. ibid. page 33
18. ibid. page 30
19. ibid. page 28
20. ibid. page 35
21. ibid. page 46
22. ibid. pages 66-67
23. ibid. page 20
24. Coleridge, Arthur Duke. *Eton in the 1840's,* page 46. 1896
25. ibid. page 420
26. Tucker. op. cit. page 9
27. Wilkinson, C.A. *Reminiscences of Eton,* page 19. 1888
28. Tucker. op. cit. page 9
29. ibid. page 17
30. ibid. page 17
31. ibid. page 15
32. ibid. page 15
33. Ainger. op. cit. page 163
34. Tucker. op. cit. page 118
35. Wilkinson. op. cit. page 21
36. Tucker. op. cit. page 24
37. ibid. page 106

38. ibid. page 70
39. ibid. op. cit. page 71
40. ibid. page 64
41. Wilkinson. op. cit. page 23
42. Tucker. op. cit. page 96
43. ibid. page 22
44. ibid. page 96
45. ibid. page 140
46. ibid. page 169
47. Chandos, John. *Boys Together,* page 206. 1985
48. Tucker. op. cit. page 67
49. ibid. page 40
50. Wilkinson. op. cit. page 164
51. ibid. page 171
52. Gathorne-Hardy. op. cit. page 59
53. Wilkinson. op. cit. page 164
54. Tucker. op. cit. page 130
56. Wilkinson. op. cit. page 129
57. ibid. page 136
58. ibid. pages 142-143
59. ibid. page 328
60. ibid. pages 324-325
61. ibid. page 51
62. ibid. pages 311-316
63 ibid. page 73
64. ibid. pages 330-331
65 Coleridge. op. cit. page 91
67. Lyte, H.C. Maxwell. *History of Eton College,* page 419. 1911
68. ibid. page 401
69. ibid. page 403

CHAPTER TWO : KEATE

1. Benson, A.C. *Fasti Etonenses,* page 297. 1899
2. ibid. page 285. Quoting A.W. Kinglake's *Eothen*
3. ibid. page 286
4. ibid. page 287
5. Tucker, W.H. *'Eton of Old',* page 155. 1892
6. Benson. op. cit. page 287
7. ibid. page 288
8. ibid. page 28

9. Tucker. op. cit. page 187
10. Wilkinson C.A. *Reminiscences of Eton,* page 51. 1888
11. Tucker. op. cit. page 8
12. Wilkinson. op. cit. page 62
13. ibid. page 257
14. ibid. pages 100-105
15. Chandos, John. *Boys Together,* page 202. 1985
16. ibid. page 205
17. Wilkinson. op. cit. page 97
18. Chandos. op. cit. page 223
19. Tucker. op. cit. page 193
20. ibid. page 201
21. ibid. page 203
22. ibid. page 204
23. ibid. pages 205-206
24. Wilkinson. op. cit. page 41
25. ibid. page 15
26. Chandos. op. cit. page 202
27. Tucker. op. cit. page 84.
28. ibid. page 183
29. Wilkinson. op. cit. page 20
30. ibid. page 20
31. Tucker. op. cit. page 183
32. Chandos. op. cit. page 228
33. Brinsley-Richards, James. *Seven Years at Eton,* page 402. 1883
34. Tucker. op. cit. page 181
35. Wilkinson. op. cit. page 46
36. Tucker. op. cit. page 176
37. Chandos. op. cit. His account of the fight followed closely.
38. Tucker. op. cit. page 187
39. ibid. page 184
40. ibid. page 165
41. Brinsley-Richards, op. cit. page 403.
42. Tucker. op. cit. page 125
43. ibid. page 116
44. Wilkinson. op. cit. page 116
45. ibid. page 127
46. Tucker. op. cit. page 130
47. Benson, A.C. op. cit. page 296
48. Tucker. op. cit. page 188
49. Chandos, op. cit. page 217
50. Lyte, H. C. Maxwell. *History of Eton College,* pages 384-5. 1911

NOTES

51. Brinsley-Richards. op. cit. page 422
52-56. Wilkinson. op. cit. pages 33-39
57. Tucker. op. cit. page 181
58. ibid. page 72
59. Chandos. op. cit. page 218
60. Benson. op. cit. page 302
61. Chandos. op. cit. page 219
62. ibid. page 220
63. ibid. page 197
64. Wilkinson. op. cit. page 17
65. Tucker. op. cit. page 194
66. ibid. page 210
67. ibid. page 159
68. ibid. page 167
69. Wilkinson. op. cit. page 124
70. Tucker. op. cit. page 155
72. Wilkinson. op. cit. page 4
73. Benson. op. cit. page 283
74. Tucker. op. cit. page 169
75. ibid. page 228

CHAPTER THREE : ROUGH AND TUMBLE

1. Chandos, John. *Boys Together,* page 80. 1985
2. ibid. page 80
3. ibid. pages 81-82
4. Markham F. *Recollections of a Town Boy at Westminster,* page 195. 1903
5. Chandos. op. cit. pages 88-89
6. ibid. page 82
7. Taylor, D.J. *Thackeray,* 1999
8. Chandos. op. cit. page 156
9. Chandos. ibid. page 133
10. Chandos. ibid. page 88
11. Browne, Janet. *Charles Darwin,* page 23. 1995
12. Bamford, T.W. *The Rise of the Public Schools,* page 73. 1967
13. Markham. op. cit. page 236
14. Johnson, Paul. *Spectator column*
15. Coleridge, Arthur Duke. *Eton in the 1840's,* page 10. 1896
16. Turner, David. *The Old Boys,* page 61. 2015
17. Chandos. op. cit. pages 101-102
18. Smith, Sidney. *Edinburgh Review.* 1810
19. Brinsley-Richards, James. *Seven Years at Eton,* page 407. 1883
20. Glendinning, Victoria. *Trollope,* page 23. 1992
21. Chandos. op. cit. page 95
22. Taylor. op. cit. page 40
24. Gathorne-Hardy, Jonathan. *The Public School Phenomenon,* page 57. 1977
25. Johnson, C. *The Ely and Littleport Riots,* page 22. 1893
26. Benson, A.C. *Fasti Etonenses,* page 321. 1899
27. Chandos. op. cit. page 183
28. ibid. pages 186-189
29. Benson, A.C. op. cit. page 290
30. Gathorne-Hardy. op. cit. pages 102-105
31. Newsome, David. *Godliness and Good Learning,* page 82. 1961
32. Chandos. op. cit. pages 149-150
33. Gathorne-Hardy. op. cit. page 58
34. Briggs, Asa. *The Age of Improvement,* page 215. 1959
35. Chandos. op. cit. page 89
36. Norman, F. *At School and at Sea,* page 8. 1899
37. Markham. op. cit. page 80
38. ibid. page 86
39. ibid. pages 77-78
40. ibid. page 150
41. ibid. page 66
42. ibid. page 64
43. ibid. page 37
44. ibid. pages 164-165
45. ibid. pages 34-35
46. ibid. page 151
47 ibid. pages 45-47
49. ibid. page 44
50. ibid. page 140

CHAPTER FOUR : VOICES OF PROTEST

1. Pearson, Hesketh. *The Smith of Smiths,* page 44. 1984
2. ibid. page 45
3. ibid. page 47

4. ibid. page 21
5. ibid. page 22
6. ibid. page 26
7. Edinburgh Review, 1810
8. Chandos, John. *Boys Together*, pages 38-39. 1985
9. Gathorne-Hardy. *The Public School Phenomenon*, page 56. 1977
10. ibid. page 56
11. Pearson. op. cit. page 52
12. ibid. pages 49-50
13. ibid. page 51
14. Chandos. op. cit. page 38

21. Shrosbee. op. cit. page 65
22. Young, G.M. *Portrait of an Age*, page 59.
23. ibid. page 59
24. Armytage. op. cit. page 53
25. ibid. page 82
26. ibid. pages 83-84
27. ibid. page 83
28. Heffer. op. cit. page 76
29. ibid. page 79
30. ibid. page 79
31. ibid. page 415
32. Armytage. op. cit. page 113

CHAPTER FIVE : DIVERSE SCHOOLINGS

1. Shrosbee, Colin. *Public Schools and Private Education*, page 2. 1988
2. Bamford, T.W. *The Rise of the Public Schools*, page 204. 1967
3. Armytage, W.H.G. *Four Hundred Years of English Education*, page 61. 1965
4. Turner, David. *The Old Boys*, page 65. 2016
5. ibid. page 87
6. Gathorne-Hardy, *The Public School Phenomenon*, page 79 1977
7. Turner. op. cit. page 88
8. Rothblatt, Sheldon. *The Revolution of the Dons*, pages 42-43. 1968
9. i bid. page 37
10. Armytage. op. cit. page 82
11. Rothblatt. op. cit. pages 65-68
12. Honey, J.R. de S. *Tom Brown's Universe*, page 119. 1977
13. Rothblatt. op. cit. page 103
14. Heffer, Simon. *High Minds*, page 446. 2014
15. Rothblatt. op. cit. page 212
16 ibid. page 188
17. ibid. page 136
18. ibid. pages 33-35
19. Armytage. op. cit. page 93
20. Vindiciae Wykamicae, 1818. Quoted by E.C. Mack, *Public Schools and Public Opinion*. 1938

CHAPTER SIX : ETON AND KING'S

1. Compton Mackenzie, Faith. *William Cory*, page 13. 1950
2. Morris, Christopher. *King's College – A Short History*, page 38. 1989
3. ibid. page 39
4. ibid. pages 24-25
5. ibid. page 25-26
6. Harrison, Ross. *Our College Story*, page 72. 2015
7. ibid. page 2
8. Morris. op. cit. page 44
9. ibid. page 45
10. ibid. page 38
11. ibid. page 44
12. Harrison. op. cit. page 94
13. ibid. pages 66-78
14. ibid. pages 79-80
15. Morris. op. cit. page 36
16. ibid. page 35
17. Harrison. op. cit. pages 72-73
18. Compton Mackenzie, Faith. op. cit. page 14

CHAPTER SEVEN : AGENTS OF CHANGE

1. Young, G.M. *Portrait of an Age*, page 32. 1961
2. Chambers Biographical Dictionary. 1997

NOTES

3. Newsome, David. *Godliness and Good Learning*, page 8. 1961
4. ibid. page 80
5. ibid. page 8
6. Heffer, Simon. *High Minds*, page 5. 2013
7. Chandos, John. *Boys Together*, page 275
8. Newsome. op. cit. page 41
9. ibid. page 42
10. Heffer. op. cit. page 6
11. Chandos. op. cit. page 253.
12. ibid.. page 118
13. Newsome. op. cit. page 29
14. ibid. page 40
15. Heffer. op. cit. page 13
16. Armytage, W.H.G. *Four Hundred Years of English Education*, Page 108. 1965
17. Chandos. op. cit. pages 255-6
18. ibid. page 257
19. ibid. page 256
20. ibid. pages 256-7
21. Heffer. op. cit. page 3
22. Pearson, Hesketh. *The Smith of Smiths*, page 155. 1984
23. Turner, David. *The Old Boys*, page 37. 2012
24. ibid. page 89
25. ibid. page 65
26. Bamford, T.W. *The Rise of the Public Schools*, page 44. 1967
27. Heffer. op. cit. page 12
28. Newsome. .p. cit. page 17
29. Chandos. op. cit. page 268
30. ibid. page 256
32. Heffer. op. cit. page 30
33. Armytage. op. cit. page 61
34. Shrosbee, Colin. *Public Schools and Private Education*, page 136, 1988
35. Bamford. op. cit. page 131
36. Shrosbee. op. cit. page 150
37. Turner. op. cit. page 66
38. Chandos. op. cit. page 191
39. ibid. page 191
40. Turner. op. cit. page 67
41. Chandos. op. cit. page 192
42. ibid. page 194
43. ibid. page 194
44. ibid. page 192
45. ibid. page 42
46. ibid. page 157
47. Benson, A.C. *Fasti Etonenses*, page 279. 1899
48. Thackeray, F. St. J. *Memoir of Edward Craven Hawtrey*, page 133. 1896
49. ibid. 144
50. Chandos. op. cit. page 70
51. Benson. op. cit. Page 390
52. ibid. page 398
53. Chandos, op. cit. Pge 211
54. Thackeray. op. cit. page 77
55. Lyte, H. C. Maxwell. *History of Eton College*, page 408. 1911
56. Thackeray. op. cit. page 79
57. ibid. page 91
58. ibid. page 76
59. Lyte. op. cit. page 434
60. Benson. op. cit. page 365
61. Thackeray. op. cit. page 80
62. Coleridge, A.D. *Eton in the Forties*, page 274. 1896
63. Chandos. op. cit. page 216
64. Benson. op. cit. page 378
65. ibid. page 368
66. Compton Mackenzie, Faith. *William Cory*, page 20. 1950
67. Lyte. op. cit. page 418. Quoting *Quarterly Journal of Education*, 1834
68. Lyte. op. cit. page 416
69. Benson. op. cit. page 379
70. Lyte. op. cit. page 420.
71. Coleridge, quoted in *Floreat*, Eric Parker, page 24. 1923
72. Thackeray. op. cit. page 75
73. ibid. page 143
74. Benson. op. cit. page 383
75. Green, W.C. *Memories of Eton and King's*, page 35. 1905
76. Coleridge, op. cit. page 294
77. Benson. op. cit. page 424
78. Lyte. op. cit. page 408.
79. Benson. op. cit. page 378
80. Lyte. op. cit. page 437
81. Ainger, A.C. *Eton Sixty Years Ago*, page 105. 1916
82. Thackeray. op. cit. page 133

83. Fletcher, C.R.L. *Edmond Warre*, page 14. 1922
84. Coleridge. Quoted in *Floreat*. op. cit. page 24
85. Benson. op. cit. page 391
86. ibid. page 394
87. ibid. page 404
88. Coleridge. Quoted in *Floreat*. op. cit. pages 24-25.
89. Compton Mackenzie. op. cit. page 26
90. Ainger. op. cit. page 224
91. Chandos. op. cit. pages 211-212
92. Thackeray. op. cit. Quoting G. G. Green, page 153
93. ibid. page 155
94. ibid. page 128
95. ibid. page 167
96. ibid. page 96
97. Coleridge. op. cit. page 363
98. Green. op. cit. page 47
99. Thackeray. op. cit. page 56
100. Brinsley-Richards James. *Seven Years at Eton*, pages 53-54. 1883
101. Compton Mackenzie. op. cit. page 15
102. Lyte. op. cit. page 426
103. Benson. op. cit. page 370
104. Coleridge. op. cit. page 312
105. Thackeray. op. cit. page 99
106. Coleridge. op. cit. page 302
107. Benson. op. cit. quoting Thackeray. page 374.
108. Tucker. *Eton of Old; or Eighty years since 1811-1822*, page 3, 1892
109. Benson. op. cit. pages 375-376
110. ibid. page 376
111. ibid. pages 376-377
112. Chandos. op. cit. page 206
113. ibid. page 208
114. ibid. page 209
115. Thackeray. op. cit. page 93
116. ibid. page 115
117. ibid. page 117
118. ibid. page 116
119. Stone, E.D. quoted in *Floreat*, op. cit. page 23

CHAPTER EIGHT : MID-CENTURY ETON

1. Ainger A.C. *Eton Sixty Years Ago*, page 194. 1916
2. Brinsley-Richards, James. *Seven Years at Eton*, page 12. 1883
3. Ainger. op. cit. pages 89-95
4. Green, W.C. *Memories of Eton and King's*. 1905
5. Brinsley-Richards. op. cit. page 8
6. ibid. pages 13-14
7. ibid. page 11
8. ibid. page 14
9. ibid. pages 25-26
10. ibid. pages 33-34
11. ibid. page 11
12. ibid. page 12
13. ibid. pages 27-28
14. ibid. pages 71-72
15. ibid. pages 66-68
16. ibid. pages 35-36
17. Ainger. op. cit. pages 96-96
18. Brinsley-Richards. op. cit. page 57
19. ibid. pages 22-23
20. ibid. page 17
21. Green. op. cit. page 32.
22. Ainger. op. cit. page 44
23. Brinsley-Richards. op. cit. pages 178-190
24. Ainger. op. cit. page 267
25. Brinsley-Richards. op. cit, pages 47-48
26. Ainger. op. cit. page 266
27. Brinsley-Richards. op. cit. page 48
28. Ainger. op. cit. page 267
29. Brinsley-Richards. op. cit. pages 162-165
30. ibid. pages 166-168
31. ibid page 166
32. ibid. page 89
33. ibid. pages 95-96
34. ibid. pages 98-99
35. Ainger. op. cit. page 176
36. Brinsley-Richards. p. cit . page 347
37. Markham, F.M. *Recollections of a Town Boy at Westminster*, pages 92-96. 1903
38. Major, Sir John. *More than a Game*, page 125. 2007

NOTES

39. Coleridge, A.D. *Eton in the Forties*, page 261. 1896
40. Major. op. cit. page 260
41. Ainger. op. cit. page 149
42. ibid. page 155
43. Brinsley-Richards. op. cit. pages 90-93 and 100-101
44. Coleridge. op. cit. page 127
45. ibid. page 137
46. ibid. page 147
47. Markham. op. cit. pages 142-143
48. Ainger. op.cit. pages 179-181
49. Coleridge. op. cit. pages 384-385
50. ibid. page 279
51. ibid. page 384
52. Thackeray, F. St. J. *Memoir of Edward Craven Hawtrey*, page 135. 1896
53. Brinsley-Richards. op. cit. pages 393-395
54. Ainger. op. cit. pages 221-222
55. Brinsley-Richards op. cit. pages 174-176
56. Ainger. op. cit. pages 240-241
57. ibid. page 236
58. ibid. page 238
59. ibid. page 225
60. Benson, A.C. *Fasti Etonenses*, page 453. 1899
61. Ainger. op. cit. pages 236-239
62. Wortham, H.E. *Victorian Eton and Cambridge*, page 190. 1927
63. ibid. page 20
64. ibid. page 12
65. Ainger. op. cit. pages 6 & 9
66. Wortham. op. cit. page 26
67. ibid. page 19
68. Young, G.M. *Portrait of an Age*, page 94. 1936
69. Wortham. op, cit. pages 22-23
70. ibid. page 33
71. ibid. page 19
72. ibid. page 31
73. Compton-Mackenzie. *William Cory*, page 19. 1950
74. ibid. page 18
75. Brinsley-Richards op. cit. page 19
76. ibid. page 19
77. Compton-Mackenzie. op. cit. page 18
78. Brinsley-Richards. op. cit. page 182
79. ibid. page 173
80. Brinsley-Richards. op. cit. page 173
81. Morris, Christopher. *King's College, A Short History*, page 43. 1989
82. Chandos. op. cit. page 156
83. ibid. page 157
84. Chandos. op. cit. page 330 n.
85. Green. op. cit. page 32
86. Chandos. op. cit. page 330 n.
87. Brinsley-Richards. op. cit. pages 127-128
88. ibid. pages 128-129
89. ibid. page 129
90. ibid. page 130
91. Chandos. op. cit. page 330 n.
92. Ainger. op. cit. page 218
93. Green. op. cit. page 18
94. Lyte, H. C. Maxwell. *History of Eton College*, page 475. 1911
95. Brinsley-Richards. op. cit. pages 126-127
96. Ainger. op. cit. page 84
97. Brinsley-Richards. op. cit. page 135
98. ibid. pages 132-133
99. ibid. pages 125-126
100. ibid. pages 308-309
101. Chandos. op. cit. page 233
102&103. Brinsley-Richards. op. cit. page 77
104. ibid. page 207
105. ibid. page 77
106. ibid. pages 142-146
107. ibid. page 342
108. ibid. pages 354-361
109. ibid. pages 278
110. ibid. page 277
111. ibid. pages 254-257
112. ibid. pages 137-140
113. Green. op. cit. page 52
114. Coleridge. op. cit. page 213
115. Lyte. op. cit. page 480
116. Coleridge. op. cit. page 91
117. ibid. page 97
118. ibid. page 95
119. ibid. page 288
120. ibid. page 216
121. ibid. page 234
122. ibid. page 216
123. ibid. page 253

124. ibid. page 121
125. Benson. op. cit. page 353
126. Brinsley-Richards. op. cit. page 249
127. ibid. page 200
128. ibid. pages 290-293
129. ibid. pages 296-300
130. ibid. pages 321-322
131. ibid. page 427
132. ibid. page 284
133. ibid. page 440
134. ibid. pages 441-442

CHAPTER NINE : TROUBLE AHEAD

1. Walter, John. https://en.wikipedia.org/
2. Benson, A.C. *Fasti Etonenses,* pages 432-433. 1898
3. Coleridge, A.D. *Eton in the 1840's,* page 279. 1896
4. Benson, A.C. op. cit. page 435
5. Honey, J.R. de S. *Tom Brown's Universe,* page 135. 1977
6. Johnson, William. *Cornhill Magazine.* March 1861
7. *Cornhill Magazine.* May, 1860
8. *Saturday Review.* December, 1860
9. *Cornhill Magazine.* December, 1860
10. *Westminster Review.* April, 1860
11. *Fraser's Magazine.* April, 1860
12. *Edinburgh Review.* April, 1861.
13. *Cornhill Magazine.* December, 1860
14. Tiverton Lecture. September, 1860
15. *Edinburgh Review.* April, 1861
16. *Edinburgh Review.* April, 1861
17. *Edinburgh Review.* April, 1861
18. Chandos, John. *Boys Together,* page 322. 1984
19. Eton College Founder's Statute
20. *MacMillan's Magazine.* February, 1861
21. *Westminster Review.* April, 1861
22. *Westminster Review.* April, 1861
23. *Cornhill Magazine.* March, 1861
24. Turner, David. *The Old Boys,* page 84. 2015
25. *Saturday Review.* December, 1860.
26. *Quarterly Review.* October, 1860
27. *Edinburgh Review.* April, 1861
28. Young G.M. *Portrait of an Age,* page 98. 1961
29. *Saturday Review.* December, 1860
30. *Saturday Review.* December, 1860
31. *The Times.* June 6, 1861
32. Ainger, A.C. *Eton Sixty Years Ago,* page 228.
33. *Quarterly Review.* October, 1860. 1917
34. *Westminster Review.* April, 1861
35. Chandos. op. cit. page 320
36. Heffer, Simon. *High Minds,* page 450. 2014
37. Brinsley-Richards, James. *Seven Years at Eton,* page 349 n. 1883
38. Turner. op. cit. page 80
39. ibid. page 111
40& 41. Turner. op. cit. page 109
42. ibid. page 80
43. ibid. pages 112-113
44. *MacMillan's Magazine.* February 1861
45. *Westminster Review.* April 1861
46. Chandos. op. cit. page 322 n.
47. *Quarterly Review.* October, 1860.
48. *Quarterly Review.* July, 1864
49. Fletcher C.R.L. *Edmond Warre,* page 12n. 1922
50. Ainger. op. cit. page 13
51. Chandos. op. cit. page 56
52. Young. op. cit. page 96
53. Chandos. op. cit. page 58
54. Ainger. op. cit. page 11
55. ibid. pages 8&9
56. ibid. pages 9&10
57. Honey. op. cit. page 127

CHAPTER TEN : SETTING UP THE COMMISSION

1. Ainger, A.C. *Eton Sixty years Ago,* page 27. 1916
2. Green, W.C. *Memories of Eton and King's,* page 22. 1905
3. ibid. page 23
4. Coleridge A.D. *Eton in the Forties,* page 332. 1896

NOTES

5. Benson, A.C. *Fasti Etonenses,* pages 453-454. 1899
6. Chandos John. *Boys Together,* page 41. 1985
7. ibid. page 229
8. Shrosbee, Colin. *Public School and Private Education,* pages 86-87. 1988
9. ibid. pages 87-88
10. The Times, June 7th, 1861. *Hansard Report*
11. ibid. June 1861
12. Shrosbee. op. cit. page 77
13. Briggs, Asa. *The Age of Improvement,* page 378. 1959
14. Shrosbee. op. cit. page 93
15. ibid. page 94
16. Armytage, W.H.G. *Four Hundred years of English Education,* page 128. 1965
17. Chandos. op. cit. page 324
18. Thackeray, F. St. J. *Memoir of Edward Craven Hawtrey,* page 204. 1896
19. ibid. page 204
20. Shrosbee. op. cit. page 83
21. Thackeray. op. cit. page 200
22. Ainger. op. cit. page 37
23. Benson. op. cit. page 403

CHAPTER ELEVEN : ETON INVESTIGATED

1. Robert Rhodes James. *Rosebery,* page 29. 1963
2. The Clarendon Report, page 58
3. ibid. page 58
4&5 ibid. page 59
6-9. ibid. page 60
10. ibid. page 61
11. ibid. page 62
12. ibid. page 63
13. ibid. page 101
14&15. ibid. page 102
16&17. ibid. page 103
18. ibid. page 104
19. ibid. page 64
20. ibid. page 67
21&22. ibid page 66
23&24. ibid. page 65
25. ibid. page 67
26&27. ibid. page 66
28. ibid. page 68
29-32. ibid. page 105
33. ibid. page 106
34. ibid. pages 292-296
35. ibid. page 70
36. ibid. page 71
37. ibid. page 72
38&39. ibid. page 108
40 - 43. ibid. page 109
44&45. ibid. page 110
46&47. ibid. page 72
48&49. ibid. page 73
50&51. ibid. page 74
52. ibid. page 48
53. ibid. page 124
54. ibid. pages 127-128
55. ibid. page 111
56. ibid. page 75
57. ibid. page 112
58. ibid. page 111
59&60. ibid. page 113
61&62. ibid. page 80
63. ibid. page 78
64&65 ibid. page 80
66. ibid. page 79
67. ibid. page 80
68. ibid. page 81
69. ibid. page 82
70. ibid. page 83
71&72. ibid. page 83
73. ibid. page 84
74. ibid. page 85
75&76. ibid. page 86
77. ibid. page 113
78&79. ibid. page 114
80. ibid. page 116
81. ibid. page 95
82. ibid. page 116
83. ibid. page 117
84. ibid. page 113
85. ibid. page 87
86. ibid. page 88
87-89. ibid. page 89
90-92. ibid. page 90
93. ibid. page 91

94. ibid. page 92
95. ibid. page 91
96. ibid. page 94
97. ibid. page 76
98. ibid. page 93
99-101. ibid. page 118
102. ibid. page 176
103. ibid. page 94
104. ibid. page 96
105&106. ibid. page 95
107. ibid. page 97
108. ibid. vol. 2. items 308-310
109. ibid. page 98
110-113. ibid. page 99
114. ibid. page 119
115-116. ibid. page 120

CHAPTER TWELVE : THE OTHER CLARENDON EIGHT

1. The Clarendon Report. Vol. 1. Page 134
2. ibid. page 139
3. ibid. page 137
4. ibid. page 140
5&6. ibid. page 138
7. ibid. page 145
8&9. ibid. page 152
10. ibid. page 155
11. ibid. page 136
12. ibid. page 140
13. ibid. page 136
14. ibid. page 155
15. ibid. page 141
16. ibid. page 161
17. ibid. page 164
18. ibid. page 165
19. ibid. page 160
20. ibid. page 161
21. ibid. page 162
22&23. ibid. page 163
24. ibid. page 164
25. ibid. page 162
26. ibid. page 173
27. ibid. page 169
28. ibid. page 170
29. ibid. pages 70 &171
30. ibid. page 175
31. ibid. page 177
32. ibid. pages 179&180
33. ibid. pages 178&179
34. ibid. page 182
35. ibid. page 183
36. ibid. pages 103-104
37. ibid. page 177
38. ibid. page 184
39. ibid. page 189
40. ibid. page 190
41. ibid. page 197
42. ibid. page 191
43&44. ibid. pages 193&194
45. ibid. page 193
46. ibid. page 189
47. ibid. page 200
48. ibid. page 199
49. ibid. page 192
50. ibid. page 196
51. ibid. page 202
52. ibid. page 205
53&54 ibid. page 204
55&56. ibid. page 205
57&58 ibid. page 207
59. ibid. page 208
60. ibid. pages 210-211
61. ibid. page 211
623. ibid. page 209
63. ibid. page 210
64. ibid. page 209
65. ibid. page 211
66. ibid. page 220
67&68. ibid. page 222
69&70. ibid. page 227
71. ibid. page 226
72. ibid. page 224
73&74. ibid. page 225
75. ibid. pages 305&306
76. ibid. page 321
77. ibid. page 310
78. ibid. page 306
79&80. ibid. page 312
81. ibid. page 314
82. ibid. page 307
83. ibid. page 319
84. ibid. page 320

85. ibid. page 321
86. ibid. page 320
87. ibid. page 309
88. ibid. page 315&316
89. ibid. page 308
90. ibid. page 309
91. ibid. page 307
92. ibid. page 319.
93. ibid. page 234
94. ibid. page 319
95. ibid. page 234
96. ibid. pages 234&235
97. ibid. page 227
98. ibid. page 234
99. ibid. page 230
100. ibid. pages 268&269
101. ibid. page 230
102. ibid. page 232
103. ibid. page 231
104. ibid. page 262
105. ibid. page 261
106. ibid. page 273
107. ibid. pages 255&256
108. ibid. page 257
109. ibid. pages 257&258
110. ibid. page 258
111. ibid. page 259
112. ibid. page 256
113. ibid. page 267
114. ibid. pages 265-267
115. ibid. page 283
116. ibid. page 284
117. ibid. page 282
118-119. ibid. page 287
120. ibid page 273
121. ibid. page 274
122. ibid. page 275

CHAPTER THIRTEEN : JUST WHAT GOT LEARNT ?

1. Public Schools Commission Report, 1864, Vol. I., page 12
2. ibid. page 28
3. ibid. page 212
4. ibid. page 181
5. ibid. page 251
6. ibid. page 246
7. ibid. pages 238&239
8. ibid. page 204
9. ibid. page 37
10&11. ibid. page 227
12. ibid. pages 226&156
13. ibid. page 249
15. ibid pages 214&215
16. ibid. pages 144&206
17. ibid. page 15
18. ibid. page 39
19. ibid. page 216
20. ibid. page 251
21. ibid. page 311
22. ibid. page 16
23. ibid. page 238
24. ibid. page 216
25. ibid. page 144
26. ibid. page 238
27. ibid. page 204
28. ibid. page 190
29. ibid. pages 252&253
30. ibid. page 279
31. ibid. pages 212&213
32. ibid. page 243
33. ibid. page 279
34. ibid. page 191
35. ibid. page 22
36. ibid. page 36
37. ibid. page 26
38. ibid. page 53
39. ibid. page 34
40. ibid. page 26
41. ibid. page 36
42. ibid. page 34
43. ibid. page 55
44. ibid. page 33
45. ibid. page 26
46&47. ibid. page 23
48&49. ibid. page 24
50&51. ibid. page 25
52. ibid. page 24
53. ibid. page 31
54. ibid. page 45

CHAPTER FOURTEEN : DEBATE RESUMED

1. *Hansard.* House of Commons. May 6th. 1864
2. *Fraser's Magazine.* June 1864
3. ibid.
4. ibid.
5. *Hansard.* House of Lords. May 27th. 1864
6. ibid.
7. ibid.
8. *Hansard.* House of Commons. May 6th. 1864
9. *Quarterly Review.* July 1864
10. Williams E.P. *Remarks upon the Report of the Public Schools Commission.* 1865
11. *Blackwood's Magazine.* June 1864
12. *Hansard.* House of Lords. May 27th. 1864
13. *Hansard.* House of Commons. May 6th. 1864
14. *Fraser's Magazine.* June 1864
15. *Hansard.* House of Commons, May 6th. 1864
16. *Edinburgh Review.* July 1864
17. *Westminster Review.* July 1864
18. *Public Schools Commission Report.* page 45
19. *Fraser's Magazine.* June 1864
20. *Hansard.* House of Commons. May 6th. 1864
21. *Fraser's Magazine.* October 1865

CHAPTER FIFTEEN : THE PUBLIC SCHOOLS ACT : 1868

1. Colin Shrosbee. *Public Schools and Private Education,* page 117. 1988
2. ibid. page 178
3&4. ibid. page 181
5. ibid. page 184
6. ibid. page 181
7. ibid. page 187
8. ibid. page 189
9. ibid. page 191
10. ibid. page 198
11. ibid. page 198
12&13. ibid. page 198
14. ibid. page 202
15. ibid. page 205
16. ibid. pages 205&206
17. ibid. page 206

CHAPTER SIXTEEN : DEPARTURES

1. Fletcher, C.R.L. *Edmond Warre,* page 7. 1922
2. ibid. page 14
3. ibid. page 13
4. ibid. page 15
5. ibid. page 14
6. ibid. page 20
7. ibid. page 25
8. ibid. page 37
9. ibid. page 40
10. ibid. page 41
11. ibid. page 42
12&13. ibid. page 45
14. ibid. page 47
15. ibid. page 48
16. ibid. page 51
17. ibid. page 75
18. Lees-Milne, James. *The Enigmatic Victorian,* page 8. 1986
19. James, Robert Rhodes. *Rosebery,* page 18. 1963
20. Lees-Milne. op. cit. page 46
21. ibid. page 8
22. Ainger, A.C. *Eton Sixty Years Ago,* page 232. 1916
23. Compton Mackenzie, Faith. *William Cory,* page 25. 1950
24. ibid. page 25
25. ibid. pages 30-32
26. ibid. pages 29&50
27. ibid. page 25
28. ibid. page 44
29. ibid. pages 34&35
30. ibid page 61
31. James. op. cit. page 27
32. Compton Mackenzie. op. cit. page 60

NOTES

33. ibid. page 61
34. James. op. cit. page 28
35. ibid. pages 26&27
36. Compton Mackenzie. op. cit. page 43
37. Lees-Milne. op. cit. page 12
38. ibid. page 12
39. ibid. page 16
40. ibid. page 18
41. ibid. page 20
42. ibid. page 14
43. ibid. page 21
44. Chandos, John. *Boys Together*, page 338. 1984
45. Turner, David. *The Old Boys*, page 146. 2016
46. Lees-Milne. op. cit. page 14
47. Fletcher. op. cit. page 88
48. Coleridge, A.D. *Eton in the Forties*, page 387. 1896
49. Compton-Mackenzie. op. cit. page 176
50. Wortham H.E. *Victorian Eton and Cambridge*, page 39. 1927
51. ibid. page 39
52. ibid. page 49
53. ibid. page 73
54. Wortham. op. cit. page 49
55. ibid. pages 49&50
56. ibid. page 63
57. ibid. page 67
58. ibid. page 53
59. Honey, J.R. de S. *Tom Brown's Universe*, page 111. 1986
60. Wortham, op. cit. page 54
61. ibid. pages 63&64
62. ibid. pages 71&72
63. ibid. pages 72&73
64. ibid. pages 69&70
65. ibid. page 70
66. ibid. page 79
67. ibid. pages 80-82
68. ibid. page 82
69. ibid. page 84
70. ibid. pages 84&85
71. ibid. pages 101&102
72. ibid. page 102
73. ibid. page 111
74. ibid. pages 107&108
75. Turner, David. *The Old Boys*, page 142. 2016
76. Wortham. op. cit. pages 115&116
77. ibid. page 117
78. ibid. pages 120-122
79. ibid. page 124
80. ibid. page 127
81. ibid. pages 130&131
82. ibid. pages 130&132
83. ibid. pages 138-140
84. ibid. page 141
85. ibid. page 144
86. ibid. page 59
87. ibid. page 133
88. ibid. pages 148&149
89. ibid. page 146

CHAPTER SEVENTEEN : LATER LIVES

1. Compton Mackenzie, Faith. *William Cory*, pages 58&59/66/69. 1950
2. ibid. page 63
3. ibid. page 63
4. ibid. page 86
5. ibid. page 65
6. ibid. page 71
7. ibid. page 65
8. ibid. page 64
9. ibid. pages 92-94
10. ibid. pages 66&67
11. ibid. page 78
12. ibid. pages 87&88
13&14 ibid. page 139
15. ibid. page 77
16. ibid. pages 79&80
17. Wortham, H.E. *Victorian Eton and Cambridge*, page 149. 1927
18. ibid. page 225
19. ibid. page 296
20. Morris, Christopher. *King's College: A Short History*, page 46. 1988
21. Wortham. op. cit. page 168
22. Morris. op. cit. page 48
23. Wortham. op. cit. pages 169&170
24. ibid. page 171
25. ibid. pages 170 & 171

26. Morris. op. cit. page 48
27. James, M.R. *Eton and King's,* page 107. 1926
28. ibid. pages 185-188
29. ibid. page 109
30. ibid. page 158
31. James. op. cit. page 120
32. ibid. page 120
33. Morris. op. cit. page 51
34. James. op. cit. page 114
35 ibid. page 125
37. ibid. page 127
38. Morris. op. cit. page 52
39. Harrison, Ross. *Our College Story,* page 97. 2015
40. ibid. page 96
41. Morris. op. cit. page 48
42. Lees-Milne, James. *The Enigmatic Victorian,* page 28 1986
43. ibid. page 95
44. ibid. page 46
45. ibid. pages 47-50
46. ibid. pages 29-32
47. ibid. page 37
48. ibid. pages 51&52
49. ibid. pages 54&55
50. ibid. pages 55-58
51. Ensor, David. Oxford History of England, 1870-1914, pages 81-83.
52. Lees-Milne. op. cit. page 66
53. ibid. pages 63-67
54. ibid. page 69
55. ibid. page 87
56. ibid. page 76
57. ibid. page 72
58. ibid. pages 73&74
59. Compton Mackenzie, Faith. *William Cory,* page 121. 1950
60. Lees-Milne. op. cit. page 73
61. ibid. pages 77-82
62. ibid. page 75
63. ibid. page 110&111
64. ibid. page 139
65. ibid. pages 85&86 seq.
66. ibid. pages 87&88
67. ibid. pages 91&113
68. ibid. pages 76&77
69. ibid. pages 70&71
70. Compton Mackenzie. op. cit. page 96.
71. ibid. pages 1 00-105
72. ibid. pages 102, 103, 107
73. ibid. page 102
74. ibid. page 105
75. ibid. page 108
77. ibid. page 107
78. Wortham. op. cit. page 17
79. James. op. cit. page 120
80. Wortham. op cit. page 179
81. ibid. page 163
82. ibid. page 181
83. ibid. pages 182&183
84. ibid. page 274
85. ibid. page 233
86. ibid. page 239
87. ibid. page 165
88. ibid. page 189
89. ibid. pages 203&204
90. ibid. page 206
91. ibid. page 209
92. Compton Mackenzie. op. cit. page 112
93. ibid. page 73
94. ibid. page 120
95. ibid. page 128
96. ibid. page 135
97. ibid. page 133
98. ibid. page 137
99. ibid. pages 132&156
100. ibid. page 142
101. ibid. page 144
102. Fletcher, C.R.L. *Edmond Warre,* page 119. 1922
103. ibid. pages 107&108
104. ibid. page 53 n
105. ibid. page 67
106. ibid. page 57
107. ibid. page 65
108. ibid. page 139
109. ibid. pages 131-136
110. ibid. page 67
111. ibid. page 160
112. ibid. page 181
113. ibid. page 177
114. ibid. page 162
115. ibid. page 162

NOTES

116. ibid. page 161
117. ibid. page 136&137
118. Heffer, Simon *High Minds*, page 45. 2013
119. Fletcher, op. cit. pages 149&150
120. ibid. page 194
121. ibid. page 150
122. ibid. page 180
123. Honey, J.R. de S. *Tom Brown's Universe*, page 197.
124. Fletcher. op. cit. page 213
125. Chandos. John. *Boys Together*, page 340. 1984
126. Fletcher. op. cit. pages 129&130
127. ibid. page 150
128. ibid. page 151
129. ibid. page 194
130. ibid. page 194 n
131. Wortham op. cit. page 179
132. ibid. page 186
133 ibid. page 291
134. ibid. page 190
135. ibid. pages 226&227
136. ibid. pages 244-246
137. ibid. pages 251&252
138. ibid. pages 286-288
139. ibid. page 285
140. ibid. pages 257
141. ibid. page 256&257
142. ibid. pages 264
143. ibid. pages 80&282
144. Compton Mackenzie. op. cit. pages 50-153
145. ibid. page 51
146. ibid. pages 156&157
147. ibid. page 126
148 ibid. page 170
149. ibid. pages 161&162
150. ibid. page 155
151. ibid. page 146
152. ibid. page 164
153. ibid. pages 170&171
154. ibid. page 161
155. ibid. page 171
156. James, Robert Rhodes. *Rosebery,* page 335. 1963
157. Ensor. op. cit. page 216
158. James. op. cit. pages 347-349
159. ibid. page 343
160. Compton Mackenzie. op. cit. page 25
161. Lees-Milne. op. cit. page 96
162. ibid. page 97
163. ibid. pages 98&99
164. James. op. cit. pages 359-362
165. ibid. page 381
166. ibid. page 383
167. ibid. page 384
168. Lees-Milne. op. cit. page 100
169. Fletcher. op. cit. page 111
170. ibid. pages 120-122
171. ibid. page 115
172. ibid. pages 141-148
173. ibid. page 147
174. ibid. page 148
175. ibid. page 144
176. ibid. pages 142&145
177. ibid. pages 145 - 147
178. ibid. pages 148&149
179. ibid. pages 154&155
180. ibid. page 153
181. ibid. page 166
182. ibid. pages 156-159
183. ibid. page 158 n
184. ibid. page 207
185. ibid. page 192
186. ibid. page 203
187. ibid. page 204
188. ibid. page 216
189. ibid. page 215
190. ibid. page 189
191. ibid. page 211
192. ibid. pages 208&209
193. ibid. page 195
194. Lees-Milne. op. cit page 95
195. ibid. pages 101&102
196. ibid. page 108
197. ibid. page 104
198. ibid. page 105
199. ibid. page 115
200. ibid. page 126
201. ibid. page 131
202. ibid. page 130
203. ibid. page 134
204. ibid. page 135

205. ibid pages 135&136
206. ibid. page 146
207. ibid. pages 157&158
208. ibid. page 168
209. Pollock, John. *Kitchener,* pages 320&321. 1998
210. Lees-Milne. op. cit. pages 106&107
211. ibid. page 149
212. ibid. page 225
213. ibid. page 154
214. ibid. pages 227-232
215. Morris. op. cit. page 54
216. Morris. op. cit. page 67
217. James. op. cit. pages 231-233
218. Mould, Alan. *The English Chorister,* page 202. 2007
219. Case, *Thomas H. Memoirs of a King's Chorister.* 1899

Quoted in *In Celebration of King's College Chapel,* compiled by Graham Chainey. 1987.

220. James. op. cit. pages 233&234
221. Henderson, R.J. *King's College School,* page 38. 1981
222. James. op. cit. page 238
223. Cox, Michael. *M.R. James. An Informal Portrait,* page 134. 1983
224. Wortham. op. cit. pages 264&265
225. ibid. page 296
226. ibid. page 297
227. ibid. page 311
228. ibid. page 314
229. ibid. page 303
230. Lees-Milne. op. cit page 190
231. ibid. page 177
232. Ensor. op. cit. page 431
233. Lees-Milne. op. cit. page 242
234. ibid. pages 220-222
235. ibid. pages 223&224
236. ibid. page 246
237. Fletcher. op. cit. page 168
238. ibid. page 130
239& 240 ibid. page 220
241. ibid. page 253
242. Honey. op. cit. page 236
243. Fletcher. op. cit. page 115
244. ibid. page 229
245. ibid. page 302
246. ibid. page 237
247. ibid. page 236
248. ibid. page 237
249. ibid. page 242
250. Chandos. op. cit. page 344n
251. Turner, David. *The Old Boys,* page 67. 2016

CHAPTER EIGHTEEN : GLADSTONE'S TABLE TALK

Source : Benson, A.C. *Fasti Etonenses,* pages 497-505. 1897

CHAPTER NINETEEN : A.C. BENSON'S JUDGEMENT

Source : Benson A.C. *From College Window,* chapter nine.

CHAPTER TWENTY : AFTERWORD

1. Chandos, John. *Boys Together,* page 20 1985
2. ibid.
3. Turner, David. *The Old Boys,* page 60. 2016
4. Glendinning, Victoria. *Trollope,* page 32. 1992
5. Taylor, D.J. *Thackeray,* page 40. 1992
6. Stevenson, R.L. poem. *'The Iron Steed'*
7. *The Times.* June 6th. 1861
8. *Edinburgh Review.* April 1861
9. Benson, A.C. *Fasti Etonenses,* page 488. 1899
10. *Edwardian Excursions.* Extracts from diaries of A.C. Benson, edited David Newsome, page 102. 1981

Bibliography

PRIMARY SOURCES

Blackwood's Magazine June 1864
Contemporary Review January 1867
Contemporary Review March 1868
Cornhill Magazine May 1860
Cornhill Magazine December 1860
Cornhill Magazine January 1861
Cornhill Magazine March 1861
Edinburgh Review vol. 16 1810
   Edinburgh Review April 1830
Edinburgh Review April 1861
Edinburgh Review July 1864
Fortnightly Review October 1865
Fraser's Magazine April 1861
Fraser's Magazine March 1868
Fraser's Magazine June 1864
Hansard Vol. 162 April 1861
Hansard Vol. 163 June 1861
Hansard Vol. 175 May 1864
Hansard Vol. 177 February 1865
Hansard Vol. 178 February 1865
Hansard Vol. 178 April 1865
MacMillan's Magazine February 1861
Quarterly Review October 1860
Quarterly Review July 1864
Report of the Public Schools Commission 1864
Saturday Review December 1860
The Times June 6th 1861
Westminster Review April 1861
Westminster Review July 1864
Williams, E.P. 'Remarks upon the Report of the Public Schools Commission'. Privately published. Eton. 1865

SECONDARY SOURCES

Ainger, A.C. *Eton Sixty Years Ago* 1917
Armytage W.H.G. *Four Hundred Years of English Education* 1965
Bamford T.W. *The Rise of the Public Schools* 1967
Benson, A.C. *Fasti Etonenses* 1899
Briggs, Asa *The Age of Improvement* 1959
Browne, Janet *Charles Darwin* 1995
Carleton, J.D. *Westminster* 1938
Chandos, John *Boys Together* 1984
Coleridge, A.D. *Eton in the 1840's* 1896
Compton Mackenzie, Faith *William Cory* 1950
Cox, Michael. *M.R. James. An Informal Portrait.* 1983
Curtis S.J. *History of Education in Great Britain* 1961
Ensor, R,C.K. *England 1870 - 1922* 1936
Farrar, Frederic W. *Eric, or Little by Little* 1858
Firth J. D'E *Winchester College* 1936
Gathorne-Hardy, Jonathan *The Public School Phenomenon* 1977
Gimson, Andrew *Gimson's Prime Ministers* 2018
Glendenning, Victoria *Trollope* 1992
Green, W.C. *Memories of Eton and King's* 1905
Harrison, Ross *Our College Story* 2015
Heffer, Simon *High Minds* 2014
Henderson R.J. *King's College School* 1981
Honey, J.R. de S. *Tom Brown's Universe* 1977
James, M.R. *Eton and King's.* 1926
James, Robert Rhodes *Rosebery* 1963
Johnson, C. *The Ely and Littleport Riots* 1893
Lamb, G. F. *The Happiest Days* 1959
Lyte, H.C. Maxwell *History of Eton* 1911

Mack, E.C. *Public Schools and British Opinion vol. I* 1938
Major, Sir John. *More than a Game* 2007
Markham, F.M. *Recollections of a Town boy at Westminster* 1903
Morris, Christopher *King's College: A Short History* 1988
Newsome, David *Godliness and Good Learning* 1961
Norman, F.M. *At School and at Sea* 1899
Parker, Eric *Floreat: An Eton Anthology* 1923
Parry, Gambier *Annals of an Eton House* 1907
Pearson, Hesketh *The Smith of Smiths* 1984
Pollock, John. *Kitchener.* 1998
Richards, James Brinsley *Seven years at Eton* 1883
Rothblatt, Sheldon *The Revolution of the Dons* 1968
Shrosbee, Colin *Public Schools and Private Education* 1988
Taylor, D. J. *Thackeray* 1999
Thackeray, F. St. J. *Memoir of Edward Craven Hawtrey* 1896
Thackeray, W.M. *Irish Sketch Book* 1842
Thomson, David *England in the Nineteenth Century* 1950
Tucker, W.H. *Eton of Old; or Eighty Years since 1811 to 1822* 1892
Turner, David *The Old Boys* 2015
Wilkinson, C.A. *Reminiscences of Eton* 1888
Wortham, H.E. *Victorian Eton and Cambridge* 1927
Young, G.M. *Portrait of an Age* 1936

Index

A

Abercromby, James, 40
'Academus', 99, 187
 Cory poem,
Adelaide, Queen, 46
Afghanistan, 207
Agadir crisis, 252
Ainsworth's Dictionary, 118
Albert, Prince, 36, 51, 57, 73, 99, 108, 251
'Alice in Wonderland' 183
Allen, George, publisher, 231
Alpine Club, 189
America, 44, 258, 260
Ampleforth College, 118,
Anderson, Mary, actress, 219
Angell, Norman, pacifist author, 253
Anglicanism, 53, 57, 214
Anne, Queen, 191
Armenian massacres, 235
Army in India, 261
Arnold, Dr. Thomas, 26, 41, 60-65-66, 68, 79, 93, 107, 159, 164, 181, 227, 251, 256
Arnold-Foster, H.O., Liberal minister; grand-son of Dr. Arnold, 251
Ascham, Roger, 4
Ashley, Lord, see Shaftesbury
Asquith, H.H, Prime Minister 216, 250, 252,
258-260,
Astronomer-Royal, 173
Austen, Jane, 202
Ayrton, Acton, M.P., 178

B

Balfour, Arthur, Prime Minister, 245-246, 250, 252
Barker, Westminster, 42
Barker, fictional boy, 117
Baldwin, Stanley, Prime Minister, 262
Balliol College, Oxford, 148, 175, 180, 240, 254
Baron's Down, Dulverton, 236, 237, 254, 273
Barnstaple, 6
Bartrum, Janet, 8
Barton, Cambridge, 229
'Basil', school novel, 117
Bayreuth, 225
Beaumont School, 124
Bedford, town, 202, 218
Bedford, Duke of, 38
Beethoven, 215
Belloc, Hilaire, 250
Bendyshe, virulent Kingsman, 205
Benham, Benjamin, Headmaster of King's College Choir School, 249
Benson, A. C. 57, 70, 85, 99, 247, 251, 264, 267-271, 273, 276-277, 279-283,
290-291
Benson, Edward White, Headmaster of Wellington College and Cantuar, 60, 240
Berkhamsted School, 46
Bertie, Lord, 259, 260
Bexhill, 250
'Billy', Harrow master, 4
Biarritz, 260
Bird, Rugby master, 62
Birmingham Social Science Congress, 1884 215
Bleriot, Louis, 255
Block Club, 226
Bloomsbury, 246
Board of Education, 216
'Boating Song,' 89, 186
Bond Street, 233
Boer War, 239, 258
Bonney, Rev. T.G., 41
'Bolshevik' unrest, 260
Botany Bay, 105
Bow Street Magistrates Court, 90
Bowen, Edward, Harrow master, 191

293

Bradley, Dr. G.G., Headmaster of Marlborough, 165
Bradshaw, Henry, 183
Bradshaw's Railway Guide, 221
Brahms, Johannes, 188
Branker, Thomas, Shrewsbury scholar, 67
Brett, Sir Baliol, First Viscount Esher, 206
Brett, Reginald, Second Viscount Esher, 182, 184- 186, 200-201, 206-213, 231, 234-236, 241-246, 250-253, 257-262
Brett, Dorothy, daughter, 246, 262
Brett, Eleanor, wife, 207, 241-242, 260, 262
Brett, Maurice, son, 211, 243, 244, 246, 253, 260-263
Brett, Oliver, son, 211, 246, 260, 262, 263
Brett, Silvia, daughter, 246, 262
Bridgewater, Robert, 'thunderguts', 107
Brighton College, 186
Brinsley-Richards, James, (Murray, R. G.) 77, 81-84, 86-87, 89-90, 99-101, 104, 107, 109, 144, 181, 276-277, 280-282
British Empire, 116, 130, 153, 158, 169
British Museum, 14, 261- 262
Broadbent, Doctor, 234
Bronte, Charlotte, 202
Brooke, Margaret, 246
Brooke, Rupert, 204
Brooke, Vyner, 246
Brougham, Lord Henry, 44, 46- 48, 52, 66, 114, 119, 122-123, 127
Browne medal, 26, 31, 67
Browning, Malvina, 165
Browning, Oscar, 92, 94, 107, 119, 131, 135-136, 141, 143, 170, 173, 187, 189-197, 202, 204-205, 221, 228, 256
Browning, William, 92, 117
Brownsover, 158
Buckingham Palace, 43-244
Buckle, George, 121, 210
Burgis, Laurence, 247
Busby, Richard, 62
Busby Library, 46

Butler, Dr. Samuel, Headmaster of Shrewsbury School, 36, 39, 62, 65-69, 70, 79
Butler, Montagu, Headmaster of Harrow, 165
Byron, Lord, 8, 93

C

Cairo, 201
Callander, 246
Canning, George, 266
Campbell, Westminster master, 38
Cambridge, 3, 50, 67, 117, 151, 156, 176, 183, 228, 231, 267
Cambridge, Duke of, 209
Camilla, Irish mare, 75
Cannon Place, Hampstead, 230
Carlisle, Lord, 241
Carlyle, Thomas, 269
Carter, William, Bishop of Zululand, 241
Cassel, Ernest, 244, 251
Cathedral Commissioners, 122
Catholics, 28, 52, 107, 231
Cato Street plot, 41
Chancery Court, 50
Chandos, John, 100, 108, 275-283, 287, 289-291
Chamberlain, Joseph, 207, 243
Chancellor's Medal, for English verse, 58, 67
Chapel Royal, 248
Charity Schools, 52
Charity Commission, 122

CHARTERHOUSE
35, 38, 41, 48-49, 111, 118, 123, 149, 151, 63-164, 272
Clarendon Report, 150, 163

Chatham, Lord, (Pitt the Elder), 37, 266
Cheltenham College, 33, 118
Christ Church, Oxford, 112, 141, 149, 168, 173, 208
Christian Science, 214
Church, Rev. Geddington Head, 120

INDEX

Churchill, Randolph, 210
Churtin, Rev.W.R., 213
City of London School, 118
Civil list, 261
Civil Service Exam, 113
Clarendon, Lord, 118, 123-124, 177-178
Clarendon Report, 150, 157, 159, 176, 189, 196, 223, 274, 283-284
Clarendon Schools, 49, 123, 157, 159, 171, 178
Clark, Sir George, 245
Classical Tripos, 57, 67, 187
Cleveland House Brothel Scandal, 210
Colchester, Lord, 94
Coleridge, Sir John, 113-114, 124, 127
Coleridge, Samuel, T., 38
Coleridge, Mary, 217-218, 230, 232
Colet, Dean, 152
'College John', 4
Collini, Stefan, 63
Coltman, Thomas, 39
Committee of Imperial Defence, 245, 251
Conduit Close, 158
Coningsby, novel, 90
Constitution Hill, 243
Cornish, Margaret, 209, 217
Cornwall, 210
Corps of Aviation, 251
Cory, (Johnson) William, 6, 55, 58, 75, 79, 86, 88, 93-94, 93-94, 99-100, 102, 112, 117, 128, 131, 134-137, 140-142, 170, 182-186, 197, 200-202, 207, 208, 210, 212, 216, 224, 230, 233-234, 236, 275
Cory, Andrew, son, 213-214, 231
Cory, Rosa, 202, 212-213, 216-217, 230-233
Craven scholarship, 26, 58
'Coningsby', novel, 90
Cornhill Magazine, 112, 115, 282, 291
Cornwall, 210
Cotton, Dr. George, Marlborough Head, 66
Cranleigh School, 124
Crawley, Lord, 241
Crimean War, 123, 180

Cromer, Lord, 223
Cromwell, Oliver, 235
Crystal Palace, 214
Curragh Mutiny, 253

D

Dare, Zena, actress, 246
Darwin, Catherine, 3, 36
Darwin, Charles, 3, 36, 68,
Darwin, Erasmus, 36
Datchet, 69
Day Training Centre, 216, 230
Dent, Edward, 204
Derby, 14th Earl of, 3, 177, 234
Derby, The, 234
Devon, county, 216
Devon, Earl of, 123, 177
Diamond Jubilee, 242
Dickens, Charles, 41, 54, 111-112
Dilke, Sir Charles, 207, 210
Disraeli, Benjamin, 90, 93
Dissenting Academies, 53
Dobson, fictional Headmaster, 117
Dodgson, Charles, 181
Domesday Book, 6
'Dotheboys Hall', 120
Douro Vineyards, 237
Downing College, 228
Downing Street, 234, 236
Drogheda, 235
Drummond, Mrs, 232
Drury, Joseph, Headmaster of Harrow, 64
Dulverton, 236
Duff, Grant, M.P., 171, 177-178
Durdans, The, 234-235

E

Eagle House, Prep. School, 119
East Sheen Prep. School, 119
Edgeworth, Maria, 53
Edinburgh, 48, 207, 233
Edinburgh Academy, 118
Edinburgh Review, 3, 44-46, 48, 122, 124, 277-278, 282, 286, 290-291
Edinburgh University, 207

Education of the Lower Orders, report, 52, 127
Edward V1, 155
Edward V11, 239-240, 244, 245, 251
Elba, Island of, 90, 213
Elcho, Lord, 108
Eldon, Lord, 50, 51
Elgin Commission, 245
Ellison, doctor, 75
Emmanuel College, Cambridge, 55
Encyclopaedia Britannica, 223
England, 1, 32, 45, 47, 54, 60, 69, 115, 129, 177-178, 233, 251, 255, 258, 260, 262, 288, 291-292
'Eric,' or 'Little by Little', Novel by F.W. Farrar, 81,117
Esperanto, 214

ETON COLLEGE:
Clarendon Report 127-145
 164, 168, 170
Other refs: 6-18, 19-33, 40, 55, 58, 61, 66, 69-78, 81-110, 111-120, 121-123, 147, 171-173 177-178, 180-186, 87-197, 202- 203, 212, 214, 218, 219-228, 234, 237, 238-241, 243, 250, 253-256, 268-272

Provosts and/or Headmasters
Balston, E. 109,116, 118, 136, 137-138, 140-141, 172, 181, 186
Godolphin, Henry, 128
Goodall, Joseph, 18-19, 32, 58, 70-71, 101, 128, 273
Goodford, Charles Old,15, 38, 100-105, 112-113, 115, 127-128, 130-132, 134, 136, 138, 140-143, 170-171, 187, 191, 196, 226
Hawtrey, Edward,18, 58, 60, 69-77, 79-80, 84-85, 89-90,100-102, 107, 124-125, 134-135, 137-138, 193,196, 266,
 273-274, 279, 281, 283, 292
Heath, G.R., 29
Hodgson, Francis, 70-72, 79, 100, 134
Hornby, Dr. J.J., 184, 186, 190-197, 214, 219,221, 223, 238-239

Keate, Dr. John, 1, 7-9, 11, 16-33, 39-40, 58, 62-63, 69-73, 75-76, 100, 103, 105,
 264-265, 267, 276
Lyttleton, Edward, 255
Roderick, Charles, 56-57
Warre, Dr. Edmond, 219-228, 236-241, 253-257,
Wotton, Sir Henry, 128

Fellows and Governors
Anson, Sir William, 238-239, 253
Bethell, George, 14
Eliot, W.L., 228
Green, Mr. 22
Hunt, Mr. 122
Huxley, T.H., 225
Peck, 'Pedestrian', 106
Plumptre, George, 91,107, 122
Wilder, J., 106, 127, 235

Masters
Abraham, C.J., 76
Ainger, A.C., 81-82, 85-86, 90, 120, 192, 200
Bethell, George, 14
Birch, A.F., 108
Browning, Oscar, (at Eton) 119, 131, 135-136, 141, 143, 170, 173, 187, 189-197
Carter, William A.,Lower Master, 134, 137, 142
Coleridge, Edward, 22, 77, 100, 132, 34, 137
Cookesley, W.G.,74-75, 92-93, 111-112
Day, Russell, 91
Drury, Ben, 23, 90
Dupuis, G.R. 33, 88, 117, 122, 127
Durnford, F.E., 91, 142
Eliot, W.L., 82-83, 101, 104, 109, 144, 228
Frewer, George, 86
Green, Mr., 22
Hale, Edward, 70, 91, 138, 224
Hawtrey, John, 83
Hawtrey, Stephen, 73-75, 135
Hexter, Major, 73-74,137

INDEX

James, C.C, 90-91, 131, 137, 141, 144, 195
Johnson, Wm. *see Cory in main index*
Joynes, J.L., 91, 104
Knapp, H.H., 21, 29, 32, 90, 264-265
Luxmoore, H.E., 119, 172, 182, 200, 237
Mitchell, R.A.H., 143
Marriott, W.B., 27, 39, 92, 180-181, 190
Rawlins, F.H., 255
Salt, Henry, 226
Stone, E.W.D, 79, 135, 200,
Tarver, Frank, 6
Tarver, H, 35, 138
Vidal, F., 180
Walford, J.T., 102
Warre, Edmond, 180-181, 186-190,195, 197, 203, 214
Wayte, W., 85
Wolley-(Dods),C., 83, 85,89, 144, 190, 192-194
Yonge, J.E., 92, 99

Boys
Ainger, A.C., 81-82, 85-86, 90, 120, 192, 200, 275
Anson, 238
Arkwright, 108
Ashley, F., 25-26
Bagge, 85
Barker, 11
Barrington, 85
Bickersteth, 200-201
Bligh, J.D., 15
'Blazes', 86-87,89,108
Booth brothers, 26
Branwell, 72
Brett, Oliver, 211
Brett, Maurice, 211
Brett, Reginald, 182, 184-186
Brinsley-Richards, James, 7, 81-84, 86-87, 89-90, 99-101, 104,107, 109, 144, 181
Browning, Oscar, 92-94
'Cherry', 83, 109
Coleridge, A.D.,72,73, 76, 90, 130, 182
Collins, 18

Coombe, 91
'Croppie', 104-105
Curzon, N.G., 192-193, 207, 229, 243, 245, 250, 253
Dalmeny, Lord, 127, 183-184, 235
Dent, J.C., 32-33
Dickens, Charley, 111-112
Eden, 33
Elliott, Francis, 183-184, 200
Farrer,T., 221
Gaskell, J.M. 25, 119-120, 266
Gladstone, W.E., 28, 37, 264-267
Goodriche, H., 24
Graham, 102
Green, W.C. 69,73, 82,85
Hall, 82,86
Hayes, 12
Heath, 264
Herbert, R., 185
Kean, 11
Lybbe, 144
Lyttleton, N.G., 81
Mansfield, J.S. 37
Marriott, 22,39
Montagu, Charles, 77
Moore, 12
Munro, 28
Murray, J. 81,88
Neville, 83
Northcote,Stafford,100
Palk, L., 23
Parker, 'Inky', 91, 223
Parry, Charles Hubert, 214,292
Paston, William, 2
Paul, Herbert, 182
Pochin, 2, 96
Praed, Wm., 28
Probyn, 185
'Pug' 83, 106
Roxburgh, Duke of, 15
Rowles, 37
Scott, George, 225
Selwyn, G.A., 12, 266
Seymour, Edward, 211, 246
Shelley, P.B., 14
Sturgis, H., 210
Swinburne, A.C., 74

Taunton, T., 26
Thomas, Morgan, 102
Trench, A.C., 189
Tucker, W.H., 3, 6-15, 17-18, 20,24-28,
  31-32, 39-40, 71-72, 78
Walker, S. 73
Warre, Edmund, 180
Wilkinson, C.A., 3, 11, 13-17, 20, 23, 25,
  29-32, 268
Williams, Rowland, 16
Willoughby, Christopher, 11
Wood, Charles, 183
Wood, Frederick, 183, 185, 200, 231

Awards/ exams
Collections, 141, 222
King's Scholarships, 131, 136, 141
Newcastle Scholarship, 21, 55, 76, 94,
  140, 180
Tomline Maths Prize, 221
Trials, 70, 133, 134

Eton Topography
Agar's Plough, 240
Brewhouse Yard, 239
Carter's Chamber, 7,11
Chapel,20, 27, 74, 77, 93, 106, 109,115,
  142-143
Cloisters, the, 58, 121, 239
Drury's House,106, 238
Election Chamber, 124
Eliot's House, 82-83, 101, 104, 109, 144
Evans' House, 112,144
Long Chamber, 6-18, 35,71-72, 76, 78,
  92, 103
Lower Chapel, 106, 238-239
Lupton's tower, 121
Memorial Hall, 239, 255
Provost's Lodge,17, 255
Savile House, 238
Weston's House, 238
Wolley-Dod's House and nearby, 238

Nearby
Brown's 'Sock' shop, 83
Brown, deaf tailor, 105
Castle Hill, 101

Castle Hotel, 109
Christopher Inn,9,26,77
Denman,tardy tailor,105
'Picky' Powell, cad, 16
Runicles shop 105
Salt Hill, 78, 83
'The Tap', 143, 189
Towers shop, 105
White Hart Hotel, 109
Williams, E.P, stationer, 105, 176

Eton College servants
Atkins, 76
Cartwright, 23
'Crab' – maid, 101, 108
'Drab' – maid, 83
Finmore, 74, 102-103
Grey, chapel clerk, 200
Goodman, 'Billy', boat-builder, 89
Hill, carpenter, 109
Worthy, cook, 9

Events
Check Nights, 104
Election Saturday, 9,14, 102, 109
Founder's Day, 124
Fourth of June, 240
Leaving Books, 75, 109,114, 135
Liberty Nights, 16
Montem, 77-79
Oppidan dinner, 103
Pig Fairs, 30

Bodies
Eton College Royal Volunteer Corps, 108
Hackney Wick Mission, 254
Literati, 28
Pop, 82, 109, 180, 253

Edward VI, 155
Edward VII, 239-240, 244-245, 251
Egypt, 201, 258
Eldon, Lord, 50,51
Ellis, Tom, 237
Emmanuel College, Cambridge, 55
'Esher Committee,' 243, 244
Eton High School, 107

INDEX

Evangelicalism, 65
Exeter College, Oxford, 189

F

Farrar, F.W., 191, 291
Fay, Kingsman, 229
Fergusson, Dr. 26
Finchampstead, Herts., 254
Fisher, Admiral, 241, 245, 251-252
Footlights, The, 214
Forsan, Headmaster of Berkhamsted, 46
Foundation boys, 177
Forster, W.E., 178
France, 201, 209, 252, 259, 260
French, General Sir John, 257-258
French Lyceum, 174
French Revolution, 38, 189, 191
Funchal, Madeira, 212, 216
Furse, Charles, 231

G

Gabell, H.D., 39
Gaisford, Dr. 112
Gallipoli, 258
Garton Foundation, 253
Gautier, Theophile, 197
'Geoffrey Davenant', 117
George I, 11, 4, 13, 18, 20, 118
George IV, 71, 160
George V, 251-252
George, Prince, (future George V), 240
General Strike, 262
Germany, 251-252, 261
Ghost Club, 214
Gladstone, Herbert, 236
Gladstone, John, 183
Gladstone, Mary, 236
Gladstone, W.E, 3, 24-25, 28, 30, 37, 55, 65, 67, 78, 104, 169, 183, 207-209, 224, 233, 236, 240, 242-243, 264-267
Goddard, Dr. Winchester, Headmaster, 147, 149
Gordon, General, 208-209

Graham, Gwendoline, 217
Grand Mogul of China 45
Granta, magazine, 247
Gray's Inn Fields, 158
Great Exhibition, 3, 79
Great Stink, 49
Green, W.C. 69, 73, 82, 85
Greece, 201
Gresham Chair, 206
Grey, Sir Edward, 231, 251
Guille, Mrs, 202, 212
Guille, Hubert, 232
Guille, Rosa, *see Cory*

H

Habeas Corpus Act, 38
Haig, Field Marshal Sir Douglas, 258-262
Haldane, R.B., 45, 251-252
Halsdon, 182-3, 185-187, 200-202, 217
Hampstead, 216-217, 230-231, 254
Hampton Court, 244
Hankey, Maurice, 262
Harcourt, Lewis, 'Loulou', 246, 261
Harcourt, Sir William, 210, 233-235
Hardisty, Mr. tutor, 111
Hardy, Thomas, 262

HARROW SCHOOL
Clarendon report 153-155, 163-168
Other refs.. 4-5, 11, 35, 42, 49, 82-83, 123-124, 176, 191, 272

Hartington, Lord, 207-208
Hawarden, 264, 267
Hawkins, Mr. Justice, 242
Hazelwood School, 52
Headmasters' Conference, 241
Heathcote, Sir William, M.P., 122
Henley Regatta, 104
Henry V1, 56, 225
'Heraclitus', elegy, 99
Herbert, Auberon, 241
Heversham G.S, 52
Heygate, Rev. W.E. 117
Hickleton, 183
Higgins, Matthew, 112-114, 124, 176

Hill, Thomas Wright. 52
Hill, Rowland, 52
Hind, Peter, King's, 47
Hinde, Mr., tutor, 32
H.M.S. Encounter, 216
Hobbs, John, tenor, 27
Holyrood, 242
Home Park, Windsor, 240
Home Rule, 210, 233, 235
Hooke, Robert, 64
House of Commons, 2, 47, 52, 54, 122, 171-172, 196-197, 207, 209, 23, 285-286
House of Lords, 52, 94, 122, 172, 176, 178, 229, 235, 285-286
Huggett, Roger, 127
Hugo, Victor, 229
Hyde Park, 255

I

Ince, Rev. Exeter College, Oxford, 189
India, 6, 183, 208, 245
India Office, The 208
Industrial Revolution, 3
Inner Temple, 58
Inter-Allied Council, 258
'Ionica', Cory poems, 231
Ironbridge, 3
Ireland, 66-67, 123, 182, 233, 253
Irving, Sir Henry, 202
Italy, 209, 229

J

Jamaica, 241
James 1., 151
James Dr. M.R., 205, 214, 221, 247, 249, 255
James, Robert Rhodes, 236
Jebbb, Richard, 188
Jeffrey, Francis, 44
Joffre, Marshal, 258
John Lyon School, 155
Johnson, Charles, 6
Johnson, Ernle, 208
Johnson, Wellington, 6, 212, 231

Johnson, William, *see Cory*
Jowett, Benjamin, 240
Judson, Harrow boy, 4
'Julius Caesar', 202

K

Kabul, 207
Kandahar, 208
Kendal Dissenting Academy, 53
Kennedy, Benjamin, 69, 156-157, 174, 223, 256
Kensington School of Art, 219
Keynes, J.M. 247-248
Khartoum, 209
King's, Cambridge, 18, 55-59, 70-71, 78, 92, 106, 113-114, 117, 122, 147, 169, 183, 186, 197, 202, 202-203, 206, 213- 227, 229-230 238, 247-249
King's College Choir School, 206, 248-249
Kinglake, A.W., 30, 32, 276
Kingsley, Charles, 60
Kitchener, Lord, 245, 257-258, 262
Knatchbull- Hugessen, M.P., 195-197
Knollys, Francis, 252
Kruger, Paul, 226
Kynaston, Dr., Headmaster of St. Paul's,152

L

Laleham, 60
Lancashire, 158, 183
Latymer, Lord, 203, 250
Lawrence, D.H. 262
League of Nations Armaments Comm. 261
Lee, Sir Philip, 262
Leeds G. S., 50
Lees-Milne, James, 210, 286-290
Leigh, Augustus Austin, 206, 231, 237, 247
Leigh, Boughton, 41
Leopold, King of the Belgians, 233

Lewis, Sir George Cornewall, 122, 124, 246, 261
Liddell, Mr., Westminster Headmaster, 2, 241
Lisbon, 231
Literis Humanioribus, 67
Liverpool, 35
'Liverpool Lurch', 213
Lloyd George, 259-260
Locke, John, 60
Lyte, Sir H. Maxwell, 25
London, 7, 38, 41-42, 53- 54,58, 68,79, 90,103, 105, 111, 118, 128, 149-150, 158, 177, 188, 191, 193, 206, 217, 228, 239-240, 257, 262, 265
London, Bishop of, 177
London Fire Brigade, 240
London Territorial Volunteers, 257
Lyell, Charles, 51
Lyon, John, 153-155
Lyttleton, Lord, 123, 177

M

Macadam, 6
Macaulay, G.M., 46
MacDonald, Ramsay, 262
MacDonald, Ishbel, 262
Mackenzie, Faith, 135
Mackenzie, Osgood, 237
Madeira, 207, 210, 212-213, 216, 219
Magdalene College, Cambridge, 268
Mahdism, 241
Majuba, battle of, 216
Mall, The 242
Malim, 2, 100
Malory Towers, 81
Malvern School, 124, 208
Manchester Grammar School, 51,174
Mansion House, 239
Mansfield, J.S. 37
Maples store, 217
March, Rugby boy, 62-63
Marco, gondolier, 211
Markham, Capt. F., 2, 4, 36,42-43, 88-89,
Markham, Dr. Cantuar, 4
Marlborough College, 40, 191

Marshall, Mr., Westminster master, 43
Marshall, Rugby boy, 63
Mary, Princess, 228
Mary, Queen, 250
Mayfair, 207
Melbourne, Lord, 65,71
Mentmore House, 235
Mercers Company, 151, 177

MERCHANT TAILORS SCHOOL
Clarendon Report 152-153
Other refs: 164-168, 123, 149, 177

Meredith, George, 202,262
Merivale, Charles, Harrow boy, 272
Merton College, 76
Messiah, The, 46
Meyrick, Westminster boy, 150
Midland Railway, 158
Middlesex, 159
Milan, 229
Mill, John Stuart, 60, 66, 187, 208
Millicent, Duchess of Sutherland, 211
Milton, John, 166, 269
Minet, Charles, 41
Ministry of Health, 242
Moberley, George, Headmaster of Winchester, 49, 62, 146-148, 166, 174,
Montem, 77-79
Monro, Rev. E. 117
Montrose, Duchess of, 102
Morley, John, 210
Morris, William, 188
Mozart, 215
Murray, John, 81, 88

N

Napier, Sir Charles, 93
Neate, Charles, M.P., 177
Nevinson, H.W, 36
Newark, 38
New College, Oxford, 113, 147-149
Newcastle, Duke of, 38, 266
Newman, Cardinal, 107, 183
Newmarket, 235

Newton, Isaac, 56
New Mexico, 262
New Zealand, 241
Nicholson, Harold, 263
Nivelle, General, 259
Nixon, J.E., 205-206
Nonconformists, 52, 234, 247
Norman, Capt. Francis, 1, 5, 253
Northcote, Sir Stafford, 100, 123, 172-173, 175
Nottingham Castle, 38

O

Office of Works, 236, 242, 247
Ogle, Rev. O. 247
Okes, Richard, 56, 121, 186, 204-205
Omdurman, battle of, 241
Orchard Lea, 12, 246
Osborn, Sergeant, 222
Osborne, Isle of Wight, 223
Oval Ground, 153
Oratory of St. Philip of Neri, 201
Ord, Boris, 247
Oxford, 50, 65, 67-68, 94, 117, 122, 129, 151, 176, 183, 208, 228,
Oxford Movement, 65
Oxford University Commission (1857), 147-148
Oxford University Royal Volunteer Corps, 180

P

Pall Mall Gazette, 209-210
Palmerston, Lord, 36, 99, 180, 234
Paris, 30, 207, 233, 259-260
Paris Embassy, 242
Parkinson's disease, 253
Parliament Bill, 1910-11, 252
'Paterfamilias', 112, 114-115, 124
Peking, 209, 241,
Pell, Albert, 51
Pelham, Bishop of Lincoln, 265
Peninsular War, 13
Penryn and Falmouth constituency, 208

Pepys, Samuel, 64
Percival, John, Head of Clifton College, 186
Perse School, Cambridge 46
Perth, 246
Peterborough, Dean of, 60
Peterloo, 38
Phillips, King's student, 229
Pilgrim's Lane, 230, 232
Poincare, President, 259
Polhill, Rev. A, 241
Political Society, Cambridge University, 226
Ponsonby, Sir Frederick, 209
Pope, The, 183, 250
Port Arthur, 241
Portsmouth, 229
Portsmouth, Lord, 197
Portland, Duke of, 9
Preparatory Schools, 6, 131, 133, 170, 172
Price, Professor, 169
Prideaux, Ada, 217, 219
Privy Council, 52
Prothero, George, 213
Prussia, King of, 72
Prussia, 38, 91
Public Schools Bills, 176-178
Public Schools Act, 1868, 186, 195-197, 267
Purcell, Henry, 64

Q

Quarterly Review, 116, 172,
'Queen Mary' – play, 202
Queensberry, Marquess of, 235
Queen's Victoria's Golden Jubilee, 240
Quidnuncs Cricket, 109

R

Ragged School Union, 53
Ramsay, Professor G.G. 224
Radcliffe, Philip, 204
Redistribution Bill, 209
Reeve, Henry, 1 14-115, 119, 127

INDEX

Red Cross, 259
Reform Bill (1832), 106
Repington, Colonel, 258
Richmond G.S., 51
Roberts, Rev. Dr. 119-120
Roberts, Field Marshall,
　First Earl, 239, 251
Robertson, Sir William,
　Field Marshal, 259-260
Robinson, Dr., 205
Rome, 183, 185, 229, 250
Rosebery, 5th Earl of, see Dalmeny for
　Eton 186, 210, 224,233-236, 243,
　246, 251, 260
Ross, Robbie, 247
Rothschild, Hannah de, (Rosebery's wife)
　235
Royal Commission into Oxford &
　Cambridge
　Universities (1850), 56,58
Royal Mint, 56
Royal Fusiliers, 260
Royal Society, 46
Ruault,Harrow master, 65

RUGBY SCHOOL
Clarendon Report, 158-62, 163-168
Other refs : 3, 26, 38, 41, 60-66, 111, 123

Runciman, W., 241
Ruskin, John, 195
Russell, Lord John, 38, 123
Russia, 208

S
___

St. Andrew's University, 183
St. Catherine's College, Cambridge, 206
St. David's Day, 43
St. Edward's School, Oxford, 124
St. George's Chapel, Windsor, 30, 70, 104, 142, 255
St. John's Ambulance, 260
St. John's Church Windsor, 106
St. John's College, Cambridge, 68, 157
St. Mark's School, Windsor, 73

ST. PAUL'S SCHOOL
Clarendon Report,151-152
Other refs: 123, 149, 164, 166, 177

St. Petersburg, 123
Salford, 53
Salisbury,Lord, 236, 245
Salvatore, gondolier, 211
Sandhurst, 141
Sandringham, 243-245, 263
Saturday Review, 116
Scarsdale, Lord, 193
Scotland, 260
Scott, Rev C.B., Headmaster of
　Westminster School, 150
Scott, Sir Walter, 164
Sedbergh School, 241
Selwyn, G.A., 12, 266
Shaftesbury, Lord, 53
Shakespeare, 166,202
Shelley, P,B., 14, 202
Sheriff, Sir Lawrence, 158

SHREWSBURY SCHOOL
Clarendon Report, 155-158,165.
Other refs : 36, 39, 49, 65-69, 111, 123,135

Shropshire, 155
Shrosbee, Colin, 3
Sichel, Edith, 218
Sidgwick, Arthur, 188
Sidgwick,Henry,118,190
Simeon, Rev. Charles, 58, 267
Slough, 239
Smith, Adam, 48
Smith, Bobus, 64
Smith, Douglas, 64
Smith, Rev. Sydney, 37-38, 44-46, 64, 113
Smith, W.H., 237
Snith, Mr., Westminster master, 38
Smithfield, 41
Smollett, Tobias, 60
Somerset, county, 236
Somerset, Lord Arthur, 210
Somme, battle of, 259

303

South Kensington Museum, 242
Spain, 123
Spanking Sam, 43
'Speedyman,' the, 13
Stamford G.S., 69
Stamfordham, Lord, 261
Stanhope, 5th Earl, 172-173
Stanley, Dean, 66
Stanley, Venetia, 259
Stead, W.T., 209-210, 234
Stephen, Sir James FitzJames, 197
Stocker, doctor, 144
Stonyhurst College, 118
Sturgis, Howard, 210
Sudan, 208-209, 233
Suffragettes, the 255
Sutherland, Millie, Duchess of, 211
Switzerland, 216, 241

T

Tait, Dr. A.C., Headmaster of Rugby, 63, 159, 165
Taunton Commission, 50
Temple, Frederick, Headmaster of Rugby, 159, 161
Temple Gardens, 59
Temple Grove School, 119, 120
Tennyson, Lord, 183, 202, 240
Territorial Force, 252
Test Act, 52
Thackeray, Rev. Francis, St. George, 86, 91, 181
Thackeray, George, 56-57, 121
Thackeray W.M., 3, 35, 202
Thames, The, 77, 103, 108, 239, 257
'The Great Illusion' 253
'The National Review', 252
'The Standard', 245
'The Times', 102, 116, 119, 210, 219, 258, 273
'The Whirlwind', 228
'The World', 252
Thistlewood, Arthur, 41
Thompson, Prof., 123
Thorpe School, 92
Thring, Edward, 227, 241

Tilley, Arthur, 247
Tilney Street, Mayfair, 207-208, 241, 262
Tiverton, 113-114, 124
'Tom Brown's Schooldays', 35, 117
'Tom Sawyer', 213
Torrington, 6, 200, 202, 217
Tours, 183
Trinity College, Cambridge, 51, 184
Trinity College, Dublin, 68
Tripos week, 228
Trollope, Anthony, 37
 175, 202
Trollope, Frances, 37
Trollope, Tom, 37
Tsar Nicholas 11, 261
Tuckwell, Rev. W., 3
Twistleton, Edward, 123

U

University College, London, 53
University College, Oxford, 141
University Test Act, 247
Uppingham School, 41
Upton, 19, 121
Utilitarianism, 60

V

Van de Weyer, Eleanor, Brett's wife, 206
Van de Weyer, Madame Sylvain, 206
Vaughan, Charles, 4, 49, 11, 153-155
Vaughan, Halford, 123
Venables, Charterhouse boy, 272
Verdun, siege of, 259
Victoria, Queen, 36, 51, 65, 79, 116, 123, 204, 209, 239-240, 242-243, 262, 272
Victory ball, 261
Von Hugel, Baron, 216

W

Wagner, Richard, 215
Wales, Prince of, (later Edward VII),

INDEX

87, 104, 142
Wales, Prince of (later Edward VIII), 258, 262-263
Walpole, Sir Robert, 57
Walter, John, 111, 219
Walters, A.F., 224
Walthamstow, 81
War Cabinet, 259
War Office, 208
Ward, George, Winchester prefect, 37
War Office, 208-209, 225, 242-243, 245, 251-252
Warrington Dissenting Academy, 53
Warwickshire, 158-159
Waterloo, battle, 30, 39
Waterfield, Mr. 132
Wellington College, 60
Wellington, Duke of, 13, 20, 116
Wells, Cathedral, 254

Wells, Dean of, 208
Wells, H.G., 250
Westminster Abbey, 205, 208
Westminster Cloisters, 58
Westminster Review, 174,

WESTMINSTER SCHOOL
Clarendon Report, 149-150
Other refs : 2, 4, 5, 10, 35-36, 38, 41-42, 49, 64, 69, 88, 89, 123, 149

Wexford, 235
Whewell, Prof. William, 51, 52
Whitechapel, 219
Whitting, Fred, King's, 205, 249
Wickham, Rev. Edward., 119
Wilde, Oscar, 235, 247
Wilhelm, Kaiser, 230
Wilkins, William, 57, 206

Wilkinson, Rev., Headmaster of Marlborough, 40
William IV 71, 89
Williams, E.P., 105, 176
Williams, (Puffer), Winchester master, 39
Williamson, Charles, 185, 200, 208, 211, 258, 263
Wilson, Woodrow, 260
Wimbledon, 108

WINCHESTER COLLEGE
Clarendon Report, 146-149, 164, 166, 168, 196
Other refs : 3, 10, 35-37, 49, 66, 111, 118, 122-123, 137, 146, 177, 241, 242

Winchilsea Constituency, (Brougham's seat), 46
Winchilsea, Lady, 201
Windsor, 8, 11, 13, 33, 73, 79, 102, 130, 197, 202, 236, 240
Windsor Castle, 104, 108, 239,
Windsor Fair, 2, 74, 104
Windsor Forest, 207
Windsor Great Park, 212
Wolseley, Viscount, Field Marshal, 209
Wood, Sir Charles, 183
Wood, Colonel, 26
Wooll, Dr., Rugby Headmaster, 61, 63
Woolwich, 141
Worcester, Mayor of, 33
Wordsworth, Christopher, Harrow Headmaster, 4, 67
Wordsworth, canon, 42
Wordsworth, Wm. 38
Wortham, H.E., 221, 228
Wright's Public House, 42
Wyse, Sir Thomas, 54

Y

York, Duke of, 123
Young, G.M., 52, 60

Printed in Great Britain
by Amazon